Decision Making

Published in association with
the Chartered Institute of
Management Accountants

Other titles in the CIMA series

Stage 1

Economics for Accountants
Keith West

Foundation Accounting
Mark Lee Inman

Quantitative Methods
Kevin Pardoe

Stage 2

Cost Accounting
Mark Lee Inman

Financial Accounting
Peter Taylor and Brian Underdown

Information Technology Management
Krish Bhaskar and Richard Housden

Management in Practice
Cliff Bowman

Stage 3

Advanced Financial Accounting
Peter Taylor and Brian Underdown

Business Taxation
Neil Stein

Company Law
Julia Bailey and Iain McCullum

Management Accounting Techniques
David Benjamin and Colin Biggs

Stage 4

Control and Audit in Management Accounting
Jeff Coates, Ray Stacey and Colin Rickwood

Financial and Treasury Management
Paul Collier, Terry Cooke and John Glynn

Management Accounting: Strategic Planning and Marketing
Patrick McNamee

Decision Making
A management accounting perspective

Stage 4

Roland Fox, Alison Kennedy and Keith Sugden
Lecturers, University of Salford

Butterworth-Heinemann Ltd
Halley Court, Jordan Hill, Oxford OX2 8EJ

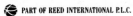 PART OF REED INTERNATIONAL P.L.C.

OXFORD   LONDON   GUILDFORD   BOSTON
MUNICH   NEW DELHI   SINGAPORE   SYDNEY
TOKYO   TORONTO   WELLINGTON

First published 1990

British Library Cataloguing in Publication Data
Fox, Roland
    Decision making.
    1. Accounting. Decision making
    I. Title   II. Kennedy, Alison   III. Sugden, Keith   IV. Series
    657

ISBN 0 7506 0035 7

Printed and bound in Great Britain by
Butler & Tanner Ltd, Frome and London

Contents

Preface   ix

Part One   *Management Decisions*

1   Corporate objectives   3

   1.1   Introduction   3
   1.2   Objectives and decisions   4
   1.3   Organizational goals – classifications   6
   1.4   Organizational goals – what are they?   8
   1.5   Whose goals?   9
   1.6   Summary and conclusion   14
         References and further reading   14

2   Decisions – context and process   15

   2.1   Introduction   15
   2.2   The decision process   15
   2.3   Decision types   24
   2.4   Information for decisions   27
   2.5   Human judgement   33
   2.6   Summary   38
         References and further reading   38

3   Decision making – theory and basic techniques, Part 1   40

   3.1   Introduction   40
   3.2   The problem of measurement   40
   3.3   Decisions under certainty   43
   3.4   Decisions under uncertainty and risk   53
   3.5   Summary and conclusions   90
         References and further reading   90

4   Decision making – theory and basic techniques, Part 2   93

   4.1   Introduction   93
   4.2   Modelling   93

4.3	Cost–benefit analysis	101
4.4	Techniques for improving efficiency	104
4.5	Accounting information for decisions	108
4.6	Conclusions	115
	References and further reading	116

Questions for Part One   **118**

Part Two   Capital Budgeting

5   Investments in a risk-free world   **129**

5.1	Introduction	129
5.2	Net present value and investment	130
5.3	Other investment criteria	135
5.4	Non-discounting techniques	135
5.5	Internal rate of return (IRR) (yield)	141
5.6	Summary of other techniques v NPV	150
5.7	Capital rationing	150
5.8	Identification of cash flows	153
	References and further reading	160

6   Investments in a risky world   **161**

6.1	Introduction	161
6.2	Portfolio theory	161
6.3	The capital asset pricing model	169
	References and further reading	181

7   Real asset investments in a risky world   **184**

7.1	CAPM and real asset investment	184
7.2	Capital market imperfections and real asset investment: the adjusted present value approach	195
7.3	Relationship between 'cost of capital' and CAPM discount rate and the former's use in investment appraisal	203
7.4	Leasing	208
	References	216

8   Project management   **218**

8.1	Project definition and selection	218
8.2	Cost implications of project approval	220
8.3	Management of project implementation	220
8.4	Post-audit of projects	223
8.5	Project abandonment	224
8.6	Final post-audit report	229
	References	230

Questions for Part Two   **231**

Part Three   Prices and Values in Decisions

9   Changes in price levels   **239**

    9.1   Introduction – problem outline   239
    9.2   General price-level changes   240
    9.3   Specific price-level changes   247
    9.4   Price-level changes and year-end accounts   257
        References and further reading   264

10   Transfer pricing   **265**

    10.1   Introduction   265
    10.2   The transfer pricing problem   266
    10.3   The transfer pricing decision   273
    10.4   Conclusion   276
        References and further reading   276

11   Pricing policy   **278**

    11.1   Policy determinants   278
    11.2   Cost-plus pricing   289
    11.3   Marginal cost-plus pricing   297
    11.4   Pricing and markets   301
    11.5   General policy issues   320
        References and further reading   327

Questions for Part Three   **329**

Part Four   Performance Feedback

12   Internal performance measurement   **341**

    12.1   Decentralization   341
    12.2   Return on investment   342
    12.3   Residual income   347
    12.4   Divisional profit   349
    12.5   Divisional investment   350
    12.6   Alternatives to ROI and RI   359
        References and further reading   361

13   Ratio analysis   **363**

    13.1   Introduction   363
    13.2   Liquidity ratios   365
    13.3   Operating ratios   367
    13.4   Gearing ratios   371
    13.5   Stock market ratios   373
    13.6   Univariate and multivariate analysis   374
    13.7   Users of accounts   375
    13.8   Some general problems of ratio analysis   375
        References and further reading   376

14   Value-added statements   **377**

    14.1   Introduction   377
    14.2   Method   378
    14.3   Applications   380
    14.3   Conclusions   382
          References and further reading   383

Questions for Part Four   **384**

Index   389

Preface

Some aspects of decision making, such as investment, are a familiar part of accounting; other aspects, such as non-economic approaches to pricing and decision analysis are somewhat underdeveloped in existing texts. In fact, the divergence of approaches has been such that an accountant would find difficulty in recognizing much of the analysis of decisions by a management scientist or a marketing specialist. This book brings together these disparate strands to present a comprehensive view of the decision-making problem.

Our special concern has been to apply theory to 'reality' without consciously sanitizing the problem. Such should be the mission of any relatively advanced book in this area. As a result, we hope that the messy, conflicting and complex problems encountered in practice have found their way into this text, and that our analysis has, at least, shed some light on the issues behind them.

Inevitably our 'solutions' are not complete – questions will always remain. To some readers, addicted to a diet of neat problems and right or wrong answers, this approach will be a little difficult at first, but, we trust, interesting and even refreshing. By contrast, we have made every attempt to make our explanations of the various solutions as simple as possible. Formal proofs, mathematical derivations, have been kept to a minimum and, for the most part, set aside in favour of simple examples illustrating the ideas in action.

In general, we hope, through this text, to impress upon the reader that decisions worthy of analysis rarely have a single best solution. Rather, we would characterize the process as choosing from among a number of second-best solutions. The choice depends upon the problem and a thorough understanding of the bases of these solutions.

We have assumed a grasp of such basic statistics as variance, covariance and linear regression, as well as an understanding of the principles of linear programming (for certain aspects of transfer pricing); these topics are contained in any book on basic statistics, though we recommend Biggs, C. and Benjamin, D., *Management Accounting Techniques* (Heinemann, 1989). Also, we assume that the reader understands how basic accounting data is compiled to form the accounting report. We recommend Biggs and Benjamin (*op. cit.*) or a traditional cost-accounting tome such as Horngren, C. T. and Foster, G., *Cost Accounting – A Managerial Emphasis*, 6th ed. (Prentice-Hall, 1986) or Drury, C., *Management and Cost Accounting* (VNR). Our concern here is to answer the question 'Having prepared the data, how can we use it to take decisions?'

To CIMA students

Appendices and sections marked with an asterisk (*) go somewhat further than the syllabus. We recommend these items, as a fuller understanding generally affords a better grasp of earlier stages; but we defer to the student's judgement as to what is practical for him or her.

Thanks for comments, encouragement and advice are owed to Professors Tony Christer (Salford University), Simon French (Leeds University), Kenneth Gee (Salford University), Geoffrey Lockett (Manchester Business School), Robert Scapens (Manchester University), Michael Theobald (Birmingham University) and Wenbin Wang (Harbin Institute, China), and to our willing and able undergraduate, Jonathan Smith, though we strongly claim sole rights on all errors.

Special thanks are also due to Doris Meek and Imelda Day for virtuoso performances on the word processor.

Roland Fox
Alison Kennedy
Keith Sugden

Part One   Management Decisions

This section introduces the many problems of decision making in organizations. General decision models are developed, under both certainty and uncertainty, where the decision maker can specify what factors are important in a decision, as well as determining the relative importance of the factors and the uncertainty associated with them.

1 Corporate objectives

1.1 Introduction

Analysis of financial decisions to be found in textbooks is almost invariably based upon the assumption of profit maximization – a term which we will take to include wealth maximization (Collier *et al.*, 1988, p. 4) and maximization of the present value of net cash flows (Arnold and Hope, 1983, p. 9). It is appropriate to start therefore by considering whether it is right that we should confine our objectives to profit maximization.

There are many organizations where the role of profit is either indirect or non-existent (see Table 1.1). The substitution of cost-effectiveness is sometimes suggested as a means of re-establishing the relevance of profits, and its accompanying body of analysis, under another name. Unfortunately, cost-effectiveness and other related financial measures are unable to compare changes in non-financial benefits with changes in costs. Their applicability is therefore severely limited.

Let us illustrate this point by considering a decision by a health authority to centralize the treatment of a particular complaint to one of the hospitals in its area. This act may save on staff and equipment costs, but it will also mean patients having to make longer journeys to the hospital, with a possible detrimental effect on treatment, and even fatalities. Relatives, on average, will also have to make longer journeys, which are likely to be fewer in number, with an adverse influence on patient morale. This, in turn, may make recovery rates slower. We cannot reduce staff and equipment without considering the effect on all the objectives of the hospital service. In doing so, we have to ask such questions as: 'Is the saving in cost worth the extra suffering?' Cost-effectiveness cannot make such judgements.

In general, financial and other goals in a not-for-profit organization are not equivalent to the profit motive in the commercial sector. Costs are incurred to further the often ill-defined, but nevertheless important, goals of the organization. As a result, the decision maker is inevitably drawn into weighing up the effect of investment and savings on difficult-to-measure goals, and making assumptions about trade-offs between these goals.

Even in commercial organizations, the profit motive may not always be easily associated with decisions. For example, let us take a decision to reduce transport costs between a factory and its retail outlets. If, in order to reduce these costs, the factory proposes to reduce the number of deliveries and increase the size of average stocks in the outlets, there is likely to be an effect on the presentation of goods within the retail outlet, the seriousness of stockouts, and the product planning by retail outlets (they would have to plan further ahead). These changes would have consequences that are difficult to measure. For instance, if the company is selling fashionable clothes, it may currently present limited amounts of stock in a fashionable setting. What, one wonders, would be the effect of presenting garments in large storage bins in the shop through lack of space? Clearly, the whole image of the company would be altered.

If we try to evaluate the problem using profit as the only goal, then we are forced into asking the shop managers questions such as 'What will be the effect on profits of not being able to order different lines as quickly?' or 'How will profits be affected by the different presentation of goods?' These are very difficult questions to answer directly. Would it not be easier to divide the question into two parts, by inserting a more tangible goal by asking 'What will be the effect on our image of not being able to change lines as often, and altering our presentation?' and then 'What effect will such a change in image have on our profits?' For this, and most other significant decisions, a more indirect series of questions seems inherently more attractive, as it can address a whole range of goals that are tangible to the manager. In this case, the decision to change transport policy can be related to all the elements of the marketing mix. These elements can then be related to profits.

Our two examples demonstrate that, in both commercial and non-commercial decisions, a model capable of incorporating more than one objective is desirable.

1.2   Objectives and decisions

Although we commonly talk about 'the goals of a decision', it should be said that it is really the decision maker, not the decision, that has goals. A decision has consequences; the equivalent term used in the literature on decisions is 'attributes'. All significant decisions have many attributes. If we were to list them all, taking a decision would indeed be a lengthy process: much time can be saved by using goals to select the important attributes. By implication therefore, if an attribute is not making some contribution, whether positive or negative, towards a goal, we should ignore it.

The relation between decision attributes and goals can present difficulties. Let us take as an example the decision to purchase a company car. In the simple case there will be a one-to-one correspondence between goals and attributes. Thus, if one of the goals is that the purchase price must be below £12,000, then clearly the attribute to be used is the purchase price of the car (though even here there may be problems, as some purchase prices are inclusive of number plates, delivery and road tax, but others are not). If we take a similar goal, that the car should be economical, then the problem is more difficult. There are several attributes that contribute to economy, the main ones being purchase price, petrol consumption and service costs. In this case, combining these attributes will be relatively straightforward. Providing that the firm has sufficient borrowing facilities, economy may be measured as the total present value of these expenses.

A third goal might be that the car should be safe. What attributes contribute towards this goal? A possible list might include the following: antilock braking, reinforced doors, quality of manufacture and reputation for safety. Meeting this goal has two further problems: measurement and association. The first two attributes are easily measured. In contrast, quality of manufacture and reputation for safety are subjective, and hence more difficult to measure. Perhaps we should construct a scale of 1–10 and ask various experts to make judgements. This raises a further problem. How do we combine such judgements to develop an effective measure? Will one expert's '5' be the same as another's? Probably not. It would, however, be wrong to ignore an attribute simply because it presents measurement difficulties. The decision maker is therefore forced into the position of having to accept that relevant data for decisions are not always objective.

The second problem we have is that of association. How do we combine the various aspects of safety in order to construct a measure? Again, this is really a matter of subjective judgement. The problem of association also occurs in weighting our three goals of initial purchase price, economy and safety. In this example, the first goal is a constraint – as long as the price is below £12,000, we can ignore it. If it is above this figure, the car is unacceptable. Assuming that we limit our choice to cars below £12,000, we can weigh up the remaining goals of economy and safety by asking the relatively straightforward question 'How much is the decision maker willing to pay for safety?' Such simplification will unfortunately not always be possible, if we include another goal, such as security, the problem becomes complex once more. Succeeding chapters will elaborate the problems presented here. To summarize, in looking at how decisions further our goals we must address the following problems:

1   Selecting relevant attributes that measure our goals.
2   Measuring those attributes.
3   Where there are a number of attributes, combining them to represent the particular goal adequately.
4   When there are a number of goals, combining them to arrive at a ranking of possible options.

The reader may well feel that this process is unduly complex. However, a moment's reflection should prove sufficient to establish that even in the seemingly straightforward decision considered here, we will indeed be presented with all these difficulties. In practice, we may choose to ignore certain problems if the cost of investigation is likely to be higher than the benefits. In this example, for instance, it would probably make no sense spending days distinguishing between two cars that were both very safe. Nevertheless, such simplications are not without risk; the meticulous decision processes of the Japanese serve as a reminder of the potential benefits.

1.3   Organizational goals – classifications

There are many different ways of looking at the concept of goals. Each of the following classifications holds implications for the decision-making process.

1.3.1   Operational and non-operational goals

An operational goal is one that is suitable for guiding decisions. It indicates clearly the attributes of a decision that will be relevant to the problem. A non-operational goal is one that is relevant to a decision, but does not help us to choose between various options. Let us look again at our car purchase example (section 1.2) to illustrate this distinction. Profit maximization may be seen as the corporate goal in selecting a car; but it does not, of itself, tell us which model to choose. Those who think that it may indicate that the cheapest is the most appropriate are implicitly conjuring up a picture of senior management driving around in battered second-hand vehicles, no doubt also having frequent accidents due to worn brakes and loose steering. Clearly, such a state of affairs would affect company morale and image. The goal of profit maximization needs interpretation. In other words, it is non-operational as regards this decision and needs to be translated into operational goals, which is what we did in section 1.2.

The distinction between operational and non-operational goals can only be made with respect to the decision. Goals may be operational for some decisions but not for others. For example, although we have said that profit maximization is non-operational for the problem of selecting a company car, it may well be a useful goal for other activities, such as choosing between investments in the stock market.

Finally, the degree to which a goal is operational may vary. Thus the operational goals of price, economy, safety and security were suggested as suitable for selecting a company car. The first two goals had a relatively straightforward link with the measurement of the various attributes. By contrast, safety and security were much more difficult to measure. With respect to safety, we proposed composite measures which were not wholly satisfactory, but were better than nothing. As a goal it was barely operational.

1.3.2   Strategic, managerial and operational goals

This classification refers to the structure of goals in an organization. The three concepts are normally presented in the form of a pyramid, and are used to classify goals, decisions and control systems (see Figure 1.1). The pyramid shape obviously invokes the idea of a hierarchy. At the bottom are the large number of operational goals that are appropriate for the many small, detailed decisions that are taken by the more junior levels of management. The choice of these goals will be guided by the next level, the managerial goals. In general, the pursuit of operational goals should lead to the achievement of the managerial goals. Similarly, pursuit of managerial goals should lead to the achievement of strategic goals. An example of this relationship is illustrated in Figure 1.1.

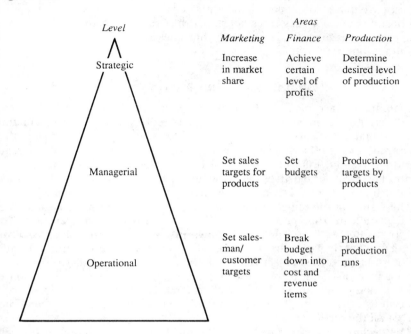

	Marketing	Finance	Production
Strategic	Increase in market share	Achieve certain level of profits	Determine desired level of production
Managerial	Set sales targets for products	Set budgets	Production targets by products
Operational	Set sales-man/ customer targets	Break budget down into cost and revenue items	Planned production runs

Figure 1.1

1.3.3 Proxy goal

The chief characteristic of a proxy goal is that it is measurable, and therefore serves as a useful substitute for one that is difficult to measure. There is a counterpart in the decision, namely, a proxy attribute (Keeney and Raiffa, p. 41). This represents the more measurable aspects of a decision: for example, standard cost is a proxy attribute for incurred cost.

1.3.4 Formal and informal goals

This distinction may alternatively be termed stated/unstated or overt/covert. These terms all refer to the possible difference between the goals that a decision maker actually follows (informal goal), and the goals that he or she professes to follow (formal goal).

Although a firm may claim to be striving for profit maximization, the facts sometimes indicate otherwise. For example, when Clive Thornton took control of a major daily newspaper, he found that the expenses of senior managers taking each other out to lunch came to more than the profits of the paper. Another example is provided by sales maximization, which has been put forward as being an informal goal of higher rank than profit maximization

(Baumol, 1977, p. 378). One of the reasons for believing that maximizing sales may be the main purpose of a commercial decision, is that managers' salaries are more closely correlated with sales than with profits. Such causal connections are not easy to establish. In this case, for instance, a firm may well prefer sales to profits on the basis that sales improve market position and maintain long-term profits.

1.4   Organizational goals – what are they?

Questionnaires are often sent out by researchers asking firms to list their goals; such an exercise is known as a self-report study. The problem that this method of research poses is that there is always the suspicion that organizations list the goals that they think the researcher would like to read. Almost certainly, informal goals will be excluded where they are seen to contradict formal objectives. For the goals that are included, both their relative importance and their precise interpretation are rarely made clear.

The results of the self-report studies for profit-making firms are sometimes held to indicate that profit is not the most important consideration. The Corporate Report (see Table 1.1) shows just over half the surveyed firms listing profit as their primary objective. However, it would not be unreasonable to interpret the other objectives of 'survival' and 'service offered' as proxy goals for profits, and in the 'other replies' category, 'the interests of share-holders' was predominant. In other words, in this survey at least, the concept of profit (or its near neighbour, shareholder wealth maximization), underlies almost all the replies.

The declared objectives of United Biscuits provide the second of the self-report studies. Their list translated profit maximization into a number of more tangible goals, and reveals the problems of conflict and the associated need to establish trade-offs. What would management do, for example, if investing 5 per cent of sales led to cash flow problems, so that loans exceeded the 40 per cent limit of capital employed? Alternatively, what if a return on capital of 20 per cent could only be achieved by increasing sales at a reduced profit margin?

In the public sector both the NHS and the police only state very general goals (Day and Klein, 1987). If there are more detailed goals, they are not disclosed. Both omit the need to keep within spending limits, and any mention of responsibilities to their employees. With these objectives added, the possibility for conflict is greatly increased. As with the commercial sector, single goals cannot be considered in isolation.

For all these organisations, declared objectives are in no way sufficient to guide decisions. The following point made by the Royal Commission on the NHS has a measure of general applicability:

> The absence of detailed and publicly declared principles and objectives reflects to some degree the continuing political debate about the service. Politicians and public alike are agreed on the desirability of a national health service, but agreement often stops there. Instead of principles, there are policies, which change according to the priority of the government of the day and the particular interest of the minister concerned.

Table 1.1   Stated objectives

Organization	Objectives	Source
155 commercial companies from Times 1000	Profit 58%, service offered 19%, survival 10%, other 13%.	Corporate Report
United Biscuits	Return on Capital employed (target 25% minimum 20%). Increase sales while maintaining profit margins; invest 5% of sales in capital expenditure; dividends should grow with profits; loans should not exceed 40% of capital employed; overseas assets should be matched by liabilities.	P. McNamee, p. 112
National Health	Encourage and assist individuals to remain healthy; provide equality of entitlement to health services; provide a broad range of services to a high standard; provide equality of access to these services; provide a service free at the time of use; satisfy the reasonable expectations of its users; remain a national service responsive to local needs.	Report of Royal Commission on NHS
Police	1 The maintenance of law and order and the protection of persons and property. 2 The detection of criminals and associated functions within the judicial process (now superseded by the Crown Prosecution Service). 3 The conduct of prosecutions in many minor cases (not in Scotland). 4 The control of traffic and advice to the local authority on such matters. 5 Certain duties on behalf of central government, for example some immigration enquiries. 6 By long tradition, to befriend people who need help, and to cope with minor or major emergencies.	Royal Commission on the Police

Politics plays a part in every organization. Where the goals of decision makers conflict, decisions may be taken without a clear formulation of objectives. Such process are likely to lead to poor decisions.

1.5   Whose goals?

1.5.1   *Individual goals*

Thus far, goals have been referred to in the context of organizations and decision makers. In looking at the concept of formal and informal goals (section 1.3.4), it was suggested that decision makers hold a number of informal, unstated goals that constitute a hidden part of the decision-making process. Casual observation is enough to establish the potential importance of these unstated personal goals. Many large profit-making organizations are founded and developed by one person, e.g. Amstrad (A. M. Sugar), Habitat (T. Conran), and Virgin Records (R. Branson). Despite having made large personal fortunes, these entrepreneurs continue in the same business, their decisions clearly motivated by more than just profit maximization (McNamee, 1988, p. 115). We may also note that all decision makers have a personal goal of survival and, at the very least, maintenance of remuneration. Certainly, the authors have yet to hear of pay cuts that have been entirely voluntary, or of managers dismissing themselves for being unproductive!

The relation between people and organizations has been eloquently expressed by Cyert and March (1963), who claim that 'people have goals ... collectivities of people (i.e. organisations) do not'. This remark was made at a time when the analysis of firms concentrated almost exclusively on formal organizational goals, and its effect was to direct attention to the relation between people and organizations. The behaviour of employees, i.e. their goals, decisions and actions, was increasingly seen as being the concern of the economist and the accountant, and not just the behavioural scientist.

A more formal expression of the relation between people and organizations can be found in agency theory, which came to prominence a few years after Cyert and March's observation. Although there are many implications of this theory – e.g. for incentives, for the provision of information, and for auditing – we include it here for its statement about goals, and in particular goal conflict; the other aspects are beyond the scope of the present text.

In agency theory, the firm is seen as being a network of people acting as agents. Briefly, when a shareholder is not able to manage the firm alone, he appoints an agent – the director. The director cannot in turn handle all the information he receives so he hires a sales director, production director, financial director and so on, to act as his agents in processing information and taking a certain level of decisions on his behalf. These directors, in turn, cannot handle all the information they receive, so they appoint managers as agents to help manage the data and take the less important decisions. This process continues down the hierarchy to the foreman and line workers, where it is physical work and the obeying of rules that are delegated, rather than information and decisions.

The model analyses the relation between principal and agent, or employee and immediate superior. In particular, it assumes that each agent is a self-interested party, implying that he has joined the organization to earn money and to minimize his effort in doing so. This introduces the possibility of what is politely termed 'moral hazard': if the cost is acceptable, i.e. there are no significant sanctions or loss of benefits, the employee will pursue his own goals to the detriment of the organization. Thus managers may spend money on expensive offices, trips with their wives abroad, prestigious cars, planes for personal as well as company use. All these expenditures are, in many cases, not strictly necessary for the pursuance of stated organizational objectives, despite protestations to the contrary. Thus we have a model built upon individual rather than organizational goals.

The employment contract is seen as the principal means by which moral hazard is avoided. To this end incentive schemes have received much attention. In effect, the scheme buys goal congruence or harmony between the individual and his superior, by making the opportunity cost (or lost incentive money) of just pursuing one's own goals too high. Congruence may also be achieved through control systems and monitoring, or post-audit of decisions – the stick as well as the carrot!

It is interesting to note that Japanese management styles place considerable emphasis on avoiding moral hazard and achieving goal congruence. 'From the selection process to the early morning exercises, the emphasis is on being a good team member' (Gabb, 1988). The Japanese decision processes of *ringi* and *nemewashi* place great emphasis on harmonizing goals:

'*Nemewashi* "Binding of the roots", refers to the "informal processes of bargaining, persuasion, the seeking of support, the long term trading of favours, and reciprocal obligations etc." (Trevor, 1983). *Nemewashi* can be considered as "pre-clearance" with all interested groups before a firm decision on any matter is taken.

"In the *Ringi* process a proposal will often be initiated by a departmental head". After discussion with other members of his division he will pass the proposal to another department along with an accompanying *Ringi* document, which he will stamp. As the proposal moves up, and across, the organization, it will be continually discussed and *nemewashi* processes will result in alterations to the initial proposal. At each stage on the route to the company president the *Ringi* document will be stamped.' (Buckley and Mirza, 1985.)

For our purposes, the significance of agency theory is that failure to maximize profit indicates more than mere inefficiency. Thus, the second-best decision may be selected because of its personal consequences for the decision maker, spending decisions on office furniture may be above what is strictly required, and so on. The organization does not disintegrate, as there is enough common interest to keep it together; but to understand decisions, we must be prepared to admit personal as well as corporate goals, and to accept a degree of goal conflict.

1.5.2   Group goals

Important decisions in organizations tend to be taken by committees or groups. In addition to the personal goals of agency theory, each committee member will usually pursue his own particular subset of managerial goals. Thus the sales manager will value decisions that increase the sales budget, the production manager will prefer decisions that lead to increased or more efficient production, and so on (Hopwood, 1974, p.130). How can we harmonize these goals? Is there a method that will meet everyone's preferences, or, failing that, which method will minimize possible conflicts?

The most obvious response to any conflict is to vote on the possible decisions. Even here, the results can be inconsistent. Let us suppose that there are three possible decisions facing managers. Decision A increases sales, Decision B reduces costs and Decision C improves productivity. Each decision can be seen to express the pursuit of a particular goal. Suppose that the group taking the decision comprises the sales director, finance director and production director, and that the ranking of projects is as shown in Table 1.2.

Table 1.2   Group voting
(1 indicates most preferred and 3 least preferred)

	A *increase sales*	B *reduce costs*	C *increase productivity*
Sales director	1	3	2
Finance director	2	1	3
Production director	3	2	1
Average rank	2	2	2

Average ranking will not separate the decisions. Discussion and comparison may produce apparent majority agreement. Thus a majority prefers B to A and prefers C to B; C appears to be preferred to or dominant over B and A (via B); but, unfortunately, a direct comparison between C and A shows that A is dominant over C. This is known as Condorcet's paradox and serves as a warning that group voting may not always lead to consistent ordering of preferences.

The problem of determining group goals was the subject of a famous study by K. J. Arrow, who concluded that, given a certain set of assumptions designed to ensure a democratic process, there was no method of ranking which always produced a consistent democratic ordering of preferences. In other words, situations could always be devised where selection could only be made by treating one of the participants unfairly. This result is known as Arrow's Impossibility Theorem. The implication is that goal conflict can only be settled by undemocratic means. In the preceding example, for instance, one of the directors may be regarded as senior and his preferences may prevail. Alternatively, the strength of preference may be tested – the finance director may agree to vote with the sales director providing the latter's salesmen collect more debts. In effect, the sales director will have bought the finance director's support. In doing so it is clear that the production director has not been treated fairly.

When groups are taking decisions, we should not look for a magical technique that will always give acceptable results. Differences have to be recognized or overcome in some manner. Broadly, we indicate two approaches to this problem: the first calls for consensus-building through political bargaining processes (see section 2.2.4), and the second incorporates the problem of consensus as part of the decision-making technique (see chapter 4). Where the problem is not specifically addressed, it will be assumed that the decision maker, whether an individual or committee, has a stable set of preferences that can be obtained by questioning (we shall see in section 2.5.3 that there

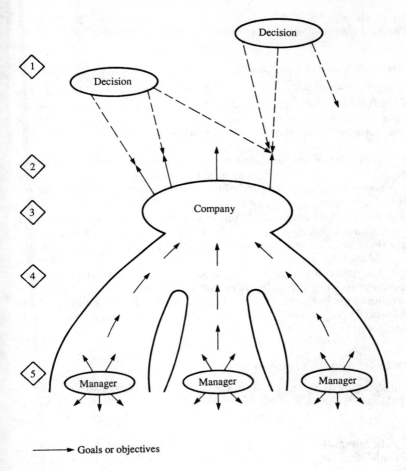

Figure 1.2   *Corporate objectives and decisions*

are strong group and social influences to encourage such stability). Without such an assumption our analysis would be virtually impossible.

1.6   Summary and conclusion

We have established that the purpose of decision making is to further corporate objectives. Ascertaining, measuring and relating objectives to decisions are integral parts of the decision process. It does, however, give rise to a number of problems which we now itemize (see Figure 1.2):

1   The relation between decisions and goals can present difficulties. Decisions have consequences or attributes, and determining how far attributes contribute to goals may require subjective scaling and the combination of several attributes.
2   A single goal will usually not be sufficient to evaluate decisions. We need to establish a set of relevant goals whose achievement can be measured.
3   Where there is more than one goal, we have the problem of combining them in order to reach a decision.
4   Where 'the decision maker' is a group of people or committee, we have the added problem of obtaining consensus.
5   Ascertaining goals is not an easy process. There is great potential for conflict between personal, unstated goals and the formal goals of an organization.

References and further reading

Accounting Standards Steering Committee (1975) The Corporate Report.
Arnold, J., Hope, A., *Accounting for Management Decisions*, Prentice-Hall, 1983.
Baumol, W. J., *Economic Theory and Operations Analysis*, 4th edition, Prentice-Hall, 1977.
Buckley, P. J., Mirza, H., 'The Wit and Wisdom of Japanese Management: An Iconoclastic Analysis', *Management International Review*, Vol. 25, pp. 16–21, 1985.
Collier, P. A., Cooke, T. E., Glynn, J. J., *Financial and Treasury Management*, Heinemann/CIMA, 1988.
Cyert, R., March, J., *A Behavioural Theory of the Firm*, Prentice-Hall, 1963.
Day, P., Klein, R., *Accountabilities – Five Public Services*, Tavistock, 1987.
Fox, R. P., 'Agency Theory – A New Perspective', *Management Accounting*, 1984.
Gabb, A., 'Komatsu Makes the Earth Move!', *Management Today*, April 1988.
Hopwood, A., 'Accounting and Human Behaviour', *Accountancy Age*, 1974.
Keeney, R. L., Raiffa, H., *Decisions with Multiple Objectives*, J. Wiley and Sons, 1976.
McNamee, P., *Strategic Planning and Marketing*, Heinemann/CIMA, 1988.
Report of the Royal Commission on the NHS, CMND 7615, HMSO, 1979, Para. 2.6.
Royal Commission on the Police, CMND 1728, HMSO, 1962.
Trevor, M., *Japan's Reluctant Multinationals*, Frances Pinter, 1983.

2 Decisions – context and process

2.1 Introduction

In chapter 1 we established that the purpose of taking decisions was to further the decision-makers' goals. Before looking at the theory and technique by which this aim may be pursued, we need to develop an appreciation of the 'real world' within which decisions are taken. To this end, we begin by examining the general decision process (section 2.2) and the main types of decisions that are taken (section 2.3). From this analysis it is clear that information and judgement are major inputs into decisions; the remaining two sections (2.4 and 2.5) examine the contribution of these inputs, again with the emphasis on the 'real world' aspects of the problem.

2.2 The decision process

It is perfectly possible in an organization for there to be an exhaustive decision process, with the most sophisticated reviews and decision techniques, which results in the selection of what proves to be an inferior option. Equally, it is possible for a manager to review the same problem, make an 'educated guess', and select the best option. No decision process guarantees success.

The evaluation of such processes in organizations is made difficult by the problem of determining what in fact was the right decision, as one cannot rerun the past. We may, with the benefit of hindsight, be able to identify a mistake, but this does not necessarily mean that our methods were at fault. A decision process can only be said to be inferior if there was information economically available at the time of the decision that was either ignored or misused. Even then, as we have noted, good fortune may yet salvage an inferior method.

The most obvious approach to determining a suitable decision process is to observe the practices of successful firms. Unfortunately there seems to be no single process uniquely correlated with success. For example, a survey by Scapens *et al.* (1982) found that in the UK nearly 50 per cent of their sample of 205 firms (with an average turnover of £239m) used payback, the accounting rate of return, and/or non-financial criteria rather than some form of discount cash flow analysis to evaluate investments; in fact no single method predominated. This result confirms the more detailed analyses of case studies, which show that successful firms employ a variety of decision-making styles and techniques with no particular process emerging as superior (see Sizer and Coulthurst, 1984).

In the literature, there have been many decision models advanced as frameworks to understand decisions. The most common is what we shall call the 'rational model'. This is a normative model; in other words, advocates maintain that it provides the structure for the way decisions ought to be taken. The alternative, positive models presented in this chapter have greater descriptive power, but lack the analysis and insight of the normative approach. For these reasons we do not develop these alternative models further than this chapter; but they are not to be dismissed, serving rather as useful critiques of normative methods.

2.2.1 The rational model

The rational model is comprehensive, logical and plausible. There are as many versions of the rational model as there are texts. This one, described in Figure 2.1, is no exception; we offer it merely as a typical example of the rational process rather than a definitive version. The model is, in fact, more complex than Figure 2.1 suggests, for within each box is a series of further normative processes.

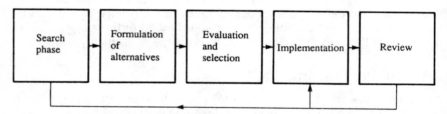

Figure 2.1   *The rational model of decision making*

The main feature of the model is that it is circular. The activities are seen as being sequential, starting with the search phase, and ending either with a review that leads back to the search (a full circle), or to implementation (creating a smaller circle).

The *search phase* seeks fundamental change, and begins with a capability profile. This is often analysed under the headings of strengths, weaknesses, opportunities and threats or SWOT analysis (McNamee, 1988, p. 148). It is both an internal and environmental analysis (Sizer, 1981, p. 80). The organization's position with respect to its markets, products and competitive strategy is reviewed, usually by means of a series of matrices, as in Figure 2.2.

For further analysis of these matrices, the reader is referred to the references and section 2.3.1. For our present purposes, it should be evident from Figure

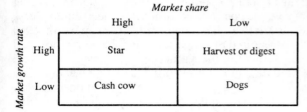

(a) Product portfolio and market strategy

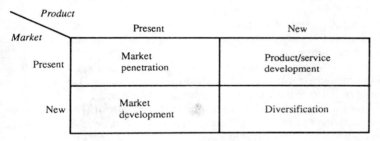

(b) Product market development

Prospects

	Unattractive	Average	Attractive
Weak	Disinterested	Phased withdrawal	Double or quit
Average	Phased withdrawal	Custodial	Try harder
Strong	Cash generation	Growth	Leader

Competitive capabilities

(c) Business sector prospects

Figure 2.2   *The search phase*

2.2 that the process directs a search for suitable courses of action to specific areas. There is then an identification of all available opportunities within the chosen strategies or 'boxes' in Figure 2.2. Again, rational processes are applied. For instance, Ansoff *et al.* (1969) analyse a strategy of diversification through merger (see Figure 2.2(b)). Suitable firms, they suggest, are found by first selecting an industry with the best merger prospects (this is achieved by assessing industries against a series of significant factors), then conducting a comprehensive search of suitable companies within the selected industry.

Once a set of possible alternatives has been outlined, a more detailed formulation of alternatives is required as preparation for the evaluation and selection process. This stage calls for the gathering of relevant data and estimates. The selection of data, and the eventual course of action, are determined by the *evaluation* model, e.g. the net present value model (section 5.2) requires an estimation of future cash flows, an accounting rate of return model (section 5.4.2) requires an estimation of future accounting profits, a multi-objective model (section 3.3.2) may need estimates of cash flow, quality, compatibility and other attributes. All these models will provide a ranking of the courses of action.

The process of evaluation relates the attributes of the various alternatives to the goals of the decision maker. For instance, the net present value model selects the estimated cash flow attributes of the decision, and this data is 'scored' in relation to the goal of increasing wealth by discounting the cash flows at an appropriate rate.

When the course of action has been selected, the decision process is completed by *implementation* followed by a review exercise. These two elements form the basis of control within the organization. In Figure 2.3 this process is outlined. The review exercise compares measures of output with the objectives. This comparison leads to the 'small loop' and 'big loop' of Figure 2.1, that is, a revision of implementation or strategic search, respectively. Thus the origins of the decision-making process are contained at the last stage – the review of implementation.

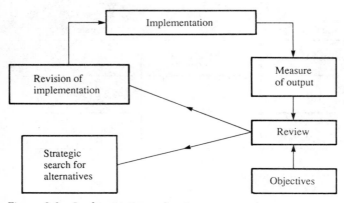

Figure 2.3   *Implementation and review*

Although the evaluation and selection stages are normally considered predominant in decision making, it should be clear that the rational model includes, in varying degrees, virtually all aspects of the firm. The treatment of decisions in many texts is entirely devoted to explaining the rational approach. Indeed, one might be forgiven for thinking that, in practice, a form of rational process predominates. It is true to say that in most organizations there is a formal decision process, and that elements of the rational model exist in every decision. Yet, it is often felt by managers that such rational processes do not fully describe actual decision making. The following quote from a manager typifies this view:

> Thank God it's over; now let's get back to work! This is my third strategy review. Same damn outcome. Nothing resolved. Every year we get together, fill in the forms – some of which don't even fit my business ... Nobody really cares what's in the strategic plans. We must put on a good show, appear to be innovative, and go through the ritual. (Lenz and Lyles, 1985.)

This has led many researchers to seek alternative explanations of the decision-making process, ones that more closely match observed behaviour. It is to these that we now turn.

2.2.2   The constraints model

This approach provides an alternative to the assumption of a single objective, or set of objectives, with known trade-offs – an assumption that, as we shall see, underlies the rational process. It was first advanced by Simon (1969), who suggested that the selection of projects should be based upon the linear programming model (see Biggs and Benjamin, 1989).

The model is made up of an objective function, followed by a number of constraints. The objective function is clearly a goal, so in business, for instance, it may be cost minimization or profit maximization; but the constraints are goals too. Recall from chapter 1 that one of the goals to be met in purchasing a car was that the price should be below £12,000. This is really a goal. However, once met, its weighting is reduced to zero and it no longer affects our choice. The treatment of goals as constraints conforms to Simon's view that people are satisficers with respect to goals rather than maximizers, i.e. the decision maker seeks certain levels of profits, sales, costs, etc. beyond which he or she has little interest. In this light, the linear programming model is a multi-objective decision-making model where constraints also represent the goals of the various interested parties. The objective function could be interchanged with any one of the constraints, e.g. a firm might seek to maximize sales, subject to a profit constraint, or maximize profits, subject to a minimum sales constraint.

The actual decision in Simon's model lies within the 'feasible area', which is that area that meets all constraints. To distinguish between alternatives within this area, he suggests the use of concepts such as Pareto optimization (see section 3.3.2). In our simple example concerning profits and sales, options within the feasible area that have higher sales and higher profits are to be preferred, though no solution is offered where one option has higher sales and lower profits within the feasible area. Although not suggested by Simon, goal programming would offer a similar but more discerning model; the technique makes it possible to weight the deviation from the constraints, and hence build in trade-offs between objectives. In some respects this brings us back to the traditional approach, for then the problem is of finding the weights. This is a complex problem for which certain algorithms have been suggested (Ashton (1985)).

Simon's constraints model has great intuitive appeal; but it is at best a partial description of the problem. Nevertheless, it does represent an important attempt to admit to the possibility that decisions may address more than one goal, and that these goals may conflict.

2.2.3   Muddling through

This highly descriptive model propounded by Lindblom (1964) will, by the nature of the title alone, evoke much sympathy from practitioners at least! Its particular critique of the rational approach is that in practice there is not a formal search phase followed by the formulation of alternatives. Such a process requires an excess of 'intellectual capacity and sources of information that men simply do not have'. He criticizes this as a 'root' method – in other words with every problem faced there is a building up from basics. The alternative process he advocates is the 'branch' method, whereby decisions are seen as a process of successive limited comparisons between an existing 'policy' and a proposed modification.

The choice of action, Lindblom suggests, is by agreement by the decision makers on the policy or action itself, 'without their agreeing that it is the most appropriate means to an agreed objective'. There is a marked similarity between this comment and the Commission on the National Health Service (section 1.4) and also the political model (section 2.2.4).

As a method of decision making the branch, or successive limited comparisons, method is not held to be ideal, in particular: 'i) Important possible outcomes are neglected. ii) Important alternative potential policies are neglected. iii) Important affected values are neglected' (Lindblom (1964)). Despite these drawbacks, it is thought by many to be both a good description of actual practice, and therefore a more realistic framework for analysing decisions. In addition it draws welcome attention to the importance of an organization's limited ability to process data and to generate agreement.

2.2.4   The political model

The political model characterizes the decision-making process as one of pursuing personal goals by obtaining agreement from those involved. Conflict is viewed as normal, there being no set of effective organizational goals. Thus action results 'from games among players who perceive quite different faces of an issue and who differ markedly in the actions they prefer' (Allison, 1971).

Strategies for obtaining agreement revolve around the use of power in a discreet fashion. The following strategies are a selection of those that have been observed by Pfeffer (1981):

1   *The selective use of criteria.* The basis upon which a decision is made is seen as an important means of legitimizing one's choice. For example, suppose project A is preferred to a number of other projects because it benefits the decision maker personally. Obviously this cannot be the overt reasons for the choice, so it is justified on more acceptable grounds, say,

because it has the fastest payback. If the project had the poorest net present value, then the decision maker would seek to exclude the net present value as a selection criterion. Thus, it is quite common in committees for an issue to be discussed not in terms of the benefits of the various alternatives, but rather, at one remove, in terms of which selection criteria should be used.

2   *The outside expert.* Influence in the decision process may be strengthened by co-opting an outside expert who will support the desired viewpoint. The apparent lack of direct interest in the outcome gives added weight to the opinions expressed. There are likely to be indirect interests by which agreement may be procured. Thus the outside expert may be a management consultant whose views are biased by a desire to retain the account, or a supplier, or a customer, both of whom may be anxious to maintain favourable trading terms.

3   *Coalition building.* One of the consequences of conflict is the building of coalitions and alliances. Not all parties to an agreement will be equally affected. Those with less at stake may 'sell' their agreement to one or other of the more interested parties in return for an understood reciprocal support over issues when the interests are reversed.

4   *Controlling the agenda.* In certain organizations it may be possible to defeat an issue by simply keeping it off the agenda. A variation of such a tactic would be to consider an issue in a subcommitte, where the selection of members may be a deciding factor. Another method is to control the order of presentation of issues. Pfeffer suggests that if weaker, less favoured options are presented first, the committee's critical powers and decision-making abilities are exercised in rejecting the proposals. Furthermore, a relatively low set of standards is set, favouring acceptance of the desired proposal. Also, many committees are limited by time and 'norms of fair play and fair treatment argue that the actor doing the proposing should get at least something from the meeting. This will be easy to rationalise as the second (stronger) issue has more merit' (Pfeffer, 1981, p. 152).

Many readers may be rather shocked by this Machiavellian approach to decisions. Nevertheless, few would deny that these strategies, or like strategies, are practised in every decision-making organization to varying degrees. We should perhaps conclude by reminding the reader that this is essentially a descriptive model, and in no way suggests how decisions ought to be taken.

2.2.5   *Agency and M form hypothesis*

We have already discussed the general agency framework in section 1.5.1. As regards the decision process, agency theory implies that responsibility for decisions ought to be delegated to the agent or manager most able to take the decision. The structural implication for the organization has given rise to the multidivisional (M form) hypothesis, which maintains that an organization 'attains optimal divisionalisation through the allocation of strategic operating decisions to different managerial levels, and the use of an appropriate control apparatus' (Ezzamel and Hart (1987), p. 253). This ideal state was developed by Williamson (1975) as the best of six possible means of classifying large corporate structures. These are:

1   Unitary (U-form): a traditional, functionally organized enterprise, including those with measures of diversification which account for less than a third of the firm's value added.
2   Holding company (H-form): a divisionalized enterprise for which the requisite internal control apparatus has not been provided because of the subsidiary nature of divisions.
3   Multidivisional (M-form): a divisionalized enterprise in which a separation of operating from strategic decision making is attained and for which the requisite internal control apparatus has been provided and is systematically employed.
4   Transitional multidivisional (M'-form): an M-form enterprise in the process of adjustment and learning.
5   Corrupted multidivisional ($\bar{\text{M}}$-form): an M-form enterprise with the requisite control apparatus but where the central management participates extensively in operating activities.
6   Mixed (X-form): an enterprise in which H-form structure, M-form divisions, and even centrally supervised divisions, may simultaneously exist.

The M form organizations ought to be more successful by virtue of their better structure. Empirical tests lend some support to this proposition, though there are considerable measurement problems. For a useful review see Ezzamel (1985).

2.2.6   *Conclusions – the gap between theory and practice*

Many readers may well feel rather bewildered by this array of models. On the one hand, there is the rational normative model which has analytical power, but is not necessarily a good description of reality. On the other hand, there are a number of competing positive models, all claiming to present a realistic picture of decision making.

Let us clarify the position by suggesting that we begin by accepting one of the positive, descriptive models for implementation. Whichever one we choose, it will only be a partial picture of the process, e.g. the constraints model offers little on the original search, and 'muddling through' has little to say on implementation and review. Moreover, each model could be improved upon in what it does say. The political model, for instance, hardly appears likely to generate and select the best opportunities in the long run, even for those who win the political struggle.

Each positive model could in some sense be refined and developed. But how is one to achieve this? To the pure positivist the only solution is to conduct further empirical study, with the hope of finding an improvement in practice that has not yet spread to the main body of organization literature. There is something of this in tests of the M form hypothesis; but such an approach is exceedingly demanding on statistical data, and is unlikely ever to produce wholly convincing results. An alternative to the positivist solution is to adopt a normative approach, and say what ought to be done. For example, one might introduce zero base budgeting (ZBB) where the 'muddling through' philosophy is thought to predominate, thereby forcing a greater element of 'root' analysis.

Taking this approach admits to two beliefs: (a) social processes are capable of being changed by directive, and (b) that one can construct by means of introspective contemplation an improvement to existing practice. Both these points are debatable. It should not be assumed, for instance, that if ZBB were introduced, the result will necessarily be ZBB. It may well amount to a sham of no real relevance. Despite these reservations, we suggest that the normative or rational approach that we have outlined is the most important of the methods of analysing decisions, as it is the only practical way by which real situations may be improved. It can do this in several ways. Those generally suggested are:

1   *The useful tools approach* (Watson and Buede (1987), p. 52). Normative methods produce many imaginative answers to problems. A manager does not have to use the approaches suggested, and there is no suggestion that a normative model will necessarily improve any particular decision-making scenario. Nevertheless, he or she may use a normative approach if desired.
2   *The educational approach.* Normative methods provide a rational approach that seems inherently desirable. By applying the model, we may be persuaded that our original choice and method was wrong and can be improved upon (French (1989), p. 37), or, as more crudely put by Keeney and Raiffa (1976, p. 1), 'the aim of the analysis is to get your head straightened out!'
3   *Communication and advocacy.* Organizations have formal decision processes which will be of varying degrees of effectiveness, but are unlikely to be wholly ignored. Managers need to communicate and persuade those involved in the decision and others not involved but who are nevertheless affected. A normative model is a useful vehicle for such advocacy (Keeney and Raiffa (1976), p. 442).

Most of the analysis in this book is normative in nature. We are therefore obviously in agreement with these reasons for taking a normative approach, though, as we have said, the more positive descriptive approaches may serve as a useful starting point and critique of the normative view.

In practice, many managers would subscribe to the view 'forget the theory, this is how we really do it'. We hope that we have persuaded the reader that this attitude is both shortsighted and arrogant. All methods are capable of improvement; the analysis presented here may at times seem idealistic, but even when it is only an ideal, it is nevertheless a valuable guide to enable managers to improve existing practices.

2.3   Decision types

Although decisions may pass through the same process, they can present markedly different problems. In this section we survey the types of problem encountered by examining common classifications of decisions.

2.3.1   Decision levels and areas

In looking at objectives, it was suggested that there was a hierarchy of goals (Figure 1.1). As decisions are means of achieving goals, a natural extension is a hierarchy of decisions.

Strategic decisions are those that are taken at the senior level of the organization. As with their equivalent goals, they deal with long-term significant consequences. An important strategic decision is the *product and service mix*, i.e. the strategy that the firm wishes to adopt with respect to its products and services. The matrices in Figure 2.2(a) and (b) illustrate the type of decisions that are made when determining such strategies.

As an illustration, let us examine Figure 2.2(a). The 'cash cow' strategy refers to a dominant portfolio of products in a limited market. In that opportunities are limited, investment would be expected to produce low returns. As a result, such products or services may be used to generate cash by maximizing short-term profits with little regard for future prospects. The returns may then be invested in the 'star' products, or they may be used to increase a low market share where there is high market growth, i.e. turning products into 'stars'. Where there is no attempt to increase the market share, the firm may adopt a harvesting strategy. In such cases, the firm follows the most profitable of the 'cash cow' approach or divestment – which is a selling off of the product name and associated production activity. The second matrix, Figure 2.2(b), looks at the problems posed by adding to the existing product or service mix (for an analysis of these strategies see McNamee (1988)). In practice, each of the policies outlined serves to limit the search process, but still include a wide set of possible actions.

Once the general strategies have been selected, a number of decisions have to be taken at a less senior managerial level. Thus, for example, where directors have taken the strategic decision to invest in and develop a certain portfolio of products, the more detailed decisions relating to promoting the product will be delegated to managers with the relevant knowledge. Such decisions are equivalent to the managerial level of Figure 1.1. At this second level, there will also be decisions relating to advertising, quality, style, brand name, service level, sales promotion, etc. These may, through lack of specialist knowledge, have to be delegated further. Decisions at this level of detail are termed operating decisions.

There is no clear distinction between operating and strategic decisions, though operating decisions require detailed knowledge and are of limited effect. They also require the more general decisions at a strategic level to be made, in order to provide guidelines. For example, the allocation of sales targets to salesmen is an operating decision that requires the setting of sales levels for products, which requires strategic decisions as to product development.

Decisions also need to be co-ordinated between different areas. As an illustration, we examine the problem of deciding upon the marketing mix. All the items in Table 2.1 require decisions that need to be blended together 'into a combination that enables the organization to achieve its objectives in its target market' (McNamee, 1988, p. 258). The problem of co-ordination is potentially enormous – in this case there are twenty-one decision areas. If we limit our concept of co-ordination to the need to consider two areas together, then there are a possible 210 problems of co-ordination (calculated as $n(n-1)/2$ where n is the number of areas). Of course, in practice some areas will not require co-ordination, e.g., payment terms and brand name. Nevertheless, the problem should not be underestimated. In certain cases co-ordination can only be achieved by detailed planning, thus 'discounts and allowances' and 'sales promotion' and 'publicity' will require a degree of joint planning. In other cases, effective strategic decisions will overcome many such problems. If it is made clear that, for instance, a product is aimed at the top range in the market, decisions such as 'brand name', 'packaging', 'distribution', 'selling' and 'price level' by conforming to this strategic decision, will achieve a degree of harmony without direct comparison.

Table 2.1 The marketing mix

Product/service	Place	Promotion	Price
Quality	Distribution channels	Advertising	Level
Features and	Distribution coverage	Personal selling	Discounts and
options	Outlet locations	Sales promotion	allowances
Style	Inventory levels and	Publicity	Payment terms
Brand name	locations		
Packaging	Transportation carriers		
Product line			
Warranty			
Service level			
Other Services			

Source: McNamee (1988), p. 258.

2.3.2   Decision qualities

Some decision problems are easily solved, others seem almost intractable. One of the most enduring classification of such problems was proposed by Thompson and Tuden (1959) by means of the matrix in Figure 2.4 which we have adapted to the terminology used here.

First, let us examine the top row in the matrix of Figure 2.4 by looking at a decision to allocate fixed costs. Suppose that all managers are agreed that fixed costs should be allocated on some measure of usage. There is therefore an agreed goal. It seems reasonable to assume that after some discussion suitable bases of allocation can be found for the various elements of fixed costs, e.g. number of people for personnel costs, area for heating and so on. The outcome from the allocation process is certain, and the goal of the

*Preferences
over goals*

		Agreed	Not agreed
Decision outcomes	Certain	Decision by computation	Decision by compromise
	Uncertain	Decision by judgement	Decision by inspiration

Figure 2.4   *Styles of decision making*

exercise is stable (in that it is agreed); hence the decision is simply a matter of computation. Alternatively, if there is disagreement over goals, then there is likely to be disagreement over the basis of allocation, though the outcome from any one method of allocation is still clear. If one manager considers that 'ability to pay' should be the goal for allocation rather than usage, say, then managers will need to debate the difference of opinion; this can only be resolved by some form of compromise (the top right-hand box).

Now let us examine the bottom row of the matrix by taking the problem of selecting competing capital investment projects. Suppose that all managers are agreed that wealth maximization should be the main goal; the net present value model seems the best choice under such circumstances. However, future cash flows are uncertain, so that the decision will be by judgement aided by decision-making techniques. Some managers might argue that this form of wealth maximization is not sufficient as a goal, and that weight should be given to the appearance of the balance sheet and accounting profit. Such a view implies that some measure of accounting rate of return would also be relevant. The bottom right-hand box is now applicable. Thompson and Tuden suggest that in such circumstances organizations may be paralysed on issues and require a manager who is able to affect the way other managers view goals and 'create a new vision or image or belief, and thereby pull together a disintegrating or paralyzed organisation' (Thompson and Tuden (1959)).

This is a rather extreme view, for there are many organizational decisions where there is uncertainty and disagreement over goals, and yet there is no paralysis. In some circumstances an option may prove superior under varying sets of goals. In our example, an investment may have a better net present value and accounting rate of return. All would therefore be agreed on the favourite option, though for differing reasons. In other circumstances, a voting procedure may be devised whereby one option is shown to be the favourite. For instance, if the option with the best net present value does not have the best accounting rate of return, but only one out of the ten managers delegated to make the selection values accounting rate of return, then it seems clear that the option with the highest net present value would be chosen, despite the uncertainty over goals. Of course, there will be circumstances as illustrated by Condorcet's paradox (section 1.5.2) where there may indeed be the paralysis as described by Thompson and Tuden. In such cases, the concept of 'muddling through' or the political processes of section 2.2.4 are the only analytical frameworks that offer solutions to such dilemmas. The drawback of such approaches is that they are either undemocratic (the political model), or the choice that they offer is suboptimal ('muddling through').

As demonstrated in Arrow's Impossibility Theorem, it is not possible to provide an 'optimal' method of obtaining agreement when goals are in dispute (section 1.5.2). Accordingly, the columns in Figure 2.5 replace this aspect by the more tractable problem of single and multiple goals. The issue of goal conflict is not entirely excluded, for where there is more than one goal, the decision maker will need to establish trade-offs. The analysis in this text follows this traditional pattern.

Sections	Single goal	Multiple goal
Decisions under certainty	3.3.1	3.3.2
Decisions under uncertainty	3.4.1–3.4.6	3.4.7

Figure 2.5   *Traditional approach to decision analysis*

2.4   Information for decisions

The provision of information in an organization is one of the principal roles of the accountant. Indeed the American Accounting Association (1966) defines accounting as follows: 'The process of identifying, measuring and communicating economic information to permit informed judgements and decisions by users of the information'.

To understand the contribution of information we first examine formal models of information value and then the practical problems of obtaining information in an organizational setting.

2.4.1   *Information value*

Let us begin with a very simplified model. Suppose Firm X Ltd wishes to launch product Y. If the product is successful, X Ltd estimates that future earnings will be equivalent to a net increase of present wealth of £1 million. If the product is a failure, then it will be withdrawn within the year with an estimated loss of £400,000. From X Ltd's experience of launching similar products to Y, it is estimated that the chances of success are 60 per cent. Let us also suppose that recent research in this market confirms that '40 per cent of all new products fail'. The problem that the firm faces may be represented by the tree diagram in Figure 2.6.

The square node indicates a decision point, the firm may either launch or not launch the product. If they *do not* launch it, there will be no future costs

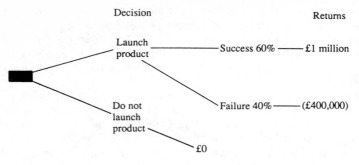

Figure 2.6   *Tree diagram*

or revenues, hence £0 return. If they *do* launch it, then they enter the risky scenario as described.

How can the returns of launching the product be represented? Suppose the manager makes the following statement: 'We launch many products; some succeed, some fail. Our general strategy is on balance to obtain a net positive return'. This suggests that some form of averaging procedure would be acceptable (but see section 3.4.2); we may represent this view by taking the expected value (EV) of returns from launching, hence:

EV (launch) = (0.60 × 1,000,000) − 0.40 × (400,000)
              = £440,000
and EV (no launch) = £0.

Thus, by our measure, X Ltd would feel £440,000 better off by deciding to launch, even though it risks losing £400,000. Suppose that X Ltd also considers test marketing the product in the South West of England. In addition, assume that the results of the test are considered to be a perfect predictor of the success or failure of the project. If we ignore the cost of the exercise for the moment, the expected value of product Y, given that a test market exercise is carried out, is:

EV (Y | test market) = 0.60 × (1,000,000) + 0.40 (0)
                      = £600,000
(the sign | means 'given that')

The test market has increased expected returns by £600,000 − £440,000 = £160,000; the gain is as a result of avoiding the losses, for if the test market report says no, then we will not go ahead with the project. By our measure, £160,000 represents the most X Ltd would be willing to pay for this perfect information. More formally:

EVPI = EV (action | perfect information) − EV (action | no information)
(where EVPI = expected value of perfect information)

Most information concerning estimates is imperfect. Let us develop this point by assuming that it is possible to express the likelihood of information being correct as a percentage. The test market exercise therefore produces information that is 100 per cent correct. Extending our example, let us suppose that the future sales of product Y can also be predicted by means of a questionnaire. This is less comprehensive as a test, so let us assume that the results of a questionnaire are likely to be correct 80 per cent of the time. If X Ltd undertakes the questionnaire, then the possible outcomes are as follows:

Report correct

a_1 questionnaire says launch, product is successful.
a_2 questionnaire says do not launch, product is unsuccessful.

Report incorrect

a_3 questionnaire says launch, product is unsuccessful
a_4 questionnaire says do not launch, product is successful.

Note that a_2 and a_4 are unobservable, though they are nevertheless distinct outcomes. The probabilities of $a_1 \ldots a_4$ are:

	Report correct		*Chances of success or failure*		
a_1	0.80	×	0.60	=	0.48
a_2	0.80	×	0.40	=	0.32

	Report incorrect				
a_3	0.20	×	0.40	=	0.08
a_4	0.20	×	0.60	=	0.12

An important point to make is that the report prediction does not affect the actual chances of success or failure. However, it does affect our chances of avoiding failure, e.g. horse racing tips (predicted information) do not affect the race itself, though they do affect our chances of avoiding failure, sometimes! So if we follow the advice of the report, the probability (Pr) of success given that the report says launch may be expressed as:

$$\text{Pr (success} \mid \text{report says launch)} = \frac{\text{Probability of success and report saying launch}}{\text{Probability of the report saying launch}}$$

$$= \frac{a_1}{a_1 + a_3}$$

$$= \frac{0.48}{0.48 + 0.08} = 86\%$$

and by similar reasoning:

Pr (failure | report says launch) $= \dfrac{a_3}{a_1 + a_3} = 14\%$

The expected value of a positive report is therefore:

EV (report says launch) $= 0.86 \, (1{,}000{,}000) - 0.14 \, (400{,}000)$
$= 804{,}000$

and the expected value of a negative report is:

EV (report says no launch) $= 0$

The probability of a positive report is $a_1 + a_3 = 0.56$ and the probability of a negative report is $a_2 + a_4 = 0.44$. Hence the expected value from using a questionnaire report is:

EV (report) $= 0.56 \times 804{,}000 + 0.44 \times 0 = 450{,}240$

By carrying out the questionnaire and following its recommendations X Ltd can expect to be better off by $450{,}240 - 440{,}000 = £10{,}240$. More generally:

EVII = EV (action | imperfect information) − EV (action | no information).
(where EVII is the expected value of imperfect information).

The gain of £10,240 may be explained as follows:

Gain in probability of success	$(0.86 - 0.60) \times £1\text{m} = 260{,}000$
Plus reduction in probability of loss	$(0.40 - 0.14) \times £0.4\text{m} = 104{,}000$
Less reduced likelihood of going ahead	
with the project by following the report	$(1.0 - 0.56) \times 804{,}000 = \underline{353{,}760}$
	Value of report $= 10{,}240$

The value of the information is in the way that it adjusts our prior probabilities of success from 0.60 to 0.86 and reduces our prior probabilities of loss from 0.40 to 0.14. The cost of this gain is the reduced likelihood of going ahead. Whereas previously we would have always gone ahead with launching Product Y, the report has only a 56% chance of recommending a launch, hence the expected benefits are less likely to be enjoyed. This analysis is based upon Bayes theorem, though we have avoided the terminology of the theorem itself (see Ezzamel and Hart (1987), for a more formal analysis). Providing that one accepts that probabilities or likelihoods can be calculated in this way, then there seems no reason why it could not be used in practice. Imagine the following conversation:

Director: I am surprised by this accounting report on Division A, I thought it was doing fine.
Manager: Well, these reports aren't always correct.

Director: They are correct about 80 per cent of the time, but I was 90 per cent sure that everything was OK.

Manager: Then by my reckoning the chances of it being OK, given that the report disagrees, are about 70 per cent. If we send it back and ask them to be 95 per cent sure about their conclusions and it comes up with the same message, then you could only be 30 per cent sure that it was really OK.

Director: Yes, let's do that.

Has the analysis helped? The reader is invited to draw his or her own conclusions. Even if the analysis is seen solely as an analytical model, there are still important insights to be made concerning the role of information in decisions. These are:

1   Information must be *relevant*; in other words, it must affect our prior probabilities of events related to the decision. In the marketing example, the information from the report affected the probability of the launch being a success. In the accounting report example, the information affected prior probabilities of the well-being of the division, which had direct implications over the decision to investigate.

2   To be worthwhile, information must be *valuable*, i.e. as well as affecting our prior probabilities, it must be worthwhile acting upon. This will not always be the case, even though information may be quite accurate. For example, in the marketing example, if the information was only 70 per cent accurate our probabilities would be affected thus:

$Pr(a_1) = 0.42$, $Pr(a_2) = 0.28$, $Pr(a_3) = 0.12$, $Pr(a_4) = 0.18$

$$Pr(\text{Success} \mid \text{report says launch}) = \frac{0.42}{0.42 + 0.12}$$
$$= 0.78$$

Pr (failure | report says launch) $= 0.22$

EV (report says launch) $= 0.78 \,(1{,}000{,}000) - 0.22\,(400{,}000)$
$= 692{,}000$

EV (report says no launch) $= 0$

EV (report) = Pr (report says launch) × EV (report says launch)
   + Pr (report says no launch) × EV (no launch)
   $= 0.54 \times 692{,}000 + 0.46 \times 0 = £373{,}680$

Going ahead without a report would yield an expected value of £440,000; hence the report is not worthwhile, even though it has caused us to revise our probabilities. By altering variables in the analysis we can see that value is made up of a combination of:

(a)   *Accuracy of information.* In this example we know that the report is valuable if it were 80 per cent accurate in its forecasts.

(b)   *Potential benefits of information.* If the benefit of a successful launch were not above £692,082, then the report would be of potential value. This might initially sound contradictory, but a moment's thought should confirm that the greater the benefits of success, the surer we would be of going ahead without any further information.

The smaller the benefits, the more carefully we need to evaluate the decision.

(c) *Potential losses.* If potential losses increased to some £635,846, then the report would be worthwhile in helping to prevent such a result.

(d) Information must be *economic*, i.e. the expected *benefits of information* must outweigh the *cost of information*

(e) *Timeliness.* To be of value, information must arrive in time for one to take a decision.

(f) Finally, and perhaps most obviously, information must be *understandable*, i.e. the implication for the decision must be clearly understood.

2.4.2   *Information gathering*

Of particular concern to the accountant is the problem of gathering information. For decision making, this exercise presents particular difficulties in that much of the information will be of a non-routine nature. An important decision is a unique event; accounting systems are cyclical in nature and cannot be expected to provide information for such unpredictable events. Information gathered from an accounting system will always have to be carefully reviewed. The technical problems of this exercise, i.e. estimating, allocating, aggregating, presenting and interpreting costs and revenues, are the very stuff of any traditional management accounting textbook (see section 4.5). In this section we complement this knowledge by looking at the organizational context.

The problem of gathering such data has been represented by researchers as creating a solicitor–informant relationship, i.e. the management accountant may solicit data from his own staff, or from the purchasing department, personnel department, production department and so on, in order to draw up a management accounting report. In analysing this relationship in the accounting context, McDonough (1971) notes that:

(a) The interests of the solicitor and informant differ, for data collection is invariably the primary activity of the solicitor while it is almost by definition a secondary activity of the informant.

(b) The informant possesses a high degree of control over the relationship.

The informant may not always view the solicitor as acting in his or her best interests. It should be remembered that it is likely that some of the data in a report may be critical of the very unit that has provided the information. If the informant is not aware or convinced of the reasons for gathering the data, a hostile intent may well be inferred. The informant may, in such circumstances, use his control over the data to frustrate the solicitor. Such action is unlikely to be overt: to pursue his own goals, the informant may adopt frustrating strategies. Three such strategies are outlined by McDonough:

1 *Delay.* Since information of an *ad hoc* nature is likely to be of a lower priority than the informant's main task, delay may be seen as a readily available strategy.

2   *Feigned ignorance.* The solicitor is not as well acquainted with the technical details as the informant. On being asked for data, the informant may either deny the existence of the data where the exact term is not used, or may provide the data but fail to inform the solicitor of a salient technical point. As a simple example, if an accountant were to ask a reluctant sales department for an analysis of sales, it is likely that the analysis would be of orders, for that is often the term used for sales in sales departments. The cancellation rate and delay between order and sale would not be provided 'because they were not asked for', though an experienced sales manager may be perfectly aware that such information would be needed.

3   Over-compliance. An informant may flood the solicitor with data, making it quite impossible to extract the relevant information. Easier methods of collecting the data may be discreetly overlooked, with little likelihood of discovery.

These strategies may also be used in combination. For instance, feigned ignorance may be used as an excuse for over-compliance: 'I'm not sure what you want, but it's probably somewhere in this lot!'

To the practitioner, these strategies will be painfully realistic. Other readers should remember that information gathering can be both costly and a source of inaccuracy, and hence affect the value of information and the decision itself. There are no simple solutions to these problems other than the exercising of the accountant's ability to 'erect and maintain bridges between levels and between functions' (McDonough (1971)).

2.5   Human judgement

Decision processes require human judgement. We have seen in section 2.4.1 that decision makers may be asked about the likelihood of a particular event. In addition, in later chapters, we will need to ask the decision maker to assess preferences, and even strength of preference. So a relevant question to consider beforehand is 'How good is human judgement?' Bayesian analysis, net present value models and like processes will be of little value if the judgemental data that they all require is badly flawed.

There have been many studies of people's ability to make estimates and take decisions from data. Unfortunately, they are in the main a catalogue of people's inability to make judgements. Before documenting these human foibles, and giving the impression that decision making is the rational interpretation of irrational data, a few points should be borne in mind: (a) most of these studies are based upon abstract questions (known as laboratory studies), it should not always be inferred that a decision maker's judgement would be as flawed when considering matters on which he or she had long experience; (b) many of the subjects are not experienced managers and may be viewed as naive; (c) there is evidence that education and incentives can improve a manager's ability to make judgements (Sage (1981), and (d) managers do make intelligent decisions, so that they cannot be subject to all of the flaws all of the time!

We shall divide our analysis of judgement into three areas: the ability to analyse data, the effect of the availability of data, and the social influences on decisions.

2.5.1   Analytical ability

Insensitivity to prior probabilities. In some experiments candidates are asked to make judgements about an item drawn from a population. A good example is estimating from a character report whether a manager is a lawyer or an engineer (Tvensky and Kahnemann (1974)); some subjects were told that the person was drawn from a population that was 70 per cent lawyers and 30 per cent engineers, other subjects were given the same population proportions only in reverse. Both groups judged the chances of the candidate being an engineer to be the same, despite the prior probabilities. Such a basis would imply that in the conversation between the manager and director in section 2.4.1, the director would typically wholly discount his prior impression of the performance of division A instead of combining the two judgements, using Bayes theorem.

Insensitivity to sample size. Judgements are often made from very small samples. A manager's own experience of one or two like situations will usually be considered sufficient for him to make confident predictions.

Illusory correlation. People see patterns where none exist. To illustrate this effect, this author used to set the following problem: last summer, which was hot, shop Q, a retail clothing outlet, found that blue was the most popular colour. This summer is confidently predicted to be cold, so should shop Q (a) order fewer blue clothes than last year, (b) order the same amount as last year or (c) order more than last year? The usual response was (a), which was explained by an inferred inverse correlation between colour association and temperature. There was no regard for the fact that the sample size was only one, and there was nothing to suggest that such a correlation existed. Response (b) is the most reasonable, as there is no reliable information justifying change. Another illustration of this effect is the tossing of a fair coin. It is often considered that a coin is more likely to show heads after a sequence of tails. Of course, the results are independent, each toss of a fair coin having a 50:50 chance of heads or tails no matter what the previous sequence of events.

Regression to mean. There is often little appreciation that results tend to vary around a mean. Tversky and Kahnemann (1973) give a graphic example concerning flight training instructors. The experience of the instructors was that harsh criticism after a bad landing usually resulted in an improved second landing, and a highly praised good landing tended to be followed by a worse landing. They inferred that harsh criticism was better than praise! The correlation is illusory. Performance tends to vary around a mean; hence one would normally expect, say, an average landing and outlying observations to be relatively infrequent. Therefore an exceptionally good landing is more likely to be followed by a worse landing and *vice versa*, whether or not there is praise or criticism.

Over-confidence. There is a tendency for decision makers to express unwarranted confidence in their estimates. To illustrate this effect, the author used to ask students to provide a high and low estimate of the number of football clubs in the four divisions of the football league such that they were 95 per cent confident that the true number was within the range. Usually, only about half the class were successful. One would expect almost all to manage this task, for, after all, the interval could be as wide as one liked. Furthermore, and this is also a common finding, having reviewed this bias the class was immediately given a similar problem (estimating the population of a town), and the over-confidence was still to be observed. In some classes it was worse! In case the reader thinks that this is a comment on students, Tversky and Kahnemann have noted similar effects among professional psychologists! None of us is immune to these biases, nor can they be easily changed.

Anchoring and adjustment. When making estimates people tend to use a starting point, no matter how random it may be. Adjustments from this initial value are generally insufficient. In an experiment where subjects were asked to estimate the number of African countries in the United Nations (Slovic and Lichtenstein (1971)), a number was chosen by spinning a wheel of fortune. First, subjects were asked whether the true number was above or below this estimate. They were then asked to estimate how far above or below the true estimate was. It was found that when the randomly selected number was high, the estimate tended to be high, and when the random number was low, the final estimate also tended to be low. Thus an anchoring and adjustment policy was pursued even when it was clearly unjustified.

Compounding estimates. Suppose a cost per unit calculation is made up of six independent costs. If there is an 85 per cent chance that each cost will be as in the budget and a 15 per cent chance it will be greater, then there is only a 38 per cent chance of achieving the budgeted cost per unit (0.85^6). This figure is somewhat less than most would estimate. Even when errors can help as well as hinder a target, the chances of meeting it are less than one would expect. For instance, Otley (1987, p. 68) gives an example of the addition of nine budgets that have normally distributed returns where there is a 30 per cent chance of achieving each budget (the tough but attainable philosophy for budgets). The chance of achieving the overall target is, however, only 6 per cent!

This result may partly be explained by falsely imputing a positive correlation between events where none exists (in the cost per unit calculation, if all costs were perfectly correlated, then there would be an 85 per cent chance of achieving the budget). In addition, the effect of multiplying probabilities produces a more dramatic shrinking than many people expect.

2.5.2   *The availability effect*

Concreteness. Managers take decisions on the information available, i.e. 'Decision makers tend to use only that information which is explicitly displayed and only in the form in which it is displayed' (Livingstone (1975, p. 117)). The accountant is correspondingly placed in a powerful position, for he can potentially affect management decisions by filtering data (Demski (1980, pp. 70–80)).

Retrievability. Managers usually absorb only a small proportion of the data presented in a report, and tests have shown that the way in which data is presented can affect this process. Making a figure difficult to retrieve reduces the chances of management using the data.

Information is also held in people's memory as well as a report, and here too the ease with which an incident is recalled will affect a manager's judgement. For example, witnessing an accident at work will make a manager overestimate the probability of such an event. In a test conducted by Tversky and Kahnemann (1973) subjects were presented with lists of people and then asked to judge whether or not there were more men than women. Judgement was found to be influenced by the number of well-known personalities in the list. Again familiarity biases judgement.

Imaginability. In estimating the likelihood of future events, some are under-estimated because they are difficult to imagine. One may think of Chernobyl, Zeebrugge, the Alaskan oil spill, Hillsborough and other such accidents and wonder whether there were insufficient safeguards simply because managers could not imagine such events happening.

Selective perception. Finally, managers tend to see only what they want to see. Unpleasant or contradictory facts tend to be overlooked.

2.5.3   Social influences

Managers, like all people, are influenced by their 'environment' – by this we mean their upbringing, education, job and by their colleagues. This has an important effect on the decisions that are taken; indeed, it has always been recognized as an important source of control. Organizations will often select people 'of a certain background' or train them in the company way to ensure a degree of cohesiveness and predictability in decision making. The point has been put more colourfully by Jay (1970), who used the selection of Roman generals as an example: 'You appoint him, you watch his chariot and baggage train disappear over the hill in a cloud of dust and that was that ... You knew that everything depended on him being the best man before he set off, and so you took great care in selecting him. But more than that, you made sure that he knew all about Rome and Roman government and the Roman army before he went'. Managers also have to take many decisions on their own, in the same manner as Roman generals.

The wider of the social influences on human behaviour are beyond the scope of this text. Here we mention briefly three sources of influence that lie within the firm.

First, there is the internal training course. Here employees are instructed directly in the company regulations and the way in which the company 'works', or takes its decisions.

Secondly, managers may be influenced by selective perception dependent on their position within the firm and, no doubt, their education. In a famous experiment Dearborn and Simon (1958) asked managers on an executive training course to identify the main problems in a case study. The majority of managers identified the principal problem as one related to their own speciality. Thus 83 per cent of sales managers saw sales as the principal problem, while only 29 per cent of other managers identified sales in this way. Our interpretation is guided by what we learn and experience.

Thirdly, in another famous series of experiments conducted between the wars at the Western Electric Company, it was demonstrated that people tend to behave in groups rather than as individuals (Mayo (1949)). In this case the group was wiring equipment, and a worker joining the group typically adjusted his or her output level to that of the group. In addition, group output was found to respond favourably to the degree of consultation and communication with the group by the researchers (this is known as the Hawthorne effect after the name of the factory). Managers too are in groups. Thus, this and like studies suggest that we can meaningfully talk about departmental or group behaviour.

In section 1.5.1 it was asserted that people and not organizations have goals. We might now modify this view by noting that people's behaviour and viewpoints are affected by outside influences, which include the organization where the decision making is located. These influences can be used to create a degree of unity between individuals. Although conflicts between a manager and an organization will always remain, it should be recognized that there are pressures in an organization to adopt a single set of goals. To assume, as we do in later analysis, that there is a single stable set of goals is not an unrealistic approximation for many organizations.

2.5.4 Conclusions on human behaviour

To some this catalogue of human failings and biases is sufficient to convince them that analysis of behaviour, including decision making, cannot be based upon the rational model, but should be by some form of social analysis using a more realistic model of human behaviour. This is a perfectly legitimate means of research, and is the reasoning behind the increase in case studies over recent years. It would be possible to attempt to understand decision making entirely by means of case studies; but it would be a lengthy and controversial process. There are two main problems. The first is that of inference. A solution to a problem found by one firm is not necessarily going to work at another, no two people are alike and no two situations are alike. The second problem is that of establishing causation. One can never be sure, for instance, whether a change in the fortunes of a company was really caused by the factors identified in the case study or whether some other variable was at work. It is not therefore surprising that attempts to analyse people in organizations in this way are part of a tradition that 'is much more concerned with the description of contexts than it is with the analysis of problems' (Gee (1986)).

In this text we boldly assume that decision makers are not subject to the weaknesses described above, i.e. we assume that managers are able to make rational estimates. In many circumstances this may not be an especially realistic assumption; but, in keeping with the rational model, we offer it as an obtainable ideal. Models based upon rational behaviour, as the reader will see, provide considerable insight into the problem of decision making and form the basis of practical techniques.

2.6   Summary

Normally we think of decision making as being the act of selecting between alternatives. In this chapter we have shown that it is much more than this – decisions require the generation of alternatives, selection, implementation and review. This is a complex organizational process, which, of necessity, we have to treat at a certain abstract level. In sections 2.2 and 2.3, we compared such abstraction with attempts to model and describe decisions and the decision making process in more realistic detail. Such alternatives provide a valuable insight, and are a useful critique of the more traditional approach that we pursue, but nevertheless they lack completeness and the analytical power of the latter.

All decisions, however described, require information and human judgement. In sections 2.4 and 2.5 we examined the role of these elements in decision making. The many difficulties raised served as a critique of our subsequent analysis, which takes unbiased data input as its starting point.

In general, the material of this chapter warns against a naive application of decision models. We have suggested that much of the succeeding analysis may be justified as providing an insight into decisions, or in some cases as tools to be used cautiously, or an ideal to be actively pursued and adopted, or even providing a language for talking about and explaining decisions – all of these reasons are justified by our main purpose, which is to aid practical decision making.

References and further reading

Allison, G. T., *Essence of Decision*, Boston: Little, Brown and Company, 1971.

American Accounting Association, 1966. Committee to Prepare a Statement of Basic Accounting Theory, A Statement of Accounting Theory.

Ansoff, H. I., Anderson, A., Norton, F. and Watson, J. F., 'Planning for Diversification Through Merger', in Ansoff, H. I. (ed.), *Business Strategy*, Penguin, 1969.

Ashton, D., 'Endowing Financial Simulation Models with Intelligence: Some Problems in Goal Programming', *Accounting and Business Research*, No. 61, Winter, 1985 pp. 3–10; and *Accounting and Business Research*, No. 62, Spring, 1986.

Biggs, C. and Benjamin, D. *Management Accounting Techniques*, Heinemann, 1989.

Dearborn, D. C. and Simon, H. A., 'Selective Perception: A note on the Departmental Identification of Executives', *Sociometry*, Vol. 21, No. 2, June 1958, pp. 140–4.

Demski, J., *Information Analysis*, 2nd edition, Addison-Wesley, 1980.

Ezzamel, M., 'On the assessment of the performance effects of multidivisional structures: A Synthesis'. *Accounting and Business Research*, Winter, 1985.

Ezzamel, M. and Hart, H., *Advanced Management Accounting*, Cassell, 1987.

French, S., *Readings in Decision Analysis*, Chapman and Hall, 1989.

Gee, K. P., *Advanced Management Accounting Problems*, Macmillan, 1986, p. xiii.

Hopwood, A. G., 'Behavioural Accounting in Retrospect and Prospect', London School of Economics Discussion Paper, 1989, No. 2.

Jay, A., *Management and Machiavelli*, Hodder & Stoughton, 1970.

Kaplan, R. S., Athinson, A. A., *Advanced Management Accounting*, 2nd edition, Prentice-Hall, 1989.

Keeney, R. L., Raiffa, H., *Decisions with Multiple Objectives*, Wiley, 1976.

Lenz, R. T., Lyles, M. A., 'Paralysis by Analysis: Is Your Planning System Becoming Too Rational?', *Long Range Planning*, August 1985, Vol. 18, pp. 65.

Lindberg, C. C., 'Transactional Conception of Fieldwork', *Human Organization*, Spring, 1968, pp. 45–9.

Lindblom, C. E., 'The Science of Muddling Through', in Ansoff, H. I. (ed.), *Business Strategy*, Penguin 1964.

Livingstone, J. L., *Managerial Accounting: The Behavioral Foundations* Grid, 1975, p. 117.

McDonough, J. J., 'The Accountant, Data Collection and Social Exchange', *The Accounting Review*, 1971, pp. 676–85.

McNamee, P., *Management Accounting – Strategic Planning and Marketing*, CIMA/Heinemann, 1988.

Mayo, E., 'Hawthorne and the Western Electric Company', in Pugh, D. S. (ed.), *Organization Theory*, Penguin, 1971.

Otley, D., *Accounting Control and Organizational Behaviour*, CIMA/Heinemann, 1987.

Pfeffer, J., *Power in Organizations*, Pitman 1981.

Sage, A. P., 'Behavioural and organisational considerations in the design of information systems and processes for planning and decision support', *IEEE Transactions on Systems, Man and Cybernetics*, September 1981.

Scapens, R. W., Sale, J. T., Tikkas, P. A., 'Financial Control of Divisional Companies', CIMA Occasional Papers Series, 1982.

Simon, H. A., 'On the Concept of Organizational Goal', in Ansoff, H. I. (ed.), *Business Strategy*, Penquin 1969.

Sizer, J., *Perspectives in Management Accounting*, CIMA/Heinemann, 1981.

Sizer, J. and Coulthurst, N., *A Casebook of British Management Accounting*, Vol. 1, ICEAW 1984.

Slovic, P. and Lichtenstein, S., 'Comparison of Bayesian and regression aproaches to the study of information processing in judgement', *Organizational Behavior and Human Performance*, 1971.

Thompson, J. D. and Tuden, A., Strategies, Structures and Processes of Organizational Decision', in Thompson, J. C. *et al.* (eds) *Comparative Studies in Administration*, University of Pittsburgh Press, 1959.

Tversky, A. and Kahnemann, D., 'Availability: An heuristic for judging frequency and probability', *Cognitive Psychology*, 1973, Vol. 5.

Tversky, A. and Kahnemann, D., 'Judgement under Uncertainty: Heuristics and Biases', *Science*, 1974.

Watson, S. R., and Buede, D. M., *Decision Synthesis*, CUP, 1987.

Williamson, O. E., *Markets and Hierarchies: Analysis and Antitrust Implications*, New York: Free Press, 1975.

3 Decision making – theory and basic techniques, Part 1

3.1 Introduction

Our main focus of attention in this chapter is on the evaluation and selection phase of the decision-making process (see Figure 2.1) – in other words, what is commonly understood by 'making a decision'. We therefore assume that the organization has searched out the options from which it has to select, and has assembled the relevant data for analysis. We also assume that the control and evaluation procedure in the firm will ensure that the estimates will be translated into reality. Thus all that is required to complete the process is the all-important selection stage.

The first general problem that we address is that of measurement. No selection can be made without some form of measure of the consequences of the various alternatives. The rest of the chapter is then a 'journey' through decision theory, starting with simple selection problems with single goals, where the consequences of options are certain, and ending with decisions where there are multiple goals – where the consequences are uncertain (sections 3.3 and 3.4).

3.2 The problem of measurement

The problem of measurement is in essence the problem of deriving a score for the various attributes of a decision. As will be appreciated from section 2.5, we want the measure to draw minimally on our limited ability to judge, and yet provide sufficient information for the particular decision process chosen. The simpler the judgements that are required, the greater the likelihood of accuracy.

A score can potentially perform two functions: it can tell us which alternative is better, i.e. it can rank alternatives; and it can also tell us how much better one alternative is than another, i.e. it can provide a measure that can be meaningfully added and subtracted. As an example, let us suppose that a

Decision rule	Net present value (£000)	Payback (years)
Project		
a_1	600	3
a_2	400	2
a_3	300	4

Figure 3.1

firm is faced with three alternatives, projects a_1, a_2 and a_3 as in Figure 3.1, and two decision rules, net present value and payback. The net present value rule provides a measure that not only ranks the alternative but also tells us how much better one is from another. Thus we can say that we would be indifferent between being offered either two a_3 projects or one a_1 project. We can also subtract the measures, e.g. we can say that if we were asked to substitute a_2 for a_1, the sacrifice would be greater than substituting a_3 for a_2. Furthermore, this is not an idle game with numbers; there is substantive meaning in these operations in that the circumstances we have outlined are not unrealistic.

The payback measure, like the net present value, is able to rank the alternatives. Payback measures a slightly different attribute to net present value (see section 5.4.1), and we should therefore not be surprised that they produce different rankings. However, unlike the net present value, we cannot meaningfully add or subtract these scores; we cannot say that a_3 is twice as bad as a_2 or that two a_1s are better than one a_2.

Both the decision rules are able to rank a_1, a_2 and a_3 but only net present value provides a measure whose differences may be meaningfully employed. A measure that only ranks is known as an *ordinal measure*; a measure that also provides meaningful differences is known as a *cardinal measure*. In that the cardinal measure 'does more', it should be evident that it is likely to draw more on the decision maker's ability to judge. Where possible, therefore, ordinal measures are preferable where they are sufficient to reach a decision. As an example, if a firm has the capacity to adopt one of the three alternatives in Figure 3.1, it can use the net present value rule as an ordinal measure. If it compares a_3 with a_2, it has merely to decide which is best; it then need only compare the winner with a_1 to decide the best of the three. In practice, questions required to determine which has the better net present value are likely to be less demanding than questions required to determine the exact net present value. Unfortunately, we cannot always just use a ranking score. In Chapter 1 we saw that a decision may meet more than one objective, and in such cases there are likely to be trade-offs, which will normally require a measure of how much of one goal we are willing to sacrifice to further another. Clearly, ordinal measures will not suffice for such decisions. The stronger cardinal measure is needed.

The act of measurement is easier for some attributes than for others. In chapter 1, we examined the effect of making fewer, larger deliveries on the image and sales of a retail clothing outlet, and we considered the varied implications of centralizing a hospital unit; in both these cases some attributes were easily measured, others were more difficult. In general, there is a *bias of measurability* towards attributes with immediate financial implications. In the car purchase problem for instance, there were greater difficulties in measuring safety than in measuring economy, and in the example of centralising a hospital unit, the saving on staff and equipment costs was a great deal easier to measure than the effect of the decision on treatment. The danger that this bias poses is that decisions will be analysed and taken on those grounds that are easily measured. This is obviously not a desirable trait for decision making.

For the accountant, this bias poses particular problems, as it is he or she who is likely to prepare much of the information. Not only is the financial data more easily measured, but it is also the very stuff of the accounting system. Textbooks, it has to be said, tend to encourage this bias. Many analyse decisions and problems with virtually no reference to the non-financial or difficult to measure aspects of problems as outlined above. At best, the effects of non-financial aspects are either assumed to be included in the financial estimates, or are relegated to some *demi-monde* of qualitative factors. Usually, such factors receive little or no attention. Even in the decisions that may seem wholly described by financial considerations there are important non-financial aspects. For example, in a recent survey of the leasing decision (Drury and Braund, 1989) 21 per cent of respondents thought that administrative convenience was of average to above average importance, and 34 per cent viewed the offering of a 'complete package' also to be of average to above average importance. Whereas textbooks dwell greatly on evaluating differing payment streams in leasing decisions, little or nothing is offered on evaluating these other factors.

All relevant consequences of a decision should be measured. Where the consequences are of a financial nature, the problems of measurement are well-documented in standard accounting texts. Where the consequences are non-financial, there may yet be a readily available measure. From previous chapters, we can cite the recovery rate from hospital operations (relevant to the relocation problem), the number of repairs (part of the car purchase problem), and the number of stockouts (part of the transport cost decision). In other cases there may not be a readily available scale. For instance, how do we measure administrative convenience in the leasing decision, or how do we measure the effect on a company's image when changing presentation of goods? The fact that these attributes are difficult to measure does not mean that they are unimportant, and is no reason for precluding them, for without being measured they cannot enter the analysis.

Thus, we argue that it is wrong to make a decision appear objective by simply omitting the more subjective aspects. They are no less important. In that accounting analysis has this bias, greater effort should be made to include non-financial measures – an argument that is not without distinguished support (Johnson and Kaplan (1987), chapter 11).

In constructing a measure, the cardinal and ordinal distinction is of crucial importance. Where an ordinal measure is being used, it will be sufficient to rank the options being considered. Where a cardinal measure is used, various techniques may be adopted. If, for instance, someone's opinion is being sought, it is useful to adopt a scale as in Figure 3.2.

Question: How safe is car A?

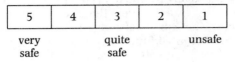

Figure 3.2   *Constructed scale*

The respondent can give his opinion as a point on the scale. Not only is such a presentation visually attractive and simple to understand, it also clearly indicates the meaning of the various values on the scale. This feature is useful when the opinions of several informants are being sought. Without such indications there is an increased risk that one person's subjective score might be very different from another's, though this will always be a problem. For instance, if we average people's scores to find it to be 3, we will always have the problem of one person's 'quite safe' being different from another's.

Where rankings are being combined, there is the further problem of the results being influenced by the options being considered. A well-known paradox, known as the Borda count (French, 1986), demonstrates that where options are chosen on their total ranking score between several judges, the choice of best option can be influenced by whether or not the least favoured option was included in the consideration. This is clearly inequitable.

As we saw in section 1.5.2, there are certain intractable difficulties when measuring and combining judgements. There is no theoretically correct method; instead there are more fair and less fair procedures. The decision maker's sense of equity is the best guide in devising appropriate means of measuring and combining estimates. As with our study of corporate objectives, analysis cannot proceed without making certain simplifying assumptions. In this case, we must assume that measurement problems have been overcome. Therefore our subsequent analysis assumes that there are no significant measurement errors.

3.3   Decisions under certainty

In Chapter 1, we pointed out that decisions have attributes rather than goals. For the remainder of this text, however, we will revert to the convention of using the terms goals and attributes interchangeably. More formally, we will assume that there is a one-to-one correspondence between goals and attributes. Thus, when we talk about the economy of a car, we will use the term both as a goal or an objective and as an attribute.

In the simplest of decisions the consequences will be single valued with respect to each attribute. If the car purchase example (section 1.2) was a decision under certainty, we would know with certainty the safety level of each car and its economy 'score'. With such decisions, any attribute of a decision will have an outcome that is known before the decision is taken.

3.3.1   *Decisions with a single goal*

The possibility of a single objective known with certainty is included for the sake of completeness. Where an option has a single relevant attribute that is known with certainty, then choice is simply a matter of computation. If, for example, a firm decides to buy the factory space closest to Manchester Airport irrespective of cost, access, etc., then the choice is determined solely by calculating distances. Much financial analysis is explained within this framework. For instance, discounted future cash flows is often used as the single attribute in selecting between actions where the discount rate and amounts are given. Although such analysis highlights the problems of computation, the reader will appreciate that there is a considerable loss of realism.

3.3.2   *Decisions with more than one goal*

Public and not-for-profit organizations are frequently faced with the problem of conflicting goals. Returning to our hospital example (section 1.1), suppose that there is a shortage of funds, necessitating cutbacks. Some proposals may call for a large reduction of staff and a small reduction in beds; other proposals may call for a large reduction in beds and a small reduction in staff. The hospital management is likely to have to make a trade off between these two attributes.

In much analysis, profit-making organizations are considered to have profit or wealth maximization as their sole objective. As explained in chapter 1, we do not disagree with profit being a goal, but, rather, question how operational it is. A profit-making organization may well find it more practical to select between alternatives, using several attributes such as direct cash flow implications, product profile, market position, management time (where this is not costed), the balance sheet appearance and so on. These attributes will then have to be combined in a manner that, in the opinion of the directors and managers, will maximize the wealth of the firm. In selecting between alternatives, managers will be faced with trade-off problems in much the same way as the hospital management. Should, for instance, management decide to develop a product which is economic on management time, improves the product profile and market position, and improves the balance sheet, but has a small cash flow directly attributable to it, or develop a rival product with a higher cash flow but which makes a lesser contribution to the other attributes? To some, the cash flows should measure the effect of all attributes; to most, we feel, the problem is better understood and analysed in this disaggregated form. After all, hospital management could equally claim that it wishes to maximize a single goal of 'social benefit' – it too is in a sense disaggregating its goals in order to address widely differing aspects of the problem.

Let us take a decision with two attributes – say hospital beds and staff, or cash flow and balance sheet appearance, or profit and safety – which we shall call a_1 and a_2. Suppose that various alternatives denoted by D_1 to D_{12} can be mapped, as in Figure 3.3.

Of the various decisions that can be taken in Figure 3.3, only D_6 to D_{11} need be considered. For all other decisions, there is an alternative that has

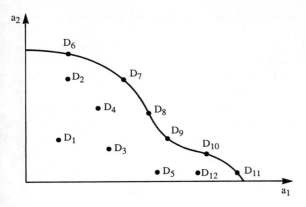

Figure 3.3

one or both attributes with a higher score and none with a worse score. Thus D_{11} has a higher a_1 and the same a_2 as D_{12}. There is no trade-off to be made between the two options; the rational decision maker would choose D_{11} as it is better or as good as D_{12} in all attributes. In comparing D_{11} and D_{12}, we say that D_{11} is dominant or 'Pareto optimal' (after the Italian economist who formulated the principle). Thus D_4 dominates D_1, and D_7 dominates D_4. No alternatives are dominant from D_6 through to D_{11}, and for this reason D_6 to D_{11} is known as the efficient set or Pareto optimal set. In selecting between the members of this set, difficult trade-offs are unavoidable: D_8, for instance, has a higher a_1 score than D_6 but a lower a_2 score – which is preferable? In order to choose the most attractive option we need to formulate a more discerning decision rule than Pareto optimalism.

Ideally, we would like our decision rule to select the best option, be easy to understand, simple to administer and, as previously mentioned, require as few judgements as possible from the decision maker. These preconditions have given rise to a host of algorithms designed to aid the decision maker in his choice. In this chapter we shall look at some of the basic solutions offered, reserving a discussion of more sophisticated techniques to the next chapter.

One simple approach suggested by Simon (1969) (see section 2.2.2) is to use constraints. In Figure 3.4 the decision maker indicates that any solution below either a'_1 and a'_2 is unacceptable; thus E_1, E_2 and E_8 to E_{14} are ruled out. Within the acceptable area, we can further rule out E_4 and E_5, as they are not in the Pareto optimal set. Our choice is therefore narrowed to E_3, E_6, or E_7. To distinguish between these elements some form of trade-off will need to be determined. For example, suppose a manager wishes to invest in machinery and selects using initial cost (a_1) and reliability (a_2) as the relevant attributes. Supposing he selects constraints such that any option above a'_1 comes within the manager's budget, and any option above a'_2 comes within the manager's view of minimum acceptable reliability (which we assume to be scored on some subjective scale). The manager may subscribe to one of three statements:

1   'I do not mind about the price of the machine so long as it comes within my budget, but I will always prefer more reliable to less reliable machines.'
2   'I am very keen to keep costs as low as possible but the machine must be of a certain level of reliability.'
3   'I have to balance reliability and cost.'

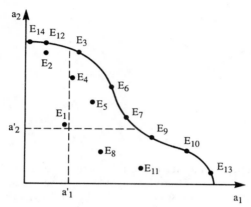

Figure 3.4

With statement 1, it seems likely that the manager would select E_3, the most reliable of the options that came within his budget. By similar reasoning, a manager who supports statement 2 is likely to choose E_7. The third statement does not allow us to select between E_3, E_6 and E_7. We can, in this case, either say that the method has gone as far as it can and the manager must make the choice; or we can ask him to make more detailed statements concerning his preferences. In pursuing the latter course, we would need to ask such questions as 'At the a'_1 level of cost, how much reliability would you be willing to sacrifice in order to save £X of initial cost?' In effect, we would be constructing an indifference curve, having first narrowed our choice (see Koutsoyiannis, 1979, for an analysis of indifference curves).

The benefits of the constraints approach lie in its simplicity. The disadvantages are that (a) there is no guarantee that the method will significantly narrow the choice, for it is possible that the constraints may be set such that the whole of the Pareto optimal set is included; (b) it may not help the decision maker, as intuition may have told him that the choice was between E_3, E_6 and E_7; and (c) he or she may not accept the idea of a constraint, the view that 'all levels of reliability have a potentially acceptable price' would effectively negate the whole approach in this example.

A variation on the constraints approach that is sometimes suggested is lexicographic ordering (Keeney and Raiffa (1976), p. 77). This method has the disadvantage of asking questions which are less likely to reflect the decision maker's preferences, but the advantage of producing a single 'winner'. The decision maker is asked to order the attributes according to importance. The best option is simply the one with the highest score for the most important attribute. If there is a tie, then the relevant options score on the second most important attribute is considered. So in Figure 3.4, if a_2 is considered to be the more important attribute, all options except for E_{12} and E_{14} would be excluded. The second attribute would then be considered; E_{12} has a higher score than E_{14} on a_1 and would therefore be judged to be the 'winner'. It seems unlikely that the decision maker would view the problem in such a simplistic manner, since the 'trade-offs' are really too crude for most problems worthy of analysis.

Let us return to the constraints approach. Suppose that the manager advocates statement 3. We suggested that one means of determining the best choice in the acceptable area would be to use an indifference curve. If this were to be done, then the problem of setting constraints could have been bypassed altogether. Economics has, since the 1930s, based the theory of economic choice entirely on the indifference curve. Applied to this problem, indifference curves might appear as in Figure 3.5. Each curve represents a

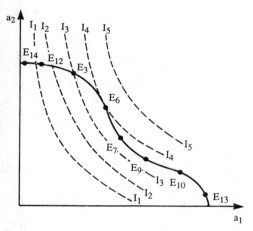

Figure 3.5

certain level of satisfaction. In order to draw up these curves, a manager must be able to make comparative statements such as 'at a particular a_2 level of safety and a_1 level of cost, I would be indifferent to giving up 1 point on my scale of safety for a machine that was £500 cheaper'. The manager is, in effect, being asked to make a series of choices that rank equally, but he is not being asked to estimate how much better one option is than another. If an option is deemed better, then it is not on the existing indifference curve but a higher one – we do not have to say how much higher, or give any notion of strength of preference, other than indifference. Thus, indifference curve analysis is a sophisticated form of ordinal ranking.

Despite the success of indifference curves in providing a basis for choice, we will continue to examine decision rules based upon a cardinal measure, as (a) it provides a general framework within which all other models can be expressed (b) it is relevant to the analysis of risk and uncertainty, and (c) forms the basis of some more recent techniques.

An important cardinal measure of decisions under certainty is known as a value function, expressed as:

$$Vi = f(a_{1i}, a_{2i} \ldots a_{ni})$$

where $a_{1i} \ldots a_{ni}$ are levels of attributes 1 to n associated with option i, and V_i represents the total score for option i achieved by some function f of the attribute levels. In this form, the model represents a guide to the decisions but no more, for all that is being specified is that attributes should be measured and combined. Preference between options is measured by their total score. To gain greater insight, we need to make further assumptions.

First, let us assume that the attributes are preference independent. The implication of this important assumption is that if we were to select any two attributes and examine preferences between various combinations (as we have been doing so far), the score for any one attribute would not depend upon a third attribute or upon the second attribute (Keeney and Raiffa (1976), p. 345; French (1989), p. 58; Buffa and Dyer (1977), p. 113).

In the example used in this section, we have talked about initial cost and reliability of a machine. Suppose we now include running costs. For most managers it is probably true to say that preference independence would not hold. If a manager were examining the trade-off between E_6 and E_7 in Figure 3.5, it would surely matter if he were told that, although E_6 has a lower initial cost, its running costs are much higher. In such a case independence could not be said to hold. If the third relevant attribute were 'safety' instead of running costs, then there would probably be preference independence. In looking at the trade-off between cost and reliability it seems reasonable to expect that varying levels of safety would not affect our trade-offs between these attributes. Furthermore, this independence condition would also apply when examining all the other possible trade-offs, i.e. cost with safety and reliability with safety. In practice, if the independence assumption is made, running costs need not be excluded. The implication is rather that, if it is relevant, initial costs and running costs should be combined into some general cost measure.

The importance of this assumption is that the model can be expressed in additive form:

$$V_i = W_1V_1(a_1) + W_2V_2(a_2) \ldots W_nV_n(a_n)$$

(the function W weights the value functions in relation to each other). We shall also assume that the value functions $V_1 \ldots V_n$ are cardinal, which implies that the differences are meaningful. Thus our value function V_i tells us not only which is the best option, but also provides a meaningful measure of how much better it is. To achieve this, we also have to assume difference independence (Dyer and Sarin (1979)). In general terms this means that not only are levels between attributes preferentially independent but also the differences. This form of value function, known as a measurable value function, is potentially of great significance. It combines the many varied consequences or attributes of a decision, giving equal treatment to both financial and non-financial aspects. To understand the measure, we need to examine the questions and judgements that the formula is asking of managers. We begin by examining $V_i(a_i)$, which is the value placed upon an individual attribute.

To formulate such values we take as an example of an attribute 'immediate financial return', the manager must be able to answer questions such as: 'Supposing you were offered £100 or £1,000, is there a value between these two amounts such that you are indifferent between the "differences"?' To clarify what is meant by 'differences' a full answer might be: 'If you exchanged my £100 reward for a £400 reward that would please me as much as exchanging a £400 reward for £1,000'.

Can a decision maker answer such questions? Some would argue that there is a danger of confusing the end result, £1,000, with the exchange (from £400 to £1,000). Another view suggests that individuals have an 'intrinsic feeling of strength of preference' (French (1986), p. 336) from which these judgements can be made. Let us assume that such questions on exchanges can be answered. It is clear that a measurable value function can then be constructed. If we assign 0 to £100 and 1 to £1,000 then £400 must be assigned 1/2 to ensure that the differences in the value scale are the same. Repeating such questions enables a curve to be sketched. For instance, a manager might be asked about his 'point of indifference' between £100 and £400 and reply: 'I would be as happy over the exchange of £100 for £170 as exchanging £170 for £400'.

By assigning 1/4 to £170, the statement in value terms, of the manager will be true. The resulting curve would look as in Figure 3.6.

The curve, as in this example, is typically concave, reflecting what economists call diminishing marginal utility or increasing satiation. In practical terms, a £1 increase is worth less to the decision maker at the £1,000 point than the £100 point. There is, in fact, little difference between the value function and classical utility. We avoid the latter term here, as we reserve it for when risk and uncertainty are involved. Where there is more than one attribute in the value function, the process is repeated for each of the attributes. A practical problem that arises when considering non-financial attributes is the assigning of the first 2 points on the scale. A common solution is to use an abstract notion of worst (scoring it as 0 out of 10) and best (with a score of 10 out of 10). This is an unnecessary complication, for the judgements are difficult enough without introducing abstract notions! A simpler approach is to assign 0 to the worst of the actual outcomes and 1 to the best outcome, remembering that it is the relative score that matters, not the absolute level.

The weights $W_1 \ldots W_n$ in the value function express the relative importance of the potential movements in the attributes (it is computationally convenient therefore that they sum to 1). Again, the relative importance is not the same as the absolute importance of the attributes. If, for instance, one attribute was safety and the other cost, cost might be weighted above safety, not because the decision maker thinks that cost is more important than safety, but rather because the *difference* in safety levels presented by the various options is judged less significant than the *difference* in cost. Remember that

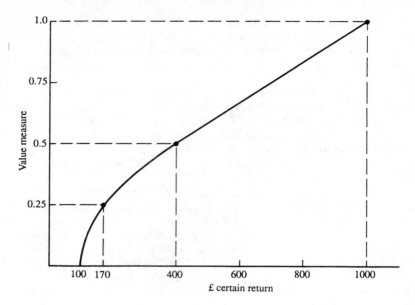

Figure 3.6

throughout it is the differences that are being measured, not the absolute
levels. To determine the weights, the total differences for each attribute
generated by the options should be presented to the decision maker. He or
she should then be asked to score their importance in, say, marks out of ten.
These scores can then be cross-checked by asking questions such as: 'Is your
8/10 score twice as important to you as your 4/10 score?' When a stable set
of scores is derived the weight is determined by the formula:

$$\frac{\text{Score out of ten for attribute n}}{\text{Total of scores}}$$

Preferences can then be determined by calculating the value V_i for each
option.

As a practical note, many decision makers are untroubled by a notion of
a worst and best level for an attribute; nor are they troubled by the problem
of weighting the various attributes by the differences they present. In such
cases, disturbing these notions for the sake of theoretical precision is probably
unnecessary. However, in a group situation these distinctions may be important, as illustrated in the previous example concerning safety and cost.

For a fuller example, let us consider a decision by a company to relocate
its offices. Suppose that three attributes are considered relevant, namely, (a)
access, (b) historical interest and (c) housing. The scores for three towns

being considered might look as they do in Table 3.1 (where 0 is the worst outcome and 10 is the best outcome).

Table 3.1

Town	Access (a)	Historical interest (b)	Housing (c)
I	7	0	10
II	0	10	0
III	10	9	5

Let us suppose that the value function (V) for each town (i) appears thus:

$$V_i = 0.25 \sqrt{a_i} + 0.25 \sqrt{b_i} + 0.5 \sqrt{c_i}$$

In words, the value function for each attribute is shaped as in Figure 3.6 (i.e. concave), and an increase from point x to y (where these are any two points on the scale 0 to 10 such that x is less than y) is ranked equally for attributes (a) and (b), but for attribute (c) is considered twice as beneficial. The scores for each town are:

$$V_I = 2.24$$
$$V_{II} = 0.79$$
$$V_{III} = 2.66$$

Thus, the access and historical interest of town III are judged to outweigh its poorer housing provision, but not by much.

As well as providing a general model whereby financial and non-financial consequences of a decision can be 'weighed up' in an unbiased manner, this method has also recently provided the basis of new approaches to decision making. Two such examples are Social Judgement Theory (SJT) and Outranking, which we shall briefly outline.

SJT is a method developed in the USA. Effectively an additive value function of the form:

$$V(a) = V_1(a_1) + V_2(a_2) \ldots V_n(a_n)$$

is constructed by presenting the decision maker with a number of hypothetical scenarios based on combinations of $a_1 \ldots a_n$; he or she is then asked to score these combinations, i.e. to estimate V(a) directly. The values of the $V_1 \ldots V_n$ parameters can then be estimated by linear regression. One should remember that the word 'estimated' includes all the problems of linear regression analysis, especially multicollinearity (Scapens, 1985), which is the problem of attribute independence in a statistical setting. The contribution of SJT is to aid the cognitive process (that is learning, understanding and judging) in order to construct the model. Hence discussion in SJT centres mainly upon effective means of presenting scenarios.

Outranking or *Surclassement* is a method developed in France which is similarly based upon a form of multi-attribute value function. It starts by assuming that a score and a weight can be derived for each attribute (again we assume that the weights add up to unity), and then tries to draw as little as possible on the information model in arriving at a selection. Two measures are used to assess whether or not one option is better than another. Say we are comparing E_6 with E_7 (see Figure 3.4), the first measure is called concordance and is simply the sum of the attribute weights where E_6 is greater than E_7 (note that if C totals 1, E_6 would be dominant). The second measure is termed discordance. This is the maximum adverse difference in attribute score (i.e. the unweighted score) from the E_6 point of view compared with E_7, divided by the maximum difference for the same attribute that the decision maker has expressed in making comparisons between other options (e.g. E_8 and E_{12} and so on). Thus our preference for E_6 over E_7 will be greater the closer concordance is to unity and discordance is to zero. The selection process is then a sequence of comparisons guided by acceptable Cs and Ds. Suitable processes have been modelled by the University of Paris in a suite of programmes called ELECTRE. Original sources are difficult to obtain, but Watson and Buede report that this method has been used successfully on the Continent. This is not the only means of manipulating weights and scores that has been suggested; but it serves as an illustration of an interesting development in decision making. For further analysis and references on both these developments, the reader is referred to Watson and Buede (1987).

We have presented the additive form of the value model. Other forms may be used, particularly when the independence conditions vital to the additive model cannot be met (Keeney and Raiffa, 1976, p. 255). Such alternatives are not generally attractive, as they lack intuitive appeal – an important quality if non-specialists are to provide useful data. For this reason it is often recommended that attributes that are independent are developed. The multi-attribute value model is the most complete expression of preferences between options. Other methods, such as indifference curve analysis, the constraints model, the lexicographical approach, SJT and Outranking, may all be viewed as simplifications of the value model.

So far, we have not mentioned a method known as pricing-out or willingness-to-pay. In measuring the contribution of non-monetary attributes we have advocated the construction of artificial scales. Another approach is to assign a monetary amount to an attribute. For example, suppose a decision

Table 3.2

	Car A	Car B	Car C	Car D
Cost	7,000	5,000	10,000	9,000
Safety (1–10)	8	5	8	5
Reliability (1–10)	7	7	10	10

maker claims to be indifferent between cars A and B in Table 3.2. In being indifferent, one can rightly say that the extra safety of car A is valued as much as the extra cost – for those are the only two differences. The temptation then is to say that an increase from 5 to 8 points in safety is worth a £2,000 increase in cost. However, such a conclusion would imply that the buyer would prefer car C to car D; but this does not necessarily follow, for the buyer may have decided that his budget cannot exceed £9,000. In this simple form, it is clear that something of a 'bent ruler' is being used to measure safety. One's attitude towards money is being confused with one's attitude towards the attribute. It is possible to adjust for this problem, but not without loss of the original intuitive appeal (Harvey, 1985).

If one does prefer an option with highest direct cost, it is correct to say that the non-financial extra level of attributes of the chosen option are worth at least the extra cost. But this statement can only be made *after the decision has been taken*. As we have seen, it is an unreliable guide to actually making the decision.

Let us conclude this section by looking at a simple multi-objective problem, say a choice of machine when price, reliability and safety are deemed important. When faced with this problem, a manager might well respond: 'Choosing between these machines is like comparing apples with pears; for instance, how can I choose between two machines one of which is safer, more reliable but more expensive?' Nothing that we have suggested will absolve the manager from the need to make such difficult comparisons. All the decision models that we have advanced here will only help to clarify the trade-offs and preferences necessary to select the best alternative – they do not take the decision for the manager. The choice of model is also a matter of the decision maker's preferences. Simpler models require more drastic assumptions; if these assumptions are appropriate all well and good, but, in general, the decision maker is faced with a trade-off between model complexity and realism. This is a decision in itself, which can only be made by means of the decision processes described!

3.4   Decisions under uncertainty and risk

In the previous section we examined problems where the attributes or consequences of a decision were known with certainty. In this section we shall examine decisions where there is uncertainty over the level of attributes of a particular option. Thus, in the previous section we assumed that in purchasing a machine, the price, safety, and reliability were known with certainty; in this section we assume that the decision maker cannot give a measure for these attributes with 100 per cent assurance. For simplicity, we shall initially examine decisions with a single goal, and add in the problem of multiple goals and trade-offs later in the analysis.

Uncertainty in the normal sense of the word means an unwillingness to commit oneself. This is clearly not a basis for examining a decision, for if the manager is unwilling to commit himself or herself to any figures, the analysis cannot begin. Analysing uncertainty is the art of deriving a method which selects the best opportunity by asking the manager to provide estimates which commit him or her as little as is needed in order to come to a decision. In making a commitment to estimates, a manager is turning an uncertain position into a risky one, i.e. one that can be analysed. The remainder of this section examines various ways in which this conversion process may be achieved.

3.4.1   Scenario analysis – strict uncertainty

We take the term 'strict uncertainty' from French (1986, p. 32), as it aptly conveys the limiting nature of this approach. In decisions of this type, we assume that the outcome of an option is known with certainty, given that we know the outcome of an uncertain event. An event commonly chosen is the state of the market; equivalent terms are 'states of nature' and 'scenarios'. In Table 3.3, we examine the cash flows that would result from actions A to E, given various market conditions. First, the reader might wish to examine

Table 3.3   Decision table showing net benefits of various actions

£000	States of nature: market conditions		
actions	bad	indifferent	good
A	5	35	100
B	40	55	55
C	25	45	90
D	30	30	85
E	2	2	2

the data and consider which action to choose. Option E can be rejected, as all other options are better in all states of the market. Each of the other options, as we shall see, is preferred by one of a number of selection models.

Maximin returns. This is probably the most popular of the selection criteria, being simply the action with the highest minimum returns. Action B fulfils this requirement; though lack-lustre in other respects, it does at least offer a minimum return of 40, and may therefore be considered a relatively safe return.

Maximax returns. By contrast, this is possibly the least popular method. It advocates selecting the action with the promise of the highest return irrespective of other possible outcomes; this is, of course, action A. The outcome under bad market conditions would, we suspect, discourage most.

Although maximax is rather reckless, maximin is perhaps rather too cautious. A middle way is the *optimism–pessimism index* (French 1986, p. 37). For this method, we choose a weight for the best and worst outcomes of a decision such that the weights add up to 1 (again, it is the relative importance of weights rather than their absolute value that matters). In Table 3.3 we might weight the worst outcome by 0.7 and the best outcome by 0.3, showing that we consider bad outcomes to be relatively more significant. Action A would score 33.5, B and C score 44.5 and D 46.5, so D would be chosen. As one might expect, D is not the action with the worst outcome, nor has it the best.

The final approach is termed *minimax regret*. It is not the absolute value of return that matters here, but the difference between what was achieved and the best that might have been achieved in the conditions, i.e. the regret. For instance, if a manager chooses option A and the market is bad, his returns will be 5. Looking at the decision table he will realize that he should have chosen B, earning 40 under bad conditions. Hence his regret will be $40 - 5 = 35$

There are many organizational settings where the concept of regret may be important. For example, one can imagine a manager's performance being subjected to a director's comment such as: 'If you had correctly anticipated that the market was going to be good, you could have achieved £100,000 profit. The trouble with you, Mr X, is that you don't know enough about the market!' The decision maker might find it difficult to explain that his actions were the best in view of the uncertainty that presented itself at the time. There is an important point at issue here, for a director will, in many situations, be unable to distinguish between uncertainty that afflicts the best of managers, and uncertainty due, in plain terms, to the manager's lack of ability. Would a better manager have been able to predict the market conditions? If so, then regret is indeed a measure of the loss. Table 3.3 shows that the maximum regret for A is 35, B 45, C 15 and D 25. Therefore C is to be preferred, as it minimizes the maximum regret.

Each of the options, apart from E, is best by one of the criteria. Option A provides the best maximax returns, B would be chosen under the maximim criteria, C minimaxes regret and D has the best optimism–pessimism index. As decision rules these methods depend upon being able realistically to characterize uncertainty in this way. If the states of nature cannot be divided in this manner, or if we cannot be very sure of the outcome, given a particular state, then this approach is not suitable. The selection of a method depends upon one's attitude towards outcomes. If one above all wishes to avoid low returns, then maximin might be suitable. If, on the other hand, one is only concerned with achieving the highest results, then maximax is suitable, and so on. We will describe this later as a choice that is dependent upon risk attitude; from a reading of section 3.4.3, the reader will appreciate that maximin and the optimism–pessimism index are forms of risk aversion and maximax is a form of risk seeing.

It is clear that most significant decisions would benefit from a more realistic description of the problem, and a more precise measure of attitude towards the results. One particular development that seems desirable is to assess, in some way, the likelihood of the various states of nature. So far, we have been careful to make no assumption as to this likelihood. If we knew, for instance, that bad market conditions were extremely unlikely, we would probably view A more favourably and B less favourably. The extent of the change would depend upon our attitude towards the results. As this raises wider problems, we defer consideration to the next section.

We conclude on a related issue. It is sometimes inferred that where no assumption is made about the likelihood of each state, it is an impartial judgement to assume that each state is equally likely. Although this was once a fashionable notion, we reject it along with most modern writers. The methods described above leave judgement on the states of nature in the realms of uncertainty. That is to say, no estimate is being made of the issue. This is clearly not the same as saying that one set of events is just as likely as another, and that the equal likelihood assumption represents some sort of impartial judgement. Yet such an approach is prevalent. For example, suppose a manager gave a high–low estimate of sales, we suspect that many would assume that the mid-point of the high–low represents an adequate single figure approximation, on the basis that, as nothing has been said about the probabilities within the range, we should assume that they are equally likely. But if the distribution is skewed or generally non-symmetrical, the mid-point

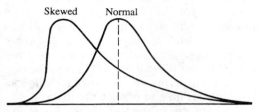

Figure 3.7   *A skewed distribution*

may be a wholly unrealistic approximation (see Figure 3.7). Decision analysis is not the art of using data and making assumptions about which no opinion either direct or indirect has been expressed. Clearly, our probabilities must be meaningful.

3.4.2   *Meaningful probability*

We have established from the previous section that it would be useful to know how likely were the various market conditions in Table 3.3. Can we devise a measure of likelihood? In fact we, along with many other texts, have simply assumed that this is possible. In section 2.4.1 we supposed that the manager was able to say that there was a 60 per cent chance of a product launch being successful. But what does this statement mean? We suggested that this information was based upon the observation that 40 per cent of all new products failed in that market. The implication therefore is that probability estimates should be based upon some notion of the frequency of occurrence. The tossing of a coin is often given as an example, since we know that there is a 50:50 chance of a head or a tail from carrying out the test a number of times. From sample tests we can infer that the true probability is 1/2 or 50:50; indeed, the whole of statistics is built up from this process of inference. To some, estimating the success or otherwise of a new product is no different. If this view were accepted, then our only problem would be collecting relevant observations from the past.

In fact, for many business problems it is not possible to collect sufficient relevant observations to infer a probability in this manner. In our product launch example, the similarity of the research reports on 'product launches' may only be superficial and the statistic spurious. For example, a manager may believe that most product failures are due to insufficient market research. If the new product being considered has been subjected to extensive research, the manager may reasonably believe that the chances of failure are much lower than 40 per cent. If the manager were to say that the chances of failure were in his estimate only 20 per cent, he could not be proven wrong in any sense. After all, if the product succeeds, both the research report and the manager have agreed that this would be the most likely outcome. If it fails, then who is to say that it was an event with only a 20 per cent chance or an event with a 40 per cent chance?

A manager may wish to use past frequences, research reports, or his own ideas on the causes of the events, or some other method, or a mixture of these approaches, we cannot reject any of these bases for making the estimation. For this reason such probabilities are termed subjective probabilities – they are not necessarily based upon objective observations such as frequencies. The term subjective does not mean that the estimates are irrational. A manager will hopefully look at all the information available, and interpret it in roughly the right manner. The net result should be a probability estimate that is more likely to lead to a satisfactory decision than one that is restricted to past frequencies. However, as we have said, the matter cannot be proven one way or the other in view of the fact that we are predicting a single future event. This leads us to an important statement on the role of decision analysis: a decision technique that uses probabilities cannot in any sense determine objectively the 'best' option; analysis merely organizes the decision maker's opinions, and derives logical inferences and interpretations in a consistent manner such that the manager chooses the option with which he or she is happiest. Without analysis, the decision maker may have a number of relevant opinions about a problem but may not know how to apply them. After analysis, the manager would probably be happier about his choice of best option.

It is now appropriate to turn to a criticism that is often made of probabilities. First let us present the correct argument. Suppose we are faced with two

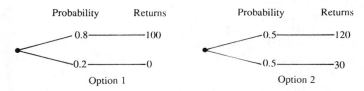

Figure 3.8

options, as in Figure 3.8 and that we valued each pound equally, e.g. that would mean that we are just as happy at receiving the last £1 of the £120 in Option 2, as receiving the first £1. Let us also assume (and we shall relax these assumptions later on) that the decision maker is a person who does not mind taking a gamble, i.e. he does not prefer Option 1 simply because one of the results has an 80 per cent chance as opposed to a 50 per cent chance. It seems intuitively reasonable to say from this that such a decision maker would be indifferent, or equally happy, between an 80 per cent chance of £100 and a 100 per cent chance of £80. In this way, we can compare the two options by converting all the returns to an equivalent 100 per cent probability. For Option 2, a 50 per cent chance of £120 is equivalent to a 100 per cent chance of £60, and a 50 per cent chance of £30 is equivalent to a 100 per cent chance of £15. Thus Option 2 is equivalent to a 100 per cent chance of £75. The manager concerned would therefore prefer Option 1 with an equivalent certain return of £80 as opposed to £75. This measure of 'equivalent certain return', or 'certainty equivalent' is not just an ordinal measure but is cardinal as well (see section 3.2 for an explanation of these terms). Therefore the difference of £5 between the two measures is a measure of the amount by which the decision maker feels better off. Put another way, he or she would be willing to pay up to £5 to be offered Option 1 rather than Option 2.

Unfortunately, the above choice is usually expressed in the following terms: the expected value of Option 1 is £80 and Option 2 is £75. An analogy is sometimes (falsely) made with tossing a coin. For Option 2 such an explanation would run like this: if we were tossing a fair coin and received £120 for heads and £30 for tails, in the long run we would expect to receive an average benefit of £75 per toss. As an explanation of what expected value means, this is reasonable. The problem is that although we use the term expected value (unfortunately) and accept the figures as being £80 and £75 respectively for Options 1 and 2, we cannot accept the explanation for two reasons. First, the option is only going to be taken once, and therefore the idea of repeated tosses of the coin and an average outcome is not relevant. Secondly, we have said that subjective probability may include an element of frequency if the decision maker thinks it to be useful, but that the concept is not exclusively restricted to the idea of frequency. It would therefore be hypocritical to justify the use of probabilities on the basis of frequency when we have said that the probabilities themselves may be based on more than just frequency. Despite the term therefore, expected value is more a measure of our happiness with the project than a statistical exercise.

And what of the criticism? It is based on the explanation of expected value that we have just rejected, and is that the problem of using expected value in, for instance, Option 1 is that the firm can 'expect' either £100 or £0 but not £80. As we have seen, this criticism is based upon a misunderstanding of what is meant by expected value in this context.

The probabilities that we have discussed so far are termed discrete, i.e. that the estimates in, say, Option 1 allow for a result of £100 or £0 but not £99 or £101 or £1 or $-$£1. In practice, of course, outcomes are unlikely to be so strictly defined; they would probably be expressed as being 'around about £100 or £0'. Therefore there is a chance that the probability is £101, etc. In such cases, the assumption is that £100 and £0 are adequate approximations. In practice, most economic events have a continuous probability − every outcome within a particular range has some probability of outcome. Discrete estimates are normally only approximations. Their value is that they are much easier to estimate and use. The nature of this approximation is illustated in Figure 3.9, using Option 1 from Figure 3.8 as an example.

The continuous line represents a probability density function in that the total area under the line adds up to 1 or certainty. The discrete approximation would, for most decision makers, be reasonable if the area between X_3 and X_4 was 75 per cent of the total area, and the area between X_1 and X_2 was 25 per cent of the total. As can be seen, this implies that the chance of observing £100 precisely is a good deal lower than 75 per cent; rather the £100 is

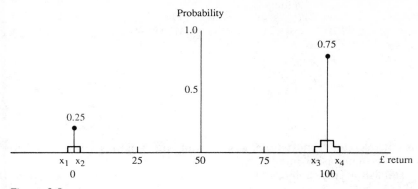

Figure 3.9

taken as a representative value from the range X_3 to X_4 for which there is a 75 per cent chance of observation.

Finally, in looking at the meaning of probability, it is useful to examine the various ways in which it can be expressed. So far, we have expressed probabilities as a percentage and a ratio. Thus, 100 per cent or 1 represents complete certainty that an outcome will occur, and 0 per cent and 0 represent complete certainty that an outcome will not occur, and values in between represent the feelings about the likelihood of an outcome. For example 80 per cent or 0.8 may be judged as 'very likely', 50 per cent or 0.5 as 'quite likely', 20 per cent or 0.2 as 'unlikely' and 5 per cent or 0.05 as 'very unlikely'. The link between descriptions and probability levels is only approximate, for, as we have said, the probabilities are subjective, and the meaning of the terms is vague. As an illustration of the range of descriptions, Moore and Thomas (1976, p. 133) report on a study of the ranking of descriptions by executives of uncertainty (see Table 3.4). It is a salutory reminder of the fickle nature of human judgement that a number of executives ranked expected above quite certain. Further, as Moore and Thomas discovered, the rankings were not

Table 3.4

Ranking expressions	Average rank	Range of ranks
Quite certain	1.10	1–3
Expected	2.05	1–6
Likely	3.85	2–7
Probable	4.25	2–9
Not unreasonable	4.65	3–7
Possible	6.10	3–9
Hoped	7.15	3–10
Not certain	7.80	3–10
Doubtful	8.60	7–10
Unlikely	8.75	3–10

	Points		
A	10	10/50 = 0.2 or	20%
B	20	20/50 = 0.4	40%
C	5	5/50 = 0.1	10%
D	15	15/50 = 0.3	30%
	50	1.0	100%

Figure 3.10

consistent over time, most respondents changing rankings when asked to perform the same task 1 month later.

In establishing probabilities, it is possible to use percentages or fractions directly. An alternative is to develop a points scale. For example, we might assign 10 points in Figure 3.10 to outcome A. If the decision maker feels that B is twice as likely as A, then we should assign 20 points to B. By the same reasoning, if C is half as likely as A, and D one and a half times as likely as A, then they should be assigned 5 to 15 points respectively. We can cross-check these ratings by asking whether the decision maker agrees that D is three times as likely as C and so on. One may combine the outcomes as well. For instance, is seeing B or C as likely as seeing A or D? Formats other than 'relative likelihood' may be used. At the risk of introducing the less desirable effects of betting, a manager may be asked if he would give odds of 3:1 against C rather than D (being 15/5), or 9:1 against C occurring and so on. The points can then be converted to fractions by dividing by the total (as in the previous section). The reason for such an exercise is that the decision maker is asked questions in a manner that he understands and finds relatively easy to answer. In general, we shall use probability on the understanding that it represents the end of a process which explains the meaning of probability to the decision maker, and ascertains estimates in a user-friendly manner.

3.4.3   Assessing risk – utility measurement

If you were presented with Options 1 and 2 in Figure 3.11, would you necessarily choose the option with the highest expected monetary value, Option 1? The second option has much to recommend it, offering the possibility of a higher return, and more importantly for most, offering a minimum return of £30. If the numbers represented £000, we suspect that few would choose Option 1.

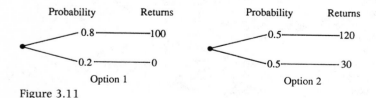

Figure 3.11

Suppose the same question were asked of a manager, only this time the figures represented profit estimates (again in £000). We suspect that most managers would also choose Option 2. The reasons would not be dissimilar to those of the personal choice. A justification might run something like this:

> I am not too concerned whether or not my profits are £100,000 or £120,000, but I am concerned about my profits showing £30,000 (Option 2) rather than £100,000 (Option 1). Obviously, there is quite a strong possibility of this happening if I choose Option 2. However, I judge this possibility to be less serious than reporting no profits, which is possible in Option 1. Despite the lesser chance of the latter event, I will choose Option 2 (principally to avoid zero returns).

Note that when we originally looked at this problem (section 3.4.2), we were careful to say that the decision maker was equally happy with every £1 received. This would make the above statement impossible, for the decision maker is saying in this example that he is more concerned about the difference between £0 and £30, than £100 and £120. Empirical tests (e.g. Swalm (1966)) confirm that the reasoning we have presented here is the more common. Evidently, when faced with a choice between risky options, choosing the option with the highest expected value is not satisfactory. In particular, it would seem that not enough account is taken of the effect of the lower returns on the decision.

This attitude can be represented by constructing a scale which would weight the difference between £100 and £120 less than the difference between £0 and £30. Then we might be able to assess the options in terms of expected value of the scores on the new scale. A suitable procedure was suggested by von Neumann and Morgenstern (1949), and the resultant measure was unfortunately given the name 'utility', a term which we shall prefix with the initials N–M to emphasize its special qualities (see section 3.4.4 for a review of utility). The scale is derived by asking a decision maker (D–M) a number of hypothetical questions in the following manner:

Analyst: If you were offered the following bet:

50 per cent chance of £150
and 50 per cent chance of £0

How much would you want to receive for certain as minimum compensation for losing the chance to enter this bet?

D–M: Well, say, £40

Analyst: If you were offered the following bet:

50 per cent chance of £40
and 50 per cent chance of £0

How much would you want to receive etc? (as above)

D–M: This is decidedly meaner than the last bet; in fact I'm not that interested in taking it, so I don't need much to dissuade me, or make me indifferent. About £5 would be my answer.

Analyst: Finally, if you were offered the following bet:

50 per cent chance of £150
and 50 per cent chance of £40

How much would you want to receive etc? (as above)

D–M: I would get at least £40 from the bet with a fair chance of an extra £110. I rather like this bet and would be a bit reluctant to lose it, so I reckon about £80.

From these questions we are able to devise a scale in much the same way as a scale was devised for the value function. First, as with any scale, we need to set two points. Let us assign the number 0 to £0 and 12 to £150 (for reasons that will become clear later). From the first bet the decision maker expresses an equivalence between the bet and £40 for certain, therefore:

$$\text{The bet} = \text{certainty}$$
$$0.5\,(0) + 0.5\,(12) = 1.0\,(A)$$
$$A = 6$$

where A is, of course, the value that our scale places upon the £40. The second bet can now be represented as:

$$0.5\,(6) + 0.5\,(0) = 1.0\,(B)$$
$$B = 3$$

B is £5, so our scale values B at 3. The third bet gives rise to the equation:

$$0.5\,(12) + 0.5\,(6) = 1.0\,(C)$$
$$C = 9$$

The value of £80 is therefore 9. The units of the scale are commonly referred to as utiles (U), and the method that we have used to derive the scale is known as mid-value splitting (Keeney and Raiffa (1976) p. 94). The aim of this approach has been to measure a respondent's reactions to risky situations. He or she is being asked to equate the risky situation, as given on the left-hand side of the equation, with a position of certainty, as given on the right-hand side. The right hand side is the *certainty equivalent*, which is usually something less than the expected value, reflecting the fact that in general people are risk averse. Before we develop this point further, let us measure these results by constructing the scale.

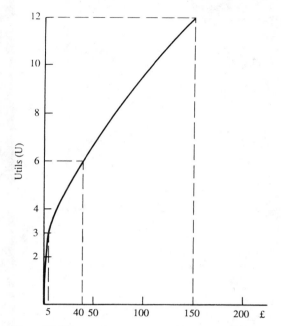

Figure 3.12

Typically, further questions, in the manner illustrated here, will yield answers whose points are then described by the line in Figure 3.12. In this particular case the line may be approximated by the equation:

$$u = \sqrt{£x}$$

Rather than choose the option which maximizes expected £s, the choice will be better predicted by maximizing expected u's, for it is the reaction to the £s as measured by the u's that is significant. All we need do is convert the £s into us using the equation $u = \sqrt{£x}$; the original bet that we considered in Figure 3.11 can now be represented as in Figure 3.13. The result is as we anticipated. Although Option 1 has a higher expected value, the relatively greater concern of the decision maker for the lower return means that Option 2 would be chosen, as it has the higher N–M utility measure.

Let us now compare the N–M utility curve of this manager with that of the manager in the previous section. The former manager's decisions were determined by the expected value, reflecting the attitude that he was not especially averse to taking a risk. Such a manager would be indifferent between the bet and the expected value and would therefore support the following equations (where ∼ means 'indifferent to'):

0.5 (£0) and 0.5 (£150) $\sim$ 1.0 (£75).$\therefore$A = £75 and 6u
0.5 (£75) and 0.5 (£0) $\sim$ 1.0 (£37.5).$\therefore$B = £37.5 and 3u
0.5 (£150) and 0.5 (£75) $\sim$ 1.0 (£112.5).$\therefore$C = £112.5 and 9u

Option 1

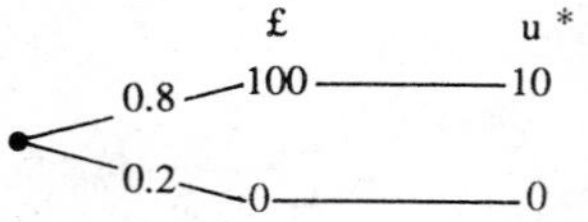

Expected value = 0.8 (100) + 0.2 (0) = 80
Expected utility = 0.8 (10) + 0.2 (0) = 8.0

Option 1

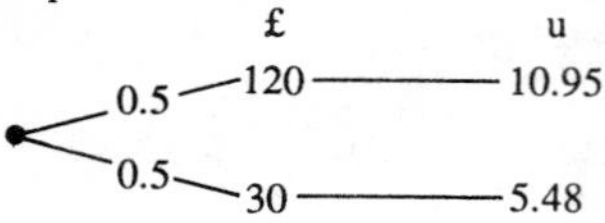

Expected value = 0.5 (120) + 0.5 (30) = 75
Expected utility = 0.5 (10.95) + 0.5 (5.48) = 8.22
* $u = \sqrt{£}$

Figure 3.13

The equation for this manager's utility curve is $u = 0.08$ (£X). Clearly, the manager's reaction to risk differs from the previous example, the two utility curves I and II are plotted in Figure 3.14.

The manager that we have just considered selects risky projects by converting (or he behaves as if he has converted) £s into utiles using curve II. The essential feature of II is that a difference in financial outcomes results in the same difference in utiles whatever level one starts from (the second derivative is 0). For instance, a gain of £10 is worth 0.8u whether it is from £0 to £10 or from £100 to £110. Curve II is not the only curve that would fulfil this requirement; in fact, any straight line would confer equal weighting on all £s and would predict the managers preferences correctly. The reader may check that the line need not even pass through the origin – thus: $u = x + 100$ (curve III) would also work. Likewise, with curve I, as long as the relative differences are not disturbed, the same predictions would be made. More formally, each N–M utility curve is a member of a separate family of curves that are unique up to a positive linear transformation, implying that:

$$u^* = \alpha(u) + c$$

where u* is a member of the same family as u and α and c are constants. Therefore, as regards curve I, the equation:

$$u = 3\sqrt{x} + 50$$

would produce the same preferences. When a curve is devised, the precise member of the family chosen depends upon the original arbitrary assignment of values to the two original points. It is reassuring that this assignment does not affect our measurement of risk.

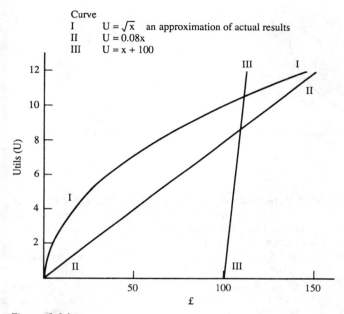

Curve
I $U = \sqrt{x}$ an approximation of actual results
II $U = 0.08x$
III $U = x + 100$

Figure 3.14

The particular interest as regards decision making is to understand the difference between curves I and II, and hence understand why the respective managers order the options in Figure 3.13 differently. Let us first of all introduce an approximate notion of risk as simply being the spread of returns, i.e. the difference between the highest and lowest outcome. The more risky the option, the greater the spread of returns. We have already established that, in answering the questions posed to devise the curve, the managers establish a certainty equivalent. If we look at Option 1 (0.8 × £100 and 0.2 × £0), the certainty equivalent for curve I is $0.8\sqrt{£100} = 8u$, which converts to £64 using the curve (we will henceforth assume that curve I is $u = \sqrt{x}$ precisely). Therefore the manager would be indifferent to accepting £64 for certain, instead of the bet. The curve II manager, by contrast, values bets at their expected value, and hence would accept £80 for certain. In other words the curve I manager will accept 80 − 64 = £16 less than the curve II manager in order to avoid the bet. The special feature of the curve II manager is, as we have noted, that he is risk-neutral. He will value bets at their expected value, *no matter how widely spread the returns are around the mean*. The £16 discount accepted by the curve I manager is therefore solely due to the fact that he is risk-averse. For this reason the amount is known as the risk premium, the price paid to avoid risk. The more risk-averse a manager, the lower his or her valuation of the bet (i.e. the certainty equivalent) as compared with the expected value. Hence the higher the risk premium.

Finally to complete the picture a third risk attitude is considered (Figure 3.15). The manager described by this curve is risk-prone.

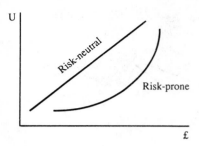

Figure 3.15

A manager who is risk-prone will only accept an amount greater than the expected value as adequate recompense. He therefore has a negative risk premium and wishes to be paid for the loss of risk. The N–M utility curve of a risk prone manager is convex, as in Figure 3.15.

These concepts of risk attitude are central to understanding decision making under uncertainty. Human behaviour encompasses all three states.

To begin with the last of the attitudes, risk-prone behaviour is well illustrated at the racecourse. The stake is always greater than the expected chances of winning. For example, the true odds of a horse quoted at 500–1 are probably closer to 10,000–1. If this were the case, a risk-neutral person would be willing to place 5p to earn £500 if the horse should win ($\frac{£500}{5p} = 10,000$); the gambler who is willing to place £1, i.e. considerably above the expected value, is therefore behaving in a risk-prone manner. Empirical tests show that risk-prone behaviour is to be found in business, particularly as regards losses. In other words it is not an uncommon finding that managers may 'gamble' to avoid losses (Swalm (1966)).

Most behaviour may be described as either risk-averse or risk-neutral. Insurance is the opposite of gambling and serves to illustrate risk-averse behaviour. Suppose that in Figure 3.16 Option I represents the prospective takings of a garden fete. There is a 90 per cent chance of fine weather when takings are estimated at £1,000, and if the weather is poor (10 per cent chance), takings will be £400. The chances of a loss of £600 revenue from bad weather are therefore 10 per cent. The risk-neutral person would only pay a premium for an insurance policy of up to £60 (600 × 0.1) to insure against this loss, leaving his expected utility at worst unaffected. The risk-averse person would be willing to pay slightly more than this. The reader may wish to check that if his utility curve were $u = \sqrt{£x}$, then he would be willing to pay up to £12.16 above the expected value in order to avoid the risk, i.e. £72.16 – the utility of 1000 – 72.16 for certain, is the same as the expected utility. The insurance company will undertake many such policies.

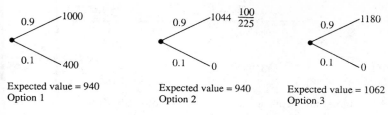

Figure 3.16

The relatively small impact of a single policy implies that it will not be particularly sensitive to the spread of possible returns that the policy offers. The insurance company will value the policy at its expected value. Therefore, the organizer of the fete is willing to pay up to £72.16 for a policy that the insurance company values at £60. The sale of the policy at any price between £60 and £72.16 would benefit both parties.

In business, risk-averse behaviour is considered the norm for decisions with significant consequences. This does not imply that managers seek to avoid risk at all costs – business, after all, *is* taking risks. What it does imply is that (a) for a given expected return managers will choose the option with the lower risk, and (b) there is a risk return trade-off. Projects with higher returns will normally offer higher risks, and whether or not the manager thinks the extra expected return to be worthwhile depends upon the extra risk. The position is illustrated in Figure 3.16. Both Options 1 and 2 have the same expected value; the risk-neutral decision maker would be indifferent between the two, but the risk-averse manager would prefer Option 1 to Option 2. In comparing Options 1 and 2, a risk-averse decision maker would weight the loss of £400 from to £0 at a 10 per cent chance more than the gain from 1,000 to 1044, $\frac{100}{225}$, at a 90 per cent chance, despite the two changes having the same expected value of £40. This is revealed by the concave nature of the risk-averse utility curve, which assigns a higher per £ utility for lower values than for higher values. The risk-averse manager would therefore prefer Option 1 to Option 2.

The choice between Option 3 and Option 1 is less clear. The expected value of the gain at the upper end is $0.9 \times £180 = £162$, and whether or not this outweighs the expected value of the loss $0.1 \times £400 = £40$ depends upon the risk-aversion of the manager. Put another way, Option 3 has a higher expected value, but a glance confirms that it is also more risky. The risk return attitude required to select between Options 1 and 2 is contained in the utility curve. Two risk-averse managers with utility functions of differing risk aversion are represented in Table 3.5. Both managers prefer Option 1 to Option 2 and are risk-averse; however, manager A is less risk-averse than manager B in that he would accept the riskier Option 3 in preference to Option 1, unlike manager B.

Accountants are in essence measurers. Therefore a natural question to ask is 'Can the degree of risk aversion be measured?' Or, more generally, 'Can risk attitudes be measured?' To get a feel for such a measure, readers should

Table 3.5

Utility function	Option 1 E(u)	CE*	Option 2 E(u)	CE	Option 3 E(u)	CE
Manager A: $U_A = \sqrt{£x}$	30.5	930	29.1	847	30.9	955
Manager B: $U_B = \log_n £x^{**}$	6.8	898	6.3	545	6.4	602

* CE is the certainly equivalent calculated in £ sterling and is the inverse of the expected utility i.e. $[E(U_A)]^2$ and $\exp E(U_B)$, where $\exp(x)$ is the same as e^x.
** The utility curve is log normal, usually denoted as ln on scientific calculators.

turn back to Figure 3.14; risk aversion evidently has something to do with the slope. However, the measure cannot simply be the slope, for the slope also depends upon the arbitrary initial assignment of two utiles to monetary values. Rather, risk attitude depends upon the relative slopes on a line – such a measure is not subject to the arbitrary choice of units. At a single point such a measure is given by the *local coefficient of risk aversion* (Pratt, 1964) which is:

$$r(x) = \frac{-u''(x)}{u'(x)}$$

where u' and u" are the first and second derivatives of the utility function. Thus:

$$r(x) > 0 \text{ risk-averse}$$
$$r(x) = 0 \text{ risk-neutral}$$
$$r(x) < 0 \text{ risk-prone}$$

The concave curve of the risk-averse decision maker has a positive slope which is declining (positive first and negative second differential), hence: $r(x) > 0$. The straight line of the risk-neutral decision maker has a 0 change in slope (a 0 second differential), hence: $r(x) = 0$. The convex curve of the risk-prone decision maker has a positive slope which is increasing (positive first and second differential), hence $r(x) < 0$.

The measure also indicates another important property of risk-aversion, namely, that people and organizations tend to be less risk-averse the higher their level of wealth. For instance, suppose we take Option 3 from figure 3.16, the risk premium for Manager B is $1,062 - 602 = £460$; if this manager now learns that he is £1,000 better off, then this is the equivalent of an option giving £2,180 at 90 per cent and £1,000 at 10 per cent (we have simply added £1,000 to all possible outcomes). This represents a definite increase in wealth of £1,000, and one would therefore expect a decrease in risk premium. This is indeed the case: the expected utility of such an option is 7.61 u (a certainty equivalent of £2,018), and the risk premium is $(£2,180 \times 0.9 + 1,000 \times 0.1) - 2,018 = £44$, a considerable reduction.

An extension of this finding is that one would expect that a wealthy company would be less risk-averse than a less wealthy company for a given risky option. This is a likely, rather than a necessary relationship, for it assumes that firms have similar attitudes towards risk at differing levels of wealth – this need not necessarily be so.

Another important conclusion, which we have already made use of, is that projects with a small potential effect on an organization's return may be approximated by the expected value alone. This is a matter of simple geometry, for a small movement on a concave curve can be approximated by a straight line – the risk-neutral attitude which values projects by expected value. This is not the same as saying that such companies *are* risk-neutral, for, no doubt, a large company will be every bit as risk-averse for a project involving significant changes of its wealth as a small company.

In practice, firms often make a distinction between small and large projects, allowing middle managers to invest sums under a certain amount. A possible justification for this rule would be that such a manager is in a position to judge and select on the basis of expected values, but does not have a sufficiently broad view of the organization to apply, in notional terms at least, a utility curve. An organization's utility curve will depend upon the total wealth position, which requires information that is beyond the scope of less senior management. There are hidden dangers in this policy. If a manager makes several investments whose returns are all correlated, then that will be the equivalent of one large investment which may have an important influence on returns (the importance of correlation is examined further in section 3.4.6). In addition, the initial cost is not always a good guide to the consequences of an investment. A small change of style or quality may not lead to great costs, but nevertheless may risk catastrophic changes in returns.

We hope that enough has been said to convince the reader that N–M utility and risk-aversion are not abstract notions. In fact they provide an understanding of much observed behaviour, and can be used as tools for improving practical decision policies within the organisation. We would go further, and suggest that they are as important as the notion of profit maximization for decisions involving uncertainty. When considering Options 1, 2 and 3 in Figure 3.16, it is not enough to know the returns and probabilities to make a decision; risk attitude is an indispensable part of the selection process.

Thus far, the measurement of N–M utility has been conducted entirely in terms of monetary units. In fact, as von Neumann and Morgenstern have pointed out, this need not necessarily be so. As an example, let us take a firm that has decided to invest £100,000 in sponsorship. Management may not feel that it is possible to measure the direct effect on profits of the various alternatives. Alternatively, they may feel able to construct a cardinal scale of 1 to 10 of benefit. Various possibilities will offer a spread of returns expressed in terms of this scale. Sponsoring a racing driver, for instance, may offer a 20 per cent chance of 10 points if he is successful, a 50 per cent chance of 6 if he performs reasonably well, and a 30 per cent change of 0 if he crashes! Sponsoring an orchestra may, by contrast, produce a 100 per cent chance of 4.5 points, a much more stable proposition. With these estimates, it is not immediately clear which option is preferable. The decision will, in part, depend upon the degree of risk the firm is willing to take in sponsoring. This may be measured by constructing an N–M utility curve in the manner described earlier on in this section, only that, instead of £s, 'units of benefit' are considered instead.

Finally, we end by stressing what N–M utility is and is not. Principally, it is a measure designed to enable decision makers to make logical and consistent choices in risky situations. Providing that one accepts that the questions posed to construct the scale are meaningful and relevant, it can be shown that maximizing expected utility provides a rational basis for choice (Bromwich, 1976). It is not the same as the utility that is to be found in economics, such a measure contemplates satisfaction on *certain* receipt of an attribute. But are they so different? After all, they both contemplate receipt, though under different circumstances. The traditional position on this question is outlined in Keeney and Raiffa (1976, p. 150). 'The utility functions we are talking about in this chapter (N–M utility) are completely different from the economist's *utility function*. Knowing one implies very little about the other. One can easily be convex and the other concave for the same attribute'.

To many, such a viewpoint raises more questions than it answers. The problem is not the role of classical utility and N–M utility in decision making, rather it is their precise meaning. This is the subject of the next section, though we stress that those who are not troubled by this issue may move directly to section 3.4.5.

3.4.4   *The utility debate**

Let us first look at the term 'traditional' or 'classical' utility. The original use of the term utility was to provide an explanation of value; it was seen as a unit of pleasure or happiness that could be derived in varying degrees by consuming a commodity. The problem that early economists faced was to link this motive for obtaining commodities, with their cost. After several false starts Stigler (1950) credits the breakthrough to the eccentric German economist Heinrich Gossen: 'A person maximizes his utility when he distributes his available money among the various goods so that he obtains the same amount of satisfaction from the last unit of money (Geldatom) spent upon each commodity'.

This is the first formulation of the famous marginal utility theory which may be more formally expressed as:

$$\frac{MU_1}{P_1} = \frac{MU_2}{P_2} = \frac{MU_3}{P_3} \dots$$

where MU_1 represents the marginal utility for product 1, i.e. the satisfaction gained from consuming the last unit of that commodity, and P_1 represents that commodity's price. If we also add the further assumption of Jevons and Walras, that marginal utility decreases with quantity consumed, then we can derive the downward sloping demand curve (Stigler (1950)).

When N–M utility was originally introduced, it was taken by some to be a

* CIMA see Preface.

means of measuring the classical utility function. The confusion was in part prompted by rather vague comments by von Neumann and Morgenstern in devising the measure (Ellsburg, 1954). Furthermore, the typical N–M curve was concave, the shape one would expect from diminishing marginal utility. As we have seen in the previous section, the concave nature of the N–M utility curve can be more plausibly explained by risk-aversion. Hence it was asserted, originally by Ellsburg (1954) and subsequently by many authors including Keeney and Raiffa (1976), that N–M utility and classical utility were quite separate concepts.

However, the idea that they are totally separate seems hard to accept. For example, let us take an apparently trivial problem which nevertheless deals with the issues that we are discussing. Suppose that an N–M utility function concerning the choice of meals was drawn up. A typical question might be: 'Would you be indifferent between a one-course meal for certain and a 50 per cent chance of a five-course meal and a 50 per cent chance of nothing?' The respondent's attitude to risk would of course be important, but so would the satisfaction received from consumption! After all, if the person did not like the menu, it would seem reasonable for him or her to choose the single course (assuming that one of the options had to be selected and consumed), rather than risk a five-course meal. If the menu were changed to a desirable one, then the same person might choose to take the risk. The most reasonable explanation for the change in choice is the different satisfaction from consumption, and not a sudden conversion to a less risk-averse approach. From this and other examples that can be devised, it would seem reasonable to propose that risk attitudes are constant, and that differences in N–M utility are caused by changes in satisfaction. It is more plausible that preferences, rather than risk attitudes, change between goods. But this would imply that N–M utility contains an element of classical utility. This is exactly the proposition put forward by the concept of *relative risk aversion*: 'A von Neumann–Morgenstern utility function confounds an individual's risk attitude with the strength of preference he feels for the outcomes' (Dyer and Sarin (1982)).

N–M utility is here seen as a function of two processes: first, the measuring of strength of preference for attribute levels (x) under certainty denoted by the function v(x); and, secondly, a risk function $U_v(.)$ defined on the value function. Thus the utility function may be described as:

$$U(x) = U_v[V(x)]$$

In this form, the N–M utility measure encapsulates an individual's attitude to certain consumption *and* his attitude towards risk. Both attitudes are normally assumed to be concave as a result of decreasing marginal utility and risk-aversion respectively (this is probably why the distinction has not been made earlier). In practice, of course, it does not seem likely that the two functions would be separated. When one is faced with a bet, for instance, the value of the prize plays an indispensable role.

Relative risk-aversion in no measure disturbs the role of N–M utility in decision making. Rather, it provides an explanation of its meaning, an explanation that provides a link between N–M utility and classical utility, as well as suggesting a reason why N–M utility curves differ over differing attributes. The development may also have measurement implications (Krzysztofowicz, 1983) though the interested reader is advised to consult French (1986, chapter 9) on such issues. Here, our interest is in the light that this development casts on our understanding of the causes of the shape of a particular N–M utility curve, as well as to show that decision making is still a developing subject.

3.4.5 Stochastic dominance*

One of the less attractive features in assessing risk is the practical difficulty of measuring the N–M utility curve. For certain comparisons, this problem may be avoided in that preference may be established for a whole class of utility functions. In other words, it may be possible to look at the probabilities and outcomes, and declare that one option is superior to another for, say, all risk-averse decision makers. In such cases there is said to be stochastic dominance.

First order stochastic dominance (FSD) applies to all positively sloped utility functions. It states that option A is preferable to B where the cumulative probabilities of A refer to a level of wealth as great as, or greater than, B. This result is demonstrated in Figure 3.17. Note that the cumulative probability of A is either equal to or lies to the right of B. The expected value in Table 3.6 also reveals the superiority of A. As $U_4 > U_3 > U_2 > U_1$, then from the A–B column $(U_3 + U_4)\, 0.1 > (U_2)\, 0.2$, so that A must have a greater expected utility than B. In general, A is superior to B as long as the cumulative A–B column is negative or 0 at all values. In practice, there will be relatively few investments rejected on these grounds, as we are including the preferences of all decision makers.

Second order stochastic dominance (SSD) applies only to risk-averse or risk-neutral decision makers, and is accordingly more discerning. Under this condition, Option A is superior to Option B if the cumulative area under the cumulative probability curve for B is at least as great as, or greater than, A, for all levels of returns. Second order dominance of A over B is demonstrated in Figure 3.18. The first order dominance condition is not fulfilled because at points I and II in Figure 3.18 (b) the cumulative probability of A is higher than B. It is easier to see this point by looking at Figure 3.18 (a). Where the returns are 5, the probability of B is higher than A; the gambler may value this difference much more highly than any of the other differences and hence may prefer B to A. Second order stochastic dominance is fulfilled, as can be seen from Table 3.7 where column 6 must be at all points less than or equal to column 7. Note that the fact that the returns are evenly spaced simplifies the calculation of columns 6 and 7, the full formulae are:

$$\text{Columns 4 \& 5: } F_1(x_i) = \sum_{i=1}^{n} f(x_i)$$

$$\text{Columns 6 \& 7: } F_2(x_i) = \sum_{i=1}^{n} F_1(x_{i-1})(x_i - x_{i-1})$$

*CIMA see Preface.

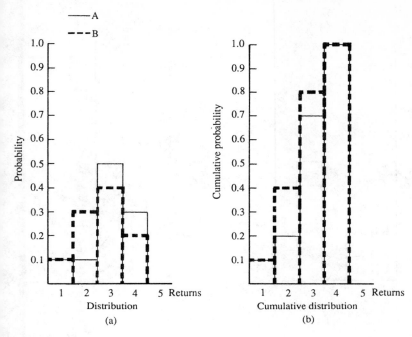

Figure 3.17

Table 3.6 Calculation of expected values where $V_i = $ NM utility of return i in Figure 3.17

A $U_i \times probability$	B $U_i \times probability$	$A-B$ $U_i \times Pr(A) - Pr(B)$	Cumulative probability of $A-B$
$U_1 \times 0.1$	$U_1 \times 0.1$	$U_1 \times \quad 0.0$	0.0
$U_2 \times 0.1$	$U_2 \times 0.3$	$U_2 \times -0.2$	-0.2
$U_3 \times 0.5$	$U_3 \times 0.4$	$U_3 \times \quad 0.1$	-0.1
$U_4 \times 0.3$	$U_4 \times 0.2$	$U_4 \times \quad 0.1$	0.0
1.0	1.0		

There will, of course, be many choices between investments where superiority depends upon the degree of risk aversion. In such cases stochastic dominance is likely to fail. It is instructive to look at such an example. Take the two investments in Table 3.8; casual inspection does not make it clear which is preferable. The full stochastic dominance process is given in Table 3.9.

FSD implies that column 4 is not greater than column 5 for every line and is less than column 5 for at least one line. This condition is violated on lines 3 and 7. This might be because risk-seeking individuals are included. SSD

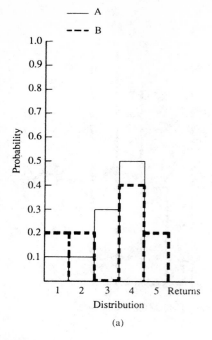

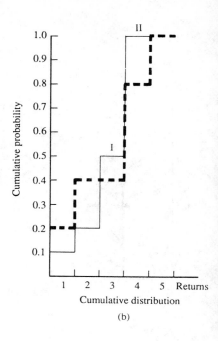

Figure 3.18

Table 3.7

1 Returns	2 Probability	3	4 Cumulative probability	5	6	7	6-7
	A	B	A	B	A	B	
x_i	$f x_i$	$f(x_i)$	$F_1(x_i)$	$F_1(x_i)$	$F_2(x_i)$	$F_2(x_i)$	
1	0.1	0.2	0.1	0.2	0.0	0.0	0.0
2	0.1	0.2	0.2	0.4	0.1	0.2	-0.1
3	0.3	0.0	0.5	0.4	0.3	0.6	-0.3
4	0.5	0.4	1.0	0.8	0.8	1.0	-0.2
5	0.0	0.2	1.0	1.0	1.8	1.8	0.0

will rule this possibility out by restricting utility curves to those where $u'(x) > 0$ and $u''(x) < 0$, which excludes the risk-seeking utility curve. For this to hold, column 6 must not be greater than column 7 for every line and must be less for at least one line. This condition is violated on lines 4 and 5.

Third order stochastic dominance. Finally, third order stochastic dominance (Whitmore, 1970) is possible where:

Table 3.8

Investment	A	B	
Probability			£ returns
0.1	11	10	
0.1	25	30	
0.6	62	50	
0.2	990	1,000	

Table 3.9

1 Returns x_i	2 A $f(x)$	3 B fx	4 A $F_1(x_i)$	5 B $F_1(x_i)$	6 A $F_2(x_i)$	7 B $F_2(x_i)$	8 A $F_3(x_i)$	9 Line B $F_3(x_i)$
10	0.0	0.1	0.0	0.1	0.0	0.0	0.0	0.0
11	0.1	0.0	0.1	0.1	0.0	0.1	0.0	0.05
25	0.1	0.0	0.2	0.1	1.4	1.5	9.8	11.25
30	0.0	0.1	0.2	0.2	2.4	2.0	19.3	15.25
50	0.0	0.6	0.2	0.8	6.4	6.0	107.3	95.25
62	0.6	0.0	0.8	0.8	8.8	15.6	198.5	224.85
990	0.2	0.0	1.0	0.8	751.2	758.0	35,264.0	359,175.25
1,000	0.0	0.2	1.0	1.0	761.2	766.0	360,202.0	366,795.25

$$F_3(x_i) = \tfrac{1}{2}\sum_{i=2}^{n} [F_2(x_i) + F_2(x_{i-1})](x_i - x_{i-1})$$

Similar conditions are required between columns 8 and 9 as between 6 and 7, with the added proviso that line 8 for column 7 must be less than line 8 for column 8. TSD excludes some, but not all, unsatisfactory risk-averse functions by restricting utility curves to risk-neutral and risk-averse functions where $u'''(x) > 0$; this includes, but is not exclusive to, decreasingly risk-averse utility functions. In our example the attempt to distinguish has failed, as column 8 is greater than 9 at lines 4 and 5. There is therefore no alternative in our example but to measure the degree of risk-aversion of the decision maker. This could be achieved by constructing an N–M utility curve in the manner described in section 3.4.3.

Simple dominance rules. We should remember that the aim of dominance analysis is immensely practical, for if dominance can be established, then there is no need to trouble the decision maker with awkward questions concerning risk attitudes (other than to establish whether he is risk-seeking, risk-neutral or risk-averse). The full procedure is rather cumbersome, but it is possible to take a number of short cuts, and we mention three. A *cannot* dominate B if any one or more of these rules apply:

1 The average of A is less than B.
2 The lowest value of A is below that of B.

3   If the averages of A and B are equal, then A cannot dominate B if it has a higher standard deviation.

Rule 1 must be so, as the risk neutral investor is not excluded by SSD or TSD and the average or expected value is the basis for selection for such an investor. If rule 2 holds, then there will be at least one errant low return for which no statement about relative utility can be made. Finally, the greater spread in rule 3, seems intuitively less attractive (Porter *et al.* (1973)).

When applied to the investments in Table 3.8, investment B cannot dominate investment A; it has a lower average and its lowest value is below that of A, so that rules 1 and 2 apply. Investment A is not excluded from consideration by these rules, and it may dominate B; but as our calculation shows, it does not. This implies that the choice between A and B depends upon how risk-averse the decision maker is. We are unfortunately forced, in this case, to ask the decision maker to consider his or her degree of risk-aversion.

Given that the method has failed to distinguish between A and B in this example, the reader might well wonder why stochastic dominance is referred to as 'an extremely important and powerful result' (Copeland and Westson (1982)). To illustrate the potential of this approach, Table 3.10 presents a slightly altered version of A, noted as A_1. The reader might like to verify that A_1 exhibits second order stochastic dominance over B, i.e. providing the decision maker is either risk-neutral or risk-averse, he or she will prefer A_1 to B. The other principal methods of evaluation, which avoid actual measurement of utilities, are the mean variance rule and the mean semi-variance rule (see section 3.4.6). As can be seen from Table 3.10, unlike dominance they are unable to select unambiguously between A_1 and B.

The particular strengths of stochastic dominance may be summarized as:

(a)   It applies to all forms of distribution no matter how irregular.
(b)   It makes minimal assumptions as to risk attitudes – detailed measurement is not required.
(c)   It does not mislead; the method makes it clear where no conclusion can be drawn.

3.4.6   *Measures of financial risk*

So far, our analysis of risk has been based on discrete returns. We have noted that in practice such returns will normally be continuous – discrete analysis is at best an approximation. An alternative approach is to use a measure of spread of the continuous distribution as a proxy for risk. In finance, the standard deviation or variance is often taken as such a measure of risk where returns are continuous. A distribution with a higher standard deviation is assumed to be more risky than one with a lower standard deviation. This idea is expressed by the mean variance rule, which states that, first, where two distributions have an equal mean the distribution with the lower variance is to be preferred for all risk-averse individuals; second, an option with a higher expected return and a lower variance is to be preferred; third, a risk return trade-off has to be established where one option has a higher expected

Table 3.10

	Investment	
	A_1	B
Returns		
10	0.0	0.1
25	0.1	0.0
30	0.0	0.1
50	0.0	0.6
62	0.6	0.0
990	0.3	0.0
1,000	0.0	0.2
	1.0	1.0
Expected value	336.7	234.0
Variance	183,032.0	146,844.0
Standard deviation	427.8	383.2
Semi-variance	54,992.0	29,493.0

value and a higher variance. These preferences are illustrated in Figure 3.19. Investment A is inferior to all points in the north-west quadrant (B,C,D), and superior to all those in the south-east quadrant (E,F,G), the points lying in the remaining two quadrants (H,I) being determined by risk return trade-off. This is the basis for deriving the efficient set in portfolio analysis (see chapter 6).

Where distributions are normal, mean and variance may be used as the basis for selecting investments, as the returns are completely described by the mean and variance (Haley and Schall (1973), p. 97). Thus, the returns of the investments in Figure 3.19 are assumed to appear as in Figure 3.20. There are two further important assumptions. First, if investments are combined, it is assumed that their combined distribution will also be normal, i.e. they are *jointly* normal. Secondly, the returns represent the total returns to the owner (or manager acting as agent). In practice distributions are unlikely to be perfectly normal and may well be markedly non-normal. In such circumstances, it would be wrong to apply the mean variance rule. To illustrate the error that can result, suppose that a manager must choose between the two investments in Table 3.11, he might make the following remarks: 'The attraction of investment A is that it offers a guaranteed level of business with a small promise of high returns. As for investment B, I would expect to have a higher return but there isn't the same guaranteed level, and the returns may be worryingly low'.

In this case, the standard deviations are identical, therefore, the mean variance rule would select B as it has the higher expected return. However, B is not stochastically dominant over A (it has a lower bottom value). If, for

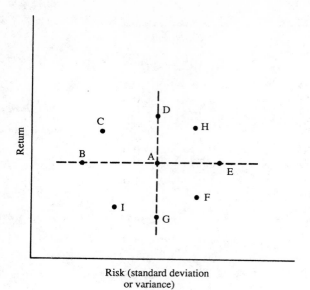

Figure 3.19

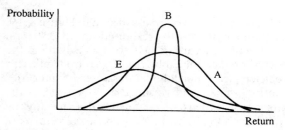

Figure 3.20

instance, the manager has a utility curve characterized by $U = \log_n(x)$, then he or she will be indifferent between the two investments and a curve such as $U = \log_n(x - 9.5)$ would imply preference for A over B despite the lower mean. Selection, as the dominance rules suggest, is dependent upon the degree of risk-aversion, a result not indicated by the mean variance rules.

Fortunately, the normal distribution, or a distribution close to being normal, may be expected to occur frequently. To illustrate the strength of the assumption, we shall take an example of a firm that sells a product in five countries. If the product is successful (50 per cent chance), the firm will earn £100,000, and if it is unsuccessful (50 per cent chance), it will earn £0. If the returns are independent, they can be expected to conform to the binomial probability distribution, which approximates to a normal distribution, as in

Table 3.11

Returns	Probability A	Probability B	
10	0.0	0.1	Where: $U = \log_n(x)$
20	0.1	0.1	$U(A) = 3.6926$,
30	0.4	0.1	$U(B) = 3.6926$
40	0.1	0.1	
50	0.1	0.1	
60	0.1	0.4	Where: $U = \log_n(x - 9.5)$
70	0.1	0.1	$U(A) = 3.3832$,
80	0.1	0.0	$U(B) = 3.1588$
Mean	44	46	
Variance	364	364	
Standard Deviation	19	19	
Semi Variance	138	226	

Figure 3.21(a). Thus, joint normal returns can be obtained even though the individual return is very non-normal (in this case it is as a rectangular distribution, Figure 3.21(b)).

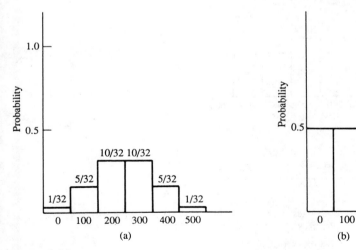

(a)

(b)

Figure 3.21

In practice, firms consider investments singly rather than in total. Does this matter? It is conceivable that a paradoxical situation may arise whereby a firm rejects an investment when considered separately, but would have accepted the investment if it were considered in combination with the other investments it is undertaking.

Reflection should confirm that the sensible answer to this question is that the total returns position should be the deciding factor. The real situation faced by the organization is the return on *all* its investments. It is therefore the effect of an individual investment on the total wealth of the organization that matters. Individual assessment may lead to suboptimal decisions.

Consider the situation where total returns both before and after the investment under consideration are considered to be sufficiently normal to be adequately described by the mean and variance; such projects are therefore jointly normal. Suppose that we are considering an investment in a sixth country with prospective returns as described by Figure 3.21(b) and that the firms existing investment in five countries has returns described by Figure 3.21(a). As investment in the sixth country is independent of the other countries, the distribution of returns will therefore be as in Figure 3.22 and Table 3.12.

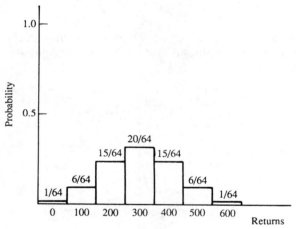

Figure 3.22

Table 3.12

	Mean	Variance
Five countries	250	12,500
Six countries	300	15,000
Effect on total returns of adding sixth country	50	2,500

If the investment were considered separately, then the mean would be £50 and the variance £2,500. Therefore the mean and variance of the individual investment also describe the effect on the total wealth position of the organ-ization. In such circumstances, the mean and variance of the individual investment is the same as the incremental effect on the total investment. Therefore, examining the mean and variance of investing in the sixth country individually, given the present position of investing in five countries, will not distort the decision. Also, as with the five countries, as long as the position both before and after the investment is normal, the non-normality of the individual investment will be of no relevance, as it will be diversified away in the total position.

Now let us consider a situation where the returns of the sixth country are not independent, but the total wealth position remains adequately normal. More specifically, if the returns of the first five countries are £200 or below, the sixth country's return is £100, otherwise the sixth country's return is 0. The distribution would be as in Figure 3.23 and the change in total returns

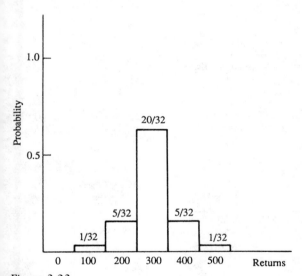

Figure 3.23

will be as in Table 3.13. The sixth country increases the mean and reduces the variance and is therefore a beneficial investment, i.e. it is in the north-west quadrant of Figure 3.19. The mean of the individual investment still reflects the change in total position; but the variance, which is still £2,500, does not. To capture the effect on total variance, the covariance of the sixth country's returns with that of the other five countries must be considered. This is calculated as in Table 3.14.

The variance of two populations X and Y added together is described by the following formula:

$$Var(X + Y) = Var(X) + Var(Y) + 2 \, cov(XY)$$

When applied to this example we have:

$$= 12,500 + 2,500 + 2 \, (-4,687.5)$$
$$= 5,625$$

which is the variance of the six countries considered together (for revision on the meaning of the term covariance, see section 6.2).

Table 3.13

	Mean	*Variance*
Five countries	250	12,500
Six countries	300	5,625
Effect on total returns of adding sixth country	50	(6,875)

Table 3.14

Pr	*Five countries' return* X	*Sixth country's return* Y	*XY*	*Pr(XY)*
1/32	0	100	0	0.0
5/32	100	100	10,000	1,562.5
10/32	200	100	20,000	6,250.0
10/32	300	0	0	0.0
5/32	400	0	0	0.0
1/32	500	0	0	0.0
				E(XY) = 7,812.5

$$\text{Cov } (XY) = E(XY) - E(X) \, E \, (Y)$$
$$= 7,812.5 - 250 \times 50$$
$$= -4,687.5$$

We can generalize this result and say that where total returns are adequately described by mean and variance (i.e. it is normally distributed), the consideration of individual investments should include the mean, variance and the covariance of the individual investment with the other investments. In circumstances where the individual investment is independent, we have a special case of zero covariance, leaving only the mean and variance as the relevant measures.

Thus far, we have assumed that the investment of the firm represents the total wealth of the owner. In practice, individual wealth is more likely to be diversified. People usually invest in their home, in their job and directly or indirectly in the stock market. Returns that are independent of the investment under consideration can be considered separately; their case is analogous to investment in the sixth country when the returns were independent of the other countries. The only connection between such investments is a general wealth effect. Thus an entrepreneur contemplating a business prospect is likely to be less risk-averse if he owns a large amount of property (yielding a return independent of his prospect), than if he has a large mortgage on his home and owns no other property. In each case, his risk attitude will not be altered towards his business prospects whether he considers them separately (given existing wealth) or adds them to a consideration of his total wealth position.

Returns that are not independent, by contrast, do need to be considered together. Such returns have a non-zero covariance, which, as demonstrated in the preceding example, can significantly affect risk attitudes.

In practice, a major area of return covariance is between different business investments. For instance, a businessman contemplating the investments discussed in this section may also hold shares in a number of other companies. It is most likely that there will be a significant degree of covariance between such investments, as they will all be affected by general market conditions. In this very important case, the businessman needs to consider the covariance between an individual share and the other shareholdings in his portfolio to assess the full impact on the risk of his returns. As the number of such investments increases, the covariances became more important than the variances (being greater in number). Many large companies are, of course, owned by shareholders. In such cases, management, acting as the shareholders' agent, will need to consider the covariance of each investment in the firm with the portfolio held by the shareholders (Rubinstein, 1974). How this might be done, and the effect on investment analysis, is examined in Part II.

We have seen that where returns are not normal, the use of mean and variance may lead to suboptimal decisions. It would be useful if another 'measure of spread' could be developed, one which would include the effect of non-normal distributions without recourse to measuring utilities.

Limited progress has been made with semi-variance (Markowitz, 1959). This measure has been suggested as a substitute for variance in the mean variance rules of Figure 3.19. It is defined as:

$$\text{Semivariance} = \sum_{i=1}^{n} [X_i - E(X)]^2 Pr(X_i)$$

where: X is the return on investment i adjusted as follows:

$$X_i = X_i \quad \text{if } X_i < E(X)$$
$$\text{and } X_i = E(X) \text{ if } X_i \geqslant E(X)$$

It measures 'downside' risk, that is where the deviation from average is negative rather than positive. This has great intuitive appeal, for variation above the mean can hardly be called risk, at least not the kind of risk that one need worry about! As regards the non-normal distributions in Table 3.11, investment A has a longer tail than B above the average, and a shorter tail below the average – hence the lower semivariance. In this example, semi-variance (unlike variance) successfully identifies the spread of A's returns as being preferable to those of B. Although for non-normal distributions semivariance will not be worse and will generally perform better than variance, it will not always be better. For example, in Table 3.10 investment A_1 has a higher expected value and a higher variance and semivariance. The mean variance and mean semivariance rule both suggest that choice is a question of trading risk for return, when in fact A_1 exhibits second order tochastic dominance over B. Therefore there is no risk return trade-off.

Another attempt to include non-normal distributions is to assume that the investor has a quadratic utility function, that is to say a utility function of the form:

$$U(x) = a + b(x) - c(x)^2$$

Then expected utility is $E[U(x)] = a + bE(x) - cE(x^2)$, and as $E(x^2) = Var(x) + [E(x)]^2$ we have $E[U(x)] = a + bE(x) - c(Var(x) + [E(x)]^2)$. With such a utility curve, the investor is only interested in the mean $(E(x))$ and the variance $(Var(x))$ of the returns. At first sight, this may seem a rather clever solution to the problem of non-normal returns – we need not worry about the non-normality of returns as the investor is not interested in them.

We include this suggestion because many texts (Keeney and Raiffa, Haley and Schall, Hull *et al.*) infer that this assumption lies at the heart of financial analysis. It could do if we so chose; but unfortunately quadratic utility functions have certain unrealistic assumptions. The function is positive (upward sloping) only so long as $2c(x) < b$ (as $u'(x) = (b - 2c(x))$); it is concave in that $u''(x) = -2c$, but it is increasingly risk-averse (see section 3.4.3) in that

$$r(x) = \frac{-u''(x)}{(u'x)}$$

$$= \frac{2c}{b - 2cx}$$

One can see by inspection that as x increases to the point where $2cx = b$, the risk-aversion factor becomes larger, which, as explained in section 3.4.3, is an unrealistic assumption.

Where distributions of total returns are not normal and are being unrealistically approximated as being normal, it is no solution to transfer this lack of realism from the distribution to the utility function.

In general, the advantage of using mean and variance or semivariance as a method of analysing risky choice is that it avoids the problems of measuring the effect of all possible outcomes on utility. As the foregoing analysis has shown, this advantage is bought at the cost of assuming a jointly normal distribution of returns. Where this assumption does not hold, it is clear that, even with semi-variance, erroneous decisions can occur for the risk-averse decision maker. To this extent, it is an imperfect substitute for utility analysis.

3.4.7   Multi-objective decisions under uncertainty

In section 3.3.2 we looked at the problem of evaluating alternatives when the attributes or consequences of proposed options were known with certainty. We now extend this analysis to examine options where the outcome is uncertain. The first example that we take is of a firm that wishes to value investments on the basis of short-term discounted cash flows, market share and balance sheet appearance (the justification for such an approach is given in chapter 1). We describe uncertainty by use of a subjective probability distribution; the estimates are summarized in Table 3.15(a). The model we develop can also be used to analyse predominantly non-financial decisions. In Table 3.15(b), we look at the problem examined in chapter 1 – the location of a hospital unit. Here we look at a mixture of objectives that are affected by the decision namely: cost, deaths due to travelling time and recovery rates. The problem is, as always, to devise a decision rule that will use this information to score each option and thereby determine an order of preference. All the elements required to address these problems have already been analysed, and this section represents a bringing together of different strands.

There are two points to make before looking more closely at the options in Table 3.15. First, we should emphasize that the choice processes that we describe are in essence theoretical. That their main purpose is to illustrate the different issues facing a decision maker. Whatever practical procedure a decision maker may adopt to interpret these issues, some position either explicit or implied will have been taken on each of the elements of the problem that we describe here. At one extreme, in practice, choice may be made by tossing a coin, thereby ignoring all the information; at the other extreme, an explicit analysis of the problem may be made in a manner close to the methods outlined here (see French (1989), for such case studies). A middle path is likely to prevail whereby a committee (formal or informal) will meet and 'discuss the issues'. Points will be made by various members of the committee that raise subjects in this chapter, though in less precise form. Thus it might be observed as regards Table 3.15(a) that Option 1 has a better balance sheet position. We can see that Option 1 has, in fact, first order stochastic dominance as regards this attribute. Another comment regarding Table 3.15(b) might be that 'Option 1 is not acceptable due to increased deaths from travelling time'. Such a statement implies that not only is there stochastic dominance of Option 2 over Option 1 in this respect, but also that the weighting given to this attribute should be such that the better recovery rate and the possibly better savings are outweighed. Another possibility is that discussion becomes confused and a decision is taken on an inadequate appreciation of the problem. This can always happen, but it is more likely to happen if the members of the committee do not appreciate the elements of the problem. A theoretical appeciation brings all the elements to the fore and shows how they are related.

A second point is that we focus, as we have done throughout this chapter, solely on the problem of evaluation and selection. That is, we assume that the decision maker has been able to formulate the problem, as in Table 3.15. We should not underestimate the considerable task that this undertaking represents. The relevant attributes have to be determined, estimates have to

Table 3.15(a)

| | Attributes or objectives | | |
Option	Short-term cash flows £s (net present value)	Market share	Balance sheet
Option 1 (attributes independent)	(0.7) £100,000 (0.3) 5,000	(0.5) big increase (0.5) no change	(0.6) improvement (0.4) deterioration
Option 2 ⟨(0.6) — 80,000⟩ ⟨(0.4) — 40,000⟩		improvement no change	no change deterioration

Table 3.15(b)

| | Attributes or objectives | | |
Option	Saving/(cost) annual equivalent £s	Recovery rate	Deaths due to travelling time
Option 1 (attributes independent)	(0.7) £200,000 (0.3) (50,000)	(0.7) big improvement (0.3) no change	(0.3) small increase (0.7) no change
Option 2 ⟨(0.8) — 100,000⟩ ⟨(0.2) — 10,000⟩		no change small improvement	no change no change

be made of the possible levels of each attribute that options are likely to attain, and subjective probabilities have to be assigned to the levels.

We now turn to the problems presented in Table 3.15(a) and (b). In the first of each of the options the attribute probabilities are regarded as occurring independently. In the second option the events are related in that there is for instance a 60 per cent chance of an £80,000 improvement in short-term cash flows, an improvement in market share and no change in the balance sheet occuring together. After a number of questions, preferences may be described as being independent. Physical interdependency, we should note, is quite different from preference independence (see section 3.3.2). We may now draw up an additive multi-attribute or multi-objective utility model as follows:

$$U = W_1 U_1(x_1) + W_2 U_2(x_2) + W_3 U_3(x_3) \ldots\ldots + W_n U_n(x_n)$$

where $x_1 \ldots n$ = the level of attribute $1 \ldots n$
$U_1 \ldots n$ = the N–M utility curve for attribute $1 \ldots n$
$W_1 \ldots n$ = the weighting or relative importance for each attribute.

The first step in applying the multi-objective model is to determine U_1, U_2 and U_3 – the N–M utility curves for each of the objectives. These are determined using the processes described in section 3.4.3. The decision maker is asked to determine the certainty equivalent of a number of hypothetical propositions concerning each objective separately. To simplify the problem of weighting, each is measured on a common utility scale. We use the most common one: 0 for the worst possible outcome and 1 for the best possible outcome, as with the determination of the value function (see section 3.3.2). In this manner, the degree of risk-aversion is measured for each of the objectives.

The next step in the process is the determination of the relative weights. The method as described for multi-objective value functions may be used. An alternative approach considered more appropriate for risky situations has been developed by Keeney (1974). This method uses gambles similar to those used to develop the N–M utility curve. To determine the weight for the cash flow attribute x_1 the decision maker would be asked to determine P such that he is indifferent between the following outcomes (Figure 3.24).

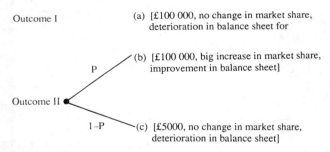

Figure 3.24

Assuming that a 0–1 scale is used for each of the objectives, Option (b) is scored 1, as it is the best of everything, and (c) is 0, as it is the worst; W_1 is therefore P as $P(1)+(1-P)(0)=P$ and outcome I is $W_1(1)+W_2(0)+W_3(0)=P$. If, for instance, the decision maker is indifferent between the two propositions at $P=0.8$, then the utility of the two propositions must be equal. The utility of the bet is 0.8 and the utility of the certain proposition is 0.8; hence W_1 is also 0.8. This procedure can be repeated for the other attributes, comparing a certain position where the measured attribute scores 1 and the other attributes are at 0 with the bet as presented above. The more highly an attribute is valued, the higher the value placed upon the certain position, and hence the greater the probability required by the decision maker that, in the bet, he or she will get the best of everything. The weights should sum to 1.0; if they do not, and the process is properly understood, then the additive model is probably inappropriate. With this final process, the multi-objective utility model is completely specified.

We can now use the data in Table 3.15 to show how the model might look. First, the scores for each of the attribute values will have been determined, assume that the results of this exercise are as in Table 3.16.

Table 3.16

Utility	Investment decision			Location of accident unit		
	Cash flow	Market share	Balance sheet	Saving/ cost	Recovery rate	Deaths due to travelling time
	U_1	U_2	U_3	U_A	U_B	U_C
1.0	£100,000	big increase	improvement	£200,000	big improve-ment	no change
0.9	£80,000					
0.8				£100,000		
0.7						
0.6	£40,000					
0.5			no change	(£10,000)	small improve-ment	
0.4						
0.3		improvement				
0.2						
0.1						
0.0	£5,000	no change	deterioration	(£50,000)	no change	small increase

Secondly, the goals must be weighted, we shall assume that after a process of questioning, as described above, the results are as in Table 3.17. It should be remembered that the weights refer to the total possible change in attributes

Table 3.17

Investment decision Attribute or weight		Location of accident unit Attribute or weight	
Goal		Goal	
Cash flow	0.6	Saving/(cost)	0.2
Market share	0.3	Recovery rate	0.5
Balance sheet	0.1	Deaths due to travelling time	0.3
Total	1.0	Total	1.0

and not to some concept of absolute levels. For example, although a decision maker may consider deaths due to travelling time as being more important than recovery rate, this is not the question being asked. The weighting is of a movement in deaths from no change to small increase as opposed to recovery rate of no change to big improvement. If the existing recovery rate is very poor indeed, then this goal may well be weighted more heavily.

Table 3.18

Investment decision as in Table 3.15(a)

Model	$U = 0.6(U_1) + 0.3(U_2) + 0.1(U_3)$
Option 1	$U = 0.6(0.7 \times 1 + 0.3 \times 0) + 0.3(0.5 \times 1 + 0.5 \times 0) +$
	$\qquad 0.1(0.6 \times 1 + 0.4 \times 0)$
	$= 0.63$
Option 2	$U = 0.6(0.6 \times 0.9 + 0.3 \times 0.3 + 0.1 \times 0.5) +$
	$\qquad 0.4(0.6 \times 0.6 + 0.3 \times 0.0 + 0.1 \times 0.0)$
	$= 0.552$

Location of accident unit as in Table 3.15(b)

Model	$U = 0.2(U_A) + 0.5(U_B) + 0.3(U_C)$
Option 1	$U = 0.2(0.7 \times 1 + 0.3 \times 0) + 0.5(0.7 \times 1.0 + 0.3 \times 0) +$
	$\qquad 0.3(0.3 \times 0 + 0.7 \times 1)$
	$= 0.7$
Option 2	$U = 0.8(0.2 \times 0.8 + 0.5 \times 0 + 0.3 \times 1.0) +$
	$\qquad 0.2(0.2 \times 0.5 + 0.5 \times 0.5 + 0.3 \times 1.0)$
	$= 0.498$

The full model and the scores for each option are shown in Table 3.18. For the investment decision Option 1 is preferred even though the expected utility of the cash flows is higher for Option 2 than for Option 1. Evidently the better performance in terms of market share and balance sheet outweighs the worse cash flow measure – to measure the options merely on the basis of direct short-term cash flows is to only have a partial view of the problem. Although accounting concerns itself principally with financial measures (U_1 and U_3), it should be appreciated from this example that financial data alone do not necessarily form a complete basis for choice.

In the second decision, Option 1 is preferred despite the fact that the savings/costs are less attractive, as are the deaths due to travelling time. In this case, the recovery is the deciding factor.

It may be felt, as regards the second decision, that a committee is unlikely to indulge in the explicit exercise of valuing a human life (which is implied in the weighting financial considerations against clinical performance). Similarly in the first decision, one might ask how likely is it that a balance sheet appearance will be openly considered as a criterion for choice. In practice these questions may be avoided, but this does not mean that they do not exist. If one ignores the problem, then these issues are simply settled by default – a position which is less satisfactory than attempting to address the problem directly.

3.5   Summary and conclusions

This chapter has traced the problem of selection in decisions from single objectives to multiple objectives, and from certain to uncertain consequences. Analysis has provided no magical solutions, but rather it has highlighted problem areas, shown how they may be solved, and how they can be put together to form a 'logical pathway' from a mass of data and opinions to a well-informed solution.

The problem can be described under three headings: measurement, estimation and preferences. The measurement problems of financial returns are well-documented in intermediate texts; these are summarized in section 4.5. However, even in a profit-making organization there will be many problems that are better understood by seeing the decision as achieving several goals, which lead in different ways to fulfilling the objective. Such 'other' goals are likely to present measurement problems, these were outlined in section 3.2.

Having devised a measurement system, we then came to the problem of estimation. Where decisions are taken by more than one person, in this chapter and in chapter 1 we have been able to do little more than point out the intractable difficulties that can arise. Although there are practical approaches to obtaining agreement (section 4.2.2), there is no theoretically correct method. A form of 'thrashing out the differences' is all that can be offered. Therefore, to proceed in analysis, we have to assume that the decision maker is either a single person or a group that is in agreement. Estimation problems also occur where the consequences of a decision are uncertain, i.e. where it is not clear what will be the cash flow or market share or value of other goals. Our analysis has suggested attaching subjective probabilities to the possible outcomes. These probabilities are not the frequentist probabilities of statistics, but reflect the 'degree of belief' in an outcome.

The final problem area is in the expression of preferences. Where there is more than one goal, the decision maker is likely to have to decide upon trade-offs. A complete statement of preferences is provided by the value function. However, dominance, constraints and goal ordering may help to simplify the problem. Where there is uncertainty, preferences have to be established between probabilistic levels of the same attribute. The N–M utility curve and the multi-objective utility function enables the decision maker to construct preferences under such conditions. Again there are concepts and techniques which can simplify this problem. We have suggested stochastic dominance, mean variance analysis and semivariance as means of avoiding the rather complex process of formulating an N–M utility curve.

References and further reading

Bromwich, M., *The Economics of Capital Budgeting*, Penguin, 1976.
Buffa, E. S., Dyer, J. S., *Management Science/Operations Research*, John Wiley, 1977.
Copeland, T. E., Weston, J. F., *Financial Theory and Corporate Policy*, 2nd ed., Addison-Wesley, 1983.

Drury, C., Braund, S., 'A Survey of UK Leasing Practice', *Management Accounting*, April 1989, pp. 40–3.

Dyer, J. S., Sarin, R. K., 'Measurable multi-attribute value functions', *Operations Research*, Vol. 28, 1979, pp. 810–822.

Dyer, J. S., Sarin R. K., 'Relative Risk Aversion' *Management Science*, 1982, pp. 875–86.

Ellsburgh, D., 'Classic and current notions of "measurable utility" ', *Economic Journal*, Vol. 64, 1954, pp. 528–56.

French, S., *Decision Theory: an introduction to the mathematics of rationality*, Ellis Howard, 1986.

French S., '*Readings in Decision Analysis*', Chapman and Hall, 1989.

Haley, C. W., Schall, L. D., '*The Theory of Financial Decisions*', 2nd ed., McGraw-Hill, 1973.

Harvey, C. M., 'Assessment of preferences by conditions on pricing out', *Operations Research*, Vol. 33, 1985, pp. 443–54.

Hull, J. C., Moore, P. G., Thomas, H., 'Utility and its Measurement', *Journal of the Royal Statistical Society*', series A, Vol. 136, Part 2, 1973, pp. 226–47.

Johnson, T. H., Kaplan, R. S., *Relevance Lost: The rise and fall of management accounting*, Harvard Business School Press, 1987.

Keeney, R., 'Multiplicative Utility Functions, *Operations Research*, Vol. 22, January–February, 1974.

Keeney, R. L., Raiffa, H., *Decisions with Multiple Objectives, Preferences and Value Trade offs*, Wiley, 1976.

Koutsoyiannis, A., *Modern Microeconomics*, Macmillan, 1979.

Krzysztofowicz, R., 'Strength of preference and risk attitude in utility measurement', *Organizational Behavior and Human Performance*, 1983, pp. 88–113.

Markowitz, H., *Portfolio Selection*, Yale University Press, 1959.

Moore, P. G., Thomas, H., *The Anatomy of Decisions*, Penguin, 1976.

Porter, R. B., Wart, J. R., Ferguson, D. L., 'Efficient Algorithms for Conducting Stochastic Dominance Tests on Large Numbers of Portfolios', *Journal of Financial and Quantitative Analysis*, 1973, pp. 71–81.

Pratt, J. W., 'Risk Aversion in the Small and in the Large,' *Econometrica*, 1964, pp. 122–36.

Rubinstein, M. E., 'A Mean–Variance Synthesis of Corporate Financial Theory', *Journal of Finance*, 1973, pp. 167–81.

Scapens, R. W., *Management Accounting: A Review of Recent Developments*, Macmillan, 1985.

Scapens, R. W., Sale, J. T., Tikkas, P. A., *Controlling Divisional Capital Expenditure*, ICMA, 1982.

Simon, H. A., in Ansoff, H. I. (ed.), *On the Concept of Organizational Goal in Business Strategy*', Penguin, 1969.

Stigler, G. J., 'The Development of Utility Theory', *Journal of Political Economy*, Vol. LVIII, 1950, pp. 307–27 and 373–96.

Swalm, R. O., 'Utility theory – insights into risk taking', *Harvard Business Review*, 1966, pp. 123–36.

von Neumann, J., Morgenstern, O., *Theory of Games and Economic Behaviour*, 2nd ed., Princeton University Press, 1947.

Watson, S. R., Buede, D. M., *Decision Synthesis: The principles and practice of decision analysis*, CUP, 1987.
Whitmore, G. A., 'Third-Degree Stochastic Dominance', *American Economic Review*, June 1970.

4 Decision making – theory and basic techniques, Part 2

4.1 Introduction

In order to illustrate the theory of the previous chapter, certain basic techniques were introduced. We now wish to augment this aspect by considering the practical implications of decision making; therefore the emphasis is on 'decision tools' rather than theory.

4.2 Modelling

A model is a simplified representation of reality where decisions can be tested. For most business problems reality is very complex, and it would be an impossible task to attempt to represent *all* aspects of a business. Of necessity, some simplifications have to be made, and a model is the inevitable result. The question for a manager, therefore, is not whether a model should or should not be employed, but rather *which* model he or she should employ. One cannot escape the process: even if a manager uses 'judgement based upon past experience' or follows a dictum such as 'keep the customer satisfied' a model of sorts is being used. We will examine the problem of modelling under two main headings: structure and information. Structure is akin to an architect's plan, in that it tells us how we are going to achieve our aims. Information is the bricks and mortar that turn the plan into reality, which in this case is the actual decision.

4.2.1 Model structures

In the 1970s, when it became clear just how powerful computers were going to be, there appeared to be the real possibility that they would be able to model all the processes of the firm. The concepts of systems theory and cybernetics also appeared to provide complete models of the firm – ideal for computerization. The future was going to be efficient, orderly and planned. As case studies document, this ideal was not achieved; the main problem was, and remains, complexity. The following comment from the largely successful experience of Blue Circle in the development of investment planning models captures the spirit of practical modelling:

> No doubt the models are far from perfect and with extra time, effort and cost they could be improved, but the question that must be asked is 'Is the extra accuracy worth the extra cost?' Our collective answer has been 'NO'. We realize the danger of trying to 'shoehorn' a problem into an already existing model, but equally we realize the danger of suboptimizing by incurring a greater cost in analysis than we can expect to save as a result' (Dolbear (1982)).

Computers have clearly not solved the problem of modelling. Therefore we still need to consider actively a number of issues when constructing a model. We list the following.

Normative/positive. A normative model is based upon an abstract analysis of the problem. It often forms the basis for what is known as a *top down* approach, whereby a simple model is devised, and detail is then added on. By contrast, a positive approach is concerned with representing the actual processes of the firm. This is often associated with a *bottom up* approach to modelling, whereby models are 'built up' from representations of the firm's actual practices. Both methods try to attain an optimum, though from opposite viewpoints. In simple terms, the normative approach begins by trying to determine how a process *ought to* operate, whereas the positive approach begins by determining how a process *actually does* operate. They then both try to improve on their initial approximations.

The benefit of the positive approach is that it is based on the tried and trusted techniques of the organization. There are, however, two main drawbacks in the resulting model. First, it is in essence an uncritical representation; there is no analysis as to whether the best decision results from this process. Secondly, It is difficult to join up positive models, for they are generally local views which do not admit necessarily to any guiding philosophy. Normative models are easier in this respect; by indulging in abstract analysis which seeks to provide a demonstrably superior solution (by providing a rational link between actions and goals), they inevitably have to address a general view of the firm, and are therefore easier to integrate. Their main weakness is precisely where the positive model is strong – a normative model may well over-simplify a problem, or in some way misrepresent the issues, for such models have not been developed 'out of' the situation being considered. Accordingly, there is no guarantee that the decisions derived from such models are better than those based upon a positive approach.

Non-numerate/numerate. Numerical models are so predominant in formal analysis of business problems that it is easy to overlook the fact that there are many non-numerate representations.

Simple examples are the principles, rules and advice as may be found in Fayol's *Principles of Management* (1971) and more recently Townsend's *Up the Organization* (1970). There is no doubt that these 'models' contain much good advice, their worth being evidenced by their popularity. A more ana-lytical non-numerate representation is frequently used in planning and strategic decision making models. Some of the more popular versions have been reproduced in section 2.2.1. As these examples show, analysis is in contingent matrix form rather than the universal rules of Townsend and Fayol. Such conditional representations can also be modelled by the flow chart, which is another more developed form of essentially non-numerate analysis.

At their best, such models can represent complex and subtle relationships in a relatively simple format. Their drawback is that they lack the precision of their numerical counterparts.

Stochastic/deterministic. Models that include uncertainty are termed stochastic or probabilistic. In this text, we have represented uncertainty by a probability distribution and measured the significant features of the distribution using mean variance rules, semivariance, stochastic dominance rules and discrete approximations. Another method, particularly suited to computers, is that of Monte Carlo simulation. The distribution of the outcome is determined by repeated 'runs' of the problem. Where a value is probabilistic, the option selected is determined by selecting a random number from a set allocated in proportion to the subjective probabilities. Thus, if event A is considered to have an 80 per cent chance and event B a 20 per cent chance, the random number might be selected from the set of whole numbers 0–99, where 0–79 inclusive follows the path of event A, and 80–99 follows event B. One run through the problems will be of little interest; normally a sample of at least 100 runs would be required to obtain a representative spread of returns.

Monte Carlo simulation has great intuitive appeal, and is a potentially useful tool. Where a decision is dependent upon a series of probabilistic events, simulation can provide a support, and in some cases a substitute, for non-computer-based methods. Its drawback is that it is time-consuming to set up, and not necessarily better at measuring the benefit of an option than the summary statistics we have used elsewhere. In particular, where probabilistic events co-vary, which is frequently the case, the simulation model can become cumbersome in that the number of pathways multiply at an alarming rate.

Deterministic models make no allowance for uncertainty. Some simple events will be deterministic, or can be approximated as such; but even where there is uncertainty, a deterministic approach may yet be useful. For example, rather than devise a probability distribution for future sales, a manager might want to see what they would look like for the next 2 years if there was a 7 per cent growth. Such 'what if' testing or sensitivity analysis is, in essence, deterministic. Nevertheless, it can provide important insights into uncertain events.

Static/dynamic. A dynamic model includes time as a variable; in a static model, time is either fixed at a single period or does not appear as a variable. For instance, net present value is a dynamic model, whereas the Capital Asset Pricing Model is a static model.

The movement and interactions of variables over time is particularly complex in most environments. Therefore, where decisions affect a single period, with no significant effect on other periods, a static model is preferable. A dynamic model's treatment of inter-temporal issues is usually very simple; accordingly, results should be interpreted with more than the usual degree of caution.

Game theoretic models. Business models usually assume a relatively simple relation between a firm and its environment. For instance, a basic cost–volume–profit model assumes that the market will accept all the units a firm can produce at a given price. More advanced formulations of demand in imperfect markets include varying demand levels at different prices. But still the relation is not complex, in that it can be expressed by the familiar downward sloping demand curve.

Game theoretic models attempt to represent a more subtle relation between an organization (including not-for-profit organizations) and its environment. A competitive scenario is often assumed whereby the environment is characterized as an opposing player who is attempting to maximize the organizations's losses on the basis that one person's gain is the other's loss. This is known as a zero sum game. In such a scenario, choosing the best course of action by conventional analysis might not be optimal if it can be effectively countered by the 'opposing player'. As an illustration, a game theoretic approach to pricing is detailed in Chapter 11.

Game theory was originally developed by von Neumann and Morgenstern (1949) in a book that has since proved to be more famous for developing a measure of utility (see chapter 3), which they did as an aside! As regards business, the results of game theory work have been disappointing. The complexity and uncertainty of business estimations makes it difficult to look more than two 'moves' ahead, and within this limit the strategies are not novel. As an illustration, the analysis of strict uncertainty (section 3.4.1) could have been presented as a two person game, where the opposing player can control the states of nature. The possible strategies are very much as examined in that section, with the best choice depending on the conditions of the game and the attitude of the players.

In spite of the lack of development, game theory is a new and interesting way of modelling a business scenario. It may yet have more widespread applications.

Heuristics. In complex situations a model can either attempt to represent complexity and derive an optimal solution by exhaustive analysis, or it can limit its analysis and apply strategies. The latter approach is that of the heuristic model. A good example is the game of chess; a computer cannot exhaustively analyse all possible combinations, so moves are evaluated in relation to certain rules or strategies that human players have found useful. One such rule is 'control of the central squares' – where there is no direct threat, the computer will prefer moves that gain control of central squares to those that only influence the side of the board. It is not possible to prove that these strategies lead to the optimal solution, as the complexity cannot be analysed. Rather, it is generally believed, or experience has shown, that the strategies are correlated positively with success. In business, the non-numerate models in planning (see section 2.2.1) are good examples of the heuristic method. The problem of using heuristic models is that, although they sometimes work, we are not sure why they work; when they go wrong, we are therefore likely to be equally baffled.

4.2.2   Estimating techniques

The accountant is in essence an information provider. As the practitioner will know, this often means delving into piles of bills, chatting with other managers, trying to reconcile opposing views, questioning people about the future, as well as quiet contemplation of the issues. In other words, the accountant is vitally concerned with estimating, or, more formally, providing input for decision models concerning future actions. We have already had much to say on the issues in question. In this section we look at practical techniques that may aid the accountant in his or her 'impossible' task.

In certain situations estimates may be made by statistical inference from historical data, using regression models or similar techniques. Such processes rely on a degree of stability in the environment within which the model operates. That is to say, apart from the variables recorded in the model, it is assumed that other factors represent no more than background noise. To many managers this is a strong assumption; markets change, new products, new competitors and new trading conditions may make data collected, say, 5 or 6 years ago not strictly comparable with the present situation. In such circumstances, past data may be useful as input into a process of subjective estimation rather than the objective processes of statistics. The statistical processes are well documented in other texts (Kaplan and Atkinson, 1989); here, we will look at some further methods for developing estimates.

If we take a problem such as an estimate of future sales, the sales manager responsible would usually be required to estimate both the level and the probabilities. In reality, future sales levels are likely to be from a continuous probability function. The manager, with the aid of the accountant/decision analyst is then faced with the problem of estimating a continuous function.

A common solution to this difficulty is to ask managers to provide high, medium and low estimates. Such information is less detailed than a continuous distribution, but it has greater intuitive appeal and is more easily manipulated. This raises the question, 'How good are three-point approximations of continuous distributions?' First of all we need to understand what is meant by a 'good approximation'. In many problems, the decision maker will be interested in the expected or mean value of the estimates, as well as a measure of their spread. We shall take the standard deviation as a suitable measure of spread. Therefore a measure can be described as 'good' if a sufficiently accurate estimate of the mean and standard deviation of the continuous distribution can be made from three-point estimates.

As one might expect, the nature of the underlying distribution is an important factor in determining the value of our methods of approximation. Where the distribution is single peaked, not too sharply pointed, with the highest point roughly in the middle (i.e. not extremely skewed), the Extended Pearson–Tukey (EPT) formula has been shown to work quite well for the mean and the Pearson–Tukey (PT) formula for the standard deviation:

$$\text{mean} = \sum_{i=1}^{3} p_i \, v_i; \text{ standard deviation} = (v_3 - v_1)/3.25$$

where p_i is the probability associated with outcome v_i, such that for the random variable X_i:

$$p_1 = 0.185 \; v_1 = 5 \text{ per cent fractile of } X_i$$
$$p_2 = 0.630 \; v_2 = 50 \text{ per cent fractile of } X_i$$
$$p_3 = 0.185 \; v_3 = 95 \text{ per cent fractile of } X_i$$

A fractile divides the distribution according to probability; thus for v_1 there is a 5 per cent probability of observing an X_i equal to or less than v_1, v_2 is therefore the median and v_3 is the value of X_i such that there is a 95 per cent probability of observing that value or less. For a normal distribution, where, for instance, there is a mean = 10 and a variance = 1, $v_1 = 8.355$, $v_2 = 0$ and $v_3 = 11.645$. The reader might like to confirm that EPT for the mean is wholly accurate (as it will be with all symmetrical distributions) and the PT estimate for the standard deviation is 98.8 per cent accurate. Tests on non-normal continuous distributions are reported in Keefer and Bodily (1983); they find similar degrees of accuracy for non-normal distributions as described above. For ease of computation, we shall illustrate the formulae by using large discrete distributions, rather than continuous ones. The results of this exercise are given in Figure 4.1 and Figure 4.2 and are reasonably good. For most applications, they represent a satisfactory level of accuracy, and hence a potentially valuable saving of managerial time and effort in avoiding the task of estimating continuous distributions.

This method applies to cases where there is only one variable, but in many business applications there will be a need to examine the effect of more than one variable. For example, the mean and variance of profit will, in a simple model, be the result of both revenue and cost variation. Where the two are independent, then the mean and variance of each variable can be estimated independently; both are additive. Where costs and revenues are related, the covariance will be non-zero, the means will still be additive, but the variance will require an estimate of the covariance (see section 3.4.6). As Keefer and Bodily report, the use of three point approximations using EPT in a decision tree or matrix format produces reasonably encouraging results, though more research is required in this area.

Much estimating of data for models is an organizational exercise. A recently introduced method for examining a decision and eliciting data is *decision conferencing* (French, 1989). Those taking the decision hold a two-day event (experience shows this to be a suitable length of time). Three support staff are employed to aid the process: a facilitator who is an analyst experienced in the theoretical and practical problems of decision making; a support analyst, who represents the problem using computer models; and a recorder, who annotates the discussion. As Buede (Watson and Buede, 1987) reports, successful decision conferencing is a process of building a consensus within a group, and is particularly suited to decisions which require inputs from across the whole organization.

There are no formal, demonstrably superior, methods of obtaining agree-

True distribution of sales:

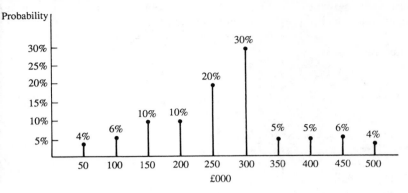

True mean   = 267.50
True standard deviation = 105.68

Extended Pearson-Tukey (EPT) estimate for mean:

Fraction (%)		Value		Probabilities	
5	=	100	x	0.185	= 18.50
50	=	250	x	0.630	= 157.50
95	=	450	x	0.185	= 83.25
				Estimated mean	259.25

Pearson-Tukey (PT) estimate for standard deviation:

$(450 - 100)/3.25 = 107.69$

Accuracy: $(1 - [\text{difference/true value}]) \times 100$

Mean: 97 per cent

Standard deviation: 98 per cent

Figure 4.1   *Pearson–Tukey estimation methods – a roughly normal distribution*

ment within a group. Most amount to a controlled form of 'thrashing the problem out' (Moore and Thomas (1986), p. 186). The *Delphi Technique* is one such method. Managers separately estimate a particular variable, and summary statistics (e.g. mean and standard deviation) of all the estimates are reported back to the managers, who may then adjust their predictions. This process is iterated until there is no further narrowing in the spread of estimates, then a meeting can be held to resolve remaining differences.

Estimating is an imprecise art; some techniques (such as linear regression) may appear more precise than others (such as EPT), and hence preferable.

Such precision, though, is often purchased at the expense of unrealistic assumptions. Only a thorough analysis of the problem and an understanding of the available techniques can determine the best method for estimating.

True distribution of sales:

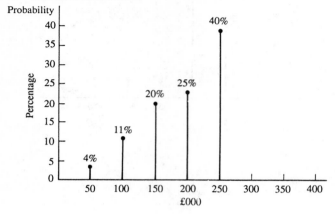

True mean   = 193.0
True standard deviation= 58.75

Extended Pearson-Tukey (EPT) estimate for mean:

Fraction (%)		Value		Probabilities	
5	=	100	x	0.185	= 18.50
50	=	200	x	0.630	= 126.00
95	=	250	x	0.185	= 46.25
				Estimated mean	190.75

Pearson-Tukey (PT) estimate for standard deviation:

$(250 - 100)/3.25 = 46.15$

Accuracy: $(1 - [\text{difference/true value}]) \times 100$

Mean: 98.8 per cent

Standard deviation: 78.6 per cent

Extended PT estimate for standard deviation (see Keefer and Bodily, 1983)

$(250 - 100)/(3.29 - 0.1[(250 + 100 - 2\{200\})/46.15]^2) = 47.28$

Accuracy: 80.5 per cent

Figure 4.2   *Pearson–Tukey estimation methods – very non-normal distribution*

4.3 Cost–benefit analysis

A common response to decisions that have financial and non-financial consequences is to suggest that some form of cost-benefit benefit (C–B) analysis be
employed. Throughout this text, we have laid great emphasis on the problem
of comparing the costs and the varying benefits that may result from a
decision; but the term also refers to a particular form of analysis developed
in economics. In the literature, there is some conflict between the methods
described in chapter 3 and cost–benefit analysis in economics (e.g. Watson
(1981)), in that for some problems both approaches may be applied. Fortunately, we can avoid this conflict by noting that cost–benefit analysis rules
itself out for virtually all accounting applications. For instance one of the
leading authorities in the C–B field writes:

> Why cost–benefit analysis? Why not plain honest to goodness profit and
> loss accounting? ... what counts as a benefit or a loss to a part of the
> economy – to one or more persons, or groups – does not necessarily count
> as a benefit or loss to the economy as a whole. And in cost–benefit analysis
> we are concerned with the economy as a whole; with the welfare of a
> defined society, and not any smaller part of it (Mishan (1971), p. 6).

In other words, cost–benefit analysis is firmly placed at the national, governmental level; whereas accounting problems are at the individual, organizational level. This difference has two important consequences: the treatment
of risk, and the application of judgement in a problem.

It was noted when discussing utility that where a project represented a
relatively small change in wealth, the expected value would produce an
acceptable ranking. In such cases the spread of returns would be of no
significance. For instance, where there is a 50 per cent chance of either A or
B, then the expected value is £100 where A = £101 and B = £99, and it is
£120 where A = − £10 and B = £250. A very wealthy person would not be
unduly worried by losing £10, and would therefore not reject the second
scenario because of this. A less wealthy person, such as this author, would
definitely prefer to avoid this possibility, though my attitude might change if
we were talking about pennies instead of £ sterling! The point to note is that
where possible returns represent a small proportion of one's wealth, expected
value is likely to be a sufficient measure of worth, there being no need to
include a measure of the spread of returns.

In relation to investment projects, the government is akin to a wealthy
person, and all projects are relatively small. The problem of risk is therefore
not likely to alter the decision maker's choice, so that the subject has only a
minor place in the C–B literature, unlike the study of finance.

The second issue is 'Whose assessments are to count?' (Dasgupta and
Pearce, 1972, p. 197). In general terms, C–B analysis attempts to apply the
judgement of the market place to non-financial items which are not sold
separately. As there is no direct evaluation, a number of techniques have
been designed which attempt to estimate the value that a market would place
on an item if it were sold separately. The result is in an estimate of people's
'willingness to pay'. To illustrate these methods, we will briefly examine how

the Roskill Commission applied C–B principles to evaluate aircraft noise in the siting of the proposed third London airport (see Commission on the Third London Airport, 1971). There were four groups of people identified as suffering:

Group	Social costs
(a) moving because of airport	S + R + D
(b) moving anyway	D
(c) remaining	N
(d) new entrants	Zero

where R = removal costs;

D = change in market price between old and new homes;

N = the sum of money which would just compensate the house owner for the nuisance suffered and make him as well off as before;

S = consumer surplus, the difference between the market value of the house and the amount you would be 'willing to pay' for it.

These figures are not easily calculated. For example, 8 per cent of the respondents in the third category would accept no compensation however large (in fact a figure of twice their house price was arbitrarily assigned). The total of the social costs of noise for each site was then added to the other financial consequences, as in Table 4.1.

Table 4.1   Summary cost–benefit analysis (1982 prices £ million).

	Cublington	Foulness	Northampstead	Thurleigh
Airspace movement costs	1685–1899	1690–1906	1716–1934	1711–1929
Passenger user costs	1743–2883	1910–3090	1778–2924	1765–2922
Other costs, including capital costs	614– 638	612– 625	626– 639	641– 653
Noise costs	23	10	72	16
Total costs	4065–5443	4222–5631	4192–5569	4133–5520

Source: Dasgupta and Pearce (1972).

Having made estimates, one then faces the problem of comparing these costs with other costs and benefits. Should '£1' of money saved by a potential user be regarded as being of equal value to '£1' of noise saved? To many it would seem invidious that the saving of £1 to someone wealthy enough to be able to fly should be regarded as equal to £1 saving of noise to a relatively poor person. This view seemed widespread in society, for there were many more protests over noise costs than there were over 'saving passenger user costs' (one of the other items being considered)!

To sum up, in practice the market is unlikely to give an unequivocal measure of non-financial items; even if it were to, it is arguable whether the market provides a fair valuation, given the imperfections in the market place and in the distribution of wealth. The 8 per cent who would not accept compensation at any price are evidence of the difficulty of trying to measure one person's inconvenience against another's.

The actual decision conformed more closely to the methods of Chapter 3. The Roskill Commission recommended the 'cheapest' of the options, Cublington, effectively weighting £1 of each cost and benefit equally. This option was rejected, and for a while the government decided that Foulness was to be the site. Interestingly, this was judged to have the least cost as regards noise (see Table 4.1. It seems that the government weighted noise costs more heavily than the C–B analysts. Eventually, of course, all the options were dropped and the existing airports were enlarged.

C–B analysis has undoubtedly provided useful information, though in this case it failed to provide the eventual solution, or even the interim solution. In particular, we might note that the evaluation and weighting of the various factors was eventually performed by the decision maker – a democratically elected body – rather than by some measure related to the market place. Ultimately, the market place was not a substitute for judgement by the decision maker. We must suspect that this is generally true.

A more direct application of the methods of chapter 3 was undertaken in connection with a similar problem in Mexico City. In this latter study, the Mexican government wanted to determine an airport policy which included the possibility of relocation. The following objectives were identified (Keeney and Raiffa, 1976; chapter 8):

1   Minimize total construction and maintenance costs.
2   Provide adequate capacity.
3   Minimize access time.
4   Maximize safety.
5   Minimize social disruption.
6   Minimize noise.

The measures chosen for each objective were as follows:

$X_1 =$ Total cost in millions of pesos, with suitable discounting.
$X_2 =$ The practical capacity in terms of the number of aircraft operations per hour.
$X_3 =$ Access time to and from the airport in minutes weighted by the number of travellers from each zone in Mexico City.
$X_4 =$ The number of people (including non passengers) seriously injured or killed per aircraft accident.
$X_5 =$ The number of people displaced by airport development.
$X_6 =$ The number of people subjected to a high noise level, defined as a composite noise rating (CNR) of 90.

The trade-offs and values placed upon each objective were not, as in C–B analysis, determined by the market place, but were left to the decision makers. The success of this project was in enabling the decision makers to build a consistent complete model from their preferences. As the study records, this led many of those involved to change their minds, following a detailed analysis of the problem. We leave the reader to judge whether this method of C–B analysis is a better method of measuring noise (for detailed report on the Mexico airport decision, see deNeufville and Keeney (1972)).

In conclusion, it is clear that cost–benefit analysis is intended for decision making at a governmental rather than an organizational level, unlike the decision techniques of the previous chapter. Its contribution to decisions by governments is also questionable, though here we have only outlined the issues by comparing the two methods. A fuller debate is beyond the immediate scope of this book – interested readers are referred to Watson (1981).

4.4   Techniques for improving efficiency

Firms do not often have to choose between substantially different investments. More typically, management are concerned with running the existing operation as efficiently as possible. This may mean reorganizing a process and thereby saving costs, investing in more efficient machines, redesigning a product to save on production costs, adjusting quality standards, implementing a default free process, investing in a marketing campaign, and so on. All these actions are investments of sorts. The choice is between the existing state of affairs and a relatively small change. Although these investments might be regarded as 'fine tuning', their effect on profits is not necessarily small, quite the contrary.

Many techniques have been developed to improve a companies' existing business, we shall examine the following: value analysis, cost-effectiveness, quality assurance, just in time production and default-free manufacturing. These are all forms of investment analysis, but their emphasis is very different from conventional analysis. Their main concern is to generate profitable or beneficial ideas, rather than examine exclusively the problem of evaluation.

4.4.1   *Value analysis and cost-effectiveness*

Value analysis has been described as 'an organized creative approach which has for its purpose the efficient identification of unnecessary cost; that is, cost which provides neither quality nor use nor life nor appearance nor customer features' (Miles, 1961). The aim of cost-effectiveness, on the other hand, is to minimize the cost of meeting a specified set of standards. Both methods have their own particular stance towards the problem of benefits. As regards value analysis, all that has to be established is that there is no reduction in existing benefits from whatever source. Cost-effectiveness, by contrast, sets levels below which benefits must not fall; these are not necessarily the existing levels.

Both methods only require a simple ranking approach to the measurement of benefits. All that has to be established is whether or not a reduction in costs will result in a ranking below existing or prespecified levels. The cost of this simplification is that we are unable to value a change in benefits. As noted in chapter 1, this limitation represents a severe restriction on the applicability of these techniques.

Because of this limitation, there are three broad categories of problem where value analysis and cost-effectiveness are not appropriate. We shall consider them in turn. First, decision makers may wish to view benefits as being variable, and may not wish to view the problem in terms of freezing benefits at a certain level and examining costs exclusively. Secondly, many projects call for expenditure to improve benefits, and these techniques are not able to compare benefits except in the very limited manner described above. Indeed it would be fair to say that these methods are rather negative and uncreative in outlook. Thirdly, where there is uncertainty as to the possible results from a cost reduction exercise, there are likely to be difficulties. For instance, if a firm selling services applies cost-effectiveness or value analysis and there is a chance, however small, that the services would fall below the set standards for each proposal being contemplated, then they would all have to be rejected. A rule-of-thumb approach might help eliminate the more unlikely adverse movement in benefits, such as ignoring possibilities which have only a $\frac{1}{2}$ per cent chance. But in many cases this may not be acceptable, as the consequences of such unlikely events may be so serious as to warrant inclusion. Such modifications are, in any case, departures from the spirit of these techniques.

With what is hopefully a balanced view of the worth of these techniques, we shall now illustrate the processes in greater detail. There is no set method of value analysis and cost effectiveness studies. All that can be given here is the flavour of such approaches as expounded in texts such as Ridge (1969).

The first step is to challenge everything. Ridge suggests that five questions be asked at every step:

1   What is done and why?
2   Where it is done and why?
3   When it is done and why?
4   Who does it and why?
5   How is it done and why?

This attitude is exercised within a job plan which may be described as having five phases:

1   The information phase.
2   The creative phase.
3   The evaluation phase.
4   The investigation phase.
5   The reporting phase.

There is an obvious similarity here between value analysis and investment analysis (see section 2.2.1).

The emphasis of value analysis is upon the function, in contrast with the cost reduction approach, which is concerned with the product or service. For example, a cost-effectiveness approach for a company making refrigerators would attempt to produce the refrigerator for less cost. Thus, a cheaper motor might be installed, or plastic and other cheaper materials might be substituted for metal parts, the design may be altered to ease construction and storage, and so on. All these alterations would be acceptable as long as there is both a saving of cost, and benefits did not fall below a certain level. Value engineering looks at the function and purpose of the refrigerator, and examines ways in which this function may be better achieved. Hence to the list of questions may be added:

6   What is the function worth?
7   What else will accomplish the function?
8   What will that cost?

This requires a degree of 'lateral thinking' (de Bono (1970)). In this case, the company might wish to consider constructing irradiation machinery, or forms of packaging or materials or chemicals that help to preserve food. Alternatively, there may be cheaper sources of cold readily available, or energy being wasted that can be used to create cold.

Once the alternatives have been outlined, there are then the more familiar evaluation, investigation and reporting phases of the decision-making process.

All organizations have a tendency to grow of their own accord. The products and services that they produce can, by a process of constant adjustment, also grow until both the organization and the products and services that they produce are unduly complex. Value analysis and cost reduction represent two means of injecting a degree of intellectual rigour into the way a company operates. The savings from this and similar exercises can often be dramatic. Tom Peters quotes Harley Davidson (manufacturer of motorcycles) as managing to reduce the number of production controllers from 27 to 1. A comparison between Japanese and American producers using comparable equipment show greater efficiency in Japan – higher output per man, greater flexibility, less downtime, and quicker throughput time (Jaikumar, 1986). The difference between profit and loss for a company in a competitive market is often only the difference in efficiency. Value analysis and cost reduction can play an important part in this respect.

4.4.2   *Quality, just in time and default-free manufacturing*

Detailed business measurement in the West is often criticized as being overly financial. Although the alternatives suggested are many, the following list contains the major proposals (Maskell, 1989). Measures should:

(a)   be directly related to the manufacturing strategy;
(b)   vary between locations;
(c)   change over time as the needs change;
(d)   be simple and easy to use;
(e)   provide fast feedback to operators and managers;
(f)   foster improvement rather than just monitor

The strategies of this section are the most successful of the methods devised to implement this perceived need for change.

The drive for improved *quality* affects both the design and manufacture of the product. It is generally accepted that poor product design is responsible for much of the quality problems. In particular, the design process is often not integrated with manufacturing – products can be made more simply and be more reliable if they are better designed. The integrated approach advocated is made all the more necessary through the introduction of computer-integrated manufacturing. When designed correctly, computers are able to check the quality of their own output, as well as produce many different designs with minimal set-up times.

In the manufacturing process, the concept of total quality control has been successfully developed by many companies. Previous thinking was that there was a trade-off between defects and the cost of output; defects were tolerated as a cost of meeting production targets. The goal of total quality control is to have zero defects. The policy affects all aspects of the business: suppliers are requested to meet default-free standards, products are designed to minimize the possibility of defects, and production processes are also reviewed to meet new standards. The effect of such an exercise is to do away with a whole panoply of checking, controls and reworking; error is no longer institutionalized or considered normal. In practice, it is generally found that implementing this policy reduces rather than increases production costs, and that throughput time is also unexpectedly reduced. In this sense firms have found that quality is free.

This movement for increased efficiency within companies has also sought to increase the productivity of capital by looking at delays in the process. The old notion of keeping a week's supply in stock has been successfully challenged by Japanese companies who have managed to reduce stock levels to a matter of hours, using the now well-known concept of *just in time* supply (Kaplan and Atkinson (1989)). Increased automation has dramatically reduced set-up times. Orders do not necessarily have to be delayed by batch production; different orders can be met by the same machines in the same day – the customer too can benefit from efficiency. Some firms, such as the Rover group, have found that a just in time policy is the key to the other features. Inefficient practices, poor quality products and workmanship are all revealed when the slack created by surplus stock at every point in the system is taken away.

The argument as regards accounting practice is that traditional methods incorporate inefficiency, and do little to encourage improvement. A standard costing system, for example, is built up from engineering measurements of the process. It is static, in that all production is assumed to have the same cost. Inefficiency, included as 'normal' wastage and idle time, is built into the system. Too often the estimates upon which standard costs are devised are the result of a 'cat and mouse' game within the firm, where those judged by the standards seek to make them as slack as possible, and those setting them attempt to make them difficult but not unrealistic. Confrontation can easily be the result, but more usually the drive for efficiency is lost in a sea of measurement problems.

Compare this approach with target costing – a practice where inefficiency is not 'built in'. Here, costing begins in the market place with a definition of the product and price that will be successful. From this price is deducted an acceptable margin, and the result is a target cost for the product. Obviously, this method does not of itself solve the problems, but it does impose an external discipline on both workers and management, emphasizing that they are working towards a common goal.

In general, such methods view greater efficiency not as a positive variance from the expected, but rather as the expectation itself. In this sense these are dynamic models founded upon specific indicators of improvement. This is a very different approach compared to the monitoring, review and evaluation functions of the more traditional methods.

4.5   Accounting information for decisions

Information produced by the traditional accounting system is used for many purposes, of which decision making is just one. Unfortunately, such accounting information is not universally applicable; a cost per unit devised for valuation in the final accounts may be very different from a cost per unit required for cost–volume–profit analysis. The problem is encapsulated in the well-known phrase 'different costs for different purposes'. Decision making, unlike control and the preparation of final accounts, is not a regular repeated process, for the information required will depend upon the decision. Accordingly, it is not possible to produce accounting information for decisions on a systematic basis (as is done for control and final accounts); each decision requires its own information set. As the accounting system is the primary source of information, this means taking information from the system and then adjusting it to the needs of the decision. In doing this, the concept of relevant cost, opportunity cost and fixed cost allocations are pertinent. In this section we shall review their contribution to decision making.

4.5.1   Opportunity cost

This is defined in the terminology (CIMA, 1974) as being: 'The value of a benefit sacrificed in favour of an alternative course of action'. The benefit sacrificed is taken as being the benefit of the most attractive alternative foregone. Thus, if a firm, say Pogey Ltd, has to choose one of the following projects:

Project	Single period cash flows (£000)
A	100
B	120
C	125

then it is clear that project C is preferable and that project B represents the opportunity cost of accepting project C. A formal statement using opportunity cost concept would read as follows:

	Cash flows (£000)
Project C	125
Less opportunity cost	120
Surplus after opportunity cost	5

Note that £5,000 surplus is not a profit or measure of the extent to which the firm is better off. Rather, it measures by how much the organization is better off with respect to its alternatives. If the figure were £100,000, or, more generally, if the surplus were a high proportion of the contribution from the best course of action, then it would be clear that the firm did not have a close alternative, and it may therefore be reasonably confident of its choice. As it is, project B is a close rival. A result such as this should cause a firm to check its calculations, and also see whether there are other objectives of a non-financial nature affected by the decision that have not already been taken into account. Thus, an opportunity cost helps in the selection process and also says something about the strength of any choice.

The most obvious comment on the preceding example is to suggest that the firm undertake all three projects, as they all have positive cash flows. If this were done, there would then be no opportunity cost as no benefit would be sacrificed. This gives us the insight that opportunity cost is created by scarcity. Because we have to make a choice due to scarcity, possible alternatives are rejected, resulting in a loss of contribution.

Students sometimes ask why should we bother with this notion when it is quite obvious that project C is the best? Is it not therefore simpler to list the alternatives, and choose the most profitable one? In this example, it is indeed easier to do this; but in more complex situations although it is always possible to list out all the options separately, the opportunity cost concept serves as a useful shorthand for including the financial effect of rejected options. We illustrate this point by extending the previous example in section 4.3. The decision to choose project C is reconsidered upon the receipt of information in Table 4.2.

Table 4.2

	Project (£000)		
	A	B	C
Sales	1,000	1,500	1,200
Less costs			
Labour (hours thousands 25:40:35)	375	600	525
Material X (units thousands 25:50:30)	375	750	450
Other relevant costs	125	5	75
Salaries	25	25	25
Surplus	100	120	125

Originally it was thought that a choice had to be made solely because of a management time shortage. It now appears that there are shortages of labour and material X.

Only 40,000 extra hours are available to Pogey Ltd. If not used on these projects, then 20,000 hours could be used on existing output, product Z. This action would increase contribution by £17 per hour before deduction of labour costs. A further 20,000 hours could also be hired out at £15.50 per hour.

Material X is also in short supply. Twenty-five thousand units can be purchased on the open market. Up to 25,000 further units could only be obtained through diverting units away from project Y, for which they have already been ordered. This would mean cancellation of the project, incurring a net loss of £20,000.

Let us produce an opportunity cost statement for the three projects being considered. By including the benefits foregone we are able to see whether undertaking A, B or C is the best course of action. A revised statement might appear as shown in Table 4.3.

Table 4.3

	Project (£000)		
	A	B	C
Sales	1,000	1,500	1,200
Less costs:			
Labour	375	600	525
Loss of net contribution of existing output of product Z £(17−15) per hour	10	40	30
Hiring out (lost contribution 15.50−15.00 = 0.5 per hour)	10	10	10
Material X	375	750	450
Loss of contribution through cancellation of project Y	–	20	20
Other relevant costs	125	5	75
Salaries	25	25	25
Net surplus	80	50	65
Select project A net surplus		80	
Less opportunity cost C		65	
Overall net surplus		15	

Note that in making these calculations the most profitable course of action is always assumed. Thus, in looking at the 40,000 hours available to Pogey Ltd, it is assumed that if any of the projects were undertaken, the firm would first use labour from the less profitable alternative, hiring out before drawing from the more profitable labour engaged to further existing output.

Each opportunity cost is in a sense a hurdle which the project has to clear. If it fails (i.e. there is a net deficit), then the resources are despatched to all those other activities that make up the opportunity cost. For example, in Pogey Ltd, suppose that revised market estimates suggest that revenues for all three projects will be 10 per cent lower than originally estimated. All three projects would have net deficits after including opportunity costs. Pogey Ltd would then use half the labour for existing output and the other half for hiring out.

Thus far, we have talked about opportunity cost exclusively in terms of benefit foregone. Often it appears as an actual cost, which can be rather confusing. In Pogey Ltd labour was costed as in Table 4.4.

Table 4.4

| | Project (£000) | | |
	A	B	C
Labour hours at £15/hour	375	600	525
Lost contribution from hiring out 20,000 hours at £0.5 per hour	10	10	10
Lost contribution to product Z (£2 per hour)	10	40	30
Total	395	650	565

An alternative presentation is shown in Table 4.5. In the alternative form, both costs are explained in terms of willingness to pay. Thus we may say that the external market is willing to pay up to £15.50 per hour for the labour. Similarly, 'existing output' is willing to pay up to £17 per hour for labour. If A, B and C are to represent the best course of action, then they must cover

Table 4.5

| | Project (£000) | | |
	A	B	C
20,000 hours at £15.50 (hiring out)	310	310	310
Value to product Z (£17 per hour)	85	340	255
Total	395	650	565

the maximum that other parties would be willing to pay. This method is a useful alternative explanation, providing it is recognized that: actual cost + contribution = willingness to pay.

Finally, opportunity cost must relate to the benefit of a real alternative. Continuing with the example of Pogey Ltd, supposing that the cost per unit for existing output was:

Product Z	£
Price	100
Material (2 units)	30
Labour (1 hour)	15
Other costs	53
Contribution	2

The contribution per labour hour, net of labour cost, is £2, as in the original example. Now let us alter the example and suppose that product Z also used material X, and that all projects can be part completed. We know that X is in short supply; only 25,000 units can be purchased on the open market, and 25,000 units through internal diversion. From the product Z cost per unit, one unit of X would increase net contribution by £1. As this contribution per unit is greater for the 25,000 units than the £20,000 they would earn if used for project Y, it would be better to charge A, B and C an extra £1 per unit opportunity cost rather than £20,000/25,000 units or 80p per unit from project Y.

But then we have the opportunity cost for both labour and materials referring to the same contribution, that of product Z. Does this matter? If we had an extra 10 hours of labour and 20 units of material X that we wanted to use on A, B or C, there would be a total apparent opportunity cost or benefit sacrificed of (10 hours × £2) + (20 units × £1) = £40. The alternative being sacrificed is product Z in both cases. We can see that in fact 10 hours of labour and 20 units of material X will produce 10 units of product Z, a lost contribution of £20 not £40. We are double counting our opportunities!

From this and our previous analysis, we can say that:

1   An opportunity cost should only be used when the resource is scarce.
2   The contribution from a unit of production, or an opportunity that is being counted as a benefit sacrificed, should attach itself to only one scarce resource as the opportunity cost.

4.5.2   Relevant cost

There are no set procedures to determine relevance. Ultimately, all that is required is an open enquiring mind and a willingness to challenge the conventions of a costing system. The following issues, nevertheless, tend to be common to most attempts to determine relevance.

Historic cost.   In the words of Stanley Jevons, 'byegones are forever byegones'. A firm may have spent £1 million on machinery, but if its use now is only as scrap worth £10, then that is its value in decisions. If someone offers £20, intending to sell the machinery as a work of art, then the firm should accept. Certainly, it should not reject the offer on the grounds that the machine cost £1 million. Such past costs are termed historic or sunk costs.

In making decisions in practice, much of the data will be historic. Does this mean that decisions are being taken using irrelevant data? The answer is probably not, for the following reasons:

(a)   An historic cost is often a good indication of the price that ought to be paid or received. It can therefore serve as a useful starting point for estimates of future prices.

(b)   Selling goods at below their historic cost is generally an admission that the activity is not worth repeating (except for capital goods). Historic costs therefore serve as an important benchmark. In this context the loss recorded in traditional accounting systems provides a correct signal. Having established that a conventional profit cannot be made from selling an item, we must accept that it is no more than common wisdom for the item to be sold at the best possible price, irrespective of its historic cost.

Byegones are still forever bygones for any particular decision. Nevertheless, this should not blind us to the fact that historic costs do give indirect clues as to performance, possible future costs and worthwhile activities. These clues should not be ignored.

Cost apportionments: A cost apportionment can be defined as 'The allotment of overhead to two or more cost centres of proportions of common items of cost on the basis of estimated benefit received' (CIMA, 1988). It is therefore an apportionment of a service cost that is only indirectly related to the level of activity. In producing a unit of output, it is likely that there will be no discernible effect on the cost of the service. Although an item may be charged with a cost apportionment, the amount does not represent a cost incurred directly by the product. The following example illustrates this point.

Computing costs in Pele Ltd are estimated to be £100,000 in the year. It has been decided to apportion this cost to departments on the basis of computer minutes used. The computing costs for department A, the production department, are estimated to be £60,000 for the year. Output is budgeted to be 30,000 units of X. Direct labour costs are £120,000, materials £150,000, power £90,000 and depreciation £30,000. All these costs are absorbed into the cost per unit. What is the cost per unit, and what is the minimum price for which the unit could be sold, without leaving the firm worse off?

The cost per unit is simply:

Product X	*£ per unit*
Materials	5
Labour	4
Power	3
Computing	2
Depreciation	1
Total cost per unit	15

The minimum price is that which will cover the direct costs incurred. Depreciation is not relevant in determining a minimum price because it is an apportionment. If production were increased, the depreciation cost to the firm would not increase, assuming that production can be met from the existing machinery. The cost per unit would appear to make this cost increase, but over- and under-recovery adjustments would bring the figure back to the £30,000.

Computing costs have every appearance of being variable when charged by the minute. If their usage were to be halved, for instance, costs would not be significantly altered from the firm's point of view. Overheads would obviously be significantly under-recovered (Inman (1989), pp. 212 and 268). When the under-recovery is apportioned, then departmental computing costs would, like the depreciation, be substantially fixed.

We may also question whether or not labour is a truly variable cost. For small changes in output, there would be no change in the workforce and, assuming that piece rates are not in operation, no change in labour costs. Traditionally, texts assume that labour is a variable cost; in practice, it is fixed over short ranges. If we make the traditional assumption and assume that labour is variable, the direct costs incurred will be:

Product X	£ per unit
Materials	5
Labour	4
Power	3
Total cost per unit	12

Any selling price over £12 will not leave the firm worse off in that some contribution will be made to overheads.

Fixed costs. For decisions that concern output, a fixed cost is invariant and is therefore by definition not relevant. This is not to say that fixed costs such as rent, rates, salaries, personnel, computing, accounting, marketing and so on, are irrelevant in all cases. Over a wide range of output, almost all costs will vary. In our last example, computing costs would vary with output if the increase or decrease in output were very large; more personnel would be needed to key in data, more computer storage space would be required, and maybe even a new computer.

Not all decisions are directly concerned with output. A restructuring of the organization might well significantly affect fixed costs such as salaries, personnel, marketing and accounting. In addition, decisions concerning quality and efficiency are likely to include changes in fixed costs. In other words, no cost is invariant to all decisions.

Incremental costs. Fixed and variable costs tend to be associated with particular categories of expenditure. By contrast, an incremental cost is one that is variable in relation to what is being considered, but it is not associated with any particular type of expenditure.

For example, if increased production meant that more factory and storage space had to be rented, and that there would have to be increases in personnel, accounting and computing costs, then these costs would be incremental to the decision to increase output. As incremental costs, they would be relevant to the decision in the same way as the variable costs of labour and materials are incremental to output. In considering both fixed and variable costs equally, the incremental cost is the closest that the accountant comes to the economist's marginal cost. The difference is that the accountant views incremental costing as an *ad hoc* exercise rather than the economist's view of marginal costing as the cornerstone of cost analysis.

Common costs. In our first example, salaries were a cost common for each of the projects being considered. In some approaches it is inferred that where a cost is common to each option being considered, it may be regarded as irrelevant. Caution is advised in ignoring such costs, for one of the options that ought always to be included is to do nothing. If the contribution from the best opportunity is less than the omitted common costs, then to do nothing would indeed be the best opportunity. A common cost is therefore only common within a restricted range. Even within this range, such a cost can affect decisions (Dillon and Nash, (1978)). Suppose we have three projects with a probabilistic outcome as follows:

	Projects (£000)		
	I	*II*	*III*
50 per cent chance	200	150	800
50 per cent chance	50	100	20

where the manager's N–M utility curve may be described as:

$$U = \log_n \frac{x}{100}$$

Where x = returns, then:

Project	*Utility*
I	0.0
II	0.2
III	0.24

If we then deduct from all outcomes a common cost of a salary of £19,000, which has previously been omitted as being irrelevant, our revised utility is:

Project	*Utility*
I	−0.29
II	0.03
III	−1.27

Project III has changed from being the most favoured to the least favoured of the options by the inclusion of a common cost. Where there is uncertainty, total value of changes in wealth matter, for the position of the decision maker on the utility curve dictates attitude towards risk.

4.6 Conclusions

Decision making within the organization is a constantly developing art. Ten years ago few had, for instance, heard of 'just in time' manufacturing, financial measures dominated decisions and many of the underlying ideas in the last two chapters were in their nascent stage. Of these developments we point to one change that is particularly significant. Although the accountant's stated aim is the 'provision of information', the tendency as regard decisions has been the 'provision of solutions'. It has been an underlying assumption in many texts and papers that the accounting system and financial decision models are able to calculate the most profitable or beneficial product, or the best course of action. By presenting rather more developed models, we have shown that there are many valuations of financial and non-financial factors, as well as trade-off judgements, which require the combination of financial and non-financial information. Such models provide a guide to decisions without giving the impression that there is a single 'best' solution. This approach enables the accountant to fulfil his or her stated role as a facilitator of the decision-making process, providing information and guidance rather than 'answers'.

References and further reading

Biggs, C. and Benjamin, D., *Management Accounting Techniques*, Heinemann, 1989.
Bryant, J. W. (ed.), *Financial Modelling in Corporate Management*, John Wiley,1982.
CIMA, *Terminology*, CIMA, 1988.
Commission on the Third London Airport, Papers and Proceedings, Vol. VII, parts 1 and 2, HMSO, London 1970; and Commission on the Third London Airport, Report, HMSO, London, 1971.
Dasgupta, A. J., Pearce, D. W., *Cost Benefit Analysis: Theory and Practice*, Macmillan, 1972.
de Bono, E., *Lateral Thinking: Creativity Step by Step*, London, Harper and Row, 1970.
deNeufville, R., Keeney, R. L., *Use of decision analysis in airport development for Mexico City*, and Morse, P. M. (ed.), MIT Press, Cambridge, Mass., 1972.
Dillon, R. D., Nash, J. F. 'The true relevance of relevant costs', *Accounting Review*, January 1978.
Dolbear, J., 'Blue Circles Investment Planning Models' in Bryant, J. W. (ed.), *Financial Modelling in Corporate Management*, Wiley, 1982.
Fayol, H., *Principles of Management in Organisation Theory*, ed. Pugh, D. S., Penguin, 1971.
French, S., *Readings in Decision Analysis*, Chapman and Hall, 1989.
Inman, M. L., *Cost Accounting*, Heinemann, 1989.
Jaikumar, R., Post-industrial Manufacturing, *Harvard Business Review*, November–December, 1986.
Kaplan, R. L., Atkinson, A. A., *Advanced Management Accounting*, Prentice-Hall, 1989, pp. 412–72.
Keefer, D. L., Bodily, S. E., 'Three-Point Approximations for Continuous Random Variables', *Management Science*, 1983, pp. 595–609.
Keeney, R. L., Raiffa, H., *Decisions with Multiple Objectives, Preferences and Value Trade Offs*, Wiley, 1976.
Maskell, B. H., 'Performance Measurement for World Class Manufacturing', *Management Accounting*, July–August, 1989 pp. 48–50.
Miles, L., *Techniques of Value Analysis and Engineering*, McGraw-Hill, 1961.

Mishan, E. J., *Cost Benefit Analysis*, Allen and Unwin, 1971.

Moore, P. G., Thomas, H., *The Anatomy of Decisions*, Penguin, 1976.

Ridge, W. J., *Value Analysis for Better Management*, American Management Association Inc., 1969.

Townsend, R., *Up the Organization*, Coronet Books, 1970.

Watson, S. R., 'Decision Analysis as a Replacement for Cost/Benefit Analysis', *European Journal of Operations Research*, 1981, 7 pp. 242–8.

Watson, S. R., Buede, D. M., *Decision Synthesis: The principles and practice of decision analysis*, CUP, 1987.

Questions for Part One

1   Pumpey plc manufactures mechanical pumps. Currently it is conducting a strategic review of its manufacturing policy for the next 5 years. The following represents a summary of a recent report.

Market
The market adopts distinct phases. Currently the firm believes it is coming to the end of a moderate phase. A strategic review of the policy options has been called for by the managing director.

Option I – continue existing policy
Fixed costs are currently some £2.5m per year, variable costs are 75 per cent of the selling price. If there is an upturn in the market, sales will be about £14m per year in real terms, assuming that the sales and promotion policy does not change. A downturn would result in sales of £10m. If there is no change, sales are projected to be £12m.

Option II – retool
Retooling would mean less wastage, reworking and more flexible production lines. Variable costs would be cut by one-third, though fixed costs, including finance would be about £5m per year over the 5 years. It is envisaged that the same pricing policy as in Option I would be pursued.

Option III – automate
This option would increase fixed costs to £6m per annum and reduce variable costs by 50 per cent. To accompany this change it is suggested that prices should be cut by 20 per cent, which would increase volume by an estimated 50 per cent in all scenarios. An appendix to this option doubts the increase in quantity, suggesting that a 'price war' would imply that the increase in quantity may only be 20 per cent. The report suggests that there is 40 per cent chance of this occurring.

Required:

(a) Construct a decision table of this problem and determine which option is best under each of the following criteria:

    (i)   maximin criterion;
    (ii) maximax criterion;
    (iii) minimax regret;
    (iv) calculate the ratio in the optimism pessimism index to change the choice in (i);
    (v) what would be your reason for rejecting Option I?

(b) Suggest reasons for using each of the criteria suggested in (a).
(c) The current beliefs of this manager are: 'Quite frankly, a downturn is as likely as an upturn, but I would say that either option is twice as likely as the situation remaining the same'.

    (i)   Calculate the expected value under each option.
    (ii) Write a brief note to the manager explaining: (a) what is meant by expected value, and (b) the relationship between choice and expected value.
    (iii) Would it be worthwhile subscribing to an economic report estimated by the manager to be 70 per cent accurate (assume that there is an equal chance of reporting the other two states of the market should the report be inaccurate)?

2 As an investment manager, you are offered two investments, A and B, with prospective net returns as follows:

	A		B
50 per cent	1,000	50 per cent	2,000
50 per cent	200	50 per cent	(200)

(a) Calculate the expected value of each investment.
(b) Caculate the variance and standard deviation of A and B.
(c) Explain how the mean variance rules would rank these two prospects.
(d) Which, in your opinion, is preferable? Explain why.
(e) Suppose that you had a utility curve of:

$$U = \sqrt{(x + 200)}$$

    (i)   draw a rough graph of the curve;
    (ii) explain the significance of its shape;
    (iii) show how the curve can be used to select between the investments.

(f)   If you could invest in A *and* B:

   (i) Draw a simple tree diagram of the total returns and their probabilities assuming that there is:

    (1) perfect positive correlation
    (2) perfect negative correlation
    (3) no correlation.

   (ii) Calculate the expected value and standard deviation for each of the returns in (i).

  (g) Explain the significance of your findings in (f) for the problem of investment analysis.

(Note: an ability to use a scientific calculator saves much calculation!)

3 Mr X wishes to replace his alloy moulding machine. There are a number of suitable replacements on the market. He has decided to use reports from trade magazines and select on the bases of:

   (i)   Initial cost.
   (ii) Reliability.
  (iii) Maintenance cost.
  (iv) Safety.
   (v) Flexibility.

Advise the manager on his selection of attributes and explain how the attributes can be used to select a replacement.

4 Mrs A is considering five competing designs of yacht to replace the existing design produced by her company Yotalot Ltd. She has outlined five criteria:

   (i)   Construction cost.
   (ii) Appearance.
  (iii) Flexibility.
  (iv) Quality.
   (v) Features.

She comments: 'The selling price of each design would be about the same with a limited allowance for quality and features of no more than £2,000. Although the profit per boat does vary between the designs, the critical factor is volume – that will depend upon selecting the best design'. After much discussion with fellow directors, the following assessments (I–V) are agreed:

Design criteria	(i) £	(ii)	(iii)	(iv)	(v)
I	13,000	good	poor	reasonable	basic
II	14,000	good	good	standard	basic
III	15,500	average	excellent	excellent	good
IV	13,500	very good	good	standard	basic
V	15,000	good	poor	excellent	good

Using this example, you are required to:

(i) Illustrate how lexicographic ordering might be used to make a selection – outline the advantages and disadvantages of this method.
(ii) How might the constraints approach be used to aid selection?
(iii) What further questions would you wish to ask in order to construct a value function? Illustrate the procedure using this problem.
(iv) The director of finance comments: 'Our main concern is making money not boats, we should select the cheapest design that meets our standards'. Identify this decision criterion and discuss its advantages and disadvantages. Is this approach necessarily better than (i) to (iii)?
(v) Compare and contrast the decision criteria of sections (i)–(iv). How might volume and profits be included in the calculations?

5   The XXTV Company is seeking ways to reduce its running costs by 20 per cent. The chairman (an ex-accountant) seeks to achieve this goal in two phases:

Phase I   cost-effectiveness and value analysis.
Phase II   a review of operations.

Phase I has led to a 10 per cent reduction in spending. To help in Phase II, the management accountant has prepared the following information:

Programme type	Existing distribution (% of weekly time)	% of weekly budget running costs	Minimum commitment (% of weekly time)
a	40	60	30
b	10	10	0
c	10	10	0
d	40	20	20
	100		

The senior management has also devised scales of 1–10 points of 'worth' to the company. These scales are based upon:

(i) audience numbers
(ii) popularity with advertisers, and
(iii) reputation for the quality of the company.

They have yet to be applied to the four types of programme.

Required:
(a) Explain how cost-effectiveness and value analysis can help to reduce costs?

(b)   Using the information provided by the accountant, outline three strategies that could be followed to implement the remaining cuts.

(c)   Explain how the managers rating system might be used in choosing a strategy.

6   A drug treatment day centre run by a charity wishes to improve the quality of its service to patients by the addition of extra facilities.

After much research it has drawn up a 'short list' of five separate possible improvements and has assessed their outcomes using the following criteria:

Criterion A: Reduced average number of waiting hours per month per patient.

Criterion B: Increased percentage frequency of seeing patients when they attend.

Criterion C: Reduced average number of 'months to cure' per patient.

Criterion D: Increased percentage frequency of patient attendance at the centre.

The assessed outcomes are:

Improvement reference number	Extra facilities	Outcome according to criterion			
		A Hours	B %	C Months	D %
1	Increase medical staff by two doctors and one nurse	4.8	35	1	5
2	Increase counselling staff by two counsellors and one nurse	6	20	1.25	10
3	Taxi service to bring patients to and from the centre	2	12	0.75	22
4	Extend by 20 hours per month the time the centre is open	4	30	1.5	10
5	Introduce group counselling sessions	–	10	1.75	15

At present the centre is open for 160 hours per month and deals with 3,000 patients. The proposed improvements will have no effect on the numbers of patients seen. The professional staff currently employed are five doctors, seven counsellors and four nurses.

The taxi service is expected to be used by 60 per cent of patients with an average attendance of one per month. Each taxi will carry an average of 1.2 patients and the cost to the centre will be £0.20 per mile.

Total distances that patients are expected to be carried per attendance are:

	Percentage of patients
10 miles	20
20 miles	40
30 miles	40
	100

The costs of extra facilities would be:

	Costs p.a. £	Associated capita equipment costs* £
Doctor's salary	22,000	5,000
Doctor's expenses	3,000	–
Counsellor's salary	16,000	2,000
Counsellor's expenses	1,500	–
Nurse's salary	10,000	1,000
Nurse's expenses	2,000	–

*These costs are depreciated over 5 years on a straight-line basis with no residual value.

Extra administration/establishment costs are £100 per month per person.

If hours are extended beyond 160 per month, overtime will need to be paid at a premium of 25 per cent on salaries (but not expenses) and an extra £4,000 per annum will be incurred for administration/establishment costs.

Group counselling sessions will require:

One specialist counsellor costing £3,000 p.a. more than ordinary counsellors.*
One assistant counsellor costing £2,000 p.a. less than ordinary counsellors.*
One nurse.

*Capital costs will be the same as for ordinary counsellors.

The centre's capital requirements will be borrowed from the bank at 12 per cent p.a. The interest and all other costs will be met by donations. The depreciation charge will be used to reduce the loan at the end of each year. Cost of working capital can be ignored.

Required:
(a) Calculate for *each* improvement the incremental cost

(i) patient per month;
(ii) for the appropriate unit of *each* of the *four* criteria.

(b) Identify the improvement with the lowest cost in (a) (ii) above for *each* of the *four* criteria.

(c) Comment on the results in (a) and (b) above with particular reference to the circumstances in which you might recommend adopting for any criterion an improvement that does not yield the lowest cost.

(d) State briefly *three* questions that you would wish to be answered concerning this cost–benefit analysis before recommending a decision.

7   As management accountant to a large manufacturing and marketing company, it is part of your work to advise on the extent to which service to customers should be improved, particularly through changes in marketing and administration.

You are required to prepare notes for a paper to the executive management committee on this subject, setting out.

(a) The approach that you would recommend in deciding whether or not to offer improved service to customers;

(b) examples (not quantified) of how this approach would be applied to *three* relevant aspects of the company's service to customers;

(c) what special benefits the management accountant can bring to the review of data on which such decisions are made.

(CIMA, May 1989)

8   A company manufacturing agricultural machinery is faced with the possibility of a strike by its direct production workers engaged on the assembly of one of its machines.

The trade union is demanding an increase of 7 per cent, back-dated to the beginning of its financial year (1 January), but the company expects that if a strike does take place, it will last 4 weeks after which the union will settle for an increase of 5 per cent similarly back-dated.

The machine whose production would be affected by the strike is sold to distributors at a discount of 20 per cent from the current recommended selling price of £3,000.

Estimated costs for the machines are:

	Fixed per year (£000)	Variable per machine (£)
Production	16,000	1,800
Distribution	1,000	100

Direct labour costs comprise 40 per cent of the variable production costs.

The budgeted output is 27,500 machines in 50 working weeks per year.

If the strike takes place the following events are expected by the company:

Maintenance staff, whose wages are included in the fixed production costs, would be used to carry out an overhaul of the conveyor system using £25,000 worth of materials. This overhaul would otherwise be undertaken by an outside contractor at a cost of £100,000 including materials.

Sales of 650 machines would be lost to competition. The balance that would ordinarily have been produced during the strike period could, however, be sold, but these machines would have to be made up in overtime working which would be at an efficiency rate of 90 per cent of normal. This would entail additional fixed costs of £10,000 and wage payments at time and one-half.

Required:
(a) (i) State, with explanations and full supporting data, whether from a purely economic point of view you would advise the management to allow the strike to go ahead, rather than agree to the union's demand.
    (ii) Explain briefly *three* factors, not considered in your above evaluation, that may have adverse financial effects for the company if the strike were to take place.

(b) Assume that the strike goes ahead, and that it lasts 3 weeks, after which agreement is reached between the company and the union for a 6 per cent pay increase back-dated to 1 January. Assume also that the anticipated loss of sales to competitors of 650 machines occurs and the balance is made up by overtime working. A newspaper reports that the cost of the strike to the company was £5 million. The trade union counters this claim by insisting that the strike was contrived by the company, to its benefit, as the machines were selling at a loss.

Required:
 (i) Comment on the statements made by the press and the trade union.
 (ii) State, with supporting calculations, whether the company was justified in using overtime working to produce the balance of machines saleable but not produced during the strike.

(CIMA, May 1987)

Part Two   Capital Budgeting

The financial evaluation of investments, whether by the Stock Market, banks or within the organization, is of crucial importance in business. This section analyses the problems that are posed by the investment decision process. In particular, we consider:

(a) The effect of differing patterns of benefits over time (chapter 5).
(b) The development and use of a market determined risk measure (chapters 6 and 7). The concept of risk to the decision maker, introduced in Part One is examined in the context of the investment community.
(c) The management problems of investment (chapter 8).

5 Investments in a risk-free world

5.1 Introduction

Any organization engaged in the provision of goods or services utilizes real assets in its operations. These assets must be maintained and renewed if the organization is to continue in existence, and must be expanded if the organization is to grow. Capital budgeting addresses two problems: how much should be spent on real assets (plant, fittings, vehicles, land etc.); and which real assets should be acquired. In deciding which assets to acquire, the organization must weigh the benefits to be gained from the acquisition against the costs that will be incurred. Often these benefits can be expressed in financial terms, e.g. when cost savings are expected, or be assessable only in qualitative terms, e.g. when expenditure on health care alleviates suffering. Whatever the measurement difficulties, some attempt must be made to express the benefits expected in a way which enables a comparison to be made *either* with the cost of the investment *or* with the benefits to be gained from a similar level of expenditure elsewhere.

Much has been written on the subject of the methods to be used in assessing capital investments, and indeed a significant proportion of this chapter will be devoted to it. But the concentration of the literature on the *evaluation* of investments should not obscure what are perhaps more important aspects of the capital budgeting process.

Figure 5.1 represents the classical view of the investment decision-making process. In this view the evaluation criterion is the *only* factor which is instrumental in determining whether or not an investment is accepted. It is not surprising, therefore, that much academic effort has been expended in refining the evaluation process.

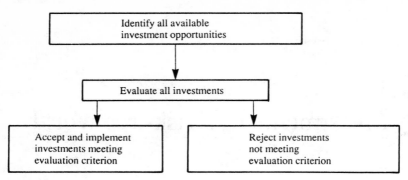

Figure 5.1

5.2   Net present value and investment

The concern of early economists was to explain the level of investment in the economy as a whole. Central to this concept of evaluation is the idea of a positive rate of interest, r, at which investors can borrow or lend money. The investor may therefore invest his funds in the market at the interest rate, r; invest his funds in real assets; undertake a combination of these two options; or borrow in order to invest in real assets. Real assets will only be attractive to a rational investor if they offer a rate of return in excess of r. By discounting the financial costs and benefits associated with real assets at this rate, the investor can determine whether a return in excess of r is available.

Consider a simple example:

Interest rate $r = 5$ per cent p.a. Projects A, B and C have a 1-year life.

	Cash outflow in year 0	Net cash inflow in year 1
Project A	£1,000	£1,100
Project B	£1,000	£1,050
Project C	£1,000	£1,000

The investor can invest in any or all of these real assets, or leave his funds in the market to earn the going interest rate. Let us assume in this chapter that all future flows are known with certainty. We can therefore compare the certain return available by investing at the market interest rate with the certain return available in the three projects. Invested in the market, £1,000 at the going rate of 5 per cent will grow to £1,050 (£1,000 × 1.05) at the end of 1 year. This represents the benchmark against which an investment in the 1-year projects should be measured. At the end of year 1, Project A offers an additional £50, B offers no gain or loss, and C earns £50 less than the market alternative. These incremental gains or losses can be expressed in present terms. For Project A the incremental gain is £50 at the end of year 1, with a present value of £50/1.05 = £47.62. There is no incremental gain or loss on Project B. Project C produces an incremental loss of £50, with a *negative* incremental present value of £50/1.05 = £47.62.

The same result is obtainable by calculating the net present value (NPV) of the investments directly:

$$NPV = \sum_{t=1}^{t=T} \frac{C_t}{(1+r)^t} - C_o \qquad \ldots \text{Equation 5.1}$$

where T is the life of the investment, C_t is the incremental cash flow in period t, and C_o is the initial investment. The discount rate r is the opportunity cost of capital. The commitment of funds for one purpose implies foregoing other courses of action. The opportunity cost of making an investment is the return foregone on the best alternative use of funds. In this simple example the market rate of interest is taken as the opportunity cost.

Using equation 5.1, the NPV of each of the three projects is:

$$NPV_A = \frac{£1,100}{(1.05)} - £1,000 = £47.62$$

$$NPV_B = \frac{£1,050}{(1.05)} - £1,000 = £0$$

$$NPV_C = \frac{£1,000}{(1.05)} - £1,000 = -£47.62$$

A net present value can be seen to be a statement in present day terms of the value of an investment to an investor. Obviously, a positive NPV represents an addition to the investor's wealth if a project is undertaken, while a negative NPV would reduce it. The objective of an investor is assumed to be the maximization of wealth. Therefore, as the NPV of a project measures the change in wealth which results from undertaking an investment, a simple decision rule follows from this: accept all investments with positive NPVs, reject all investments with negative NPVs.

5.2.1 *Net present value and aggregate real asset investment*

By means of this model, the capital budgeting problem at the national level is solved. The total investment in real assets undertaken within the economy will be equal to the funds necessary to finance the acquisition of *all* real assets investments with positive NPVs.

At the national level this is a model which can aid economic management. For example, if the Chancellor wishes to stimulate investment in the economy, this simple model shows him that he should reduce interest rates. This will lead to an increase in total investment in real assets. Conversely, an increase in interest rates will reduce investment. It is not necessary for *all* firms to increase investment when interest rates are cut for the model to have good predictive powers. So long as *aggregate* real asset investment behaves as predicted, the model is useful at a national level.

The behaviour of each individual firm has much in common with the behaviour of the economy as a whole but is not identical to it. For example, 'evaluate all investments' makes sense at a national level. It is reasonable to suppose that every investment possibility will have been considered by someone. However, it is not reasonable to assume that someone, or some firm, will have considered *all* possibilities. At national level this is of no consequence, it is not necessary to consider why it is firm A rather than firm B that evaluates a particular proposition so long as one firm carries out an evaluation. However, if the model is adopted at the level of the individual company, it is clearly *not* realistic to say 'evaluate all investment opportunities'. Individual firms will evaluate a sub-set of these opportunities. At the national level the choice of sub-set is of no significance but to the individual firm it is of vital importance.

It is arguable that the relative neglect of this aspect of the decision-making process arises from a failure to recognize that a model which is adequate in its aggregate national form may be incomplete when applied at the disaggregated level of the firm. The application of the NPV rule to the level of the individual firm leads to the maximization of shareholder wealth in that firm in the limited sense of measuring the incremental value of the investments actually *considered*. However, shareholder wealth may have been higher if a different set of investments had been considered. At the individual firm level the choice of investments to evaluate may have much greater significance for shareholder wealth than the evaluation technique used. This does not, of course, mean that evaluation is unimportant, but simply that its crucial rule at the national level is complemented by other important considerations at the level of the firm.

5.2.2   *Net present value and individual investment in real assets*

Apart from the acquisition of domestic items – houses, cars, furniture, etc. – few individuals make *direct* investments in real assets. Such investments are carried out on their behalf by companies in which they have a shareholding. In most cases these shareholdings are themselves indirect, e.g. through pension-fund contributions or the purchase of unit trusts. The ultimate owners of a large company will thus tend to be a large and motley band, yet company decision makers are theoretically charged to act in the best interests of all these diverse shareholders.

Consider a company, Dilemma Limited, which has two shareholders, each owning 50 per cent of the shares: Mr Spender and Mr Saver. Spender enjoys a high standard of living and is unwilling to reduce his current consumption to finance investment, even if the returns offered are very high. In contrast, Saver is very frugal in his habits. Once his basic needs are met, he always saves any surplus funds, irrespective of the level of return offered. Saver's current income is sufficient to satisfy these basic needs adequately.

Dilemma has a profit of £3,000 held in the form of cash, and is considering whether to distribute this profit as dividend or invest in some combination of the three projects in Example 1. Let us assume for the moment that a capital market does *not* exist, so there is no market-based rate, r, at which the company and its shareholders can borrow or lend. In this situation, the management of Dilemma would not know how to act. In the context of the NPV model as stated, the interests of Spender would best be served by distributing the £3,000 as dividend. He would then be able to use his share of the dividend to increase his current living standard. However, this distribution would not meet with the approval of Saver. He would not wish to spend his part of the dividend on current consumption, and therefore would be put to the trouble, and in the real world possible expense, of re-investing it in real assets. Assuming (consistent with the classical model) that no investment opportunities are open to him which are not open to the company, then his interests would be best served by Dilemma retaining the whole £3,000 and investing in each of the three projects. The company is thus unable to satisfy both its shareholders simultaneously.

A company can only be said to be acting in the best interests of its shareholders if the decisions it makes on their behalf coincide with the choices they would have made for themselves. In the absence of a capital market, Spender, faced with the choice of projects A, B and C, would not invest in any of these options if it meant foregoing current consumption. The introduction of a capital market, with an interest rate r, would change his stance. Spender does not need to reduce his current spending in order to invest. He can fund his investments by borrowing. Providing the investment has a positive NPV, he can, if he wishes, invest and *increase* either future or current consumption. For example, Spender can borrow £1,000 at the going interest rate to fund an investment in A. At the end of the year, the proceeds from A will enable him to repay the loan plus 5 per cent interest, i.e. £1,050, and leave him with a £50 surplus to spend in the future. If he was a real spendthrift, he would borrow £1,047.62: £1,000 would be invested in A and he would spend £47.62, the net present value of A, in the current year. At the end of the year, the £1,100 he received from A would be just sufficient to repay the loan of £1,047.62 plus 5 per cent interest.

Spender would be indifferent as to whether or not to invest in B. The cash flow from this project is sufficient to repay a loan taken out to finance it, but has no surplus. An investment in B would neither reduce nor increase Spender's opportunity to consume now or in the future: its net present value is zero.

C is a most unattractive proposition. The cash flow from C would not enable a loan to be repaid. If undertaken, Spender would have to reduce his current consumption by £50 in order to meet the interest cost in one year's time.

Let us turn now to Saver. It has been argued above that all three projects are attractive to him if his only choice is between consumption and investment in real assets. But, again, the existence of a capital market changes his position. Funds not invested in real assets can be invested at the market rate r. Saver will now consider whether the cash flows he can obtain from the real assets are greater or less than those he would obtain from leaving his funds to earn the going interest rate. This comparison would reveal A as the only project earning a surplus return.

The introduction of the market rate of interest means that the opportunity cost of capital is the same for all people *irrespective* of their individual tastes and preferences. This leads to a very important result. If the managers of a business invest in projects with positive NPVs and reject investments with negative NPVs, they will be making the decisions which the shareholders would have made for themselves. By operating this rule they are maximizing the value of the company and thus the wealth of their shareholders. Although it is up to the shareholders to decide whether to consume this wealth – Spender would incline to immediate consumption, Saver to reinvestment – the *choice* of real asset in which to invest is the same for *all* investors.

If we set aside the problem outlined above that, in reality, firms will only evaluate a sub-set of investments, then the basic NPV model thus provides a decision rule with two very important properties:

1   Maximization of net present value is equivalent to maximization of share-holder wealth.
2   Investment decision making can be delegated to agents who, by applying the NPV rule, will act in the best interests of their principals, irrespective of differences in the tastes and preferences of those principals. This is known as the 'Separation theorem' (Hirschleifer (1958)).

It is now appropriate to examine the extent to which these conclusions are dependent on the assumptions of the model. First, the discount rate must be a measure of the opportunity cost of funds for wealth maximization to result. The model assumes a single rate which reflects the opportunity cost for *all* individuals and companies. In reality we know that borrowers and lenders do *not* face the same interest rate, and therefore do not have the same opportunity cost of capital. For example, the opportunity cost for Spender is given by the cost of borrowing, while the correct discount rate for Saver is the return available on lending. Furthermore, costs and returns may differ as between individuals and organizations. In the real world, the returns and benefits are net of taxes and transaction costs, and these generally do not impact equally on all individuals or organizations. Therefore, far from having a single rate, r, which is a universal measure of opportunity cost, in reality a whole range of rates may be encountered. Decision makers will tend to choose the discount rate which measures opportunity cost for their own organization. As no single rate could coincide with the opportunity cost to all shareholders, the idea of wealth maximization for all principals will be lost, and decisions taken on their behalf will approximate to weath maximization rather than attain it.

Other features of this simple model abstract from reality. For example, not only is information assumed to be freely available and costless, so that all investments can be evaluated and forecasts are also assumed to be *certain*. With certain cash flows Spender can borrow to finance investments and still sleep soundly. The prospect of the actual investment returns being less than those forecast is assumed away: the principal, plus interest on any loan used to finance an investment with positive NPV may always be repaid from the future cash flows. In the real world, *certain* future costs and benefits are the exception rather than the rule. Risk or uncertainty surround the future, and investments in real assets by organizations are normally subject to both risk and uncertainty in varying degrees.

Both these terms refer to situations in which a range of outcomes rather than a single outcome is possible, but a distinction is made between them on the basis of the availability of past information. If a proposed course of action is identical or very similar to courses of action which have been undertaken repeatedly in the past, then the proposed action is subject to *risk*. Past experience can be used as a guide in specifying the range of possible outcomes for the action currently proposed. It can also be used as the basis for assigning probabilities to these outcomes. Where no past experience is available, then an action is subject to *uncertainty*. Any prediction of the possible outcomes of an uncertain event requires a leap of imagination. Probabilities assigned to these outcomes must be subjective, rather than statistical, probabilities. In common with most other literature the word 'risk' will be used to cover both terms from here on. The NPV model can in fact be modified to accommodate risk, as we shall see later (chapters 6 and 7), but when comparisons are made between appraisal methods, the simple risk-free method outlined above is usually taken as the standard against which other methods should be assessed.

5.3   Other investment criteria

We shall now outline the alternatives to NPV which researchers have found to be commonly used in practice. The operation of these methods will be illustrated by reference to the four projects W, X, Y and Z, whose cash flows are outlined in Table 5.1.

Table 5.1   Cash Flows

| | Projects | | | |
| | W | X | Y | Z |
Year	£	£	£	£
0	− 1,000	− 500	− 1,000	− 500
1	500	320	10	0
2	500	320	10	0
3	32	10	800	0
4	32	10	800	900

The prevailing market rate of interest is 5 per cent.

We have demonstrated earlier that under the assumed conditions of the basic model (perfect information, perfect capital markets, certainty) shareholder wealth will be maximized by accepting only projects which offer a positive NPV. Other methods must therefore be judged on their ability to lead to decisions consistent with those made using the NPV criterion. To aid this comparison, the calculation of NPV for each of the four projects W, X, Y and Z is shown in Table 5.2.

5.4   Non-discounting techniques

5.4.1   *Payback*

The payback period for a project is the length of time required for an investor to recoup the initial investment outlay. Decision makers specify a required payback period, and if an investment has a payback period equal to or shorter

Table 5.2

Year	Discount factor 5%	Cash flows (£) W	X	Y	Z	Present value (£) W	X	Y	Z
0	1.0	−1,000	−500	−1,000	−500	−1,000	−500	−1,000	−500
1	.952	500	320	10	0	476	305	10	0
2	.907	500	320	10	0	454	290	9	0
3	.864	32	10	800	0	28	9	691	0
4	.823	32	10	800	900	26	8	658	741
				NPV		−16	+112	+368	+241

than this period, the investment is accepted. If the payback period is longer than that specified, the project is rejected. If we assume that cash flows are received at the end of each year, the payback period for the four projects above is as shown in Table 5.3.

Table 5.3

Project	Initial outlay (£)	Cumulative cash flow (£) Years 1	2	3	4	Payback time
W	1,000	500	1,000	1,032	1,064	2 years
X	500	320	640	650	660	2 years
Y	1,000	10	20	820	1,620	4 years
Z	500	0	0	0	900	4 years

If, for example the required payback period is 3 years, then projects W and X are acceptable using this criterion, and projects Y and Z would be rejected.

Operation of the NPV rule indicates that projects X, Y and Z should be accepted. Only project W should be rejected. Inconsistencies thus arise in the treatment of projects W, Y and Z under the two evaluation criteria. These inconsistencies arise from the two defects of payback. First, no weighting is given to the timing of cash flows, i.e. they are not discounted. For example, the £500 inflow in year 2 of project W is accorded the same value as the £500 inflow in year 1. However, this criticism can be met by evaluating projects using 'discounted payback'. The discounted payback period is the time taken for the discounted value of the projects cash flows to equal the initial outlay. Second, cash flows received after the cut-off point are ignored, which leads to the rejection of projects such as Y and Z. Surveys of capital budgeting practice regularly report high utilization of payback. In the UK, Pike and Wolfe (1988) report that payback is becoming increasingly popular, being used by 92 per cent of firms surveyed in 1986 as against 73 per cent of firms in their 1975 survey. McIntyre and Coulthurst (1987) reported a usage rate of 80 per cent. Similar results have been reported in the USA. If, as demonstrated above, decision making using payback is so obviously inconsistent with wealth maximization, why is it so widely used?

Why is payback so popular?

1 *Simplicity.* Its operation and philosophy could easily be explained in a few minutes to someone with no financial training. To fully understand NPV, several hours study are probably required. Nevertheless, few people would be averse to investing several hours in study, if it could be shown to lead to significant financial rewards. The simplicity of payback cannot therefore fully explain its high use.
2 *Decision makers are unaware of the alternative methods.* This might be true for a minority of small firms, but surveys have generally shown that other methods are widely understood. Indeed, in most cases, payback is used in conjunction with other methods.
3 *It addresses organizational realities.* The popularity of payback may be related to the unrealistic assumptions of the simple NPV model. The single objective of wealth maximization is often an inadequate interpretation of the goals perceived to be important by management. In a multi-objective setting, payback may be taken as a good proxy measure for immediate financial viability (see chapter 1). Further, future cash flows in reality are generally neither known nor certain. The forecasting of these flows is a difficult procedure, becoming even more difficult as the flows recede further into the future, and their identification may entail an organization in considerable expense. Payback only requires that flows be forecast up to the payback point. Many firms use payback as an initial *screening* device, i.e. as a means of identifying whether it is worth committing the resources which will be required if a full evaluation is to take place.
4 *It is a means of dealing with risk.* In the simple model, all flows, whether near or distant, are assumed certain. In the real world this is not the case. Payback favours those projects with high cash flows in the early years, which can be seen as a crude way of dealing with future uncertainty.

5.4.2 Accounting rate of return (ARR)

This is the only commonly used technique in which accounting profits rather than cash flows are used as input data. To find the ARR of an investment, the *average* profit over the life of the investment is calculated. This is then expressed as a return on either the initial *or* average investment in the project. An acceptable ARR must be specified by the decision maker, projects exceeding this return being accepted, and those falling short of the return being rejected.

The data for W, X, Y and Z are in the form of cash flows and must be converted to accounting profit before the computation of ARR can be carried out. An *approximation* to profit can be found by deducting depreciation from the forecast flows. In reality, other adjustments are usually necessary before cash flows become accounting profit calculated in accordance with the accrual principle of accounting. However, for present purposes, an appreciation of the method can be obtained without these further adjustments.

Total accounting profit for each project will be taken as the sum of the cash flows minus the cost of the asset (assumed to be represented by the flow in year 0). Any proceeds from the sale of the asset will be reflected in the year

4 cash flow. The average profit is found by dividing the total profit by the life of the project.

The average accounting profits for projects W, X, Y and Z are shown in Table 5.4.

Table 5.4

Project	Total cash inflow (£)	Depreciation (£)	Accounting profit (£)	Project life (years)	Average accounting profit (£)
	(A)	(B)	(D) = (A − B)	(C)	D/C
W	500 + 500 + 32 + 32 = 1,064	1,000	64	4	16
X	320 + 320 + 10 + 10 = 660	500	160	4	40
Y	10 + 10 + 800 + 800 = 1,620	1,000	620	4	155
Z	0 + 0 + 0 + 900 = 900	500	400	4	100

The ARR can now be found by expressing the average profit as a percentage of the total investment:

Project	Accounting rate of return (based on total investment)
W	$\dfrac{16}{1,000} \times 100 = 1.6$ per cent
X	$\dfrac{40}{500} \times 100 = 8$ per cent
Y	$\dfrac{155}{500} \times 100 = 15.5$ per cent
Z	$\dfrac{100}{500} \times 100 = 20$ per cent

A variant on this calculation is to express the return as a percentage of the *average* investment. The average investment in the project is found by dividing the total investment by two. This calculation is independent of the length of the project, as Figure 5.2 illustrates.

Based on average investment, the ARR of the four projects is as shown below:

Project	Accounting rate of return (based on average investment)
W	$\dfrac{16}{500} \times 100 = 3.2$ per cent
X	$\dfrac{40}{250} \times 100 = 16$ per cent
Y	$\dfrac{155}{500} \times 100 = 31$ per cent
Z	$\dfrac{100}{250} \times 100 = 40$ per cent

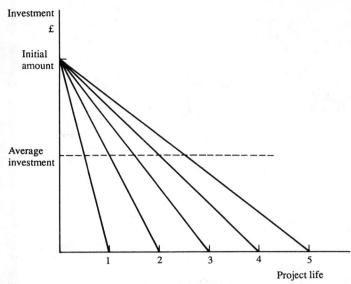

Figure 5.2

Obviously, the return based on average investment will always be twice that based on total investment (for the simple case of an initial outlay only).

Where ARR is the evaluation method, the decision maker must specify a required rate of return. In this particular case, if the market rate of interest of 5 per cent is chosen, the same set of investments will be selected, using both ARR (either total or average variant) and NPV. X, Y and Z are acceptable, and only W would be rejected. However, it must not be assumed that such consistency is the general rule. For example, if the market rate of interest were to increase from 5 per cent to 16 per cent, then only project X would have a positive NPV, as Table 5.5 shows.

By the NPV criterion, investments W, Y and Z would be rejected, and only X would be accepted. A similar increase to 16 per cent in the required ARR would lead to the selection of a different set of projects to those suggested using NPV at this new rate. Where ARR is based on total investment, a required rate of 16 per cent would lead to the rejection of W, X and Y and the acceptance of project Z. An ARR cut-off of 16 per cent based on average investment would indicate acceptance of all projects except W.

ARR and NPV use different input: accounting profit in the former case, cash flows in the latter. The methods also weight these data differently, discounting being applied to cash flows but not to accounting profit. Agreement on the selection of the same set of investments under ARR and NPV is thus purely coincidental.

As decisions based on ARR may differ from those based on NPV, the use of ARR is not necessarily consistent with the objective of wealth maximization set out in our model above. Nevertheless, surveys consistently find it to be a

Table 5.5

Year	Discount factor 16%	W	X	Cash flows (£) Y	Z	W	X	Present value (£) Y	Z
0	1.0	−1,000	−500	−1,000	−500	−1,000	−500	−1,000	−500
1	.862	500	320	10	0	431	276	9	0
2	.743	500	320	20	0	371	238	7	0
3	.641	32	10	800	0	21	6	513	0
4	.552	32	10	600	900	18	6	442	497
				NPV		−159	+26	−29	−3

widely used technique in practice. For example, Pike and Wolfe (1988) reported 56 per cent of their sample companies were using ARR. This is an increase on Pike's (1982) earlier reported usage rate of 51 per cent in both the 1980 and 1975 sample.

ARR is said to be popular for the following reason:

Businessmen are accustomed to thinking in terms of profit. Accounting profit features in many widely used measures of business performance: for example, earnings per share and return on investment both utilize accounting profit in their calculation. It is therefore argued that an evaluation method which employs profits will be more readily comprehensible to businessmen and investors than, say, discounting methods, which use cash flows.

However, a counter to that argument can be adduced. A project with a high ARR need not necessarily impact favourably on the earnings of a company or division in the short term. Consideration of investment Z illustrates this point. Despite its high ARR, undertaking Z would adversely affect a company's accounting profit for the first 3 years of the project's 4-year life. This may itself lead to confusion if it is assumed that undertaking a project with high ARR, will lead to higher reported profits in the short term.

It is unlikely that businessmen would commonly be misled in this way. The use of ARR may well indicate that a company's management is concerned with maintaining a strong balance sheet position. Such management may well screen projects by rejecting any which do not offer a high ARR in each of the early years of a project's life. The ARR in a particular year is the accounting profit in that year expressed as a percentage of the total (or average) investment. If a project does not offer a satisfactory ARR in its first or second year, its evaluation may be terminated. For example, full consideration of project Z may not take place because its ARR is negative in year 1 (and years 2 and 3). This negative ARR in year 1 arises because the accounting profit in year 1 is negative, being the cash flow of zero minus depreciation.

A policy of only pursuing the evaluation of projects with high ARRs in their early years is both a crude way of dealing with risk and a saving of limiting processing abilities.

Businessmen clearly do find ARR useful, although it is interesting to note that the number of firms using ARR appears to be declining. For example, Pike (1982) found 19 per cent of firms using ARR as their sole evaluation criterion in his 1975 survey; this figure declined to 12 per cent of the firms surveyed in 1980. His 1985 survey, reported in Pike and Wolfe (1988), found that none of the surveyed firms were using ARR as the sole evaluation technique. Despite this trend, ARR remains popular when used in combination with other methods of evaluation.

5.5 Internal rate of return (IRR) (yield)

The IRR of an investment is that rate which when used to discount the cash flows of the investment will result in a net present value of zero.

By setting NPV to zero, and substituting IRR for r, equation 5.1 becomes:

$$NPV = \sum_{t=1}^{T} \frac{C_t}{(1 + IRR)^t} - C_o \qquad \qquad \text{... Equation 5.2}$$

This equation must be solved to find the internal rate of return. Unless the cash flows remain constant throughout a project's life, the solution must be achieved by a process of trial and error. Computer programs are available to carry out this procedure, but for simple examples an approximation can fairly easily be found for projects with conventional cash flows (i.e. those with an initial outflow followed by a stream of net inflows). A methodical trial and error approach can be used by taking the following steps:

Step 1
Establish the NPV of the project at a zero interest rate. If an investment with conventional cash flows is to have a positive IRR, this must be a positive figure.

Step 2
Select a positive discount rate and calculate the NPV of the project at this rate.

Selection of this positive rate should not be entirely random. Consideration of the NPV at a zero discount rate, the life of the investment and the timing of the cash flows, should enable an informed guess to be made as to a discount rate likely to result in an NPV near to zero. For example, at a zero discount rate the NPV of project X is £140 (i.e. £640 − £500), or 28 per cent of the original investment. For project Y the NPV at zero discount rate is £620 (i.e. £1,620 − £1,000), or 62 per cent of the original investment. Both X and Y have a life of 4 years. This is a relatively short project life, and therefore the effects of discounting will not be fiercely felt except at high rates: for example, the value of £1 received in 4 years' time is still almost £0.89 at a 3 per cent rate of discount, but is reduced to only £0.48 if the rate applied is 20%. A 'guesstimate' of IRR might lead to a discount rate of around 14 per cent being tried for both project X and project Y. This is a fairly high discount rate, reflecting the ability of both projects to earn relatively high non-discounted returns on the original investment. The suggestion of the same rate for X and Y, despite the much higher non-discounted return of Y, reflects a consideration of the timing of the cash flows. The flows of X are heavily concentrated in the first 2 years of the project's life. These flows will be affected by discounting to a far smaller extent than the flows of project Y, which occur largely in years 3 and 4. So, despite the disparity in the non-discounted returns of X and Y, a discount rate of 14 per cent appears to be a reasonable starting point. The calculation of the NPV of these two projects at 14 per cent is shown in Table 5.6.

Table 5.6

Year	Discount factor @ 14%	Cash flows (£) X	Cash flows (£) Y	Present value (£) X	Present value (£) Y
0	1.0	− 500	− 1,000	− 500	− 1,000
1	.877	320	10	281	9
2	.769	320	10	246	8
3	.675	10	800	7	540
4	.592	10	800	6	473
				+ 40	+ 30

A positive NPV at this rate shows that both X and Y have an IRR greater than 14 per cent. The size of the NPV also suggests that the IRR of X is likely to be higher than that of Y: as we saw earlier, raising the discount rate will affect the NPV of Y to a much greater extent than that of X, because of the timing of the cash flows.

Step 3

Repeat the process in step 2 for one or more additional discount rates. Sketch the NPV profile and calculate an approximate IRR. Reference back to Table 5.2 shows the NPV of project X and project Y at 16 per cent. The NPV profile of the two projects is shown in Figure 5.3.

Note that the NPV profile is *not* a straight line but a concave curve. An *approximation* to the true IRR can be found by considering the change in NPV between two points near the IRR (so that the linear approximation over this range becomes more accurate).

For project X an increase in the discount rate from 14 per cent to 16 per cent results in a change in NPV of £14 (£40 − £26), i.e. over this range a 2 per cent increase in the discount rate reduces NPV by £14. To reduce the NPV of X to zero, the discount rate must be raised from 16 per cent by an amount sufficient to cause a drop in NPV of £26, i.e. from £26 to £0. An approximation of this required change can be found by assuming linearity of

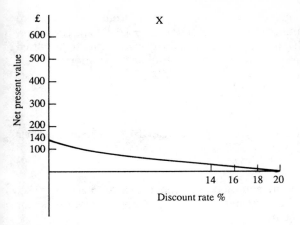

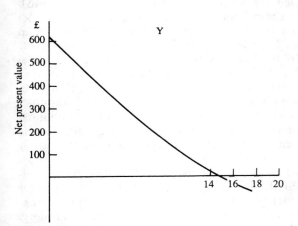

Figure 5.3

the NPV profile. Under this condition, we can calculate the required increase as follows:

$$\text{Change} = \frac{2 \times 26}{14} = 3.714 \text{ per cent}$$

The IRR of X is thus approximately 20 per cent, i.e. 16 per cent + 3.714 per cent.

For project Y, the same increase in the discount rate from 14 per cent to 16 per cent results in a change in the NPV of £59 (£30 − [− £29]). Therefore, to reduce Y's NPV from £30 to zero will require the discount rate to be raised from 14 per cent by an amount determined by a similar calculation:

$$\text{Change} = \frac{2 \times 30}{59} = 1.02 \text{ per cent}$$

The IRR of Y is thus approximately 15 per cent (i.e. 14 per cent + 1.02 per cent).

Step 4
Insert the approximate IRR in equation 5.2 and check for accuracy, i.e. whether NPV is equal to, or very near, zero. If the approximation is not accurate, more trials must be made.

The above procedure will be appropriate for determining the IRR in the overwhelming majority of cases, where cash flows are not constant throughout a project's life. However, occasionally an investment's cash profile might show a single outflow followed by a constant stream of inflows, or an approximation thereto (rental agreements are an obvious example), and under these limited circumstances it is possible to calculate the IRR direct from an inspection of discount tables. In order to do this, it is necessary to calculate the investment/inflow ratio (IIR), which is found by dividing the initial investment by the amount of the annual net cash inflow. The factor derived from this calculation is the mathematical equivalent to an annuity factor in the discount tables. The discount rate which gives this factor as the annuity for a given number of years (the number of years for which the annual net cash inflow in the IIR calculation will be received) *must* be the IRR, as the application of this factor to the annual net cash inflow will give a PV exactly equal to the initial investment, i.e. a NPV of zero.

The decision rule with IRR is to compare the projects IRR with the company's opportunity cost of funds, and accept the project if its IRR is greater than the company's cost of money and reject it if it is not. Given the assumptions that have been made so far, viz; perfect capital markets, certainty, and conventional cash flows, and the additional assumption of independent projects (i.e., no mutually exclusive projects – section 5.5.1), this decision rule would always lead to the selection of the *same* set of projects as the application of the NPV rule.

The decisions in the cases of projects W, X, Y and Z are consistent with this general rule, as Table 5.7 illustrates. However, as we shall see in the next section, conflicts can arise between NPV and IRR when the assumptions are relaxed.

5.5.1   *Mutually exclusive projects*

With perfect capital markets, and thus limitless availability of funds at the going rate of interest, projects are competing against an externally set hurdle of the discount rate. They are not competing against each other for finance.

Table 5.7

	Project			
	W	X	Y	Z
IRR	4%	20%	15%	16%
IRR decisions based on opportunity cost of funds of 5%	Reject	Accept	Accept	Accept
NPV at 5%	−£16	+£112	+£368	+£241
NPV decision	Reject	Accept	Accept	Accept

Nevertheless, some projects may be competitors for non-financial reasons. For example, various options may be put forward by the management of a company for the development of a piece of land which it owns. These options may include developing the land for recreation, development as housing, development as shops or a straightforward sale. All these options are mutually exclusive. Each option requires the use of the land, and the selection of one option automatically precludes the others.

Suppose now that X and Y are mutually exclusive projects. The decision maker must now make a choice *between* them. Looking at IRRs, project X appears to be the better investment, with a yield of 20 per cent as against a yield of only 15 per cent for Y. Perusal of the NPVs gives the opposite view, with project Y being preferred, with an NPV of £368 against an NPV of only £112 for X.

Shareholder wealth would in fact be maximized by following the guidance of NPV. As explained earlier, NPV shows the surplus available from investment after rewarding the suppliers of capital. The greater the surplus, the more beneficial to the shareholders an investment will be. IRR, however, expresses returns not as a surplus but as a rate per pound invested. It takes no account of the scale of a project. Thus £1 invested to return £1.20 in 1 year's time shows the same IRR of 20 per cent as £1 million invested to return £1.2 million in 1 year's time. But the absolute value of the two investments is very different. If the appropriate rate of interest is 5 per cent, then the surplus, i.e. the NPV from the £1 investment, is £1.20/(1.05) − £1.0 = £0.143. The surplus from the investment of £1 million is £1.2M/(1.05) − £1M = £143,000.

The *rate* of return of the two investments is identical, but the surplus wealth created is 1 million times greater with the larger investment. It must be emphasized that with mutually exclusive projects only one investment can be undertaken; acceptance of one automatically precludes the others. The rate per pound invested in such circumstances can thus be a misleading guide.

Project X earns a return of 20 per cent per pound invested on an investment of £500, but acceptance of X means that Y must be rejected, the two projects being mutually exclusive. Acceptance of X also means that the *total* investment of the company will be £500 less than if Y had been accepted, £500 being the difference between the initial investment of £1,000 in Y and £500 in X. Remember it is assumed in our example that funds are freely available at 5 per cent, so that all independent projects will be accepted and financed, provided they earn a return greater than 5 per cent (i.e. they have a positive NPV). The total capital expenditure of the company will thus be the total set of independent investments with positive NPVs, *plus* the chosen projects from any sets of mutually exclusive investments. Choosing the smaller of two mutually exclusive investments is thus the equivalent of rejecting the investment of the additional funds required by the larger investment. The cash flows of the larger investment could in fact be divided into two parts: one part is equal to the flows of the smaller investment and the remainder represents the marginal flows associated with the 'additional' investment. The flows of Y could thus be depicted as $X + (Y - X)$, as shown in Table 5.8.

Table 5.8

Year	Y	=	*Project (£)* [X	+	(Y − X)]
0	− 1,000		− 500		− 500
1	10		320		− 310
2	10		320		− 310
3	800		10		790
4	800		10		790
IRR	15%		20%		14%
NPV (@ 5%)	+£368	=	[+£112		+£256]

From this table it can be seen that rejecting Y in favour of X would not maximize shareholder wealth. Accepting X implies rejection of the notional project $(Y - X)$, which has an IRR of 14 per cent, greatly in excess of the opportunity cost of money, and a positive NPV of £256. The correct decision (i.e. to accept project Y) *could* be made by considering the IRR of X, Y and $(Y - X)$, as we have done here, but is a much more complicated procedure than a simple consideration of the individual projects' NPVs ab initio. IRR is thus more difficult to apply correctly than NPV. A mathematical property of IRR can further complicate its use in the evaluation of mutually exclusive investments, as seen at the end of the next section.

Where mutually exclusive investments have *unequal lives*, consideration must be given to the time period over which a comparison of the investments is to be made. Let us consider two investments, A and B, with cash flows as shown below:

Years	0	1	2
	£	£	£
Project A	− 15,000	+ 10,000	+ 10,000
Project B	− 15,000	+ 18,750	

A comparison of A and B can be based on the cash flows as given. A comparison can also be made over an equal time span for both investments: the lives of A and B can be equalized by assuming that the company can re-invest in another project like B at the end of year 1. The cash flows of two consecutive investments in B would be shown in Table 5.9.

	Years	0 £	1 £	2 £
Project B		− 15,000	+ 18,750	
Project B repeated			− 15,000	+ 18,750
Total cash Flow		− 15,000	+ 3,750	+ 18,750

Table 5.9

The table below shows the NPVs and IRRs of A and B under each of these circumstances.

Basis of calculation	NPV ($r = 5\%$)	IRR
(1) Unadjusted cash flows (i.e. A over 2 years, B over 1 year)	$NPV_A = +3,590$ $NPV_B = +2,857$	21% 25%
(2) Cash flows adjusted to equalize project lives (i.e. A over 2 years B over 2 years)	$NPV_A = +3,590$ $NPV_B = +5,578$	21% 25%

IRR indicates that project B is the superior choice. This conclusion holds good irrespective of the period over which the comparison is made. As the IRR is a *rate* of return per pound invested, it is obvious that that rate will be unchanged by subsequent repetitions of a project; if project B were to be repeated on 100 consecutive occasions, its IRR would remain at 25 per cent. Being an *absolute* value, this does not hold true for NPV. A comparison of the NPVs of A and B under the differing bases illustrates this point: when the lives are unequal, A has the higher NPV; when the lives are equal, B has the higher NPV.

It is not possible to specify whether mutually exclusive investments should be considered over the same time period. Each case must be judged on its merits. The choice is determined by the action the company must take at the termination of the shorter-lived project. If the company is *obliged* to re-invest in similar assets at this point, then the projects should be compared over equal time periods. If, however, there is no presumption that the company will be required, or even able, to act in this way, then comparison over differing lives may be perfectly valid.

Suppose that investments A and B are alternative machines. If it is known that the output from the machine will be required for at least 2 years, then one investment in B will not meet the company's requirements. At the end of year 1, the company will have to make an additional investment to provide the output required in year 2. A and B should therefore be compared over an equal time period, as in calculation 2 above.

Suppose now that A and B represent alternative marketing strategies for a novelty product. Project A represents a low price strategy, while B represents a high price strategy. In charging the high price, the life of the product is limited to 1 year. Clearly the product cannot be relaunched at the end of that time. The options open to the company at the end of year 1 are independent of the strategy adopted in marketing the product. It is thus valid to make a straight comparison of A and B (calculation 1 above) in such circumstances.

When mutually exclusive projects have differing lives, an explicit decision must be taken as to whether it is necessary to equalize the lives before making a comparison. If equalization is *not* required, then a choice should be made on the basis of NPV. If equalization *is* required, the project with the higher NPV should still be chosen, although equalization may alter the ranking of projects, as the example, above illustrates.

5.5.2   Multiple IRRs

Equation 5.2 is a polynomial. Solving for the IRR will lead to a unique solution when the cash flows are conventional, i.e. where there is only one change of sign (usually a cash outflow followed by a stream of inflows). However, there will be as many different IRRs which satisfy the equation as there are changes in the cash flow sign. Thus an investment which as a cash outflow, followed by an inflow, followed by an outflow, has two sign changes and may give rise to two IRRs, as the following example illustrates.

A company is considering staging an event which will require the erection of temporary accommodation and facilities, and their subsequent clearing. The cash flows associated with the project are:

Year	Cash flow (£)
0	− 29,090
1	+ 68,400
2	− 39,940

The company's cost of money is 20 per cent.

This investment has two internal rates of return, as the figures in Table 5.10 show.

Table 5.10

Year	r = 27.15% Flow	r = 27.15%	PV	Year	r = 8% Flow	r = 8%	PV
0	− 29,090	1.0	− 29,090	0	− 29,090	1.0	− 29,090
1	+ 68,400	.78647	+ 53,795	1	+ 68,400	.9259	+ 63,331
2	− 39,940	.61854	− 24,705	2	− 39,940	.8573	− 34,241
		NPV	0			NPV	0

Both IRRs, 8 per cent and 27.15 per cent, are equally valid. Therefore the decision whether or not to accept this investment cannot be made by reference to these rates alone. Again, NPV can be used to give a clear result. At the company's cost of money, the project has a positive NPV of £174, and should therefore be accepted. The NPV profile of the project is sketched in Figure 5.4.

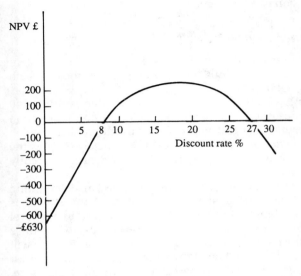

Figure 5.4

Investments with multiple sign changes are uncommon when considering investments in isolation. However, the calculation of flows on incremental projects such as (Y–X) in the previous section may often give rise to frequent sign changes, thus compounding the difficulty of using IRR in these circumstances.

5.5.3 IRR and interest rate changes

For simplicity, we have so far assumed a constant rate of interest. If the interest rate *does* change from period to period, then this changing discount rate can easily be included in the calculation of NPV. The IRR of a project is, however, an *average* return over the project's life. It is not clear whether a project is acceptable if the interest rate is greater than this average for part of the project's life, while being less than it for the remainder.

5.5.4 Popularity of IRR

Surveys consistently find IRR to be a more popular and widely used discounting method than NPV. We have shown that in many circumstances NPV and IRR will lead to the same decisions. However, we have also shown that there are some technical problems in the application of IRR which are absent with NPV. Despite this, businessmen appear to prefer IRR to NPV for two main reasons. First, it is argued that a rate of return, or yield, is an easier concept to grasp than a net present value. Second, it is argued that, in the real world, the opportunity cost of funds, and hence the discount rate, can be difficult to establish. An IRR can be calculated without a discount rate initially being specified, although the IRR must obviously be measured against *some* hurdle before a decision can be made.

5.6   Summary of other techniques v NPV

The use of non-discounting evaluation methods is theoretically inconsistent with an objective of shareholder wealth maximization. Nevertheless, such methods are still widely used in practice.

Two principal discounting methods exist: net present value and internal rate of return. In most cases, these two methods would lead to the selection of the same set of investments, but IRR has some technical problems which make it difficult to apply in certain circumstances. Theoretically, NPV is the best method of investment evaluation. In practice, IRR is used more frequently than NPV.

The NPV model shows the role played by interest rates in determining investment at a macro level. The model shows that total investment is determined by the set of available investment opportunities, and by the level of the interest (i.e. discount) rate. Any increase in interest rates will reduce the number of projects offering positive NPVs, while a reduction in rates will increase the acceptable set of investments. Policy makers know that interest rates can be used as a means of controlling aggregate investment expenditure. If individual firms respond to changes in interest rates in a way consistent with this model, it is not necessary for the behaviour of individual firms to mirror the behaviour theoretically suggested *precisely*. Indeed, we have already seen that their behaviour does not do so. Individual firms do not generally make decisions based on NPV, despite its theoretical benefits.

A possible explanation for this may lie in the divergence between the assumptions of the model and the conditions which firms face in the real world. The assumption of limitless funds at the going interest rate is clearly an abstraction from reality. Decision makers often perceive the supply of investment funds to be limited. Where an apparent lack of funds results in the rejection of some investments which would otherwise have been accepted, a situation of capital rationing is said to exist.

5.7   Capital rationing

Capital rationing can be defined as a situation in which lack of finance prevents a company from accepting all projects with positive NPVs at the going interest rate. Such rationing may be externally or internally imposed. External capital rationing has two main forms. 'Hard' external rationing is a situation in which the market places, or is perceived by the firm to place, an absolute limit on the funds it will supply to the firm in a particular period. 'Soft' rationing exists when the cost of funds to the firm increases as the firm's demand for funds increases: the interest rate to the firm rises simply as a result of the firm's total capital budget increasing, irrespective of the purpose for which funds are required. Divergence between borrowing and lending rates is also a form of 'soft' capital rationing. Clearly, any form of external capital rationing means that the capital market is less than perfect. The existence and importance of long-term *external* capital rationing is the subject of academic debate which lies outside the scope of this book. *Internal* capital rationing undoubtedly exists in many companies.

Whatever its causes, the effect of capital rationing is that projects compete against each other for limited funds, rather than competing only against the externally imposed yardstick of the interest rate.

Internal capital rationing exists when a self-imposed limit is set on a company's total capital expenditure budget. In practice, this limit is often equal to the expenditure which can be internally financed. A number of arguments can be adduced in favour of companies limiting their capital expenditure:

1 The successful implementation of investment projects demands the commitment of considerable management time. Such time is scarce. Limiting the size of the capital spend keeps the executive task of project management within reasonable bounds.
2 By limiting capital expenditure to that which can be financed by internally generated funds, firms can avoid the problems created by real or imagined external capital rationing.
3 The knowledge that investments are competing against *each other* encourages the search for good projects. This may be the case particularly in divisionalized companies, where divisions compete against each other for capital. Note, however, that the idea of a 'search' for good project ideas is not compatible with the basic investment model. The model assumes that all investment opportunities are known, and simply require evaluation. In the real world this is not the case!

Internal rationing is theoretically inconsistent with an objective of wealth maximization, because, by definition, capital rationing is a situation in which some projects whose NPVs are positive when discounted at the going interest rate are nevertheless rejected. However, the explicit and implied assumptions of the simple model – freely available and costless information, ease of project implementation, etc. – are clearly at odds with the reality of the investment environment at a micro level. A decision to limit the size of the capital budget might be a perfectly rational way of reducing complexity to manageable proportions. But the decision rule 'accept all investments with positive NPV at the going interest rate' can no longer be applied. It would lead to the selection of a set of investments which, by definition, the company would be unwilling or unable to finance.

Therefore, under capital rationing, a firm must select a set of investments which can be financed within its limited capital budget. The objective of maximization of shareholder wealth must be modified in these circumstances to maximization of shareholder wealth subject to a capital constraint.

Capital rationing dictates a policy of getting the best return per pound invested. A simple 'rule-of-thumb' method to deal with this situation is to assess projects by means of 'profitability index':

$$\text{Profitability index} = \frac{\text{Present value}}{\text{Initial outlay}}$$

This expresses the present value of a project as a rate per pound invested. Projects are ranked according to their profitability index until funds are exhausted. The profitability indices of W, X, Y and Z are:

W	X	Y	Z
$\dfrac{PV}{IO} = \dfrac{£984}{£1,000} = .984$	$\dfrac{£612}{£500} = 1.224$	$\dfrac{£1,368}{£1,000} = 1.368$	$\dfrac{£741}{£500} = 1.482$

Suppose a company had a capital constraint of £1,500 in period 0. Consideration of the profitability indices would dictate acceptance of projects Z and Y, after which the capital budget would be exhausted. The company would obtain an NPV of £609 from these projects.

Suppose now that the capital constraint is expected to extend beyond period 0, with only £200 being available for investment in period 1. In this case the profitability index would not give the optimal project choice. Considering period 0 and period 1 together, the NPV of the investments could be increased by accepting project X in period 0, in order to use the cash flows from X to finance an investment in Y in period 1. If project Y is divisible, half of Y could be undertaken in period 0 and half in period 1; if Y is not divisible, then the whole project should be deferred to period 1. Table 5.11 shows that the NPV is greater than £609 in both these cases: £703 if Y is non-divisible and £712 if Y can be divided. In fact the profitability index is only optimal when there is a single constraint, such as one period of capital rationing.

The introduction of *any* other constraint for example, mutually exclusive projects or project inter-dependencies – renders the method sub-optimal.

When resources are limited in more than one period, the problem of project choice can be solved by linear programming. The problem outlined above is one of maximizing NPV, subject to capital constraints in two periods. The simplest programs allow project divisibility, so, if x_i is the proportion of the i_{th} project accepted, for projects W, X, Y and Z the problem is:

$$\text{Maximize} - 16x_w + 112x_x + 368x_y + 241x_z$$

Subject to:

Period 0 Capital Constraint $1,500 > 1,000x_w + 500x_x + 1,000x_y + 500x_z$
Period 1 Capital Constraint $200 > -476x_w - 305x_x - 10x_y + 0x_z$

As investment in a project can only be undertaken once, and the amount of the investment cannot be negative, then:

$$0 \leqslant x_i \leqslant 1$$

Table 5.11

	Projects divisible					Non-divisible projects	
Projects accepted Expenditure £	**NPV £**	**Period 0 Expenditure**	**NPV**			**Projects accepted Period 0 £**	**£**
	X	500	112			X	500
112							
	Z	500	241			Z	500
241							
	@ Y	500	184				
353		1,500	537				1,000
Imposed constraint		(1,500)				Available funds	(1,500)
Cash to period 1		0				Cash to period 1	500
		Period 1				**Period 1**	
	@ Y	500	175	(184)		Y	1,000
350	(369)						
1.05				1.05			
Imposed constraint		(200)				Imposed constraint	(200)
Cash flow from X		(305)	(320)			Cash from period 0	(500)
			1.05			Cash flow from X	305
(320)							
1.05							
Cash to period 2		5				Cash flow to period 2	5
Total NPV			712			**Total NPV**	712
705							

Sophisticated computer programs are available to solve linear programs. An obvious refinement is the preclusion of divisible projects, which involves the use of integer programming. Mathematical programming is not widely used in practice. It could be argued that this is because of the expense of running integer programs but a more likely reason is that companies find the input data requirements too onerous. If the company cannot be certain of its future cash flows, it cannot be certain of the results obtained from a program based on its forecasts of those funds. Decision makers might well conclude that equally valid results can be obtained from rule-of-thumb processes.

5.8   Identification of cash flows

The examples given in the text so far have assumed not only that future cash flows are certain, but also that the decision maker has correctly included all the flows which are relevant to a decision, and excluded all others.

Consider a company, Investor Limited, which is contemplating the introduction of a new product, X. A new machine costing £600,000 would have to be bought to manufacture X, but Investor could accommodate all other aspects of the new production, e.g. the requirement for factory and warehouse space, within the company's existing facilities. The machine has an annual capacity of 10,000 units of X, and could be used for 4 years before being scrapped at zero value. Investor sets selling prices for its products on the basis of cost plus calculations. Its accountant has prepared the following standard cost figures to enable a target selling price to be set:

	£
Materials	50.00
Labour:	
Skilled: 10 hrs @ £6 per hour	60.00
Semi-skilled: 10 hrs @ £5 per hour	50.00
Variable overheads:	
20 hrs @ £2 per hour	40.00
Fixed overheads:	
Specific – 20 hrs @ £0.75 per hour	15.00
General – 20 hrs @ £0.75 per hour	15.00
Total	230.00
Target profit margin (30%)	69.00
Target selling price	299.00

The standards have been based on the capacity of the machine, i.e. 10,000 units p.a. The marketing department has located a distributor who would sign a 4-year contract to take all the budgeted production of X at a price of £299.00. The distributor would pay Investor for X annually in arrears, i.e. the first payment would be made 1 year and 1 day after the start of production. Investor holds 1 month's stock of materials, and on average pays its suppliers 1.4 months after delivery.

A trainee accountant has been asked to prepare a cash flow forecast and NPV calculation for the 4 years during which X might be produced. The following additional information has been provided to aid his calculations:

(a) The machine is to be financed by a loan at the going interest rate, i.e. 10 per cent p.a. The company will thus pay annual interest charges of £60,000 on the loan.

(b) The company allocates fixed overheads on the basis of direct labour hours. The general overheads represent allocations of the company's existing fixed overheads to product X. The specific fixed overhead charge is an allocation, on a straight-line basis, of the depreciation of the new machine over its 4-year life.

(c) Skilled labour is in short supply. During the first year of X's production, skilled labour would have to be diverted from existing products. Currently, the average cash contribution generated per skilled labour hour is £3.50. Skilled labour could be made available for the remaining 3 years of X's production by carrying out a recruitment and training programme during the first year. This programme would entail a one-off cost of £1,000,000, and, if undertaken, would enable the diverted labour to return to its usual work after 1 year of producing X.

(d) The current rates of corporation tax are 35 per cent on taxable profits over £750,000, 25 per cent on taxable profits below £150,000, and a sliding scale for profits in between these levels. Plant attracts an annual writing-down allowance of 25 per cent of cost or written-down value.

(e) All prices are expected to be stable over the next 5 years, i.e. there is no inflation.

The trainee accountant produces the following figures and notes:

Proposed investment in production of product X

Notes

1   *Skilled labour*

(i)   This is a scarce resource to the company. If labour is to be moved from one area of production to another, it is necessary to ensure that the contribution earned on the new production is at least equal to that which would have been earned elsewhere. Accordingly, the contribution foregone by switching skilled labour to the production of X has been included as a cost of X.

(ii)   The option to recruit and train new labour has been rejected on the grounds that the cost of recruitment and training exceeds the discounted value of the expected benefits. See calculation below.

Year		£	r = 10%	PV
				£
1 Training cost		1,000,000	.909	− 909,000
2 Additional cash contribution				
	10 × 10,000 × £3.50	350,000 ⎫		
3	,, ,,	350,000 ⎬ 2.261		+ 791,350
4	,, ,,	350,000 ⎭		
		NPV		− 117,650

2   *Taxation.* This has been ignored, because of the difficulty in establishing the rate of tax applicable to Investor Limited. Over the last decade, Investor limited has sometimes paid tax at the small company rate, sometimes at the marginal rate, and at times has had no taxable profit.

3   *General fixed overheads.* These have been excluded from the cost of production, as they are not related to product X, and will be incurred whether or not product X is manufactured.

Calculation of NPV

	£	£
Annual cash outflow		
Unit cost of production per standard cost	230.00	
Less general fixed overheads (see note 1)	15.00	
Unit cost directly attributable to production of X	215.00	

Total annual production cost	
£215 × 10,000	2,150,000
Plus: opportunity cost of using	
skilled labour (see note 2)	
10 × 10,000 × £3.50	350,000
Interest payment on loan used to finance	
machine purchase	60,000
Total annual cash outflow (Years 1–4)	2,560,000

Other cash flows

Purchase of machine (Year 0)	£ 600,000

Annual cash inflow

Payment from distributor		
in arrears (Years 2–5)	10,000 × £299	2,990,000

Calculation of NPV

Year	Cash outflow (£)	Cash Inflow (£)	r = 10%	PV(£)
0	− 600,000	–	1.0	− 600,000
1	− 2,560,000	–	.909	− 2,327,040
2	− 2,560,000	+ 2,990,000	.826	+ 355,180
3	− 2,560,000	+ 2,990,000	.751	+ 322,930
4	− 2,560,000	+ 2,990,000	.683	+ 293,690
5		+ 2,990,000	.621	+ 1,856,790
			NPV	− 98,450

Recommendation prepared by the trainee accountant: Do not purchase the machine to manufacture X.

Consideration of these calculations and notes illustrates a number of points. *Treatment of overhead allocations.* The specific fixed overhead has been included as part of the cost of product X. However, the whole of the specific fixed overhead is the depreciation of the machine (annual cost £15 × 10,000 = £150,000; cost over 4 years £150,000 × 4 = £600,000). Depreciation is *not* a cash flow; it is simply a book allocation of the original cost of £600,000. In the calculation of NPV, the cash flow associated with purchasing the machine has been correctly identified as a year zero cash outflow. To include depreciation also as a cash flow double counts the cost of an asset, and is always an error.

The exclusion of the general fixed overhead from the calculation is correct on the basis of the information given. However, in the long run, *all* costs are variable. It may be perfectly true to say that the fixed costs would initially be unaltered by the introduction of product X, but it might also be true to say that, if product X were *not* introduced, the level of fixed overheads could be reduced at some point over the 4-year period. Certainly, the longer the lifespan of an investment, the more likely it is that the investment will have a direct bearing on the future level of fixed costs of the business. Care must be taken not to apply the rules of short-term decision making to long-term situations. Identifying the increase or decrease in fixed costs over time with specific projects will always entail an element of judgement. Nevertheless, it is a truism to state that, in the long run, if a company made no investments, it would ultimately cease to exist, and therefore would have no fixed costs. By excluding all fixed costs it is also true to say that a company may be in danger of accepting projects which do not have a genuinely positive NPV. If such projects are accepted in significant numbers, the company would find itself making losses, and ultimately might be forced out of business. When establishing cash flows therefore, decision makers should pay particular attention to the identification of costs which are fixed in the short run but variable in the long run.

Alternatively, it may be argued that this last point is covered in practice by only accepting projects with significantly positive NPVs. In theory, an NPV of £1 is sufficient to justify an investment of £1M, but in reality, decision makers would reject such a marginal investment. In demanding a positive NPV from all projects, a company should ensure that it covers all its unallocated fixed costs.

Treatment of opportunity costs. When a resource is scarce, an implicit or explicit comparison must be made of the returns available from its use in alternative situations. An explicit comparison can be made by calculating the returns available from each alternative use, the highest return being selected as the basis for the chosen course of action. Alternatively, the return foregone on the best alternative course of action can be included as an implicit cost of any new proposal. If the new proposal can offer a positive return even when this additional cost is included, then it offers a return in excess of existing alternatives and should be accepted. In the example above, the inclusion of the contribution, earned on existing work as a cost, or negative cash flow, of the new alternative is correct. Skilled labour is a scarce resource, and its use of X implies a necessity, not only for the production of X to be profitable, but also for it to be more profitable than the existing work for each unit of that scarce resource.

The suggestion by the trainee that new skilled labour should not be recruited requires further discussion. On the basis of the information provided, the proposition that the investment in recruitment and training has a negative NPV is correct. However, even a small additional cash contribution by this newly trained workforce beyond year 4 would change the position. We should consider whether the labour could be used on other projects after X to earn a positive contribution. Assume, given the certain world with which we are dealing, that it would in fact be used on other projects after year 4, and could earn a further contribution of £350,000 per year for 2 years. In this case, it is clear that the training and recruitment programme should be undertaken. In the real world, it may be very difficult to predict the opportunities available to the company after the demise of X. A qualitative, rather than a purely quantitative, approach may be appropriate in this situation. If the evaluation of X takes place on the assumption that the training programme will go ahead, the basic NPV calculation must obviously be accompanied by a narrative. This narrative would include an explanation that the investment in X will provide not only the benefits quantified but, because it increases the size of the skilled workforce, it would also furnish the company with a better base from which to exploit opportunities at the end of X's life.

Taxation. An apparently simple question, such as 'What is the rate of tax applicable to the profits of an investment?', can rarely be answered unequivocally. In the UK, the corporation tax rate may vary from zero, for a company with large accumulated tax losses, to the current maximum of 35 per cent, where taxable profits exceed £1,000,000. Obviously, the actual rate payable is dependent on the outcome of *all* the company's activities, and not just the investment in question. When taxation is introduced therefore, it is impossible to look at investments individually.

Taxation also impacts on the net value of payments made by companies to the suppliers of investment funds. Again, this impact is not uniform, with debt being more favourably treated than equity (see Section 7.2).

Interest costs. The return required from a project by the suppliers of finance is given by the discount rate. A positive NPV shows that the costs of finance are covered and a surplus earned. The inclusion of an additional cash flow representing the specific interest cost of an investment thus constitutes a double counting of financing costs. The interest charges on the loan in the example above should have been excluded from the cash flow calculation.

Working capital. Undertaking an investment often alters the working capital requirements of a business. Such changes have cash flow implications, and care must be taken to include these changes in cash flow forecasts.

In the example above, the investment in X gives rise to an increase in the company's stocks. However, in this case the increase is financed by creditors, the credit period of 1.4 months being longer than the average stockholding period of 1 month. By the end of the first year, the company will have taken delivery of 13 months' supply of material: the initial buffer stock of 1 month, plus material for 12 months' production. Twelve months' supplies will have been paid for, with 1 month's delivery outstanding at the year end. In this case, the material cost included in the cost of production, actually equals the cash flow cost to the business. Obviously, payments are made to the supplier throughout the year, not simply at the year end, and a strictly accurate present value can only be found if they are discounted by the rate appropriate to the actual date on which the payments are made. Conventionally, the discount rate used in NPV calculations represents the present value of £1 received or paid at the *end* of a particular year. However, the inaccuracy introduced by using a year-end rate in cases such as this is not normally serious enough to warrant the use of a range of rates.

Cash receipts will not usually coincide with forecasts of accounting revenues. The latter will normally exceed cash inflows in the early years of a project's life, because of the growth in the level of year-end debtors as sales levels build up to their peak. Furthermore, cash from debtors will usually be received throughout the year. Nevertheless, the assumption implicit in the use of a year-end discount rate, i.e. that all cash is received at the year end, is normally made in the case of debtors, in the same way (and using the same argument) as we saw with suppliers.

In our particular example, settlement for X is by a single annual payment received 1 day after the anniversary of the start of the project. Chronologically the first payment falls in year 2. However, as the payment is received on day

1 of year 2, its present value is more accurately measured by using the year 1 discount factor, representing the value at the *end* of year 1, rather than that for year 2. The cash inflows would thus be more realistically stated by including each of them 1 year earlier than shown on the trainee's report.

A revised cash flow forecast and NPV calculation for project X, which incorporates all the above points, is shown below.

Proposed investment in production of product X

Annual cash outflow

	£	£
Unit cost of production per standard cost	230.00	
Less: specific fixed overheads	15.00	
Less: general fixed overheads	15.00	
Unit cost directly attributable to production of X	200.00	
Total annual production cost	200 × 10,000	2,000,000
Total annual cash outflow (years 1–4)		2,000,000

Other cash outflows

	£
Purchase of machine (Year 0)	600,000
Investment in recruitment and training (Year 1)	1,000,000
Opportunity cost of using skilled labour (Year 1) 10 × 10,000 × £3.50	350,000

Cash inflows

	£
Payment from distributor in arrears 10,000 × £299	2,990,000

Calculation of NPV

Year	Cash outflow (£)	Cash Inflow (£)	$r = 10\%$	PV (£)
0	− 600,000	–	1.0	− 600,000
1	− 3,350,000	2,990,000	.909	− 327,240
2	− 2,000,000	2,990,000	.826	+ 817,740
3	− 2,000,000	2,990,000	.751	+ 743,490
4	− 2,000,000	2,990,000	.683	+ 676,170
			NPV	+ 1,310,160

Notes

1 This calculation has assumed that the company will invest in recruitment and training. The life of X is not sufficiently long to enable the full cost of this investment to be recouped. Although the NPV of an investment in X would have been £117,650 higher ([£350,000 × 2.261] − [£1,000,000 × .909]) if the option to switch labour from existing production had been adopted in preference to the training option, the latter

course provides the company with an additional pool of skilled labour for use on other projects after the production of X has terminated.

2   Taxation has been ignored in this calculation.

Consideration of this example illustrates the importance of ensuring that the correct cash flow figures are used.

References and further reading

Aggarwal, R. 'Corporate Use of Sophisticated Capital Budgeting Techniques: A Strategic Perspective and a Critique of Survey Results', *Interfaces*, April 1980.

Bradley, S. P., Frey, C. S. Jr, 'Equivalent Mathematical Programming Models of Pure Capital Rationing', *Journal of Financial and Quantitative Analysis*, June 1978.

Capettini, R., Grimlund, R. A., Toole, H. R., 'Comment: The Unique Real Internal Rate of Return', *Journal of Financial and Quantitative Analysis*, December 1979.

Emery, G. W., 'Some Guidelines for Evaluating Capital Investment Alternatives with Unequal Lives', *Financial Management*, Spring 1982.

Gordon, L. A., 'Further Thoughts on the Accounting Rate of Return vs. the Economic Rate of Return', *Journal of Business Finance and Accounting*, Spring 1977.

Hirschleifer, J. (1958), 'On the Theory of Optimal Investment Decision', *Journal of Political Economy*, Vol. 66, pp. 329–72.

McIntyre, A., Coulthurst, N., 'The planning and control of capital in medium sized companies', *Management Accounting*, March 1987.

Pike, R. H. *Capital Budgeting in the 1980's*, CIMA, 1982.

Pike, R. H., Wolfe, M. B., *Capital budgeting for the 1990's*, CIMA, 1988.

Statman, M., 'The Persistence of the Payback Method: A Principal–Agent Perspective', *Engineering Economist*, Winter 1982.

Weingartner, H. M., *Mathematical Programming and the Analysis of Capital Budgeting Problems*, Englewood Cliffs NJ: Prentice–Hall, 1963.

Weingartner, H. M., 'Capital Rationing: n Authors in Search of a Plot', *Journal of Finance*, December 1977.

6 Investments in a risky world

6.1 Introduction

In the real world, present resources are usually committed in the expectation, rather than the certainty, of future returns, i.e. investments are subject to risk. As previously stated, risk refers to a situation in which a range of outcomes, rather than a single certain outcome, is possible.

When investment decisions are risky, a manager must incorporate into his decision process the attitudes of his shareholders towards risk as well as their time preferences, if he is to act in their best interests. On the face of it this seems an impossible task, given the diversity among shareholders in most companies. However, a model which seeks to establish a market price for risk, i.e. to specify the return required from a share given its risk, has been developed. The model is the capital asset pricing model (CAPM). It was originally developed for the analysis of financial assets, such as shares, but it can be extended to include real assets. If CAPM holds, then a purchase of shares in any company signifies a shareholder's willingness to accept the market risk/return trade-off. A manager can therefore use this externally set yardstick of required return in much the same way as the interest rate is used in a risk-free world: a project offering an expected return greater than the market return, given its level of risk, is acceptable; a project offering a lower expected return should be rejected.

To fully appreciate the significance and limitations of this theory, it is necessary to give an explanation of CAPM. This model, which builds on earlier work by Harry Markowitz (1952) on portfolio theory is discussed below.

6.2 Portfolio theory

Portfolio theory is a single-period model, which is concerned with the selection of financial assets that are subject to risk. Investors are assumed to be risk-averse, and to make decisions based on the distribution of an investment's expected returns. Markowitz assumed that investors' decisions were based on two parameters only: the expected return from an investment, and the variance, or standard deviation of this expected return.

Where returns are normally distributed, it is perfectly acceptable to consider only the mean and standard deviation, which will completely define the distribution of such returns. The mean, or expected value, of any distribution is given by:

$$E(x) = \sum_{i=1}^{n} p_i x_i \qquad \qquad \text{... Equation 6.1}$$

where E(x) = expected value of x,
  x_i = i_{th} possible outcome of the value of x,
  p_i = probability of i_{th} possible outcome.
  n   = number of possible outcomes.

The variance of a distribution, $\sigma^2(x)$ is given by:

$$\sigma^2(x) = \sum_{i=1}^{n} p_i (x_i - E(x))^2 \qquad \qquad \text{... Equation 6.2}$$

The standard deviation of a distribution is simply the positive square root of the variance.

Portfolio theory considers how investors can construct 'efficient' portfolios of investments. Given the assumption that investors are concerned only with the expected value and variance of their portfolios, an efficient portfolio is one which offers the maximum possible expected return for a given level of risk (as measured by the portfolio variance) or the minimum level of risk for a given level of expected return. The principles of portfolio building will be illustrated by considering the following investments, A and B. Each investment has an initial outlay of £1,000, and a range of outcomes is possible. These outcomes and their associated probabilities are shown below:

A		B	
x_i	p_i	x_i	p_i
£		£	
979.29	0.25	625.403	0.3
1,050.00	0.5	1,400.000	0.4
1,120.71	0.25	2,174.597	0.3

The expected values and variances of these investments are:

E(A) = 0.25 × £979.29 + 0.5 × £1,050 + 0.25 × £1,120.71 = £1,050
E(B) = 0.3 × £625.403 + 0.4 × £1,400 + 0.3 × £2,174.597 = £1,400
σ_A^2 = 0.25(979.29 − 1,050)² + 0.5(1,050 − 1,050)² + 0.25(1,120.71 − 1,050)²
    = 2,500
σ_A = £50
σ_B^2 = 0.3(625.403 − 1,400)² + 0.4(1,400 − 1,400)² + 0.3(2,174.597 − 1,400)²
    = 360,000
σ_B = £600

Investment A thus offers an expected value of £1,050, with a standard deviation of £50; B has an expected value of £1,400 with a standard deviation of £600.

Based on the original investment of £1,000, the rate of return offered by A is 5 per cent, with 5 per cent standard deviation; the return on B is 40 per cent, with a 60 per cent standard deviation. If A and B are divisible, these returns are not the only ones available to investors. By spreading their investment *between* A and B, investors can construct portfolios offering any expected return between 5 per cent and 40 per cent.

The expected value of any portfolio is simply the expected value of each component part of the portfolio, multiplied by the fraction of the total funds devoted to this component part, i.e.:

$$E(P_n) = \sum_{i=1}^{n} E(N)P_i \qquad \ldots \text{Equation } 6.3$$

where $E(N)$ = expected value of n th asset,

$E(P_n)$ = expected value of a portfolio of N assets,

P_i = fraction of that portfolio devoted to i_{th} asset $(\sum_{i=1}^{n} P_i = 1)$.

For example, if £1,000 is invested in a two-asset portfolio, consisting of £500 in A and £500 in B, the expected value of this portfolio is:

$$E_{(A+B)} = 0.5\ E(A) + 0.5\ E(B) = 0.5 \times £1,050 + 0.5 \times £1,400 = £1,225$$

The expected rate of return on the portfolio will be 22.5 per cent. If portfolio returns are expressed as percentages of the original investment, then:

$$E(r_p) = \sum_{i=1}^{n} E(r_i)P_i \qquad \ldots \text{Equation } 6.4$$

where $E(r_p)$ = expected rate of return on portfolio p,

$E(r_i)$ = expected rate of return on i_{th} asset in portfolio,

P_i = fraction of total portfolio devoted to i_{th} asset.

n = number of assets in portfolio.

Thus the expected return on a portfolio 50 per cent invested in A and 50 per cent in B is

$$\begin{aligned} E(r_{(A+B)}) &= 0.5E(r_A) + 0.5E(r_B) \\ &= 0.5 \times 5\% + 0.5 \times 40\% \\ &= 22.5\% \end{aligned}$$

as we saw above.

As the expected returns on A and B are constant, it can be seen that the expected return on the portfolio can be changed to any desired level between 5 per cent (total investment in A) and 40 per cent (total investment in B), by altering the balance of investment between A and B.

The expected return on a portfolio is thus a function of:
1   The expected return on the individual portfolio assets.
2   The allocation of portfolio funds between the individual portfolio assets.

Altering the allocation of funds in a portfolio between individual assets will not only change the expected return on the portfolio, but also the variance or risk of the portfolio. The variance of a portfolio is given by:

$$\sum_{i=1}^{n} P_i X_i = \sum_{i=1}^{n} P_i^2 \sigma_i^2 + 2 \sum_{i=1}^{n-1} \sum_{j=i+1}^{n} P_i P_j \text{Cov} (X_i X_j)$$

where: n   = number of assets in portfolio.
            P_i = fraction of total portfolio invested in i_{th} asset
            P_j = fraction of portfolio devoted to j_{th} asset
            X_i = i_{th} asset in portfolio
            X_j = j_{th} asset in portfolio
            σ_i^2 = variance of i_{th} asset
            Cov $(X_i X_j)$ = covariance of X_i and X_j

The variance of a two-asset portfolio consisting of assets A and B, and P_a invested in A and P_b invested in B, and $P_a + P_b = 1$, is:

$$\text{Var} (P_a A + P_b B) = P_a^2 \sigma_a^2 + P_b^2 \sigma_b^2 + 2 P_a P_b \text{Cov} (A,B)$$
                                                                        ... Equation 6.6

The portfolio variance is thus a function of:
1   The variance of the individual portfolio assets.
2   The allocation of portfolio funds between the individual portfolio assets.
3   The covariance between the individual portfolio assets.

The covariance of two random variables A and B may be defined as:

$$\text{Cov} (A,B) = E((A_i - E(A)) (B_i - E(B)))   \text{... Equation 6.7}$$

If E(A) and E(B) are superimposed on any diagram showing observations of two random variables A and B in response to an event, then the observations will fall in one of four quadrants, as shown below.

Value A	1	2	
	$A_i - E(A) + ve$	$A_i - E(A) + ve$	
	$B_i - E(B) - ve$	$B_i - E(B) + ve$	
			E(A)
	3	4	
	$A_i - E(A) - ve$	$A_i - E(A) - ve$	
	$B_i - E(B) - ve$	$B_i - E(B) + ve$	
	E(B)	Value B	

The product of $(A_i - E(A))$ and $(B_i - E(B))$ is positive in quadrants 2 and 3, and negative in quadrants 1 and 4.

    Figure 6.1 illustrates this point, showing observations of A and B which have a positive covariance (diagram a), a negative covariance (diagram b) and zero covariance (diagram c).

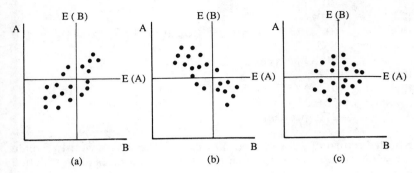

Figure 6.1

The covariance is a simple measure of how two random variables react to events or move together. However, the resulting figure often conveys little meaning to the non-statistician, as the size of the covariance is affected by the scale used to measure the variables. The correlation coefficient, ρ, also measures the movement of two random variables in response to events, but the correlation coefficient is invariant to scale, and can take values only between (and including) ± 1. The correlation coefficient is obtained by dividing the covariance by the product of the standard deviations of the two variables, i.e.:

$$\rho_{ab} = \frac{\text{Cov (A,B)}}{\sigma_a \, \sigma_B} \qquad \dots \text{Equation 6.8}$$

$$\text{Cov (A,B)} = \sigma_a \sigma_B \, \rho_{ab}$$

Substituting this term in Equation 6.6, the variance of a two-asset portfolio can be given by:

$$\text{Var} (P_a A + P_b B) = P_a^2 \sigma_a^2 + P_b^2 \sigma_b^2 + 2 P_a P_b \sigma_a \sigma_b \rho_{ab}$$
$$\dots \text{Equation 6.9}$$

Using this formula, we can calculate the variance and standard deviation of the two-asset portfolio – 50 per cent A and 50 per cent B – described above, using different values for the correlation coefficient.

(1)   If $\rho_{ab} = +1$
     then $\sigma^2_{ab} = ((0.5^2) \, (5^2) + (0.5^2) \, (60^2) + 2 \, (0.5) \, (0.5) \, (5) \, (60) \, (1)$
           $\sigma^2_{ab} = 1056.25$
           $\sigma_{ab} = 32.5$ per cent

(2)   If $\rho_{ab} = 0.5$
     then $\sigma^2_{ab} = (0.5^2) \, (5^2) + (0.5^2) \, (60^2) + 2 \, (0.5) \, (0.5) \, (5) \, (60) \, (0.5)$
           $\sigma^2_{ab} = 981.25$
           $\sigma_{ab} = 31.37$ per cent

(3)   If $\rho_{ab} = 0$
      then $\sigma^2_{ab} = (0.5^2)\,(0.5^2) + (0.5^2)\,(60^2) + 2\,(0.5)\,(0.5)\,(5)\,(60)\,(0)$
               $\sigma^2_{ab} = 906.25$
               $\sigma_{ab} = 30.1$ per cent
(4)   If $\rho_{ab} = -0.5$
      then $\sigma^2_{ab} = (0.5^2)\,(5^2) + (0.5^2)\,(60^2) + 2\,(0.5)\,(0.5)\,(5)\,(60)\,(-0.5)$
               $\sigma^2_{ab} = 831.25$
               $\sigma_{ab} = 28.83$ per cent
(5)   If $\rho_{ab} = -1$
      then $\sigma^2_{ab} = (0.5^2)\,(5^2) + (0.5^2)\,(60^2) + 2\,(0.5)\,(0.5)\,(5)\,(60)\,(-1)$
               $\sigma^2_{ab} = 756.25$
               $\sigma_{ab} = 27.5$ per cent

The expected return of 22.5 per cent in this portfolio will obviously remain constant whatever assumption is made about the magnitude of the correlation coefficient.

Figure 6.2 illustrates the relation between risk and return from our two-asset portfolio of A and B, under differing values of their correlation coefficient.

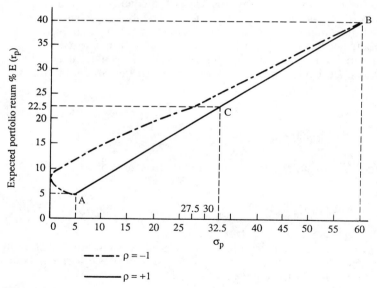

Figure 6.2

If can be seen that the risk/return relation is given by a straight line joining A and B when the returns on the assets are perfectly positively correlated. For any other level of correlation, A and B can be combined in portfolios with risk/return opportunities concave to the line. The further the correlation moves from $+1$, the more concave the risk/return relation becomes. The reader may also note that, for certain values of σ, portfolios of A and B can be constructed which have a *lower* degree of risk than an investment in A alone, despite the risk of B being much higher than that of A. This result is intuitively accessible when correlations between A and B are negative, i.e. a good outcome for A is associated with a bad outcome for B.

In this situation, the range or standard deviation of possible outcomes is reduced by combination. However, this result is not confined to situations in which ρ_{ab} is negative. For any two assets, A and B, where $\sigma_B > \sigma_A$ a portfolio of A and B can be created whose standard deviation is less than that of A alone for all values of ρ less than σ_a/σ_b. As standard deviations are positive, and $\sigma_B > \sigma_A$ then σ_A/σ_B must always be a positive fraction. In our particular example, $\sigma_a/\sigma_B = 5/60 = 0.083$. Thus for positive correlations between A and B up to 0.083, a portfolio of A and B can be created which offers a higher expected return than A alone for a *lower* level of risk – a combination which is unequivocally superior to an investment in A alone. This illustrates the benefits of combination.

Other individual assets may also exist which lie on the straight line connecting A and B. For example, consider asset C, whose expected return is 22.5 per cent, with a standard deviation of 32.5 per cent. The expected return on this asset is equal to the expected return on a portfolio of 50 per cent A and 50 per cent B, as seen above. The standard deviation of asset C equals the standard deviation of the portfolio of 50 per cent A, 50 per cent B, *if* the correlation coefficient of A and B is $+1$. For any degree of correlation of A and B *less* than 1 the expected return is still 22.5 per cent, being independent of the correlation, but the standard deviation of the portfolio is less than 32.5 per cent.

Faced with the choice between an investment in C, and an investment in this portfolio of A and B, a rational risk-averse investor would always prefer the portfolio, except in the situation where returns on A and B are perfectly positively correlated. With perfect positive correlation, the investor would be indifferent between a portfolio of A and B, or an investment in C, as both offer the same expected return with the same degree of risk. The preference for the portfolio in all cases other than that of perfect positive correlation between A and B arises because the portfolio offers the same expected return as C, but the standard deviation of this return is less than that of C. Consideration of the calculations and Figure 6.2 above illustrates this point. For all correlations other than $+1$, an investor can build a portfolio of A and B which, compared to an asset lying on the line connecting A and B, either

(a) offers a lower level of standard deviation for a given level of expected return, or
(b) offers a higher level of expected return for a given standard deviation.

This is the essence of portfolio building. A combination of assets improves the available risk/return trade-off open to investors, except in the limiting case of perfect positive correlation between the asset returns, when the combination would be neutral to this trade-off. There is *no* relation between assets that can lead to the return/risk trade-off being worsened through combination. In the two-asset case illustrated above, combinations of A and B either offer a risk/return trade-off better than that offered by individual assets lying on the line A, B (i.e. the returns available are shown by a concave curve to the left of the line connecting A and B), or they offer the same trade-off as A, B. No combinations offer returns to the right of line A, B.

As the number of assets in a portfolio increases, the principle that the addition of an asset either improves the risk/return trade-off, or is neutral to it, remains good. For example, consider a portfolio consisting of A, B and C. For simplicity, this will be illustrated on the basis of a two-asset portfolio, the original portfolio of 50 per cent A and 50 per cent B constituting one asset, and C the other.

Suppose this new portfolio is created with 50 per cent of the funds being invested in C, and 50 per cent in the portfolio of A and B. The expected return on this portfolio is:

$$E(r_p) = 0.5 \times 22.5\% + 0.5 \times 22.5\% = 22.5\%$$

The standard deviation of the portfolio depends on the correlation coefficient between the return on the portfolio of A and B, and that of C. This variance is calculated below, with differing assumptions regarding the correlation.

(1) If $\rho_{(a+b)c} = +1$

   then $\sigma^2_{(a+b)c} = (.5^2)(32.5^2) + (.5^2)(32.5^2)$
   $+ 2(.5)(.5)32.5(32.5)(1)$
   $= 1,056.25$

   $\sigma_{(a+b)c} = 32.5$ per cent

(2) If $\rho_{(a+b)c} = +.5$

   then $\sigma^2_{(a+b)c} = (.5^2)(32.5^2) + (.5^2)(32.5^2)$
   $+ 2(.5)(.5)(32.5)(32.5)(.5)$
   $= 792.1875$

   $\sigma_{(a+b)c} = 28.15$ per cent

(3) If $\rho_{(a+b)c} = 0$

   then $\sigma^2_{(a+b)c} = (.5^2)(32.5^2) + (.5^2)(32.5^2)$
   $+ 2(.5)(.5)(32.5)(32.5)(0)$
   $= 528.125$

   $\sigma_{(a+b)c} = 22.98$ per cent

(4) If $\rho_{(a+b)c} = -.5$

   then $\sigma^2_{(a+b)c} = (.5^2)(32.5^2) + (.5^2)(32.5^2)$
   $+ 2(.5)(.5)(32.5)(32.5)(-.5)$
   $= 264.0625$

   $\sigma_{(a+b)c} = 16.25$ per cent

(5) If $\rho_{(a+b)c} = -1$

   then $\sigma^2_{(a+b)c} = (.5^2)(32.5^2) + (.5^2)(32.5^2)$
   $+ 2(.5)(.5)(32.5)(32.5)(-1)$
   $= 0$

   $\sigma_{(a+b)c} = 0$

Table 6.1 summarizes the variances on the original portfolio of A and B, and the new portfolio with half the funds in (A + B) and half in C.

The summary clearly shows that, for a given expected return, the addition

Table 6.1

ρ	$\sigma\,(A+B)$	$\sigma\,(A+B)\,C$
1	32.5	32.5
.5	31.3	28.15
0	30.1	22.98
−.5	28.83	16.25
−1	27.5	0

of another asset reduces the standard deviation of the return, except where the returns on the assets are perfectly positively correlated.

As more and more assets are added to a portfolio, the curve showing the limit of available risk reduction for given returns is pushed further and further to the left. Given the assumption that all assets are divisible, and there are no transaction costs, the choice available to investors would be bounded by the curve joining the asset with the lowest standard deviation to the asset with the highest standard deviation, taken in this case to be A and B respectively. Portfolios on this frontier would contain differing proportions of all available financial assets.

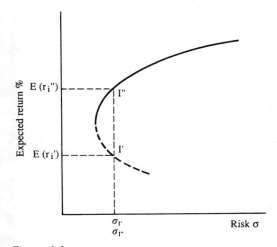

Figure 6.3

All areas bounded by the curve and the broken part of the curve in Figure 6.3 represent inefficient portfolios, i.e. portfolios which do not offer the maximum possible expected return for a given level of risk. Investors wishing to accept levels of risk associated with the broken part of the curve should build portfolios represented by the efficient frontier vertically above the desired risk level, as they will obtain a higher level of expected return, without increasing their level of risk. For example, a portfolio represented by I′ has the same standard deviation as a portfolio represented by I″. For this same level of risk, the expected return is only $E(r'_i)$ for portfolio I', but is $E(r''_i)$ for portfolio I''. As $E(r''_i)$ is in excess of $E(r'_i)$, portfolio I'' is preferable to portfolio I'. The efficient frontier represents the best possible risk/return trade-off.

For ease of exposition, the principles of portfolio analysis have been illustrated by a two asset portfolio. However, the efficient frontier theoretically contains *all* financial assets. Inspection of equation 6.5 will show that, as the number of assets in the portfolio increases, the contribution to the portfolio variance of the individual asset variance declines, relative to the contribution of the relation *between* the portfolio assets, i.e. the covariance terms. For example, in a two-asset portfolio of A and B, only the relation between A and B needs to be considered, in addition to the individual variances of A and B. Addition of another asset, C, to the portfolio trebles the number of relevant inter-relations, i.e. the covariance or correlation of A and C, and B and C, must now be included in the calculation of the portfolio variance, in addition to the covariance of A and B. The variance of a portfolio containing n assets is calculated by including n terms relating to the individual asset variances, and $(n^2 - n)/2$ terms to the relation *between* the assets. As n increases, the importance of the individual asset variances in determining the total portfolio variance decreases rapidly, while the covariance of the assets becomes increasingly important, as Table 6.2 shows.

Table 6.2

Number of assets in portfolio	Number of individual variances (n)	Number of covariance/correlation terms $(n^2 - n)/2$
2	2	1
3	3	3
4	4	6
5	5	10
10	10	45
20	20	190
50	50	1,225
100	100	4,950

It was shown earlier that, where a new asset is merely substituted for part of an existing portfolio holding, i.e. where the *size* of the portfolio remains constant but the *mix* changes, a decline in the portfolio variance is *not* dependent on negative correlations between the existing and new assets. Let us now turn to the addition of an asset with *no* consequent alteration in the holdings of other assets, i.e. to an increase in the absolute *size* of the portfolio.

Such an addition can also reduce the total portfolio variance, if the returns on the additional asset are negatively correlated with the returns on some or all of the existing portfolio assets. When the negative covariance terms introduced by the new asset are sufficiently large or numerous to outweigh the positive covariances, together with the individual variance of the new asset, the portfolio variance will decline.

6.3   The capital asset pricing model

In general, it is unlikely that the returns on financial assets will be negatively correlated. Economy-wide factors, such as the level of interest rates, general level of demand, exchange rates, etc. will affect all companies to some extent. Therefore the returns on financial assets will tend to be positively correlated. Nevertheless, there are specific factors associated with some assets which cause the returns on them to be negatively correlated with the returns on other assets, if the effects of economy-wide factors are excluded from the analysis. For example, company X manufactures and sells ice cream. The returns on this activity will obviously be affected by some or all of the economy-wide factors mentioned above, but they will also be heavily dependent on the weather. Company Y is engaged in the manufacture and sale of umbrellas. Like X, the company is affected by economy-wide factors, but its returns are also affected by the weather. Hot and dry weather is good for X and bad for Y, while cold and wet weather is good for Y but not for X. By holding both X and Y in a portfolio, the variability of returns due to the weather is eliminated.

In CAPM, a distinction is made between the variability of outcomes brought about by company-specific, i.e. asset-specific, risks, and the variability brought about by general, i.e. market-wide risks. The specific risks are known as 'unsystematic' or 'diversifiable' risks, while the general risks are referred to as 'systematic' or 'non-diversifiable' risks. A basic proposition of CAPM is that no reward can be expected from bearing unnecessary risk. By building an efficient portfolio, the specific or 'unsystematic' risks of individual assets can be diversified away. Therefore an investor holding a single asset or a portfolio consisting of a very small number of assets is bearing unsystematic risk, which could be eliminated by diversification. The investment would not lie on the efficient frontier, and no increase in expected return can result from accepting this risk.

Thus the holders of shares in the ice cream company are not rewarded for bearing the specific risks associated with the weather. This risk – the unsystematic risk – could be eliminated by holding shares in companies such as the umbrella manufacturer. Accepting specific risk must therefore be seen as a voluntary act. On the other hand, economy-wide factors which cause variability in investment returns – general risk – can only be eliminated by investing in risk-free assets (or by using hedging instruments e.g. options – beyond the scope of this book). The expected returns on risky assets must obviously be higher than the return on risk-free assets to compensate for this unavoidable systematic risk.

As we have seen, a rational investor would choose a combination of risky assets along the solid part of the envelope curve in Figure 6.3 – the efficient frontier. All points along this line contain all available risky assets but in differing proportions.

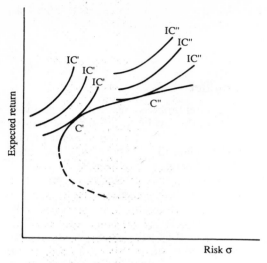

Figure 6.4

Figure 6.4 shows that an investor with the family of indifference curves IC' would choose the combination of risky assets represented by C', while the combination represented by C" would be chosen by an investor with indifference curves such as IC". Rational investors always seek to reach their highest possible indifference curve. As the shape of indifference curves is not the same for all risk-averse individuals, it follows that any point along the efficient frontier represents a rational choice for some investors.

6.3.1   The capital market line

Individuals are not compelled to invest in risky assets. Earlier, we assumed the existence of a rate of interest at which funds could be borrowed or lent. This interest rate represents a risk free asset. An investor can lend at this rate in the knowledge that his return is certain, i.e. there will be no variability in the return. When a risk-free asset is introduced into the analysis, the options open to the investor are increased and improved, as he can now:

1   Invest all his funds in the risk-free asset.
2   Invest part of his funds in the risk-free asset and part in the risky assets.
3   Invest all his funds in risky assets.
4   Borrow at the risk-free rate in order to invest in risky assets (note: it is assumed that borrowing and lending rates are equal).

For each of these alternatives, a rational investor will seek to minimize the risk associated with a given level of return.

Consider the investor whose indifference curves are shown by the family IC'. In Figure 6.5, A risk-free asset is introduced with return r_f and, by

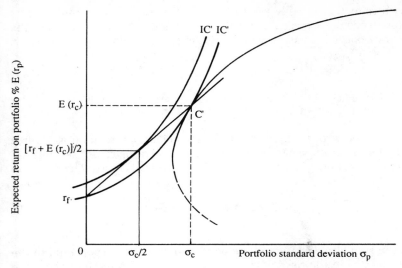

Figure 6.5

definition, a standard deviation of zero. The indifference curve passing through C' also, by coincidence, passes through r_f, showing that the investor would get the same utility from an investment in the risk-free asset as from the investment in the risky portfolio represented by C'. The higher expected return on C' is just sufficient to compensate this investor for accepting its associated risks. However, the investor could reach a higher indifference curve by investing part of his funds in the risk-free asset and the remainder in risky assets. Suppose for the moment that the investor decides to retain the risky part of his portfolio as C'; he can then build a two-asset portfolio – the first asset being the risk-free asset, and the second being the set of risky assets represented by C'. $E(r_c)$ is greater than r_f, and any desired return between $E(r_c)$ and r_f can be obtained by varying the relative proportions of the total funds invested in the two assets. For example, if a return falling midway between $E(r_c)$ and r_f was required, i.e.

$$\frac{E(r_c) + r_f}{2}$$

then this could be achieved by investing half the funds in the risk-free asset, and half in the risky portfolio. From equation 6.4, the expected return on this portfolio $E(r_p)$, is given by:

$$E(r_p) = 0.5\, r_f + 0.5\, r_c = \frac{r_f + r_c}{2}$$

But the introduction of risky asset C′ into the portfolio brings uncertainty. The return becomes expected rather than certain. From equation 6.6, the variance of a portfolio consisting of the risk free asset and C′ will be given by:

$$\text{Var}(P_1 r_f + P_2 r_c) = P_1^2 \sigma_{rf}^2 + P_2^2 \sigma_{rc}^2 + 2 P_1 P_2 \text{Cov}(r_f, r_c)$$

Where P_1 = proportion of funds in r_f,
P_2 = proportion of funds in r_c.

By definition r_f is zero, as there can be no variability of return on a risk-free asset. Furthermore, there can be no relation between the return on the risk-free asset and that on the risky asset, so Cov (r_f, r_c) is also zero. The equation is thus reduced to:

$$\text{Var}(P_1 r_f + P_2 r_c) = P_2^2 \sigma_{rc}^2$$
$$\sigma(P_1 r_f + P_2 r_c) = P_2 \sigma_{rc}$$

Thus the standard deviation of the portfolio is directly proportional to the amount invested in the risky asset. The risk premium on the portfolio – the difference beween the expected return on the portfolio and the expected return on risk-free assets – will also vary in direct proportion to the amount invested in the risky asset. A straight line can therefore be drawn connecting r_f and C′, and by altering the proportion of his portfolio invested in the risky assets, C′, an investor can construct a portfolio anywhere along this line. This enables the investor to reach a higher indifference curve, as can be seen in Figure 6.5. However, the investor could reach a still higher indifference curve if he modified his portfolio of risky assets. The line r_f C′ is not unique: a straight line can be drawn connecting r_f with *any* combination of risky assets. Portfolios can be constructed offering the risk and return shown by any line, simply by varying the proportion of risky assets. An infinite number of portfolios can therefore be constructed. However, the steeper the line connecting the risky portfolio with the risk-free asset, the better the risk/return trade-off. A straight line through r_f tangential to the envelope curve represents the steepest of all these possible lines, and thus provides the most attractive investment opportunities.

Inspection of Figure 6.6 shows that line r_fM is superior to other possibilities such as r_fC′. If an investor is prepared to accept the risk associated with C′, his best option is to build a portfolio consisting of the risk-free asset and the portfolio of risky assets represented by M. This portfolio, P, vertically above C′ on line r_fM, would have the same standard deviation as C′, but a higher expected return. The reader should note that the line r_fM offers the optimal investment opportunities to *all* investors, whatever their individual tastes and preferences.

For example, the preferred portfolio for the investor with indifference curves IC′ now lies to the left of M along r_fM; it is no longer C′ as in Figure 6.4. It reflects a portfolio in which part of the investor's funds are invested in risk-free assets, the remainder being invested in the portfolio of risky assets represented by M. The optimal portfolio for the investor with indifference curves IC″ lies to the right of M along r_fM; it is no longer C″ as in Figure 6.4.

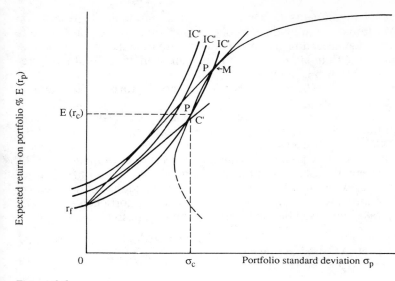

Figure 6.6

Portfolios along this section of the line reflect a situation in which the investor borrows funds at the rate r_f, in order to invest in the risky assets represented by M.

It should be noted that, although the two preferred portfolios offer different expected returns and risk, the risky part of *both* portfolios is represented by the set of risky assets at M, known as the 'market portfolio'. The adjustment for individual taste is made by varying the *proportion* of the portfolio held in risky assets, and *not* by adjusting the risky assets themselves. For all individuals the investment decision is thus divided into two distinct steps:

1 Determining the optimal set of risky assets – given by M, and described as the 'market portfolio'.
2 Determining the preferred point along the line r_fM – known as the 'capital market line' – by selecting the optimum mix between the risk-free asset r_f and the risky asset M, according to tastes and preferences.

The discovery that the investment decision in a risky world can also be divided into two separate steps – known as '(Tobin's) separation theorem' (Tobin, 1958) – is vitally important to the development of the CAPM. As all investors theoretically hold the market portfolio, M, the line r_fM (the capital market line (CML)) defines the market price for risk. It is independent of individual preferences, and thus enables general observations on the required relation between risk and return to be made. Portfolio M theoretically represents a portfolio containing all traded financial assets. It is thus a well-diversified portfolio. The specific, unique or 'unsystematic' risks of the individual underlying investments have been diversified away. But as we have seen, certain risks – the 'systematic' risks – cannot be diversified away, as they affect all investments to some extent. The variability of returns on portfolio M is thus caused by the portfolio's systematic risk. Investors require compensation for accepting the systematic risk represented by portfolio M, and this takes the form of an expected return for M in excess of the risk-free rate. This excess return is known as the 'risk premium', and is shown by the expression $E(r_m) - r_f$, where $E(r_m)$ is the expected return on the market portfolio, M.

If a portfolio is 50 per cent invested in risk-free assets, and 50 per cent invested in the market portfolio, its systematic risk would be half that of the market portfolio, and thus, as seen above, the required risk premium would also be halved. The risk premium is directly proportional to the level of the portfolio's systematic risk. Expressing this same idea in terms of return, we can say that the expected return on a portfolio is equal to the risk-free return, plus a risk premium which is directly proportional to the portfolio's systematic risk. This proposition also holds for individual financial assets, i.e.:

$$\begin{array}{llll} \text{Expected return on} \\ \text{a financial asset (A)} \end{array} = \begin{array}{l} \text{Risk-} \\ \text{free} \\ \text{return} \end{array} + \begin{array}{l} \text{Measure of} \\ \text{systematic} \\ \text{risk of (A).} \end{array} \left(\begin{array}{ll} \text{Expected return} & - & \text{Risk} \\ \text{on market} & & \text{free} \\ \text{portfolio} & & \text{return} \end{array} \right)$$

6.3.2 *'Beta' and systematic risk*

In CAPM the level of systematic risk of a financial asset is known as its 'beta' – (β). The market portfolio, M, has a β value of 1. Assets with more systematic risk than the market have a β greater than 1. If an asset has less systematic risk than the market, its β is less than 1. If an asset has the same systematic risk as the market, its β is equal to 1. The risk premium on an asset is thus directly proportional to its β so that, for any asset i its expected return $E(r_i)$ is given by:

$$E(r_i) = r_f + \beta[E(r_m) - r_f] \qquad \ldots \text{Equation 6.10}$$

where
$$\beta = \frac{\text{Cov}(r_i, r_m)}{\sigma^2_m}$$

To understand β intuitively, remember that when we are looking at the variation of a large portfolio of investments the covariance terms dominate our calculations. In other words, it is the covariance of the returns of portfolio assets with each other that determines the risk of a portfolio.

The market's perception of the risk of an *individual* share is no different. It is the covariance of the returns of an individual share with the other shares in the market that determines its risk. In the capital asset pricing model, the covariance of an individual share with the market rate of return is used as a substitute for the total of all the individual covariances weighted by their relative market values. To emphasize this point we can rewrite equation 6.10 as follows:

$$E(r_i) = r_f + \text{Cov } (r_i, r_m) \frac{(E(r_m) - r_f)}{\sigma^2_m}$$

In words, the required return, $E(r_i)$ of an individual share is made up to the risk-free rate of return r_f, plus the market's perception of the risk of an individual share Cov (r_i, r_m), multiplied by the 'price of risk per unit of variance' or

$$\frac{(E(r_m) - r_f)}{\sigma^2_m}$$

In effect, this last term converts the covariance into an interest rate which is the risk premium.

As CAPM postulates that the risk premium is a reward for bearing systematic risk, it follows that an individual asset having a particular level of systematic risk should offer the same expected return as a portfolio with the same systematic risk level. For example, let

$E(r_m)$ (expected return on market portfolio) = 25 per cent
r_f (risk free return)   = 5 per cent
σ_m (standard deviation of market portfolio) = 30 per cent

Figure 6.7 shows the capital market line consistent with this data. The investor can build a portfolio anywhere along the CML to suit his tastes. If he does not wish to accept the variability of returns associated with the market portfolio, M, he can move down the CML towards r_f. Suppose he requires an expected return of 10 per cent. This could be achieved by investing 75 per cent of his money in the risk-free asset r_f, and 25 per cent of his funds in the market portfolio. The expected return on his portfolio, $E(r_p)$ is given by:

$$E(r_p) = 0.75 \, r_f + 0.25 \, r_m = 0.75 \times 0.05 + 0.25 \times 0.25$$
$$E(r_p) = 0.10$$

The standard deviation associated with this portfolio, σ_p, is

$$\sigma_p = P_2 \sigma_m = 0.25 \times 0.3 = 0.075$$

i.e. as only 25 per cent of the portfolio is invested in risky assets, its standard deviation, at 7.5 per cent, is only 25 per cent of the market standard deviation of 30 per cent.

This portfolio is represented by point P in Figure 6.7.

If an individual share has the same expected return as portfolio P, i.e. 10 per cent, its systematic risk must also be equal to that of portfolio P. In equilibrium, expected return is a function of systematic risk. If an individual share with the same expected return as P offered investors a different risk/return trade-off to that offered by P, the share would be traded. It would be bought if its systematic risk were lower than P's, and sold if its systematic risk were higher. Purchases would drive the price of the share up, and hence the expected return down, to a level commensurate with its systematic risk.

Similarly, sales would depress the share price, and thus increase its expected return, again to a level commensurate with its systematic risk.

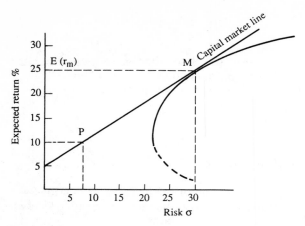

Figure 6.7

6.3.3   The security market line

The systematic risk of an individual share, as measured by its β value, can be plotted against the share's expected return. The resulting line is known as the 'security market line' (SML), shown in Figure 6.8.

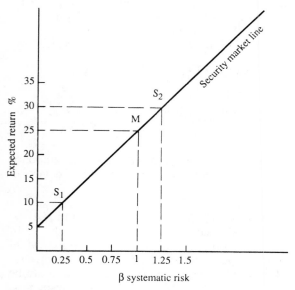

Figure 6.8

Note that the SML relates expected return to systematic risk. While systematic risk is synonymous with the variability of a portfolio, the unsystematic risk having been diversified away, it is *not* synonymous with the variability of an individual asset. For example, an individual share such as S_1, with an expected return of 10 per cent, will, if CAPM holds, have the same systematic risk as portfolio P in Figure 6.7. However, the variability of return of S_1 will be a function of both its systematic and unsystematic risk. Generally, the total risk of an individual asset will be higher than its systematic risk. Under CAPM, it is irrational for investors to hold undiversified portfolios, as they are bearing a risk for which there is no reward.

6.3.4   CAPM and the individual investor

Although CAPM requires that all investors should hold the market portfolio, M, to gain the full benefits of diversification, much of this benefit can be gained from holding far fewer shares. In fact, a portfolio containing only 15–20 randomly selected shares will eliminate around 90 per cent of the shares' unsystematic risk, as Figure 6.9 shows.

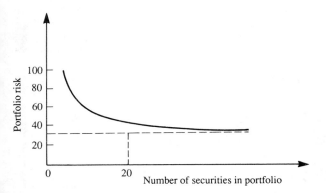

Figure 6.9

In reality many investors do not hold diversified portfolios. This has become particularly true in the UK since the introduction of the government's privatization programme. Many investors hold shares in a single privatization issue. This does not invalidate CAPM; it merely means that investors are accepting some risk for which no reward can be expected. Moreover, in the real world, diversifying a portfolio is not costless. Transaction costs are incurred in buying and selling shares, and these costs are assumed to be absent in CAPM. These costs are not only financial, they also include the effort on the part of an individual in effecting his investment decisions. As the size of the bargain decreases, transaction costs represent an increasing percentage of the value of shares traded. Such costs obviously place a disproportionate burden on small investors. To some extent, these charges can be mitigated for the small investor by investing in assets such as unit trusts, although even here an annual management charge must be paid, in addition to the initial bid/offer spread. Certainly, direct personal share ownership has shown a declining trend in the UK over this century. By value of holding, the private direct investor is now relatively unimportant in the UK market. Most shares are held by financial institutions, such as pension funds and life assurance companies, who are able to trade their shares relatively cheaply. Shares in the UK market are thus generally held by financial institutions, who hold them as part of a well-diversified portfolio.

6.3.5   *Calculating the 'beta' of a share*

The idea of systematic risk is central to CAPM. An asset whose systematic risk, i.e. its β, is larger than 1 will be expected to earn a greater 'excess' return than that offered by the market portfolio. For example, a share such as S_2 in Figure 6.8 has a β of 1.25. From equation 6.10, its expected risk premium is $1.25\,(r_m - r_f)$ i.e. $1.25\,(25\% - 5\%) = 25$ per cent. The expected return on S_2 will be the risk–free rate, 5 per cent, plus its individual risk premium, 25 per cent, i.e. 30 per cent. If the *actual* return on the market portfolio in a particular period were only 10 per cent, i.e. the market risk premium was reduced to 5 per cent ($10\% - 5\%$), then the expected return on S_2 would be $r_f + \beta\,(E(r_m) - r_f) = 5\% + 1.25\,(10\% - 5\%) = 11.25$ per cent.

An estimate of the β of an individual share, i, can be made by plotting the excess return earned on security i, $(r_i - r_f)$, against the excess return earned by investing in the market portfolio $(r_m - r_f)$.

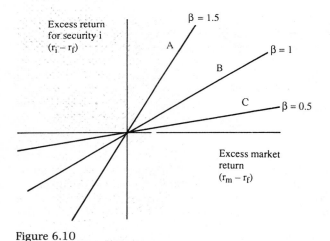

Figure 6.10

The slope of the regression line through the plotted points gives an estimate of the share's β. Figure 6.10 shows three regression lines for three shares – A, B and C. Such lines are known as 'security characteristic lines' (SCLs). In Figure 6.10 the three SCLs are shown as passing through the origin. This indicates that, when markets are in equilibrium, a zero excess return on the market portfolio will lead to a zero excess return on other shares in the market; In reality, when data for actual shares are plotted against the axes of Figure 6.10, the SCL rarely passes through the origin. The distance between the origin and the point at which the regression line cuts the vertical axis is known as the security's alpha value (α). Interpretation of α values is difficult. It may be argued that they are not inconsistent with CAPM. CAPM is based on *expected* return, but the SCL is derived from *actual* data. This may explain the existence of α values, while not invalidating CAPM. Alternatively, if CAPM fails to consider items which are important to investors when making investment decisions in the real world, the long-term existence of α values may well be caused by these ignored factors. Obviously, such an explanation would undermine CAPM as a model of reality.

6.3.6 CAPM as an economic model

At this point it may be useful to consider whether CAPM is a 'good' economic model. A good economic model is one which can be used to explain and predict economic events. It is not necessary for the assumptions of the model to be realistic. The ultimate test of any model is its capacity to explain and predict events. The basic premise of CAPM is that the expected return on any risky asset is proportional to its β. Is this consistent with observed facts? Unfortunately, it is not possible to give a simple answer to this question, as CAPM is a very difficult model to test. The testing difficulties arise from two main sources. First, as noted above, CAPM is a model of *expected* returns, but only *actual* returns can be observed. Second, the market portfolio should contain *all* risky assets. As there is no quoted portfolio containing all such assets, a surrogate for the market portfolio, such as the FTSE index, must be used. For these reasons, some researchers have argued that CAPM is a theory which cannot be tested (Roll, 1977). However, notwithstanding the methodological problems, others have tried to test CAPM, to ascertain whether the risk/return trade-off for all risky assets does actually lie along the security market line. Some studies, such as the famous Black, Jensen, Scholes paper (1972), appear to vindicate CAPM. But other studies have found CAPM to be a much more approximate representation of reality (e.g. Fama and Macbeth 1973, and Banz 1981), indicating that the model might well omit factors which are important in setting the price of risky assets. Nevertheless, despite evidence that CAPM does not include *all* the factors relevant to setting share prices, research suggests that systematic risk is an important factor. We may conclude that CAPM represents the truth, but not the whole truth. Future developments in finance theory, such as arbitrage pricing, may advance our understanding of the problem. But for the moment CAPM, provides a simple and useful model for looking at risk and return.

References and further reading

Banz, R. W., 'The Relationship Between Return and Market Value of Common Stock, *Journal of Financial Economics*, March 1981.
Best, M. J., Grauer, R. R., 'Capital Asset Pricing Compatible with Observed Market Weights', *The Journal of Finance*, March 1985.

Black, F., Jensen, M. C., Scholes, M., 'The CAPM: Some Empirical Tests' in Jensen, M. (ed.) *Studies in the Theory of Capital Markets*, Frederick A. Praeger, 1972.

Brealey, R, A., Hodges, S. D., 'Playing with Portfolios,' *The Journal of Finance*, March 1975.

Brennan, M. J., 'The Optimal Number of Securities in Risky Asset Portfolios Where there are fixed Costs of Transacting: Theory and Some Empirical Results; *Journal of Financial and Quantitative Analysis*, September 1975.

Brown, K. C., Brown, G., 'Does the Market Portfolios Composition Matter?', *The Journal of Portfolio Management*, Winter 1987.

Burgess, R. C., Bey, R. P. 'Optimal Portfolios: Markowitz full Covariance versus Simple Selection Rules', *The Journal of Financial Research*, Summer 1988.

Dickinson, J. P., 'The Reliability of Estimation Procedures in Portfolio Analysis', *Journal of Financial and Quantitative Analysis*, June 1974,

Dowen, R., 'Beta, Non-Systematic Risks and Portfolio Selection', *Applied Economics*, February 1988.

Elton, E. J., Gruber, M. J., Padberg, M. W., 'Simple Criteria for Optimal Portfolio Selection: Tracing out the Efficient frontier', *Journal of Finance*, March 1978.

Elton, E. J., Gruber, M. J., 'Non-Standard C.A.P.M.s and the Market Portfolio', *Journal of Finance*, July 1984.

Fama, E. F., Macbeth, J. D., 'Risk, Return and Equilibrium: Empirical Tests', *Journal of Political Economy*, 1973, pp. 607–36.

Fisher, L., Kamin, J. H., 'Forecasting Systematic Risk: Estimates of "Raw" Beta that Take Account of the Tendency of Beta to Change and the Heteroskedasticity of Residual Returns', *Journal of Financial and Quantitative Analysis*, June 1985.

Garven, J. A., 'CML to SML: An Alternative Approach', *Journal of Business Finance and Accounting*, Summer 1988.

Klemkusky, R. C., Martin, J. D., 'The Effect of Market Risk on Portfolio Diversification', *Journal of Finance*, March 1975.

Kroll, Y., Levy, H., Rappoport, A., 'Experimental Tests of the Separation Theorem and the Capital Asset Pricing Model,' *American Economic Review*, June 1988

Lakonishok, J., Shapiro, A. C., 'Systematic Risk, Total Risk and Size as Determinants of the Stock Market Returns', *Journal of Banking and Finance*, March 1986.

Levy, H., 'Another Look at the Capital Asset Pricing Model', *Quarterly Review of Business and Economics*, Summer 1984.

Lintner, J., 'Security Prices, Risks and Maximal Gains from Diversification', *Journal of Finance*, December 1965.

Markowitz, H. M., 'Portfolio Selection', *Journal of Finance*, March, 1952 pp 71–91.

Markowitz, H. M., *Portfolio selection; Efficient Diversification of Investment*, John Wiley, 1959.

Myers, S., Ruback, R. 'Discounting Rules for Risky Assets', Cambridge: NBER, 1987.

Roll, R., 'A Critique of the Asset Pricing Theory's Tests; Part 1: On Past Potential Testing of the Theory', *Journal of Financial Economics*, March 1977, pp. 129–36.

Rubenstein, M. E., 'A Mean-Variance Synthesis of Corporate Financial Theory', *Journal of Finance*, March 1973

Ross, S. A., 'The Arbitrage Theory of Capital Asset Pricing' pp.341–60, *Journal of Economic Theory*, December 1976

Ross, S. A., 'The Current Status of the Capital Asset Pricing Model (CAPM)', *Journal of Finance*, June 1978.

Scott, E., Brown, S., 'Biased Estimators and Unsuitable Betas', *Journal of Finance*, March 1980.

Statman, M., 'How Many Stocks Make a Diversified Portfolio?' *Journal of Financial and Quantitative Analysis*, September 1987.

Sharpe, W. F., 'Capital Asset Prices : A Theory of Market Equilibrium', *Journal of Finance*, September 1964.

Tobin, J., 'Liquidity Preference as Behaviour Toward Risk', *Review of Economic Studies*, 25: 65–86, February 1953.

7 Real asset investments in a risky world

7.1 CAPM and real asset investment

The consideration of CAPM in the previous chapter was not primarily motivated by a need for the reader to understand how shares are valued. Rather, it was undertaken to give an insight into how risk might be accommodated into the investment decision-making process of individual companies. In the absence of risk, shareholder wealth is maximized by accepting all investments whose NPVs are positive after discounting at the market interest rate. This chapter begins by considering whether it is possible to devise a rule of equal simplicity in a risky environment. Can the company decision maker act in the best interests of all shareholders simultaneously, given that their individual attitudes to risk may differ?

It has been shown (section 6.3.1) that the separation theorem provides a solution to this problem. It assumes that shareholders are risk-averse, but shows that differing degrees of risk-aversion can be accommodated by varying the holding of risk-free assets. It shows that rational, risk-averse investors will *all* hold the market portfolio as the risky part of their personal portfolio.

CAPM proposes a theory as to how these risky assets are priced. It suggests that their prices adjust until the asset's expected risk premium is directly proportional to its systematic risk, or beta (β). The expected return on the risky assets in the market portfolio is just sufficient to compensate investors for the relevant asset risk, i.e. the systematic risk.

Any investment which a company undertakes represents an addition, though a very small one, to the market portfolio. The required return on this investment will depend on its systematic risk. Thus, if a decision maker can establish the systematic risk of a project, he can establish the return which *all* shareholders would require from the investment. By using this required return as a discount rate, he can establish whether the investment offers a return adequate to compensate for its systematic risk, i.e. whether the resulting NPV is positive.

It would thus appear that a simple decision rule, analogous to that in the risk-free environment, has been devised for a risky environment, i.e. accept all projects which show a positive NPV when discounted at the rate commensurate with the individual project's systematic risk. A project's systematic risk is measured by its β. Once that is known, the required rate of return, and hence discount rate, can be established. For example, a project with a systematic risk equal to the market portfolio, i.e. with a β of 1, would have a required rate of return equal to the expected rate of return on the market portfolio, $E(r_m)$. If the NPV of an investment when discounted at this rate were positive, it would show that shareholders could obtain a return in excess of that necessary to compensate them for the project's systematic risk. The project would thus be an attractive proposition, and should be accepted. Conversely, a negative NPV would indicate that the project could not earn a return large enough to compensate for its systematic risk, and consequently it should be rejected.

The use of a risk-adjusted discount rate based on a project's β value appears to offer a simple way of taking risk into account in investment decision-making. Moreover, it provides a way of incorporating risk which is optimal for *all* risk-averse investors. Simplicity and universality provide a seductive combination. However, it would be premature to conclude that a sound and workable solution has been found to the problem of how to incorporate risk into the investment decision process. A number of theoretical and practical points must be considered.

CAPM is a single-period model, which predicts expected returns over a period – the period often being taken as 1 year. By definition, capital investment projects extend beyond a single year, i.e. capital budgeting is a multi-period activity. We must therefore determine whether a discount rate derived for a *single* period can safely be applied over the *life* of a project. We can use equation 6.10 to derive a discount rate for a single-period project, A, viz:

$$r_A = r_f + \beta_A \left(E(r_m) - r_f \right)$$

where r_A = required return on project A,
$\beta_A = \beta$ of project A,
$E(r_m)$ = Expected return on market,
r_f = risk free return.

Can this rate, r_A, be used in equation 7.1 to produce a theoretically acceptable NPV for a multi-period project, A?

$$NPV_A = \sum_{t=0}^{n} \frac{E(NCF_{At})}{(1 + r_A)^t} \qquad \ldots \text{Equation 7.1}$$

Where NPV_A = net present value,
$E(NCF_{At})$ = expected Net Cash Flow of Project A in period t,
r_A = risk adjusted required rate of return of project A.

If it is assumed that the only uncertainty in the future relates to the project's cash flows, so that, for example, β is known, the risk-free rate is known and constant throughout the project's life, then fortunately equation 7.1 can safely be used for most types of project (Fama (1977)). A discount rate derived from the single-period CAPM model can usually be employed to discount expected project cash flows, in order to arrive at a risk-adjusted net present value.

Clearly, the caveats expressed in chapter 6 concerning the validity of the single-period CAPM are equally applicable in a multi-period context. what we must now consider is whether the extension of the model to a multi-period setting imposes *additional* restrictive or unrealistic assumptions. In fact, the risk-adjusted NPV value calculated from Equation 7.1 will normally be a slight overstatement of the true CAPM risk-adjusted NPV. The change from a single-period to a multi-period situation does introduce some inaccuracy into the calculation but, assuming the correct asset β is used, the extent of the error is very small (see Myers and Turnbull (1977)), and the discount rate can be safely (if not rigorously) applied to obtain a risk-adjusted NPV.

7.1.1   *Multi-period CAPM and changes in risk*

By using a unique discount rate, we are implicitly assuming that the asset β is constant for each period of the investment's life. This might be a close approximation of the truth in many cases, but it will clearly be inappropriate when different phases of a project are characterized by different risks and thus different βs. In such cases, use of a constant discount rate should be avoided.

For example, suppose the board of the newly-privatized electricity industry is considering a proposal to build a new type of power station, using untried technology. The proposal is that a prototype model should be built in year 0, at a cost of £2.5 million. Extensive tests would be carried out on the model in year 1, costing £10 million. These tests would show whether a full-scale station would be a success or a failure, and would also provide the answer to certain technical questions. A full-scale station could not be built without these answers. Whatever the results of the tests, the model would be dismantled at the end of year 2, at a cost of £2 million. Initial research indicates that there is a 60 per cent chance that the tests will prove the design is a failure, and a 40 per cent chance that the model will show that a full-size station could operate successfully. If the trials are successful, a full-scale station could be built during year 2 at a cost of £200 million. The life of the station would be 38 years. During each of these 38 years, the expected net cash inflow from operating the station would be £34 million. The board considers this proposition worthy of evaluation, particularly as the new station would be environmentally cleaner than existing power stations. However, no attempt has been made to include environmental benefits in the cash flow computations. As the board views the proposal as 'risky', the accountant is asked to evaluate it, using a 24 per cent discount rate. It is assumed that all cash flows occur at the end of the relevant years.

Table 7.1 shows that the proposal has a negative NPV when evaluated at a 24 per cent discount rate.

The accountant has also included a calculation of the project's NPV at 14 per cent. He considers that the 24 per cent discount rate suggested by the

Table 7.1

Year	Expected cash flow (a)	Probability of expected cash flow occurring (b)	Expected cash flow x probability (a × b)	Discount factor @ PV r = 24%	PV	Discount factor @ r = 14%	PV
	£m		£m		£m		
0	− 2.5	1.0	− 2.5	1.0	− 2.50	1.0	− 2.50
1	− 10	1.0	− 10	0.806	− 8.06	0.877	− 8.77
2	− 2	1.0	− 2.0	0.65	− 1.30	0.769	− 1.54
2	− 200	0.4*	− 80.0	0.65	− 52.00	0.769	− 61.52
3–40	+ 34	0.4*	+ 13.6	1.90	+ 25.84	5.458	+ 74.23
				NPV	− 38.02		− 0.10

* Station only built if trials successful.

board has no theoretical underpinning. His 14 per cent was derived from CAPM, using the following data:

$$r_f = 0.08$$
$$E(r_m) = 0.18$$
$$\beta_{project} = 0.6 \text{ (utilities have low systematic risk)}$$
$$r_{project} = 0.08 + 0.6(0.18 - 0.08) = 0.14$$

At 14 per cent the project still has a negative NPV, indicating that the board should reject it, *certeris paribus*. However, as the NPV is not significantly negative, the board may still be attracted to the proposal because of the environmental considerations.

However, CAPM theory has not been correctly applied by the accountant in this case. The project falls into two quite distinct phases, the first being the experimental or prototype phase, and the second the full-scale station phase. The systematic risk of these two phases may differ. The second phase is connected with the generation and sale of electricity. Electricity generation has a high level of fixed production cost relative to variable cost. Fixed costs are largely impervious to market-induced changes. Thus the cost structure of electricity generation implies a lower-than-average level of cost-induced systematic risk. Similarly, revenues from the sale of electricity are subject to a below-average rate of market variability, and hence systematic risk. This is because electricity is seen as a necessity in many circumstances, which leads to a high and stable core demand. The accountant is therefore correct to observe that the second phase of the project has a β value of less than 1. For the first phase, however, no revenue-induced systematic risk can be present, as no revenues are expected. The systematic risk of this phase is determined solely by the covariability of the project costs and market returns. As noted above, the higher the level of fixed project costs to total cost, the lower will be the market-induced variability in these costs. In the experimental phase the costs will be almost totally fixed. Any variability in costs actually incurred is likely to be brought about by unique or *unsystematic* factors – for example, the need to make unforeseen design modifications – than market-induced considerations. The covariability of phase 1 costs with the market is thus likely to be extremely low – or even zero. The required risk adjustment to the risk-free discount rate will therefore be very low or zero. If the correct asset β for this phase of the project *is* zero, the appropriate discount rate is the risk-free rate.

The project's cash flows should thus be discounted at the two applicable rates, viz. 8 per cent for flows relating to the experimental phase, and 14 per cent for the flows relating to phase 2, the full-scale production phase.

It is worth examining further why the risk-adjusted rate for phase 2 should only be applied once that phase of the project actually starts. No risk can attach to an activity until that activity begins, and it begins only when resources are committed to it, or a binding undertaking to commit resources is made. Phase 2 of the electricity generation project does not start until year 2. By undertaking phase 1 of the project, the company is in no sense committed to undertake phase 2, even if the trials are a success. As no risk compensation is necessary unless and until phase 2 starts, the discount rate in phase 1 need only compensate the investor for the time value of money, i.e., the risk-free rate. Table 7.2 shows the evaluation of the two projects using differing discount rates.

Table 7.2

Year	Experimental cash flows £m	Discount factor @ r = 8%	PV £m	Full-scale plant expected cash flow £m	Discount factor @ r = 8% (years 1–2) r = 14% (years 3–40)	PV £m
0	− 2.5	1.0	− 2.5			
1	− 10.0	0.926	− 9.26			
2	− 2.0	0.857	− 1.7	− 200	0.857	− 171.40
3–40				34	6.087*	+ 206.96
		Phase 1 NPV	− 13.46		Phase 2 NPV	+ 35.56

Probability of Phase 2 occurring is 0.4
∴ Expected NPV Phase 2 = 0.4 × £35.56m = £14.22m
Expected NPV Phase 1 + Phase 2 = − £13.46m + £14.22m = £0.76m

$$*\text{Discount factor} = \frac{1}{(1.08)^2} \sum_{t=1}^{t=38} \frac{1}{(1.14)^t}$$

Table 7.2 shows that the project has a positive NPV when the discount rate is varied to reflect the differing risk, or β, of each phase of the project.

The decision to undertake phase 1 of the project provides the company with an option to undertake phase 2. The cost of the option is the present value of the experimental phase, i.e. £13.46 million. If phase 2 is undertaken, its value at time 0 is £35.56 million, considerably in excess of the cost of the option. However, if the trials are unsuccessful, phase 2 will not be undertaken, so that the value of phase 2 will be zero. When viewed from time 0, the value of the option to invest in phase 2 must be weighted by the probability of the further investment being undertaken. The expected value of phase 2 then becomes £14.22 million, which is still greater than the cost of phase 1. The project should therefore be accepted.

The above example has shown that the use of a single discount rate, implying a constant project β, is not universally applicable. Explicit consideration of this point before project evaluation will usually bring any discontinuities in project risk to light.

We must now consider the practical problem of how to establish the appropriate β value for each project or phase of a project.

7.1.2 Establishing a project beta from investing company beta

We saw earlier (section 6.3.5) how an estimate of the β of a quoted company could be made, i.e. by observing movements in the share price of the company relative to market price movements. The company β might therefore seem to be the obvious starting point in establishing a *project* beta. However, the company's own unadjusted β will rarely give a good approximation. To show why this is so, let us begin at the individual asset level, and work up to the company level.

Consider a single asset, A, with a high level of systematic risk, and hence a β value of 2. This asset is acquired by a company and is the company's sole asset. The funds to acquire A are provided by the company shareholders, i.e. the company is totally equity financed. Thus:

$$\beta_{\text{equity}} = \beta_{\text{asset}}(A) = 2$$

Suppose that the shareholders provide further funds, to buy another asset, B. B has a market value equal to A, so that the shareholders' funds are now divided equally between A and B. However, asset B is less risky than A, having a β of 1. The company now represents a two-asset portfolio, the risk of the portfolio being the weighted average of the constituent assets:

$$\begin{aligned} \beta_{\text{equity}} &= 0.5\,\beta_{\text{asset}}(A) + 0.5\,\beta_{\text{asset}}(B) \\ &= 0.5 \times 2 + 0.5 \times 1 \\ &= 1.5 \end{aligned}$$

Thus for a totally equity-financed company, the true β is simply the weighted average of the βs of the company's projects.

As this company β is an average of the *existing* project βs, it is not usually the relevant β to use in establishing a discount rate to evaluate *new* projects. Only if the proposed project has the same systematic risk as the *average* existing project will the β be appropriate to the new project. There is no *a priori* reason to suppose that this will be the case. In the example above a discount rate based on a β of 2 would have mistakenly led to the rejection of project B.

Suppose that the second asset, B, had been financed by the issue of debt. The company has now moved from being an ungeared company to being a geared company. The well-known Modigliani/Miller ($M+M$, 1958) proposition states that, in a tax-free world, the introduction of debt finance will not alter a company's weighted average cost of capital: it will remain constant irrespective of gearing levels. If the *average* remains constant then, given the lower cost of debt finance relative to equity, it follows that the cost of equity must increase when debt is introduced. This is illustrated in Figure 7.1. See also section 7.3.

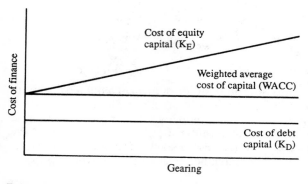

Figure 7.1

The risk of a particular asset is independent of the source of finance used to acquire it. However, the risk borne by the purchaser depends on both the asset risk and the financing source. A reconsideration of Figure 6.6 illustrates this point. An individual who invests on the CML to the right of M accepts a higher level of risk than the investor at M, even though the risky assets are *exactly* the same in each portfolio, and only the financing differs. Portfolios to the right of M are financed wholly or partly by borrowing. Should the actual return be less than the expected return, the debt will still have to be repaid, so that the variability of returns on a portfolio to the right of M is much greater than the variability of a portfolio at M (or to the left of M). However, this greater variability is brought about solely by the method of finance, as the variability of returns on the actual assets represented by M is the same in every portfolio.

When an individual buys shares in a geared company, it is akin to buying into a portfolio to the right of M: the total risk is greater than the weighted sum of the systematic risk of the underlying assets. The β of geared companies is thus higher than the β of ungeared companies, *ceteris paribus*. In fact, if we assume that the β of debt is zero – a reasonable assumption, as debt is usually fixed and does not change with varying market conditions, and further assume that there are no taxes – then:

$$\beta \text{ with gearing} = \beta \text{ without gearing} \times \frac{MV_E + MV_D}{MV_E} \qquad \text{... Equation 7.2}$$

where

MV_E = Market value of equity,
MV_D = Market value of debt.

In our example above, when the acquisition of B was equity-financed, β without gearing was 1.5. If B is financed by debt, then:

$$\beta \text{ with gearing} = 1.5 \times \frac{1+1}{1} = 3$$

After the issue of the debt, the equity-holders are bearing two sources of risk for which they can expect to be rewarded: the financing risks introduced by holding debt, and the business risk of the real assets. These two risks are independent, and in the initial evaluation of projects the financing risk should be ignored.

Observed company βs reflect both financing and business risk. If capital markets are perfect, then only the business risk is relevant in project appraisal, and observed βs should be adjusted to remove the effects of gearing. Fortunately, it is a relatively easy matter to adjust the observed β to strip out the effects of gearing, as consideration of equation 7.2 shows.

The problem created when the new project does not have the same systematic risk as the *average* existing project is not so easily surmountable, however. There are also further problems in relying on a company's own observed β. If only a small number of observations are made in establishing this β, there could be a high estimation error, i.e. the 'true' β might differ markedly from the observed β. Increasing the number of observations of price movements reduces this error. However, the number of observations can only be increased by lengthening the time span over which observations are recorded. This introduces a new problem: as the timespan is lengthened, the possibility that the company β has itself changed will increase. As seen above, once an observed beta has been adjusted for gearing, it is simply the weighted average of the βs of the underlying assets. If the type of asset investment undertaken by the company has changed significantly over time, the true company β will also have changed, invalidating the observed value.

Finally, starting with one's own company β is only possible for quoted companies. This route is not open to private companies, or companies whose shares are not actively traded.

The attempt both to determine one's own company β, and then to derive a discount rate from it, can thus be seen to be fraught with difficulties. The use of data derived from other companies eliminates or reduces all the problems outlined above. The CAPM-derived discount rate for a project can be established by adopting the procedure in the following section.

7.1.3   *Establishing a discount rate using proxy companies*

1   Identify a number of listed companies whose principal activities coincide with the proposed activity. For example, if a company is proposing to enter the construction industry, it would identify a number of companies primarily engaged in construction of the type under consideration.
2   Obtain the last 5 years' published accounts for these companies (readily available on request from the company secretary). These accounts enable an assessment to be made of:

   (i)   The similarity between the investment proposal and the activities of the chosen companies. Any companies which have significant interests *outside* the appropriate field should be eliminated.
   (ii) The level of the companies' gearing.

3   Obtain the β value for each of the sample companies. These are readily available (e.g. from DataStream or through the London Business School Risk Management Service) for every listed company in the UK, and are normally calculated over a 5-year period.
4   Adjust the obtained β value for each individual company to eliminate the effect of gearing. By rearranging equation 7.2, we have

$$\beta_{\text{without gearing}} = \beta_{\text{with gearing}} \times \frac{MV_E}{MV_E + MV_D}$$

This formula ignores taxation. In reality, the cost of debt finance is reduced by the debt tax shield (i.e. interest costs are tax-deductible) and the market value of debt must be reduced to reflect this beneficial tax shield. This represents a move from the assumption of perfect capital markets. With the introduction of tax, the formula becomes:

$$\beta_{\text{assets}} = \beta_{\text{company}} \times \frac{MV_E}{MV_E + MV_D \ (1-t)} \qquad \ldots \text{Equation 7.3}$$

where $\beta_{\text{assets}} = \beta_{\text{without gearing}},$
           $\beta_{\text{company}} = \text{Published } \beta = \beta_{\text{with gearing}},$
           $t = \text{Corporation tax rate.}$

If the companies have been carefully selected, β assets should be very similar for all of them. If any company has a β_{asset} which is significantly different from the others, it should be omitted from the subsequent calculation.

5   Calculate an average β_{assets} from the remaining selected companies.
6   Make any adjustment to this β value (as calculated in step 5), thought necessary because of differences in the systematic risk characteristics of the project under review and those of the proxy companies. This step is particularly important where proxy companies are few in number, or where the proxies are not felt to be closely representative of the proposed project. An understanding of the factors affecting the systematic risk of

all projects is necessary to determine whether an adjustment in step 6 is required.

Any project can be divided into two elements: revenues and costs. Costs can be further subdivided into fixed costs and variable costs. The total systematic risk of a project is dependent on the systematic risk of these individual elements, i.e. the way they are affected by macro-economic factors. Remember that sensitivity to company-specific factors is not relevant to systematic risk.

Fixed costs, by definition, cannot be altered in the short term. Thus, as we saw in section 7.1.1, the degree of correlation or covariance between market movements and fixed costs is likely to be very low or zero. Variable costs, however, will be responsive to market changes. A general improvement in economic conditions will tend to boost demand for all types of product. As demand increases, output and hence variable costs will increase. Conversely, a reduction in demand will lead to a drop in output, and a consequent fall in variable costs. Further, the unit price of variable cost inputs (e.g. materials) may also vary along with macro-economic conditions. For example, in times of economic buoyancy the price of crude oil, the basic raw material of the petro-chemical industry, will tend to rise. When demand slackens, it will fall back again.

Project revenues, like variable costs, will also be sensitive to macro-economic change. Obviously, the degree of revenue sensitivity will depend on the type of product being sold. Demand for the necessities of life is relatively inelastic, whereas luxury goods have a very elastic demand curve. For example, as general wealth increases, the demand for staple foods such as bread and milk is likely to show little increase (and may even decline as consumers substitute more expensive foods, such as the breakfast croissant for toast). In contrast, the demand for restaurant meals increases substantially as the economy expands. However, in bad times, people may cut back sharply on eating out, while making little, if any, adjustment to their bread and milk consumption.

A priori, the higher the revenue sensitivity of a project, the higher its systematic risk will be. For projects with high revenue sensitivity, the projects cost structure also becomes relevant in the determination of systematic risk. Where variable costs are a high proportion of total costs, a sharp drop in revenue will be accompanied by a largely offsetting fall in costs. However, where costs are mostly fixed, a fall in revenue may mean that the company is not generating a sufficient contribution to cover these costs, and significant losses can be incurred.

Projects with high revenue sensitivity and high fixed costs thus have a high level of systematic risk. High revenue sensitivity coupled with low fixed costs leads to a much lower level of systematic risk. If a project has low revenue sensitivity, its systematic risk will be below average. This observation holds for any costs structure. If the revenues are stable, the necessity to reduce costs in response to demand changes does not arise.

If the proposed project has a greater or lesser degree of revenue sensitivity than the proxy companies, the average β will need adjustment. For example, in evaluating a proposal to open a chain of delicatessens, the nearest proxy companies may be provided by supermarket chains.

However, as delicatessens operate at the luxury end of food retailing the observed supermarket β would need upward revision to provide an appropriate proxy for assessing the project.

Similarly, proxies derived from companies undertaking projects which have high revenue β will also need upward adjustment, if the proposal under consideration is more capital-intensive than the norm, i.e. if it has a higher than normal ratio of fixed to total cost. Downward adjustment will be required if the proposal is less capital intensive than the norm for the activity, i.e. if it has a higher than normal ratio of variable to total cost.

7   With the β_{asset} value calculated as above, and equation 7.4 below, establish the discount rate, r_i, to use in evaluating the proposed investment:

$$r_i = r_f + \beta_{\text{asset}} (E(r_m) - r_f) \qquad \ldots \text{Equation 7.4}$$

R_f can be established by noting the redemption yields available on government stocks with a maturity date around the termination of the life of the proposed investment. The actual risk premium, $r_m - r_f$, has been relatively stable over a long period of time at around 9 per cent.

8   Discount the expected cash flows of the proposed investment by the rate r_i calculated in equation 7.4. This provides a 'base case' NPV.

A practical criticism of the above procedure would be that it is time-consuming to establish a discount rate for every proposed investment. Unfortunately, calculation of a specific project rate cannot be avoided if a new proposal falls outside present business areas. However, for more routine proposals, a firm may use a discount rate established for the division or business area in which the proposal falls. A divisional rate, of course, is open to the same criticism as a company-wide rate. It assumes that any proposed investment has the same business risk as the average divisional investment. Nevertheless, a divisional rate offers a more accurate benchmark than a company-wide rate, and can be marginally adjusted where appropriate.

Our preoccupation so far has been to find an evaluation method which is able to distinguish those investments in real assets which *increase* shareholder wealth from those which *diminish* it. It has been shown that this objective can theoretically be achieved by accepting all investments which show a positive NPV when cash flows are discounted at the market discount rate in a risk-free world. In a risky world, a theoretical solution is to accept projects with a positive expected NPV, after cash flows have been discounted by a rate of interest derived from the capital asset pricing model. In arriving at these conclusions, certain assumptions, e.g. perfect divisibility of projects, and homogeneous expectations on the part of investors, must be made. Assumptions are always necessary in model building but, as was stressed earlier in the case of CAPM, a model may still be valid, even if its assumptions do not precisely mirror the real world.

7.2   Capital market imperfections and real asset investment: the adjusted present value approach

The assumption of perfect capital markets facilitates the separation of the choice of real asset investment from the decision as to how its acquisition should be financed. We have shown that the same choice of real asset investment will be made by all rational investors in both the risk-free and the risky world, as perfect capital markets ensure the same opportunity cost of capital for all investors. Differing consumption requirements and/or attitudes towards risk can be accommodated independently of investors' choice of real assets. Obviously, if markets are not perfect, the opportunity cost of investment may differ from investor to investor. For example, where borrowing and lending rates diverge, an investment may appear unattractive to an investor whose opportunity cost is the borrowing rate, but it may be attractive to another investor whose opportunity cost is the lending rate. In the real world, a company acting on behalf of its shareholders needs to use an 'average' rather than a unique market rate (plus risk premium where appropriate) in evaluating investments. A degree of sub-optimality for some investors must inevitably result from this. However, as investors are free to sell their shares, the sub-optimality should not be serious.

If internally generated funds are insufficient to finance investments, long-term finance is raised by issuing further equity or debt. Legal formalities must be observed in their issue, and thus transaction costs will be incurred. Where debt interest is tax-deductible, as in the UK, the cost of debt finance is less than that of equity finance – but the amount of debt which a company can issue might well be affected by the market value of the company's equity. The market value of equity is itself a function of the projects a company has already undertaken. If capital markets are perfect, the cost of finance is determined simply by the purpose for which the finance is required. When imperfections exist, the transaction costs of raising the finance, the type of finance raised – tax-deductible debt or non-deductible equity – and the existing company capital structure may all need to be considered. Capital market imperfections in the real world mean that the investment decision cannot be totally separated from the financing considerations, so that management is obliged to take their interaction into account. This may be achieved by adjusting the 'base case' NPV calculated in step 8 above. In establishing this 'base case' NPV, all financing considerations were omitted. The project was viewed in the context of an all equity financed mini-firm. The adjusted net present value (APV) approach refines the base case, by adding the NPV of the side effects of accepting the project, i.e.

Project APV = Base Case NPV + sum of net present value of the side effects of accepting the project.

Significant side effects may arise from two main sources: the transaction costs of raising finance, and the tax-deductibility of debt interest.

7.2.1.   *Calculation of adjusted present value*

Example 1

Suppose an investment of £10 million in perpetuity has a 'base case' NPV of £0.5 million. If new funds are required to provide the £10 million, the costs of raising this finance must be considered. The cost of an equity issue as a percentage of the funds raised depends on the size and type of the issue, typically being highest for relatively small issues to new investors to the company, and lowest for rights issues to existing investors. For example, it is not uncommon for issue costs to account for 15 per cent of the funds raised for issues made under the Business Expansion Scheme; for large rights issues, the percentage cost may be around 2–3 per cent of the funds raised.

Issue costs in excess of £0.5 million, for equity would render the above project unattractive. If the project were to be financed totally by new equity, with issue costs of £0.6 million, then the APV would be negative:

$$\text{APV} = \text{Base case NPV} - \text{issue costs}$$
$$\text{APV} = £0.5\text{m} - £0.6\text{m}$$
$$= -£0.1\text{m}$$

However, this analysis ignores the fact that issuing new equity increases the firm's capacity to borrow. Suppose the firm's policy is to have 40 per cent of total long-term finance (i.e. debt plus equity) in debt. Issuing £10 million of equity increases the firm's willingness to take on a further £4 million in debt. Moreover, it is widely held that the ability to issue debt has a positive value to the firm, because of the tax shield associated with it.

Assume that this company can raise perpetual debt at 10 per cent, interest is tax-deductible, the tax rate is 35 per cent, and tax is paid 1 year in arrears. The tax shield on a debt of £4 million is therefore a perpetuity of £4 million × 10% × 35%, i.e. £140,000, starting in 1 year's time. The discount rate to use in evaluating this tax shield is the interest rate charged on the debt, the assumption being that the risk on a tax shield is equal to the risk on the payments generating that shield:

$$\text{PV of a perpetuity commencing in year 1} = \frac{\text{Perpetuity}}{r}$$

where r = relevant discount rate

$$\text{PV of tax shield} = \frac{£140,000}{0.1} = £1,400,000$$

If the value of this tax shield is included in the APV calculation, then:

$$\text{APV} = \text{'Base Case NPV'} - \text{PV issue costs} + \text{PV of tax shield}$$
$$= £0.5\text{m} - £0.6\text{m} + £1.4\text{m}$$
$$= £1.3\text{m}$$

An obvious question to raise at this point is: 'Should the PV of the tax shield on debt be included in the calculation, despite the fact that the firm has not yet signalled a specific intention to issue further debt?'

The answer to this question is yes: the PV of the tax shield should be calculated on the basis of the debt which the project could support, rather than the debt which it actually does support. Debt and equity are not issued daily by a company. Many of the transaction costs of issuing debt or equity are largely fixed, e.g., the costs of preparing a prospectus for an equity issue, or drawing up a loan agreement, are substantially independent of the magnitude of funds to be raised. For this reason, companies do not normally raise long-term funds until their requirement is sizeable. Moreover, there is no necessity for them to raise new debt and equity simultaneously. A company's preferred debt ratio refers to the market value of its debt as a percentage of the market value of its debt plus equity. The actual debt ratio will obviously vary on a daily basis, as market prices alter. The preferred debt ratio is thus a target figure, giving a guide to the average level of company debt over time. It is not a precise figure which can be adhered to on a daily basis. In our example, a persistent tendency for the ratio to stray above the 40 per cent level would favour an equity issue when the company next raised funds. Conversely, a tendency for the ratio to stay below the 40 per cent level would indicate that new finance should be provided by loan capital.

Companies invest in real assets with far greater regularity than they raise new finance. The precise source of finance for a particular investment will usually be an accident of timing. Let us assume the existence of a preferred debt ratio: then, if debt is issued to finance an investment, other investments immediately subsequent to this will tend to be financed by equity. Similarly, once a number of projects have been financed by equity, the debt capacity of the company will have been enhanced, and other projects will tend to be financed by debt. Undertaking new projects increases a firm's ability to raise debt. The actual issue of the debt may precede, coincide with or postdate a particular investment. Nevertheless, as *all* investments in real assets add to a firm's debt capacity, all should gain the same relative benefit from the debt tax shield.

The reader might well assert that this same logic should be applied to equity issues, i.e. an investment which happens to be financed by an equity issue should not bear all the transaction costs of that issue, as it is only an accident of timing that the investment was not financed from retentions, or indeed by debt. In the example above, the company has a target ratio of 40:60 for debt:equity. *If* the project had been financed in this ratio, £4 million of debt would have been raised, and £6 million of equity issued (ignoring retained earnings). In arriving at the APV figure of £1.3 million, the tax shield on the £4 million notional debt was taken into account. Thus the APV effectively includes the costs and benefits of £14 million of finance – £10 million equity + £4 million debt – not just the £10 million actually needed. A rule-of-thumb approach to dealing with this problem would be to include only 60 per cent (in this example) of the actual issue costs of equity in the APV calculation. The costs of raising £6 million in equity, and the benefits of the tax shield on £4 million of debt would then be accounted for. The costs associated with the remaining £4 million of equity actually issued could be included in the evaluation of the next £6.67 million of company investments (£4 million being 60 per cent of £6.67 million).

There are a number of problems with this approach. First, we only have the transaction costs of raising a notional £6 million in the APV calculation, rather than the costs of the £10 million actually raised. The implicit assumption here is that there are no transaction costs associated with issuing debt – clearly an invalid assumption in the real world. Although the transaction costs of raising debt will usually be less than the costs of raising equity, the differences may well not be so great that the cost of the equity issue cannot stand as a useful proxy for it. Leaving the issue costs unadjusted would cause this to happen automatically.

Second, adjustment of the issue costs is administratively burdensome. It necessitates records being kept of the proportion of the current issue costs to be carried forward, and these costs to be matched up with future investments Moreover, additional adjustments may be necessary. In the present example, if the next investment happened to require £6.67 million, then the whole of the notional issue costs of the £4 million brought forward could be matched against it. However, if this later investment were financed entirely by the issue of *debt*, the refined approach would include only 40 per cent of the transaction costs (the remaining 60 per cent being carried forward), with the brought forward equity issue costs being substituted. The costs excluded from the calculation of the APV – 60 per cent of the cost of raising debt – might well approximate to the equity cost brought forward and put in its place. This cumbersome approach might thus have little practical value.

It seems to the authors that, as a *practical* approach, it is adequate to let the PV of any issue costs stand unadjusted in the calculation of the APV.

Example 2

A company is considering an investment of £100,000 in capital equipment. the project is expected to yield positive net cash flows of £50,000 before tax each year for 3 years. The equipment will have zero scrap value at the end of its 3-year life.

The company has established that projects of this type fall within an industry category with an average beta value of 1.325, and an average debt:equity ratio of 1:2. Corporation tax is 35 per cent, and a writing-down allowance of 25 per cent on cost is available on capital expenditure. Assume that tax is paid without delay in the year in which the revenue is received. The after-tax rate of return on government stocks with a 3-year maturity date is 7 per cent. The after-tax risk premium is expected to be 8 per cent.

Let us calculate the 'base case' NPV for this project.

Referring back to the procedure outlined above, we can see that the data for steps 1–3 are actually given in the question. Equation 7.3 in step 4 (p. 192) can therefore be solved for the project beta:

$$\beta_{asset} = 1.325 \times \frac{2}{2 + 1\,(1 - 0.35)}$$
$$\beta_{asset} = 1$$

(Note: equation 7.3 assumes that all cash flows are perpetuities. Clearly this is not the case in this example, so an element of error is introduced. However, the error is unlikely to be serious.)

All the data are now available for solving equation 7.4 (p. 194), in order to find the discount rate to use in calculating the base case NPV:

$$r_i = 0.07 + 1 (0.08)$$

(Note: $(E(r_m) - r_f)$ is the risk premium, given in the example as 8 per cent.)

$$r_i = 0.15$$

Thus the project cash flows should be discounted at 15 per cent. Obviously, the cash flows will need to be adjusted for tax. They will be subject to tax at 35 per cent, so the after-tax cash flow each year is $0.65 \times £50,000$, i.e. £32,500. Furthermore, the capital expenditure gives rise to tax benefits, as calculated below:

Writing-down allowances (WDA)
(Assume capital outlay on day 1 of year 1)

Capital cost	£100,000	
WDA @ 25%	25,000	Tax benefit @ 35% = £8,750 (year 1)
	75,000	
WDA @ 25%	18,750	Tax benefit @ 35% = £6,562 (year 2)
Balancing allowance	56,250	Tax benefit @ 35% = £19,687 (year 3)

Total base case cash flows

Year	Project flows £	Tax on cash inflows @ 35% £	Tax relief WDA £	After-tax cash flows £	$r_i = 15\%$	PV £
0	(100,000)			(100,000)	1.0	(100,000)
1	50,000	(17,500)	8,750	41,250	0.870	35,887
2	50,000	(17,500)	6,562	39,062	0.756	29,531
3	50,000	(17,500)	19,687	52,187	0.658	34,339
					NPV	−243

Base case NPV = −£243

The base case NPV does not present this project as an attractive opportunity to the company. However, the APV approach requires that side effects from the project should be taken into consideration before making a final decision.

Financing side effects of project
Assume that the project would be financed by a mixture of debt and equity, using the proportions prevailing for projects of this type (as given in the data), i.e. 1/3 debt, 2/3 equity. Further assume that debt can be raised with an 11 per cent coupon, the issue costs of debt are 1 per cent of the total loan raised, and the issue costs of equity are 5 per cent of the total equity raised.

Present value of capital issue costs

Loan $\dfrac{£33,333}{99} \times 1 = £337$ [total loan raised £33,333 + £337]

Equity $\dfrac{£66,667}{95} \times 5 = £3,509$ [total equity issued £66,667 + £3,509]

Present value of tax shield on debt

Annual interest	£33,670 × 0.11 = £3,704
Annual tax relief	£3,704 × 0.35 = £1,296
P.V. of tax relief	£1,296 × 2.444* = £3,167

(*2.444 is the annuity factor for 11% over 3 years. The *pre*-tax cost of debt is used as the discount rate, because tax relief has already explicitly been taken into account in the calculation; to use an after tax cost of debt would thus double-count the benefit.)

Adjusted net present value

	£
Base case NPV	(243)
Issue costs debt	(337)
Issue costs equity	(3,509)
P.V. of debt tax shield	3,167
Adjusted net present value	(922)

The APV of the project is even less desirable than the base case NPV, showing that the project should be rejected.

Alternative financing proposals

Suppose now that the proposed investment was to be undertaken in an area of high unemployment. To encourage investment in such areas, the government is prepared to offer loans of up to one-third of the capital value of a project, at an interest rate of only 4 per cent. The loans are repayable at the termination of the project's life.

Let us recalculate the APV of the investment on the assumption that the company takes maximum advantage of this cheap loan, i.e. it borrows £33,333 at 4 per cent from the government, rather than issuing other forms of debt. There are no issue costs or arrangement fees on the government loan. Equity financing would remain as before.

Calculation of APV with government loan arrangements

Base case PV and equity costs are unaltered, but the calculations for debt must be reworked.

PV of tax shield on government loan

Annual interest	£33,333 × .04 = £1,333
Annual tax relief	1,333 × .35 = £ 467
PV of tax relief	467 × 2.444* = £1,141

(*The annuity factor for 11 per cent is still used to evaluate the PV of the tax relief, as this is the relevant interest rate for the risk. The 4 per cent rate is artificially low, being even lower than the risk-free rate.)

The discount rate used in calculating the base case NPV expresses the market cost of financing the project. If a project can be financed at below-market rates, this represents a financing *subsidy*, which must also be included in the calculation.

PV of loan subsidy
After-tax saving on market interest rate

$$£33,333 \ (0.11-0.04) \ (1-0.35)=£1,517$$

$$\text{PV of interest rate savings } £1,517 \times 2.444^* = £3,707$$

(*Again, the 11 per cent interest rate is relevant.)

Adjusted present value under government loan provisions

	£
Base case NPV	(243)
Issue costs: equity	(3,509)
PV of debt tax shield	1,141
PV of loan subsidy	3,707
Adjusted NPV	+1,096

Under these assumptions, the financing side effects have made this project worthwhile, and it should be accepted on financial grounds.

7.2.2 Value of debt tax shield

The calculations above have assumed that the debt tax shield is worth 35 per cent, i.e. the full corporation tax rate, of the interest payment. It rests on the assumptions set out in Modigliani and Miller (1963), which include corporate taxation but exclude consideration of personal taxes which financiers may suffer on dividends or interest. When personal taxation is introduced into the analysis, it can be shown that the value of the debt tax shield is reduced and under certain assumptions may actually be of zero value (Miller, 1977). However, it is generally accepted that the shield *is* valuable, but its value is difficult to establish, owing to its dependence on factors such as the probability of a company's being tax-exhausted, the recoverability of advance corporation tax, the personal tax position of the company's shareholders, and the relative tax rates on dividends, capital gains and interest income. In practice, a company would have to make a judgement as to the value of the debt tax shield in the light of its own circumstances, and that of its shareholders.

7.2.3 *Discount rate applicable to financing side effects*

The reader will have noted that the discount rate used to evaluate the side-effect cash flows differs from the discount rate used to calculate the base case NPV. This is because the systematic risk of the side effects differs from the systematic risk of the base case cash flows. For example, the obligation to pay interest on debt finance exists irrespective of any environmental changes affecting the fortunes of a firm. Although the tax shield value of these interest payments may differ from firm to firm, as we have seen above (section 7.2.2), the tax shield itself has the same low systematic risk as the interest payments, and should therefore be discounted at a relatively low interest rate.

7.2.4 *Valuation of components rule (VCR)*

The technique of using different discount rates for the various parts of an investment proposal is sometimes referred to as the valuation of components rule (VCR). The logic may be applied to the evaluation of the base case NPV as well as to the evaluation of side effects. If a project's costs were subject to significantly less systematic risk than its revenues, for example, two discount rates could be used: a lower one for the costs, and a higher one for the revenues, to reflect the different systematic risk levels of each. However, as it is more difficult to establish a beta value for the component parts of a project than for the whole project, this procedure is usually only considered for very large or unusual projects.

However, companies may consider using a differential rate when discounting the value of capital allowances. For multi-project companies, the value of a capital allowance may be independent of the financial performance of the specific project giving rise to it. For example, a company with large unutilized tax losses is unable to benefit from capital allowances in the short term. Conversely, for a company with high taxable profits, the allowance is valuable, even if the profits of the specific project under review are insufficient to absorb all of them as they arise. In section 7.2.1, example 2, the balancing allowance in year 3 is greater than the year 3 net cash inflow (assumed, for simplicity, to equate to taxable profit before capital allowances). If this were the company's only project, the value of the balancing allowance would be diminished, because of the lack of taxable profits against which to offset these allowances. Nevertheless, in determining the base case NPV, the full benefit of this balancing charge has been recognized.

This method implicitly assumes not only the existence of taxable profits elsewhere in the company, but also that these profits are large enough to require the company to pay tax at the full corporation tax rate. In fact, a company can face any one of four effective tax rates in a year: zero (when the company is tax exhausted); the small company rate; the marginal tax rate levied on profits lying in the band between the small company rate and the full rate; and the full company rate.

In reality, when evaluating the base case NPV, a company should forecast both the year in which capital allowances may be offset against profits, and also the tax rate to use in determining the benefit of this offset – no easy task in view of the interdependencies, as we saw in section 7.2.2.

However, these considerations of value and timing do not affect the choice of discount rate to be used in evaluating the flows. In the example above, the benefits of the capital allowance were discounted at the rate reflecting the project's systematic risk, i.e. 15 per cent. At this rate the base case project has a negative NPV. However, a reduction of only 1 per cent to 14 per cent of the discount rate applied to the tax relief in WDA is sufficient in this case to give a positive Base Case NPV, as Table 7.3 shows.

This example illustrates that a failure to recognize that a single discount rate may not always be appropriate for all cash flows associated with a project can be critical in determining whether or not a project is acceptable.

7.3   Relationship between 'cost of capital' and CAPM discount rate and the former's use in investment appraisal

The cost of capital to a company is the weighted average price which it must pay to persuade suppliers of funds to provide it with finance. In a risk-free world with perfect capital markets and no taxes, all suppliers of funds will be satisfied with the going interest rate. This interest rate is a true reflection of the opportunity cost to suppliers of allowing the company to use their funds. Thus the company's cost of capital is this going rate. When risk is introduced, all other assumptions remaining as above, the suppliers of capital require compensation for accepting the risk. Funds will only be supplied in the form of equity to companies if there is an expectation that the companies can earn a return in excess of the risk-free return, to compensate the shareholders for risk.

If the risk premium is determined in the manner suggested by the capital asset pricing model, i.e. the premium on the risk-free return compensates for the systematic risk being accepted, then the cost of capital for an all equity-financed company equals the CAPM-derived discount rate. Under these circumstances, an all equity-financed company's cost of capital is not only compatible but is also synonymous with the CAPM 'cost of capital' or discount rate. Therefore, for an all equity-financed firm, as the company's cost of capital equals the CAPM discount rate, the use of this cost of capital as the discount rate in project appraisal is only appropriate if the project under consideration has the same risk characteristics as the company's average existing project. If this is *not* the case, then the risk compensation contained in the discount rate is inappropriate.

In an all equity-financed firm, the company's cost of capital equals the return required by the ordinary shareholders on their investment. When debt financing is introduced, the cost of capital to the company is the weighted average cost of the debt and equity financing, as the equation below shows:

$$K_O = \frac{K_E V_E}{V_E + V_D} + \frac{K_D V_D}{V_E + V_D} \qquad \ldots \text{Equation 7.5}$$

where
K_O = weighted average cost of capital,
K_E = cost of equity capital,
K_D = cost of debt,
V_E = market value of equity,
V_D = market value of company debt.

Table 7.3

Year	A Project flows inflows £	B Tax on cash inflows at 35% £	(A–B) £	$r_1 = 15\%$	PV of (A–B) £	C Tax relief on WDA £	PV of (C) [at 15%] £	$r_1 = 14\%$	PV of (C) [at 14%]
0	–100,000		–100,000	1.0	–100,000				
1	+50,000	(17,500)	+32,500	0.870	+28,275	8,750	7,612	0.877	7,674
2	+50,000	(17,500)	+32,500	0.756	+24,570	6,562	4,961	0.769	5,046
3	+50,000	(17,500)	+32,500	0.658	+21,385	19,687	12,954	0.675	13,289
					– 25,770		+ 25,527		+ 26,009

NPV when (A–B) and (C) both discounted at 15% = – £25,770 + £25,527 = – £243
NPV when (A–B) discounted at 15% and (C) discounted at 14% = – £25,770 + £26,009 = + £239

There are a number of models for ascertaining K_E. However, the important point to note is that, in a world without taxes, the Miller/Modigliani (1958) proposition shows that the cost of capital, K_O, is independent of the company's gearing (see Figure 7.1). Without taxes, K_O represents the return which must be earned by the company on its projects, given the systematic risk of those projects.

This given level of project risk must be borne by those who finance the assets. If some of those financiers are able to provide funds to the company on terms which largely release them from accepting this asset risk, as total risk will remain unchanged, it follows that the risk borne per unit of financing supplied by others must necessarily increase. For example, a debenture holder in a company is guaranteed a particular rate of return, and can usually force the sale of the company's assets to recover his funds if the company defaults on its interest payments. Thus debenture finance is relatively risk-free to the supplier of debenture finance.

The corollary is that, as the debenture-holder's return is effectively guaranteed, the rate paid to him will hardly differ from the risk-free rate, as a premium above this risk-free rate will only be paid as compensation for bearing risk. As the proportion of the company's assets financed by debt increases, the total level of risk is spread over a reducing proportion of equity finance. As gearing increases (i.e. as $V_D/(V_E + V_D)$ increases), the rate demanded by holders of equity (K_E) will increase to compensate the equity holders for the increased proportion of the total asset risk carried by each unit of equity, as relatively risk-free debt finance is substituted for equity. However, this increase in the rate required by equity shareholders does not change the cost of capital (K_O) to a company in a tax-free world. As Figure 7.1 showed, the extra return demanded by shareholders as gearing increases is exactly offset by the benefit derived from substituting cheap debt finance for more expensive equity finance.

This has a number of implications for capital investment. In a tax-free world, if a company knows its cost of capital (K_O), it can use this as the discount rate for new projects with the same systematic risk as the average existing project. Changes in the gearing level of the company will change the rate demanded by shareholders (K_E), but will leave K_O, and hence the discount rate, unaffected.

Similarly, in a tax-free world, changes in a company's gearing will affect its beta. The change in the company beta will reflect the change in return required by shareholders in response to the different risk they bear as gearing increases/decreases. However, as we saw earlier (section 7.1.3, step 4), the gearing effect on beta must be stripped out in arriving at an asset beta to use in deriving a discount rate. In perfect capital markets without taxes, the CAPM-derived discount rate will again be equal to K_O, even if the firm engages in gearing, i.e. the rate reflects only the business risk of the company's assets. If the project under consideration does not have the same systematic risk as the average existing project, then a discount rate (by whatever method it has been derived) based on the risk of this average existing project is not the appropriate discount rate to use when appraising the new project. The appropriate rate should reflect the systematic risk of the new project, and may be established by using data on proxy companies, as outlined in step 1 (section

7.1.3). Use of proxy companies enables the correct discount rate for the project to be found, either by establishing the weighted average cost of capital (WACC) of the proxy companies or by deriving a CAPM discount rate from proxy company data. In both cases, given perfect capital markets and a tax-free world, the discount rate arrived at should be the same. It is therefore immaterial which of the two methods is used to derive the rate.

This equality of rate rests on the proposition that K_0 is constant, i.e. gearing does not affect the cost of capital to the company. If K_0 is *not* constant, but changes as the level of company gearing changes, the WACC becomes a function of two factors – the systematic risk of the business assets, and the level of the company's gearing.

In deriving the CAPM discount rate, this second factor is always eliminated from the calculation, as step 4 (section 7.1.3) showed. Thus the proposition that the WACC equals the CAPM derived discount rate is true if, *and only if*, the WACC is independent of gearing.

As discussed earlier, the Miller/Modigliani (1958) proposition is that the WACC *is* independent of gearing in a tax-free world. However, in the real world, companies are subject to corporate taxes. Furthermore, in many countries, including the UK and USA, debt and equity are treated differently for tax purposes: the interest on debt is a tax-deductible expense, whereas the dividends paid to equity holders are not. If a company can offset its interest payments on debt against its taxable profits, it benefits from the so-called debt tax shield. The actual value of this shield is the subject of academic debate, but it is generally agreed that the debt tax shield does have a positive value; its precise amount need not concern us here.

The tax treatment of the interest paid by the company to the debt holders has no implications for the risk borne by ordinary shareholders, and therefore does not affect their required rate of return. It is thus intuitively obvious that a move from a tax-free world to one in which there is a tax subsidy on debt and no subsidy on equity will lead to a decline in the cost of debt to the company, with no offsetting increase in the cost of equity. In a tax-free world, debt is cheaper than equity *only* because of the differing risks attached to the two sources of finance. In a taxed world, where debt interest is tax-deductible, this is *not* so. Debt becomes relatively cheaper simply because of its tax advantages to the company (considerations of personal taxation are ignored in this argument). Thus if WACC is constant in a tax-free world, it will *not* be constant in a taxed world with debt interest tax-deductibility. Here, the tax advantage attaching to debt implies that the WACC will decline as gearing increases. The increase in the rate demanded by shareholders as the proportion of debt increases will continue exactly to counteract the cost advantage of debt bought about by its differential risk level, but will not remove the cost advantage of debt brought about by its tax-deductibility. In a taxed world, therefore, WACC will decline as gearing increases.

The logical conclusion which follows from this proposition, of course, is that rational decision makers would wish to gain the maximum possible advantage from the debt tax shield, and companies would thus be almost totally financed by debt. However, such high levels of corporate gearing are not the norm. This may be because important real-world considerations, e.g. bankruptcy costs, were omitted in evaluating the risks of high levels of gearing. Indeed, the greatest area of academic contention centres around the behaviour of the WACC at high gearing levels.

In the foregoing discussion of the role of WACC as a discount rate in project appraisal, the important point at issue was not *how* the WACC changes with gearing, but *if* it changes with gearing in a taxed world. The vast majority of academics accept that, in a taxed world, WACC *does* vary with gearing. There is strong support for the view that, at low levels of gearing, the tax-deductibility of debt leads to a reduction in the WACC as gearing increases. Acceptance of the proposition that WACC in a taxed world is a function of the company's level of gearing has important implications for the use of the WACC as a discount rate in project appraisal. For example, if a company is considering an investment in a new project, which has the same systematic risk as its average existing project, the use of the company's WACC as the discount rate for the new project is valid only if the company's gearing, and hence its WACC, would be unchanged by undertaking it. For small projects, this may be a reasonable approximation to reality. However, for larger projects, such an assumption can introduce significant inaccuracies, and the company may wish to finance the project in such a way that the gearing level remains unchanged after the project's acceptance. Unfortunately, this is not as straightforward as might at first be thought.

In a perfect capital market, undertaking an investment will increase the value of a company's equity by an amount equal to the NPV of the new project. If the new project is financed in the company's existing debt:equity ratio, undertaking it will normally change the company's gearing level.

Consider a company which currently has a debt: equity ratio of 1:2 i.e., the market value of the equity, MV_E, is twice that of the debt, MV_D. Financing a new project with positive NPV, with funds in this same ratio 1:2 will, in fact, alter the company's gearing as Table 7.4 shows.

Table 7.4

	Debt	Equity	Gearing
Pre project	MV_{D_1}	MV_{E_1}	$MV_{D_1}/MV_{E_1} = 1:2$
New project finance	Δ_D	Δ_E	$\Delta_D/\Delta_E = 1:2$
Post project	$MV_{D_1} + \Delta_D$	$MV_{E_1} + \Delta_E + NPV$ new project	$(MV_{D_1} + \Delta_D)/(MV_{E_1} + \Delta_E + NPV$ new project$) \neq 1:2$

Only when the NPV of a new project is zero will financing the project in accordance with the company's existing debt:equity ratio leave the company's gearing unchanged. Gearing is held constant for a successful project, i.e. one which has a positive NPV, where:

$MV_D : MV_E =$ New debt finance : New equity finance + NPV new project

Thus, for acceptable projects, gearing will be maintained by raising relatively more debt and relatively less equity than is implied by the existing capital structure.

In reality, the ability of a company to raise debt depends on the security which can be offered to the lender. Where loans are secured on particular assets, this security lies in the ability of the lender to find a market for the asset if the borrower defaults on his payments. The ease with which assets can be realized will obviously vary considerably. For example, residential property has a ready second-hand market, and difficulties are rarely found in disposing of it at a level approaching its purchase price. Conversely, large specialized machinery may be very difficult to sell, and may raise only a fraction of its purchase price. Thus lenders may be prepared to advance, say, 80 per cent of the cost of a house to a borrower, but may only be prepared to lend, say 20 per cent of the cost of a specialized machine. The proportion of the assets's cost which a lender is prepared to advance is known as its 'debt capacity'.

In our discussion of gearing so far, it has been assumed that companies can decide on a desired level of borrowing, and that the required finance will be forthcoming, regardless of the debt capacity of the company's assets. This is probably unrealistic, and a further reason for the absence of high observed levels of gearing in the markets: companies may simply be unable to raise funds once their debt capacity has been exhausted, whatever their preferences may be.

As assets have differential debt capacities, the value of the debt tax shield will also vary from asset to asset, being highest for those with a high debt capacity, and lowest for those with a low debt capacity. The WACC includes the value of the debt tax shield to a company, based on its existing level of gearing. Where the asset under consideration has a debt capacity which differs from this existing gearing level, the use of the WACC as a discount rate ignores the difference. The value of the debt tax shield to the project will thus be under- or over-estimated. Use of the APV approach – a CAPM-derived discount rate with separate consideration of financing side effects – can easily accommodate differences in debt capacity.

7.4   Leasing

7.4.1   Introduction

A lease can be defined as a contractual relationship between the legal owner of an asset (the lessor) and a separate individual or firm that enjoys the exclusive use of that asset (the lessee) over a given period of time. By paying a rental to the lessor, the lessee is able to gain the benefits of an asset's use without assuming the obligations of ownership. The rental will be calculated to compensate the legal owner of the asset for the capital cost of acquisition, the time value of the funds tied up in the asset, and the risk of default by the lessee.

There are two types of lease: financial (or capital) and operating. In a *financial* lease, the asset is effectively 'purchased' through the rental payments: the contract is intended to recover the *full* costs of ownership until the end of the asset's useful life. In contrast, an *operating* lease will be for a period shorter than the asset's economic life, or will allow the lessee to terminate the contract before the recovery of its full costs.

An operating lease will not affect a company's gearing – it is the equivalent of a conventional rental agreement. A finance lease, on the other hand, *will* affect a company's gearing, as it is obviously the equivalent of debt. Indeed, SSAP 21 specifically requires finance leases to be capitalized on the face of the balance sheet, and thus gives explicit recognition to its status in this respect.

7.4.2 *Leasing and the separation theorem*

As we saw earlier (section 6.3.1), the separation theorem states that, in a world of perfect capital markets, the value of an asset is independent of the way it is financed. All financial instruments, including leases, would have an NPV of zero, and a company would be indifferent between leasing a new asset and buying it outright by means of a loan. Lessor and lessee would be in a so-called zero-sum game, as the following example illustrates:

Example 3. A company wishes to acquire an asset which costs £1.2m and has an economic life of 6 years with no residual value. A finance company has offered to supply the asset on a financial lease for six annual rental payments of £250,000, payable in advance. We shall assume that both parties are full corporation taxpayers, that the corporation tax rate is 35 per cent and tax is paid annually in arrears, and (for the sake of simplicity) the annual writing-down allowance is the same as straight-line depreciation:

Lessee
£000s

Year	Investment	Rental payment	Tax shield on rental @35%	Tax shield lost on WDAs (200 p.a. @35%)	NCF
0	1,200	(250)			950
1		(250)	87.5	(70)	(232.5)
2		(250)	87.5	(70)	(232.5)
3		(250)	87.5	(70)	(232.5)
4		(250)	87.5	(70)	(232.5)
5		(250)	87.5	(70)	(232.5)
6			87.5	(70)	17.5
					(195)

Lessor

£000s

Year	Investment	Rental payment	Tax on rental @35%	Tax shield on WDAs (200 p.a. @35%)	NCF
0	(1,200)	250			(950)
1		250	(87.5)	70	232.5
2		250	(87.5)	70	232.5
3		250	(87.5)	70	232.5
4		250	(87.5)	70	232.5
5		250	(87.5)	70	232.5
6			(87.5)	70	(17.5)
					195

The cashflows have not been discounted, as discounting would clearly not affect the outcome in this example. We shall discuss the appropriate rate to apply to particular situations at a later stage.

7.4.3 Why is leasing popular?

Despite recent research evidence (Drury and Braund, 1989) that many companies are not fully aware of the relevant issues in the lease-versus-buy decision, and a significant number of actual lessees are using an incorrect discount rate in its evaluation, the sheer size of the leasing market in the UK – £6,000m of new capital investment in equipment in 1987 was carried out by means of lease contracts – would indicate that it is not a zero-sum game. Let us turn therefore to an examination of the reasons why leasing is so attractive.

Convenience. Operating leases allow companies the flexibility to acquire the use of equipment as and when needed. The expense and effort required to purchase the asset and resell it shortly thereafter is avoided, as is the alternative of purchasing it and having funds tied up in idle equipment. In this situation, the lessor effectively acts as an intermediary who is able to reduce transactions costs by dealing in specialized assets with a wide range of customers.

Technological risk minimization. Companies often perceive operating leases as advantageous in situations of rapid technological change, where there is a substantial risk of obsolescence – the computer market is a good example. However, it would be naive to assume that the lessor is unaware of this risk, and his own exposure on cancellation or termination of the contract, and the rentals will obviously reflect these factors. Nevertheless, there can be a financial advantage to the lessee, inasmuch as the cost to the lessor of 'insuring' against these risks may be significantly lower than that to the lessee, particularly where the asset has alternative uses in other markets, or where the risk can be spread over a large number of contracts.

Bankruptcy cost minimization. A financial lease contract is similar to a debt repayment schedule for the purchase of an asset by a loan, in that the company is obliged to make a series of fixed payments. However, in the case of default in the payment of *lease rentals*, the asset is simply repossessed by the lessor. If financial difficulties cause a company to default on a debt repayment schedule, the result could be a petition by the creditors to wind up the company.

Difficulties in raising finance. It can be difficult for relatively new companies, without an established track record for credit-rating purposes, to raise finance for capital purchases. Leasing provides an easily obtainable alternative to borrowed funds, as adequate security is provided for the lessor by the retention of ownership of the asset. Furthermore, it can be a relatively cheap source of finance if the benefits of lower administration and transaction costs are passed across to the lessor in reduced rental payments. For example, a lessor who specialized in a particular type of asset can safely extend the finance (i.e. lease the asset) without the necessity of conducting a detailed analysis of each lessee's business: although lessees will differ in size and risk, the underlying asset is the same in each case, and costly investigative costs can be avoided. The use of simple, standard lease contracts will also keep down the administrative and legal costs.

Guarantees and maintenance. The lessor may be able to provide some additional service as part of the lease contract that makes it more attractive than an outright purchase. However, it would again be naive to assume that the rental payments would not reflect the value of this, at least in part. The fundamental question, whose answer is a matter of fact (though not necessarily easy to determine), is whether the service can be performed at a lower cost by the lessor than by the lessee (or an independent firm acting for the lessee), so that the total package from the lessor is more attractive than the alternative of a loan plus service payments.

Market imperfections. The example above assumed perfect capital markets. As soon as this assumption is relaxed, transaction costs, differential interest rates between lending and borrowing, and differential tax rates between lessor and lessee (looked at separately under 'tax advantages' below) conspire to make leasing a less costly source of finance in some situations than borrowing and buying.

Tax advantages. In certain circumstances, imperfections in the tax system, giving rise to differential tax rates for lessor and lessee, can be used to advantage in a financial lease. When a company buys an asset, it obtains a tax shield from the future capital allowances on that asset. Capital allowances are an allowable deduction against taxable profits, and thus reduce the tax payable by the company. However, if a company happens to be tax-exhausted, the benefit of the tax shield will have to be carried forward until such time as the company is due to pay taxes again, and thus the PV of the capital allowances will be reduced, perhaps dramatically so. On the other hand, if the company *leases* the asset under these circumstances, and the lessor *is* a full taxpaying company that can obtain the tax benefits of ownership without delay, in a competitive leasing market the lessee should be able to negotiate a rental charge that reflects a large part of the value of the tax shield to the lessor. Thus leasing provides a means by which a taxpaying lessor transfers some of the tax benefits of purchasing an asset to a tax-exhausted lessee through lower rentals.

7.4.4   Capital budgeting and leasing

Let us now turn to the question of how leasing can influence the capital budgeting decision, and how a financial lease should be evaluated. The first point reduces to two further questions. 'Is leasing more profitable than borrowing and buying?' 'Could lease financing turn an otherwise unprofitable project into a profitable one?' The second question recognizes that an investment could have a negative NPV based on a purchase, but a positive NPV when combined with a lease. If the first of these calculations has already taken place, then the size of the negative NPV will be known and can simply be compared with that of any positive NPV from a subsequent lease-versus-buy analysis, and if the latter exceeds the former then the project should be undertaken by means of a lease. Obviously, if the result of the subsequent lease-versus-buy computation is a *negative* NPV, i.e. a purchase is to be preferred to a lease, then an even larger negative NPV would result from funding the project by a lease contract, and the project should be rejected. However, if this first calculation has not been performed, then the better of the two alternatives from the lease-versus-buy computation should be used for the subsequent project analysis.

7.4.5   What is the appropriate discount rate to use in leasing calculations?

Before we go on to look at the different methods for evaluating a financial lease, we must consider the discount rate to be used in the calculation, and the impact of taxation on that rate. The discount rate should be the borrowing rate that the firm would have to pay if it took over a secured loan on the asset repayable on the terms implicit in the lease contract: we recognize the equivalence of lease financing to debt financing by discounting at the borrowing rate on a comparable loan. In other words, if the cash flows associated with the decision to lease have a risk equivalent to those associated with servicing the same level of debt, the appropriate rate to use to discount those cash flows is the borrowing rate which would apply to that debt. In the case of a full taxpaying lessee, the net incremental cash flows should be discounted at the *after*-tax borrowing rate, because interest charges are tax-deductible, and a taxpaying firm would be able to take advantage of them. In the case of a tax-exhausted firm, there are no taxable profits to absorb the tax-deductible interest payments, and thus their deductibility has no value and the *pre*-tax borrowing rate should be used.

7.4.6   Lease evaluation

Evaluation of lease by straight PV comparison with borrowing and buying
This is the first of the methods referred to above. Let us take the data from our earlier example, and assume that an appropriate borrowing rate to apply in the calculation is 10 per cent. Let us further assume that the lessee is a full taxpaying company, and thus use the *after*-tax borrowing rate as a

discount rate, i.e. 6.5 per cent (10 per cent less tax at 35 per cent). The computation would be as follows:

£000s

Year	Invest- ment	Rental payment	Tax shield on rental	Tax shield on WDAs lost	NCF	Discount factor at 6.5%	PV
0	1,200	(250)			950	1.0	950.00
1		(250)	87.5	(70)	(232.5)	0.9390	(218.317)
2		(250)	87.5	(70)	(232.5)	0.8817	(204.995)
3		(250)	87.5	(70)	(232.5)	0.8278	(192.463)
4		(250)	87.5	(70)	(232.5)	0.7773	(180.722)
5		(250)	87.5	(70)	(232.5)	0.7299	(169.702)
6			87.5	(70)	17.5	0.6853	11.993
						NPV	(4.206)

The negative NPV indicates that borrowing and buying the asset outright is to be preferred to leasing.

Let us now look at the same data from the viewpoint of a tax-exhausted lessee, for whom the appropriate discount rate would be the full pre-tax borrowing rate of 10 per cent. Obviously, in the case of tax-exhaustion, it would be inappropriate to include in the calculation of cash flows either the benefit of the tax shield associated with the rental payments, or the opportunity cost of the tax shield on the capital allowances foregone, both of which are a function of taxpaying status. The cash flows are thus limited to the cost of the investment and the gross rental payments:

£000s

Year	Investment	Rental payment	NCF	Discount factor @ 10%	PV
0	1,200	(250)	950	1.0	950
1–5		(250)	(250)	3.7907	(947.67)
				NPV	2.33

The NPV has now become positive, indicating that, on these data, leasing is to be preferred to borrowing and buying when the lessee is tax-exhausted. Here we see an example of differential tax rates between lessor and lessee being used to the advantage of *both* parties to the lease contract. The lessee has a positive NPV of £2,330, and the lessor a positive NPV of £4,206 (the mirror image of the lessee's negative NPV in the previous table). Obviously, the lessor's NPV will only be this mirror image if the interest rate used as the basic for the discount rate in its calculation is the same as that used in the lessee's analysis. Fortunately, this is easily seen to be the case, despite one's natural belief that the lessor should be able to borrow at a cheaper rate than the lessee. Whether this is the case or not is irrelevent to the argument. The lessor is comparing the lease to the equivalent loan which a lessee could obtain on the security of the same asset, in exactly the way that the lessee effectively compares the lease with a loan that could be obtained from a bank or other lender for its purchase. Both parties assume the same borrowing rate, although their after-tax interest rates will differ if they find themselves in differing taxpaying positions.

Evaluation of lease by equivalent loan (or loan balance) method
This is an alternative method for obtaining the NPV of a lease which is entirely consistent with the pre- and post-tax discount rate approach of the previous method. Its objective is to determine the capital sum that, together with interest at the relevant rate, would be fully repaid from the net cash flows associated with the lease. Looking at this another way, it is the capital sum that, when invested at the relevant rate, would be just sufficient to pay the net cash flows of the lease. This capital sum represents the PV of the lease, and the difference between this amount and the initial investment will be the NPV of the lease. If the PV of the lease exceeds the initial investment, the NPV will be negative and leasing more expensive than borrowing and buying – and *vice versa*. The calculation is simple, and requires only that the net cash flows be discounted at the appropriate pre- or post-tax rate. The following table uses the NCF data from our earlier example, and give exactly the same answer as the last method:

Table 7.5

	Full tax-paying lessee				Tax-exhausted lessee		
£000s				£000s			
Year	NCF	Discount factor @ 6.5%	PV	Year	NCF	Discount factor @ 10%	PV
1	(232.5)	0.9390	(218.317)	1–5	(250)	3.7907	(947.67)
2	(232.5)	0.8817	(204.995)				
3	(232.5)	0.8278	(192.463)				
4	(232.5)	0.7773	(180.722)				
5	(232.5)	0.7299	(169.702)				
6	17.5	0.6853	11.993				

	Full tax-paying lessee		Tax-exhausted lessee
Equivalent loan	(954.206)	Equivalent loan	(947.67)
Investment	950.00	Investment	950.00
NPV	(4.206)	NPV	2.33

The following loan repayment schedules prove that loans of £954,210 and £947,670 can in fact be fully repaid from the respective net cash flows of the lease:

Full tax-paying lessee

£000s

Year	Loan outstanding at beginning of year	NCF	After-tax interest payment @ 6.5%	Capital repayment	Loan outstanding at end of year
1	954.21	(232.5)	62.02	170.48	783.73
2	783.73	(232.5)	50.94	181.56	602.17
3	602.17	(232.5)	39.14	193.36	408.81
4	408.81	(232.5)	26.57	205.93	202.88
5	202.88	(232.5)	13.19	219.31	(16.43)
6	(16.43)	17.5	(1.07)	(16.43)	—
				954.21	

Tax-exhausted lessee

£000s

Year	Loan outstanding at beginning of year	NCF	After-tax (= pre-tax) interest payment @ 10%	Capital repayment	Loan outstanding at end of year
1	947.67	(250)	94.77	155.23	792.44
2	792.44	(250)	79.24	170.76	621.68
3	621.68	(250)	62.17	187.83	433.85
4	433.85	(250)	43.39	206.61	227.24
5	227.24	(250)	22.72	227.28	0.04*
				947.71	
				(0.04)*	
				947.67	

*Rounding.

One obvious advantage of the equivalent loan method is that it will facilitate the evaluation of a lease in less simple situations – such as temporary (as opposed to permanent) tax exhaustion – for which a unique discount rate is difficult to determine.

Evaluation of lease by IRR

The two methods we have looked at so far have used the NPV to determine the value of a lease. However, as we saw earlier in chapters, the IRR method is employed more frequently in capital budgeting than NPV, and we must discuss its use in lease evaluation. The IRR will be the discount rate that gives an NPV of zero for the relevant net cash flows from the lease. The particular figures we have chosen fortunately save us the trouble of working this out, as it is obvious from Table 7.5 that the IRR is just over 6.5 per cent in the case of the taxpaying lessee (where the NPV at 6.5 per cent was (£4,206)) and marginally under 10 per cent for the tax-exhausted lessee (where the

NPV was £2,330 at 10 per cent). These IRRs represent the after-tax cost of leasing, and will be compared with the after-tax cost of borrowing (6.5 per cent in the case of the tax-paying lessee and 10 per cent in that of the tax-exhausted lessee – remember that after-tax = pre-tax in the case of the latter), and the alternative which shows the lower rate should be selected. In our example, borrowing is to be preferred to leasing for the full taxpayer, and leasing to be preferred to borrowing for the tax-exhausted lessee. However, there are a number of problems with the IRR method that serve to make its use in lease evaluation an unsatisfactory and, in some cases, impractical proposition:

1   As we saw earlier, the IRR method of investment appraisal is unsuitable for comparisons between mutually exclusive projects: when the alternative with the highest IRR does not happen to have the highest NPV, the analysis gives the wrong signal to the firm. Obviously, a company might find it necessary to compare bids from different lessors involving leases with differing lifespans, and in this situation, selection of the alternative with the highest IRR is no guarantee that the correct choice has been made.
2   We know that there is no unique rate of return when the net cash flows after the initial period show changes in sign from negative to positive – as is the case in our example, when the outflows for the tax-paying lessor in years 1–5 are followed by an inflow in year 6. There will be as many IRRs as there are sign changes, complicating the lease evaluation unnecessarily.
3   When a company is tax-exhausted for only part of the timespan of the lease, more than one after-tax borrowing rate will be applicable to the cash flows in the analysis. It is far from clear which of these different rates should be used for comparison with the IRR, making it difficult to determine whether the lease would be profitable.

We do not suggest that IRR should *never* be employed in lease evaluation, but would point out that NPV does not suffer from the ambiguities inherent in IRR when the analysis is less than straightforward.

References and further reading

D. R. Chamber, R. S. Harris and J. J. Pringle. 'Treatment of Financing Mix in Analysing Investment Opportunities', *Financial Management*, Summer 1982.

De Jung, D. and Collins, D. W. 'Explanations for the Instability of Equity Beta: Risk Free Changes and Leverage Effects' Journal of Financial and Quantitive Analysis, March 1985.

Drury, C., Braund, S., 'A Survey of UK Leasing Practice', *Management Accounting*, April 1989, pp. 40–3.

Fama, E. F., 'Risk-Adjusted Discount Rate: Capital Budgeting under Uncertainty', *Journal of Financial Economics*, August 1977, pp. 3–24.

Gahlon, J. M. and Gentry, J. A. 'On the Relationship Between Systematic Risk and the Degrees of Operating and Financial Leverage' *Financial Management*, Summer 1982.

Hill, N. C. and Stone, B. K. 'Accounting Betas, Systematic Operating Risk, and Financial Leverage: A Risk-Composition Approach to the Determinants of Systematic Risk', *Journal of Financial and Quantitative Analysis*, September 1980.

Klemosky, R. C. and Martin, J. D. 'The Adjustment of Beta Forcasts', *Journal of Finance*, September 1975.

Martin, J. D. and Scott D. F. Jr, 'Debt Capacity and the Capital Budgeting Decision', *Financial Management*, Summer 1976.

Miller, M. H., 'Debt Taxes', *Journal of Finance*, vol. 32, August 1977, pp. 261–76.

Modigliani, F. M., Miller M. H., 'The Cost of Capital, Corporate Finance and the Theory of Investment', *Accounting and Economic Review*, June 1958, pp. 261–97.

Modigliani, F. M., Miller, M. H., 'Corporate Income Taxes and the Cost of Capital: A Correction', *Accounting and Economic Review*, June 1963, pp. 423–43.

Myers, S. C., Turnbull, S. M., 'Capital Budgeting and the Capital Asset Pricing Model: Good News, Bad News', *Journal of Finance*, 1977, pp. 321–3.

Reilly, F. K. and Wright, D. J. 'A Comparison of Published Betas', *The Journal of Portfolio Management*, Spring 1988.

Rendleman, R. J. Jr, 'Ranking Errors in CAPM Capital Budgeting Applications', *Financial Management*, Winter 1978.

Taggart, R. 'Capital Budgeting and the Financing Decision: An Exposition', *Financial Management*, Summer 1977.

8 Project management

8.1 Project definition and selection

In common with most textbooks which deal with capital budgeting, we have devoted a substantial amount of space to the subject of project evaluation. However, this consideration was prefaced with the warning that 'the concentration ... on the *evaluation* of investments should not obscure what are perhaps more important aspects of the capital budgeting process' (section 5.1). Many surveys of capital budgeting practice have been undertaken in both the UK and USA. These surveys also have tended to focus on the investment evaluation technique employed by companies. Comparatively few have made any attempt to ascertain which aspects of the capital budgeting procedure present most difficulty to managers in practice, and which aspects are considered by them to be most critical to an investment's success. However, these questions were specifically addressed by Gitman and Forrester (1977). They divided the investment process into four stages, as shown in Table 8.1. Despite its overwhelming prominence in the academic textbooks, 'financial analysis and project selection' (which equates to evaluation) was considered to be the most difficult aspect of the appraisal process by a mere 15 per cent of the respondents, and only 33 per cent considered it to be the stage most critical to a project's success.

The results of this survey, which are consistent with the findings of Fremgen (1973), clearly show that project definition and cash-flow estimation were regarded both as the most difficult *and* the most critical part of the capital budgeting process.

The disparity between the central role given to project evaluation in the academic literature, and the more peripheral importance it holds for practitioners, may be explained by comparing the theoretical premises on which project selection is based with the realities of organizational life.

Large organizations almost invariably have a capital budget, and projects can only be undertaken after obtaining the authority to spend against it. In most organizations, the authority to sanction capital expenditure against the

Table 8.1   Most difficult and most important stages of capital budgeting process

Stage	Responses	
	Most difficult (%)	Most critical (%)
Project definition and cash-flow estimation	64	52
Financial analysis and project selection	15	33
Project implementation	7	9
Project review	14	6
Total responses	100	100

budget is retained by top management. However, is the ability to *sanction* expenditure synonymous with project *selection?* In a narrow sense this is obviously the case, as top management can accept or reject the proposals brought before them. But surveys of practice have repeatedly found that rejection rates are very low, which suggests that some process ensures that only 'good' projects are ever submitted for approval. *Real* project selection must therefore take place much lower down the organization.

Many project 'ideas' originate at the operating level. For example, a production manager working in a divisionalized company might be aware that profitability could be improved by further investment in his production facilities. The means of improvement may range from a slight modification of existing equipment to a complete refitting of the facility with machines utilizing a new, but unproven, technology. Although the latter could well offer the highest expected NPV to shareholders, the manager might refrain from proposing this particular course of action, as he might perceive the plan as one which carries great *personal* risk. Should the project have a bad out-turn (perfectly consistent with a high expected NPV), blame might well attach to him as the instigator of the project and his career prospects might be damaged. He may also be unwilling or unable to devote the necessary time to collecting the data to support the case. Furthermore, if he works in a division evaluated on the basis of return on investment (ROI), he may be conscious of potential antagonism from his divisional manager, who could oppose the investment on the grounds that it would initially depress the divisions' ROI by heavily increasing the capital base. Therefore, if the operating manager is currently able to earn a satisfactory return on the assets in his charge, he may in fact decide to do nothing.

Investment opportunities are thus filtered at lower levels in organizations. Managers do not submit investments for approval unless they are confident that the proposals will meet the company's investment criteria. Moreover, they may refrain from submitting proposals which would otherwise be acceptable, if they feel that the proposals call for a high degree of personal effort or risk on their part.

Top management does not therefore select a sub-set of investments from all available opportunities, as theory suggests. 'Selection' in its normal sense does not actually take place at the *approval* stage, so this may explain why this phase is considered to be relatively unimportant in practice.

8.2   Cost implications of project approval

For large-scale projects, formal approval may be a two-stage process: the first stage is the sanctioning of a feasibility study, and the second is the sanctioning of the project itself. The final request to sanction capital expenditure should contain plans for the the project's implementation. The plans should define in detail the three related elements of a project: its scope, the time schedule for its completion, and its estimated cost. Project implementation is simply the execution of these plans.

It has been estimated that, for large-scale engineering projects, around 80 per cent of the total project cost is unalterably fixed at the final approved stage, i.e. if the plans are followed, there is only limited scope for altering the costs. In other types of project, approval may fix a much higher percentage of the total investment cost – for example, approval to buy a particular machine at a specified price would imply a commitment to 100 per cent of the project's total costs. It can thus be seen that, as the bulk of project costs are committed by the acceptance of the plan at the approval stage, project cost control is most effectively exercised *before* this point is reached, rather than during implementation. This would explain why relatively few of Gitman and Forrester's respondents regarded implementation as the most critical or difficult phase of the capital budgeting process. Certainly, if the original estimates of cost built into the plan turn out on implementation to be unrealistically low, even the most effective project management will not turn a bad investment into a good one: efficient implementation can never be a substitute for proper planning.

8.3   Management of project implementation

Where approval of a project commits the company to less than 100 per cent of total project costs, steps should be taken to ensure that *actual* costs are as low as possible. As we know, an expected cost is not a point estimate, but a weighted average of all possible outcomes. The expected cost is therefore higher than the least possible cost, and lower than the highest possible cost. Active project management during implementation will seek to ensure that the final cost is at the lower rather than the higher end of this spectrum.

8.3.1   *Role of project manager*

For large projects, a project manager should be appointed to oversee the implementation of the project. The necessity of having a single person with responsibility for implementation may not at first be apparent. We have argued that, where good planning exists, implementation is no more than following the detailed plans prepared before the project was approved. However, as the scale of the project increases, so does the complexity of the plans.

The technical details of engineering projects are normally set out in a 'project specification'. Each element of a project requires its own specification. For very large projects, such as the building of the power station in our earlier example (section 7.1.1), the size and complexity of the construction would be such that the project specifications would run into several books. The construction plan would show how the myriad parts are to be assembled into a whole. Most construction work is sub-contracted. The project manager is responsible for ensuring the effective co-ordination of all necessary work at each stage of the project. Failure to sequence work correctly can result in costly delays, and various methods have been devised to assist in the work scheduling, e.g. Gantt charts, critical path analysis (CPA), project evaluation and review technique (PERT), and precedence networks.

However, detailed plans – in terms of technical requirements, work scheduling and expected cost – are a *necessary*, but not a *sufficient* condition for successful project implementation. Hitches in execution are an inevitable accompaniment to all complex plans. The project manager plays a vital role in foreseeing and, where possible, forestalling difficulties, and in ensuring that any deviations from the plan which *do* occur do not have serious 'knock-on' consequences for the rest of the project. The role of a project manager has been likened to that of the conductor of an orchestra. The conductor makes no direct contribution to the music itself, as he does not play an instrument. If he were removed, the orchestra *might* continue to play harmoniously for a short time, but the longer and more complicated the piece, the more inevitable it becomes that cacophony will result. In project management terms, the equivalent of this cacophony will be rapidly escalating project costs. Project management is thus often regarded as synonymous with project cost control.

Instances of projects suffering serious cost overruns are legion, including such famous examples as the development of Concorde and the building of the Sydney Opera House. Both these projects broke new ground: Concorde was the first supersonic passenger jet, and the Sydney Opera House was architecturally unique. With innovative projects of this type, although it is possible to specify the ultimate 'output' of the project, it is much more difficult (feasibility studies notwithstanding) to specify *in exact detail* the plan to be followed to achieve the desired end result. However, the less tightly drawn the initial plans, the greater the likelihood that costs will escalate during implementation, reinforcing our earlier point that project cost control is most effectively exercised at the planning and approval stage, rather than at implementation.

Nevertheless, even the best and most detailed plans may require revision as the project progresses. It is part of the project manager's job to ensure that no revisions are undertaken until they have been shown to be necessary and appropriate, and have been properly sanctioned. A distinction should be drawn between those changes to a plan which are known as 'scope changes', and the ones which are referred to as 'extra works'. The latter may occur on any project. They are additional work done within the *scope* of the project, but not included in the original specification. For example, plans for a building will specify the required number of drains. If, on excavation of the site, the ground is found to be much wetter than had been anticipated, the project manager must determine whether this necessitates the laying of additional drains. If extra drains are required, and the work is being sub-contracted, he must ensure that the specification and cost of these additional drains is negotiated with the sub-contractor *before* the work is done. He must also make any necessary amendments to the work schedule of the project to accommodate the additional time taken in drain-laying.

'Scope' changes are more serious than 'extra works', as they relate to changes which fundamentally alter some part of the approved plan. These changes are more likely to be required in innovative projects, but many also occur in more conventional situations. Changes in scope should be avoided wherever possible, as alterations to complex plans are inevitably costly. The authority to sanction changes in scope should be vested in the body which sanctioned the original expenditure, thus ensuring that costs do not escalate without the authorizing body's knowledge. Where scope changes are authorized, it is again up to the project manager to organize the work schedule to accommodate these changes.

The project manager thus constantly *reviews* implementation plans, as well as overseeing current work. He also provides progress reports to the authorizing body. In addition, detailed financial information on project costs will be provided to this body by the accounting staff. Systems which enable costs to be identified with particular projects must be established. However, this is cost reporting, not cost control. Nevertheless, it is an important activity. Top management require independent confirmation that the project manager is correctly reporting project progress. Statements of costs incurred to date, and certificates of work completed, help provide this information.

8.3.2   Role of internal audit

The internal audit section also has a role to play in monitoring the organization and progress of a project. The audit team will review the financial systems of the project, to ensure that expenditure on the project is correctly recorded, and that payments to suppliers and contractors are *bona fide*. However, the work of internal audit should not be confined to financial and accounting matters. The team should also review the manner in which work on the project is progressing. If the audit team does not contain technical experts, it may employ consultants to help with these reviews. Technical assistance will probably be necessary in verifying the project manager's estimates of the amount of work which has actually been completed. This will always be in excess of the amount of work which has been paid for, so financial records cannot provide this check.

Audit reports, like the project manager's report, should go to the sanctioning body. They may be produced less frequently than those of the project manager, but they should provide a wider-ranging review.

8.4   Post-audit of projects

In many organizations, responsibility for carrying out a post-audit of a project will rest with the internal audit section. A post-audit reviews all aspects of a completed project, to assess whether it lived up to initial expectations in terms of revenues and costs. The post-audit report analyses the causes of deviations of actual from planned results. Its main purpose is to enable the experiences – good or bad – gained during the life of one project to be made available for the benefit of future projects. The role of post-audit is thus essentially a forward-looking one, which seeks to establish lessons from the past for the future benefit of the organization.

Nevertheless, reviews by the post-audit team *before* a project is complete may yield benefits for the current projects as well as future ones. This is particularly true when projects are running over budget. It is a matter of semantics whether any project review undertaken *prior* to the time at which a project is fully 'on stream' can be called a *post*-audit. This semantic point is unimportant: what does matter is that a project which is running over budget should be the subject of a wide-ranging, independent review. This may be termed an interim post-audit.

The review will seek to determine the underlying causes of cost overruns. Detailed reasons should have already been set out in the project manager's progress reports, but too much detail can obscure general trends. In a minority of cases, the project progress reports may not be entirely accurate. The manager might minimize the reporting of current difficulties, in the hope of making compensating changes later on.

A further function of the interim review is to assess whether the project is still viable. This is a point which will *not* be addressed by the project manager. His job is to make progress toward the goal he has been set, not to question that goal. The wisdom of continuing with a project which is going badly wrong should be considered by the sanctioning body, but there are powerful reasons why it may try to avoid doing so. We pointed out earlier that few project proposals are ever rejected, and suggested that this was because 'bad' ideas failed to gain initial informal acceptance, while ideas perceived to be 'good' gained support and sponsorship as they moved towards the sanctioning stage. The project's supporters become increasingly committed to a project as preparations are made to submit it for sanction. This increasing commitment gives the proposal a momentum of its own, making it very difficult to stop. The reader can imagine how much greater this momentum becomes once a project has been started, and significant amounts of expenditure have been incurred. It requires a considerable amount of courage to admit to mistakes of such magnitude, and abandon a project. As Davis (1985) observes: 'The number of bad projects that make it to the operational stage serve as proof that their supporters often balk at this decision'.

The post-audit team does not itself have the power to abandon projects, but it can bring the implications of severe project problems to the attention of the sanctioning body in a way which forces the body to consider this possibility.

8.5 Project abandonment

In this book it has been advocated that the decision whether to invest in a project should be taken by reference to the project's expected net present value, i.e. accept investments with a positive expected net present value and reject those with a negative expected net present value. The decision whether to abandon a project can easily be accommodated within this framework. Abandonment should take place where the net expected proceeds from abandonment are greater than the net expected proceeds from continuing with the project, i.e., abandon if:

$$A_t + \sum_{t=t+1}^{t=n} \frac{NCF_{At}}{(1+r_A)^t} \quad > \quad \sum_{t=t}^{t=n} \frac{NCF_{Pt}}{(1+r_p)^t} \qquad \ldots \text{Equation 8.1}$$

expected value of   expected value of
abandoning project   continuing with
                                 project

where:

A_t = net benefit of abandonment in period of abandonment, t,
NCF_{At} = future expected net cash flows in period t from abandonment,
NCP_{Pt} = future expected net cash flows in period t from continuing with project,
r_A = discount rate appropriate to abandonment cash flows,
r_p = discount rate appropriate to project cash flows.

Example 1

Table 8.2

Year (t)	NCF_p (£)	r_p = 18%	ENPV (£)
0	(1,175)		(1,175)
1	+1,000	0.8475	848
2	+1,000	0.7182	718
3	+1,000	0.6086	609
	Expected net present value		+£1,000

Consider the investment, I, whose cash flows are shown in Table 8.2. The initial investment of £1,175 in year 0 in investment I represents the purchase of a specialized machine whose purchase price is known with certainty. The second-hand market for such machines is very poor, so the purchaser would be unable to sell the machine for more than £300 even if it was re-sold immediately after the initial purchase. There would be no further costs or revenues associated with a resale. Thus immediately after the machine is acquired:

$$A_t = £300 \text{ and } \sum_{t=t+1}^{t=n} \frac{NCF_{At}}{(1+r_A)^t} = 0$$

i.e., the expected value of abandoning the project is £300. Compare this with the expected value of continuing with the project. Inspection of Table 8.2 shows that the value of continuing is £2,175, the expected net present value of I, less than initial (negative) flow.

As would be expected, the benefits of continuing with the project greatly outweigh the returns from immediate abandonment. Indeed abandonment, *ceteris paribus*, can only be an attractive proposition in the early days of a project's life if the initial outlay on the project can be resold almost immediately for a sum greater than:

$$\sum_{t=1}^{t=n} \frac{NCF_{pt}}{(1+r_p)^t}$$

Clearly an investment would not be undertaken initially unless the ENPV was positive i.e. unless:

$$\sum_{t=1}^{t=n} \frac{NCF_{pt}}{(1+r_p)^t} > \text{initial investment outlay}$$

If future expectations of costs and revenues are unchanged, immediate abandonment thus implies that an asset can quickly be resold for a sum in excess of its purchase price. This would represent a very unusual state of affairs, as the resale price of productive assets is normally less than their purchase price.

There are, of course, many examples of assets bought at one price and then quickly resold at great profit. Tales of goods bought for a few pounds in flea markets or junk shops which are later auctioned for vast sums are often reported in the press. However, such stories rarely relate to *productive* assets. Rather they concern individual sales of items of artistic merit whose original vendor was unaware of the exact nature of the item in his possession. The ultimate buyer must pay the price demanded by the lucky (or shrewd) purchaser as he cannot go to the original seller for an identical item. For manufactured goods the position is different. Assets can be replicated so that a buyer has a choice of supplier. He can trade in the second-hand market or go direct to the manufacturer. Clearly some financial inducement is required to persuade him to take the second-hand item. Thus for manufactured goods, such as machinery, immediate abandonment or salvage value is usually lower than original cost. How much lower depends on the specific type of asset. The more specialized the item, the greater the difficulty of finding a buyer and the lower the second-hand value is likely to be.

If the possibility of the abandonment value being higher than the costs incurred is set aside, then abandonment will be signalled as a result of revised expectations of future revenues and costs. These revisions may be consistent with the data on which the original investment decision was made or may represent an alteration to earlier expectations. Let us now examine the former case.

8.5.1   *Planned project abandonment*

The layout below shows the possible outcomes of the investment in example 1, and the associated probability, p, of these outcomes:

Time 0	1	2	3
	p=.33 + £1,500	p=.33 + £1,500	p=.33 + £1,500
−£1,175	p=.33 + £1,000	p=.33 + £1,000	p=.33 + £1,000
	p=.33 + £ 500	p=.33 + £ 500	p=.33 + £ 500

(NCF)
$$
\left.\begin{array}{l}1{,}500\times.33\\1{,}000\times.33\\500\times.33\end{array}\right\} £1{,}000 \quad \left.\begin{array}{l}1{,}500\times.33\\1{,}000\times.33\\500\times.33\end{array}\right\} £1{,}000 \quad \left.\begin{array}{l}1{,}500\times.33\\1{,}000\times.33\\500\times.33\end{array}\right\} £1{,}000
$$

It can be seen that at time 0 the expected return in each year is £1,000, i.e. .33 × £1,500 + .33 × £1,000 + .33 × £500. Suppose now that there is perfect correlation between the results of each of the 3 years. This means that a result of + £1,500 in year 1 guarantees the same result in years 2 and 3. In time period 0 the investor can calculate the *expected* net cash flow in years 2 and 3 but with perfect correlation of flows between years these flows are known with certainty at time period 1. Clearly if the first year result is + £1,500 or £1,000, then the *actual* NPV of the project will be positive. However if the first year outcome is + £500, then the investment will have a negative NPV, i.e. − £1,175 + £500 × 2.174 = − £88. This outcome does not, of course, invalidate the decision taken at time period 0 to undertake the investment. Nevertheless, if the actual result is £500 in year 1, the benefits of continuing with the project should be compared with the benefits of abandonment. If the project is continued through years 2 and 3, the company will receive £500 in each of these years. At time period 1 these flows are no longer uncertain, so that their present value at time period 1 can be found by discounting back to period 1 using the risk-free rate. Let this rate be 10 per cent. The present value at time period 1 of continuing is thus:

Value of continuing at = £500 × £1.7355 = £868
time period 1 (period
1 outcome is known at
£500)

This must be compared with the abandonment value of the project, which in this case is the resale price of the machine. As this is no greater than £300, the project should be allowed to run its course, i.e. abandonment is not justified.

Suppose now that the supplier of the machine is eager to make a sale and is prepared to incorporate a buy-back clause into the sale agreement. The terms of the clause being that he will repurchase the machine for £950 at any time up to and including the first anniversary of the sale. In these circumstances the abandonment value of the project at the end of year 1 is £950. A comparison of this sum with the £868 present value of continuation shows that, under the later conditions, the company should *plan* to terminate the project at the end of year 1 if the actual outcome of that year is £500. The possible outcomes of example 1 when the buy-back option is included are shown below:

Time 0	1	2	3
	$p=.33+£1,500$	$p=.33+£1,500$	$p=.33+£1,500$
$-£1,175$	$p=.33+£1,000$	$p=.33+£1,000$	$p=.33+£1,000$
	$p=.33+£\ \ 500$	$p=.33+£\ \ \ \ 0$	$p=.33\ \ £\ \ \ \ 0$
	$+£\ \ 950$		

NCF$_p$			
$\left.\begin{matrix}1,500\times.33\\1,000\times.33\\1,450\times.33\end{matrix}\right\}$ £1,317	$\left.\begin{matrix}1,500\times.33\\1,000\times.33\\0\times.33\end{matrix}\right\}$ £ 833	$\left.\begin{matrix}1,500\times.33\\1,000\times.33\\0\times.33\end{matrix}\right\}$ £ 833

By including abandonment in the plan, the ENPV of the project is increased by £46 as Table 8.3 shows. The revision of expectations of outcomes in year 2 and year 3 in the revised example 1 which take place at the end of year 1 arises from the knowledge gained during year 1. This does *not* mean that

Table 8.3

Year	E (NCF$_p$) (£)	$r_p=18\%$	PV (£)
0	(1,175)		(1,175)
1	1,317	0.8475	1,116
2	833	0.7182	598
3	833	0.6086	507
		ENPV	£1,046

expectations in year 0 were in any way incorrect. In year 0 it was known that one of three results was equally likely in year 1, and that the passage of time would reveal the actual result of year 1 and hence (because of the perfect correlation between years) the results of years 2 and 3. This situation contrasts with one in which events in year 1, or any other year, cause an *unforeseen* need to amend later years' forecasts.

8.5.2   *Unplanned project abandonment*

Suppose in revised example 1 that a new tax is announced during the course of year 1. This tax will have the effect of reducing the project's revenues after year 1 by 50 per cent. The annual outcome in years 1, 2 and 3 will thus now be £750, £500 or £250. The outcome in year 1 will still determine which of these results will be achieved.

As previously shown, a cash flow in years 2 and 3 of £500 (or less) indicates that the project should be abandoned. The introduction of the tax means that

£1,000 in year 1 will now be followed by only £500 in years 2 and 3. In this situation abandonment is the appropriate action at the end of year 1 for an actual outcome of £1,000 as well as an outcome of £500. This situation was not, and could not have been foreseen at the time the project was being considered.

Should the actual outcome in year 1 be £1,000, it is unlikely that there would be any resistance in the company to the idea of terminating the project. Although such action was unforeseen, it has become necessary because of external events for which no one in the company can be held responsible.

The need for previously unplanned abandonment can be much more difficult to acknowledge and accept when it is necessitated by revision in future expectations which arise from errors in the original forecasts or in project implementation. It is in these circumstances that the internal audit team can have a significant role to play in highlighting changed circumstances.

Consider a company which plans to undertake a project, A, with the expected cash flow pattern at the time of the project's approval as shown in

Table 8.4

Project A year	Expected present value of annual costs (£m)	Expected total present value of net revenues (£m)
1	5.0	
2	10.0	
3	15.0	
4 ⎫		
5 ⎬		34 (revenue exceeds cost in
6		each of years 4–7)
7 ⎭		

Expected net present value of project A = £34m − £(5 + 10 + 15)m = + £4million

Table 8.4. Suppose that great difficulties are experienced in implementing the project plan in year 1, the actual costs incurred during the first year being £10 million. The crucial question which must then be asked is 'Does the actual outcome in year 1 necessitate any revision in the expected outcomes of later years?' If no revision is required, then, at the end of year 1, further costs of £25 million (year 0 value) must be incurred to secure inflows of £34 million (year 0 value). Thus the expected present value of continuing with project A beyond year 1 is £9 million (year 0 value). (Adjusting the figures to year 1 values increases the expected NPV, strengthening the case for continuation. For ease of exposition this adjustment has been ignored.)

The expected present value of continuing must be compared with the salvage value of the year 1 expenditure. It may be assumed that in this example the salvage value is zero, i.e. costs incurred in abandoning the project equal the revenues received from abandonment. The company should therefore continue with the project.

If costs and revenues are as predicted beyond year 1, then the result of the investment will, of course, be negative; the excess spending of £5 million in year 1 is greater than the expected net present value originally forecast. However at the end of year 1 this excess expenditure is a sunk cost and, as such, plays no part in the decision whether to continue with the project or not.

The premise that the events of year 1 carry no implications for the forecasts of later years should be subjected to close scrutiny before being accepted. Actual costs in year 1 were twice their estimated size; if this were to be repeated in years 2 and 3, then continuation of the project would not be justified. Project costs beyond year 1 would be £50 million (year 0 values) against forecast revenues of £34 million (year 0 values). Abandonment would clearly be the correct course of action in such circumstances.

As previously suggested, those intimately involved with a project may be reluctant to admit, even to themselves, that early problems are likely to continue. A disinterested assessment of the situation by the post-auditors can prove invaluable in these circumstances.

When problems are being experienced in implementation, there may well be a tendency to focus almost exclusively on a project's costs. However, the post-audit team, unencumbered with day to day operational worries, can consider both future costs *and* future revenues. By checking the continuing validity of both forecast costs and revenues the team is in a position to advise the sanctioning body as to the wisdom of continuing along the basis of the original plan. The interim post-audit report can draw the attention of the sanctioning body to projects where revisions to cost and/or revenue forecasts are required. The sanctioning body is then able to consider the appropriate response to these changed circumstances, including the possibility of abandonment.

The presence of the post-audit team should encourage honesty in facing problems at all levels of the organization, as attempts to ignore or hide realities should be uncovered by the team during its investigations.

8.6 Final post-audit report

The final post-audit report is the last link in the project control system. It provides a history of the project from inception to completion, and constitutes the formal means by which the experience gained on any particular project is made available for the benefit of future ventures. These reports will distinguish between projects which have a good outcome due to good planning and management, and those whose good outcome is the result of good fortune. Similarly, the causes of bad outcomes will be fully disclosed. Past experience is helpful in making future decisions, particularly – as was stressed in section 8.2 – as it is at the planning stage that project control is most important and effective.

References

Davis, D., 'New projects, beware of false economies', *Harvard Business Review*' March–April, 1985.

Fremgen, N. J. 'Capital Budgeting Practices: A Survey' *Management Accounting*, May 1973.

Gitmann, L. J, Forrester, J. R. 'A survey of capital budgeting techniques used by major U.S. firms', *Financial Management*, Fall, 1977.

King, P., 'Is the Emphasis of Capital Budgeting Theory Misplaced', *Journal of Business Finance*, Winter 1975.

Questions for Part Two

1   A well-diversified company is considering an investment in its construction division. The beta value of total equity financed companies in the construction industry can be taken as 1.2. The current risk-free rate of interest is 10 per cent per annum and this is not expected to change over the next 2 years. The overall return on equities over the next 2 years is expected to be 15% per annum.

(a)   Calculate the appropriate discount rate to be used in evaluating the investment.

(b)   Suggest whether the company should undertake the investment if the expected cash flows are as shown below. (Cash flows are perfectly correlated betwen years).

Year	Cash flow (£m)	Probability of cash flow occurring
0	−4.5	1
1	4.0	0.8
1	1.0	0.2
2	4.0	0.8
2	1.0	0.2

(c)   Discuss the implications of the capital asset pricing model for the choice of discount rate to be used by a company when evaluating potential investments. Include a consideration of any practical difficulties in establishing this rate.

2   An analysis of historic data in Company Z, which is totally equity financed, yields the following results:

	Company Z
β	0.9
Yearly standard deviation of return	19.0%

The expected market rate of return is 16 per cent, with a standard deviation of 20 per cent, and the return on risk-free assets is 10 per cent.

(a) What is the expected return on buying a share in Company Z?

(b) As the standard deviation of return in Z is less than that of the market, outline the advantages and disadvantages of holding a single share such as Z rather than the market portfolio.

(c) Discuss whether the return you have calculated in (a) would represent an appropriate discount rate for use in the company's DCF calculations when evaluating potential investments.

3   Tepo plc is currently considering four independent investments. Data on the expected return and risk of these investments is shown below:

	A	B	C	D
Return (%)	10	14	8	12
Systematic Risk (%)	7.5	17	4.5	10

(a) Given a risk-free rate of return of 6 per cent and an expected market rate of return of 15 per cent, with standard deviation of 18 per cent, which, if any, of these investments should the company undertake? Support your answer numerically.

(b) Discuss the view held by several board members of Tepo that, as the average rate of return achieved by Tepo in recent years has been 12 per cent p.a., only project B offering 14 per cent is worthy of consideration.

(c) Briefly discuss the advantages and disadvantages of basing large investment decisions on a consideration of alternative possible scenarios rather than on a consideration of risk and return figures of the kind shown above.

4   A company is proposing to acquire a piece of office equipment which has a life of 5 years, after which it would need to be replaced. The purchase price of the equipment is £5,000. It will have no residual value at the end of its life and for tax purposes the capital allowances are assumed to be at 20 per cent per annum on a straight-line basis.

If it were to buy the equipment, the company would need to borrow the total sum from the bank. Repayments would be by a standard annual amount at the end of each year. This amount would comprise repayment of principal and interest at 16 per cent per annum before tax.

The equipment is also available on a standard 5-year lease at an annual payment of £1,529.

The company is not certain that it will require the equipment for the full 5 years because it is considering a more elaborate system that would make this equipment redundant. In these circumstances:

1   The equipment could be sold at the end of any year for 80 per cent of its book value.

2   A special lease can be taken at the same annual cost as for a standard lease but with the facility to cancel at the end of any year. There is, however, a penalty of £1,850 if the lease is cancelled at the end of the first year and a penalty of £1,000 if it is cancelled at the end of the second year. There are no penalties for cancellation at the end of the third or fourth years.

The company assesses the probability of its keeping the equipment

for one year	0.2
for two years	0.3
for three years	0.2
for four years	0.2
for five years	0.1
	1.0

You are required to advise the company whether it should lease or buy the equipment

(a) if it is certain to keep the equipment for the whole five years and is considering a standard lease, and

(b) if it is uncertain of the time the equipment will be kept and it is considering the special lease.

Notes
Assume that interest payments are made net of tax at 50 per cent and that tax of 50 per cent on profits applies and that it is paid in the year in which profits are earned.

Ignore the risk differentials other than those explicitly stated in the question.

All workings should be shown to the nearest £.

(CIMA May 1987)

5   RS Ltd is considering using a machine made by BC Ltd. The machine would cost £60,000 and at the end of a 4-year life is expected to have a resale value of £4,000, the money to be received in year 5. It would save £29,000 per year over the method that RS Ltd currently uses. RS Ltd expects to earn a DCF return of 20 per cent before tax on this type of investment.

RS Ltd is currently earning good profits, but does not expect to have £60,000 available to spend on this machine over the next few years. It is subject to corporation tax at 35 per cent and receives capital allowances of 25 per cent on a reducing balance basis.

Required
(a) Recommend whether, from an economic viewpoint, RS Ltd should invest in the machine from BC Ltd.

(b) Calculate which of the following options RS Ltd would be financially better off to adopt:

Option 1 – buy the machine and borrow the £60,000 from the bank, repaying at the end of each year a standard amount that would comprise principal and interest at 20 per cent per annum.

Option 2 – lease the machine for 4 years at an annual lease payment equal to the annual amount it would need to pay the bank under *Option 1* above;

Show your calculations.

(c) Recommend, with explanations, which of the two options in (b) above RS Ltd should adopt, assuming that such a lease was available, but that it would not give RS Ltd the right to acquire the machine at the end of the lease period.

Note: Assume that lease payments or loan repayments are made gross at the end of each year and that tax is paid and tax allowances received one year after those profits are earned.

(CIMA, November 1989)

6   In the context of capital budgeting, *you are required* to explain:

(a) the meaning of 'beta';
(b) the function of 'beta' in the capital asset pricing model;
(c) what one might do to overcome the difficulty that 'beta' for a proposed capital expenditure project is not necessarily the same as that for the company as a whole.

(CIMA)

7   A theatre with some surplus accommodation proposed to extend its catering facilities to provide light meals to its patrons.

The management board is prepared to make initial funds available to cover capital costs. It requires that these be repaid over a period of 5 years at a rate of interest of 14 per cent.

The capital costs are estimated at £60,000 for equipment that will have a life of 5 years and no residual value. Running costs of staff, etc. will be £20,000 in the first year, increasing by £2,000 in each subsequent year. The board proposes to charge £5,000 per annum for lighting, heating and other property expenses, and wants a nominal £2,500 per annum to cover any unforeseen contingencies. Apart from this, the board is not looking for any profit, as such, from the extension of these facilities, because it believes that this will enable more theatre seats to be sold. It is proposed that costs should be recovered by setting prices for the food at double the direct costs.

It is not expected that the full sales level will be reached until year 3. The proportions of that level estimated to be reached in years 1 and 2 are 35 per cent and 65 per cent respectively.

You are required to

(a) Calculate the sales that need to be achieved in *each* of the 5 years to meet the board's targets.
(b) Comment briefly on *five* aspects of the proposals that you consider merit further investigation.

Ignore taxation and inflation.

(CIMA, May 1987)

Part Three   Prices and Values in Decisions

The pricing decision and the cost of resources will affect the wealth of all organizations. This section examines how pricing decisions are made and how the prospective cost of resources affects decisions.

9 Changes in price levels

9.1 Introduction – problem outline

Comparative static analysis in micro-economics, that is analysis of the firm using demand curves, marginal cost and total cost curves, etc., advocates that a change in price of inputs should be accompanied by alterations to the selling price (where the market permits) and to output levels, in order to maximize profits (see section 11.1.3). Although such analysis provides useful insights into what is a very complex picture, it should not necessarily be taken as a direct prescription for practice.

Any manager who has organized a change in selling price or output will know that production, sales and marketing managers as well as financial managers and the directors of the company have to be consulted in order to determine the extent of any such changes. Discussions can be long and difficult, for no production manager wants to decrease output, and no sales manager wants to raise prices. Extensive calculations have to be made, sales literature has to be altered, salesmen informed, production plans must be changed, bonus schemes adjusted and future estimates of both output and revenue revised. Special exercises may be required, such as a reduction or increase in labour force, the discontinuing of a product and a discount sale. The general exercise is expensive and risky; an error in a price increase can lose valuable customers, an ill-timed price decrease can also seriously damage a company's performance.

On the cost side, where there is an increase in cost and a cheaper alternative supplier, the advice of conventional analysis is to use the cheaper alternative. Again, in practice the picture is rarely so simple. A supplier will often be producing to the firm's own specification. A just-in-time default free supply policy may have been developed (Kaplan and Atkinson, 1989), and changing to an unknown supplier will require increased inspection and extensive discussions. If there are 'teething problems', the knock-on effects can be very costly. In addition, the alternative supplier may not be cheaper for very long, but may be pursuing a pricing policy to attract customers (see section 11.4).

It would be wrong to infer from this description of the practical problems of changes in price levels that a firm should never change its prices or alter its buying policy. Of course, there will be circumstances where to do nothing would be suboptimal; but equally there will be many circumstances where a change is too costly. It is the understanding of these circumstances and their effect on decisions that is the focus of this chapter.

In discussing price changes, we shall divide our consideration between general and specific change. A general price change is a uniform uplift or decrease in prices due to general economic conditions. Firms will periodically review their prices with a view to adjusting for this effect. The intention of such changes is to maintain the real value of returns. As regards decision making, the prospect of a general change in prices should not affect decisions, as general inflation is a measurement rather than a valuation problem. For instance, if all prices and incomes were to double no item would be cheaper or more expensive and hence no decision need alter.

A specific price-level change occurs when a cost or a selling price moves independently of other prices. In this case an item may become relatively cheaper or more expensive than a comparable alternative. By contrast therefore, the prospect of specific price-level changes will affect our decisions.

9.2   General price-level changes

9.2.1   Real and monetary rates

Decisions are potentially distorted by comparing costs and revenues at different times without adjusting for general inflation. For instance, if a firm is offered an agreement to purchase Product A at £5 each for the next 5 years and the current selling price is £4.80, which is expected to keep pace with inflation, the offer is not necessarily unprofitable. The cost of £5 is the actual money amount that will be paid and is known as the *monetary rate*. The revenue of £4.80 is the current selling price, and general inflation of, say, 8 per cent per annum, would mean that at the end of 4 years we could expect to be selling product A for £6.53 (i.e. 4.8×1.08^4) whereas our cost of £5 would not have altered. In fact, after only the first year there would be a small trading profit (see Table 9.1). The value of the revenue in terms of purchasing power would not have changed (this is normally expressed as the *real value* of sales); however, the monetary rate of sales would have changed. As regards cost the £5, the position is reversed: the real value over time declines as inflation continues but the price does not change – in other words, the monetary rate is constant.

Clearly, in planning and decision making we must not mix monetary and real rates: either our figures are expressed in monetary terms – the actual cash amounts paid and received – or in real terms, i.e. today's prices. These two methods are illustrated in Table 9.1, using the example given above. It is assumed that inflation during the year is 8 per cent per annum and that one item is bought and sold at the end of each year. The profits are identical, except that the real rates are given in today's money and the monetary rates are stated at estimated actual amounts paid and received. For example, the real and monetary profits in the fourth year are related by the inflation rate,

thus:
$$\text{monetary profit} = \text{real profit} \times \text{inflation}$$
$$1.53 = (1.12) \times (1.08)^4.$$

Table 9.1 Real and monetary valuations, assuming 8 per cent inflation

		0 (ie now)	1	Year 2	3	4
Real rates	Selling price	4.80	4.80	4.80	4.80	4.80
	Cost	5.00	4.63*	4.29	3.97	3.68
	Profit	(0.20)	0.17	0.51	0.83	1.12
Monetary rates	Selling price	4.80	5.18	5.60	6.05	6.53
	Cost	5.00	5.00	5.00	5.00	5.00
	Profit	(0.20)	0.18	0.60	1.05	1.53

*£5 in 1 year's time will buy £4.63 worth in 1 year's time in present values.

What if we wanted to calculate the net present value of the figures in Table 9.1? To do this, we assume that the example represents cash flows. Our only problem therefore is to decide the appropriate discount rate. In general, the discount rate (i) is made up of three elements: time preference (tp), inflation (f) and risk (r). The relation is multiplicative – hence: $(1+i) = (1+tp) \times (1+f) \times (1 \times r)$. Both monetary and real rates include time preference and risk, and the monetary rate also includes inflation. If we take the bank rate (currently at 12 per cent) as an indication of time preference and expected inflation, and individual risk is estimated to be an extra 2 per cent, then the total monetary discount rate will be $(1.12) \times (1.02) = 1.1424$ or 14.24 per cent. When applied to the monetary cash flows in the conventional way, the net present value expressed in pounds sterling at year 0 will be:

$$NPV = (0.2) + \frac{0.18}{1.1424} + \frac{0.60}{(1.1424)^2} + \frac{1.05}{(1.1424)^3} + \frac{1.53}{(1.1424)^4}$$
$$= 2.02$$

In order to calculate real rates we will need to include a discount rate that comprises time preference and risk, but not inflation, as all the figures are expressed in current values and hence do not include any estimate of future inflation. We therefore need to take 8 per cent out of our monetary discount rate. As the relationship is multiplicative, deduction is achieved by division:

$$\frac{1.1424}{1.08} = 1.057.$$

The rate of 5.7 per cent is therefore inclusive of time preference and risk only. Discounting the real returns at the real discount rate gives:

$$\text{NPV} = (0.2) + \frac{0.17}{1.057} + \frac{0.51}{(1.057)^2} + \frac{0.83}{(1.057)^3} + \frac{1.12}{(1.057)^4}$$
$$= 2.02$$

The result using real rates is the same as using monetary rates, which is what one would expect, for both methods ultimately express the value of the project in present-day money.

The mistake that is often made is to apply the monetary discount rate to real prices. The reason for this error is that rates of interest quoted on the financial markets are monetary rates (apart from index-linked government bonds); also, we usually think of values at today's prices. It seems a natural development therefore to plan in terms of the values that we normally use and apply the discount rate which is quoted in the market (adjusted for the risk of the project). But such an approach is to commit the folly of mixing real and monetary returns. Unfortunately, this error is made all too often in practice. To illustrate the problem in context, we offer the following extended example.

Example 1
Hookway Ltd provides service X to the public and is wondering whether or not to open up a branch in Monton. The estimated fee income in current values would be £100,000, which would be expected to rise by 20 per cent per year. After 3 years, for legal reasons, the service would be discontinued. The office would be leased at a fixed annual rate of £10,000; a manager and three assistants are required, and salaries for the current year are £20,000 for the manager, and £9,000 for the assistants. Assistants' salaries have kept pace with general inflation of 10 per cent; managers' salaries have increased in real terms by about 2 per cent owing to general skills shortages. Stationery and other services will cost a further £20,000 per year. This cost is again expected to keep pace with inflation. Finally the cost of setting up the project is estimated to be £40,000.

There are a number of similar projects that Hookway Ltd could undertake. a constraint on senior management time means that projects will have to be selected according to profitability. It has been decided to use the net present value criterion, with a required real rate of return of 20 per cent.

Calculate the net present value, using both monetary and real rates, assuming that all cash flows occur at the year end (except for the initial set-up costs).

The first step is to decide which costs in the question are in real terms and which are at monetary rates. The fee increase is a monetary rate, as it refers to the actual revenue that the firm expects to collect. The lease is also a monetary rate, as £10,000 is the actual contractual amount that will have to be paid. The salaries and stationery costs are real rates; they are both expected to change over the years as a result of inflation. The initial cost is a present-day cost, the only point at which real and monetary rates are the same.

Calculations based upon monetary rates are:

	t_0	t_1	t_2	t_3
Fee income		120000	144000	172800
Lease		(10000)	(10000)	(10000)
Manager's salary				
(monetary rate = $(1.10) \times (1.02)$)		(22440)	(25178)	(28249)
Assistants' salary (1.10)		(9900)	(10890)	(11979)
Initial costs	(40000)			
Net cash flows	(40000)	77660	97932	122572

Required monetary rate of return $= (1.10) \times (1.20) = 1.32$ i.e. 32%

$$\text{Net present value} = (40000) + \frac{77660}{1.32} + \frac{97932}{1.32^2} + \frac{122572}{1.32^3}$$
$$= 128331$$

Calculations based upon real money rates are:

	t_0	t_1	t_2	t_3
Fee income $(1.2/1.1)$		109090	119008	129827
Lease $(1/1.1)$		(9090)	(8264)	(7513)
Manager's salary (1.02)		(20400)	(20808)	(21224)
Assistants' salary		(9000)	(9000)	(9000)
Initial costs	(40000)			
	(40000)	70600	80936	92090

The required real rate of return $= 1.20$ i.e. 20 per cent.

$$\text{Net present value} = (40000) + \frac{70600}{(1.2)} + \frac{80936}{(1.2)^2} + \frac{92090}{(1.2)^3}$$
$$= 128331$$

The two methods should always produce the same results.

9.2.2 *The use of indices*

A common way of measuring the effect of price changes is the use of a price index. To calculate the inflation rate over a particular period the following formula is used:

$$100 \times \left(\frac{\text{end of period index}}{\text{beginning of period index}} - 1 \right).$$

Thus, if we wanted to calculate the inflation of retail prices in 1986 using the Retail Prices Index, the rate is:

$$100 \times \left(\frac{385.9}{373.2} - 1 \right) = 3.4 \text{ per cent,}$$

where 385.9 is the index for 1986 and 373.2 is the index for 1985.

Price indices are published by the Central Statistical Office in its *Annual Abstract of Statistics*. It is worth noting how they are constructed. In a simple case the index will measure the increased price of a single homogeneous product. For instance, in calculating the cost of diesel fuel, the government will take a weighted average of the market prices. Outlets for diesel fuel that are more popular than others will be given a higher weight. For example, the price of the fuel sold next to a refinery might be especially low, but as not much is sold through this output, it would have a lower weighting than London diesel fuel prices.

The prices are then converted into an index number as follows:

1986 Price (P)	Weight	Price × weight
150	0.1	15.0
165	0.7	115.5
155	0.2	31.0
	1.0	161.5

The weighted 'typical' price of £161.5 is then compared to the price in the base year (which is arbitrarily given the index number 100). Suppose that the price in 1980 was £104.9. The amount by which our price is greater than the 1980 price is

$$100 \times \left(\frac{161.5}{104.9} - 1 \right) = 54 \text{ per cent.}$$

As 1980 is given the index number of 100, then our 1986 price should be 54 per cent higher, which is simply 154.

A complex index relates to a whole range of goods. In the Retail Prices Index (RPI), for instance, each item considered in the index will have various prices throughout the country weighted as for diesel fuel, the weighted price for each product being considered will then, in turn, have to be weighted according to its popularity in the retail market. In the RPI, weights are given according to various sectors, e.g. food in 1986 was given a weight of 185/1,000 compared to tobacco of 40/1,000. Thus the typical consumer spent 18 per cent of his or her income on food and 4 per cent of his or her income on tobacco. In the case of the RPI, these weights are revised annually from the Family Expenditure Survey.

The Tax and Price Index (TPI) is similar to the RPI, except that it includes changes to direct taxes (including National Insurance) as well as retail prices. The index measures the amount by which gross income would have to increase in order to maintain its real value in purchasing power. If, for instance, there is a rise in prices which is offset exactly by a fall in taxation for the average taxpayer, then there would be a rise in the RPI but no change in the TPI.

The TPI was designed for use in wage negotiations. Whether it or RPI is used is a matter of who should benefit. In the case of tax cuts and inflation, the employer would benefit by using the TPI, as it would increase by less than the RPI. The employee might well feel that it is the employer rather than the employee who benefits from employee tax cuts by this method, for the employees' purchasing power would remain the same in spite of the tax cuts, whereas the employer's wage bill would decline in real terms. Where there are tax increases, the TPI will allow for the extra burden, but the RPI will not; the preferences of the employer and employee will thus be reversed.

As well as the two retail indices, there are, as we have said, a host of producer price indices. Managers ought to be aware of the indices for the types of expenditure under their control, and this knowledge should be used for the prediction of future price levels in the planning process. The range of

Table 9.2 Price indices and rates of change.

	1980	'81	'82	'83	'84	'85	'86
RPI	263.7	295.0	320.4	335.1	351.8	373.2	385.9
Annual inflation (%)		11.9	8.6	4.6	5.0	6.1	3.4
TPI	139.4	161.2	170.5	178.0	183.9	192.4	197.1
Annual increase (%)		15.6	5.8	4.4	3.3	4.6	2.4
Copper	100	91.9	89.9	111.6	109.7	117.4	99.5
Annual increase (%)		(8.1)	(2.2)	24.1	1.7	7.0	(15.2)
Real change* (%)		(17.9)	(10.0)	18.7	(6.4)	0.9	(18.0)
Cars	100	108.7	115.9	119.7	127.2	136.8	146.7
Annual increase (%)		8.7	6.6	3.3	6.3	7.5	7.2
Real change* (%)		(2.8)	(1.8)	(1.2)	1.2	1.4	3.7

*The increase after dividing by the RPI index.

price indices is illustrated in Table 9.2. The pattern of price changes can differ markedly; although the most important factor will normally be the general price-level change, there are exceptions. In Table 9.2, for instance, the price of copper has little correlation with the general rate of inflation; the variation in car prices, on the other hand, has moved much more closely with the general rate.

Models for predicting price movements, whether intuitive, statistical or heuristic, will clearly differ according to the product.

9.2.3 Timing of price-level changes

A firm sets prices for its product or service and also determines the rates of pay, unless controlled by national agreement. An important element in determining prices and rates is their timing.

The claim, for instance, that rates of pay have kept pace with inflation may have a variety of implications as regards total cost. At one extreme the firm may adjust a rate or price for the coming year's level of inflation. At the other extreme, the firm may only adjust for inflation at the end of the year. The cost of adjusting pay levels is illustrated in Figure 9.1. The line DB represents the daily pay rate, assuming that it is adjusted each day for the rate of inflation. The area EDBF represents the cost of constantly maintaining the

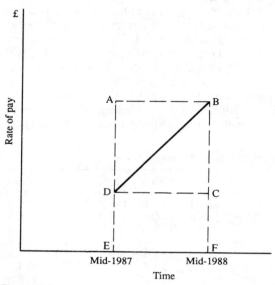

Figure 9.1

same rate of real pay. Immediate adjustment leaves the worker relatively better off by ABD; late adjustment leaves the worker worse off by DBC. In all cases the rate of pay at the end of the year will have kept pace with inflation. The amount of pay received will, however, be very different.

A similar problem prevails in the timing of price increases and its effect on revenue. Increases may be small and frequent, following the DB line, or larger and less frequent, going via point A or C. If a single price change of 1/2DA is made, then the lost business by being above the DB line must be compared to business gained in the latter half of the year by being below the DB line. The relative changes in demand will depend upon the market's price-sensitivity. Where the market is very price-sensitive, it is likely that changes will have to be small and frequent to keep pace with other prices, e.g. petrol. Where the market is less sensitive, small differences in price over time may well not significantly affect demand. Such prices need not be adjusted as frequently, thereby reducing the cost of adjustment (see section 9.1).

The implications for decisions are relatively clear. An annual 10 per cent increase in price levels, rates of pay, etc., does not necessarily mean that the total cost will increase by 10 per cent. A single increase at the end of the year will not change costs at all, whereas a beginning of the year increase will increase costs by the full 10 per cent.

9.3 Specific price-level changes

9.3.1 Demand analysis

One of the main difficulties faced by a company setting prices is predicting market reaction to a real change in selling price (i.e. change other than one to keep pace with general inflation). If a price is increased relative to the general price level, will there be a dramatic or slight fall in the quantity demanded? Equally, if there is a decrease, how great will be the increase in demand? As we will see in chapter 11, in practice this is a complex decision which requires a consideration of all the elements in the marketing mix. Nevertheless, we can highlight some important aspects of this problem by examining basic micro-economic analysis of demand.

Let us start by representing the relationship between changes in retail prices and quantity demanded in the form of graphs (see Figure 9.2). There are two extremes of the price–quantity trade-off between which many prod-

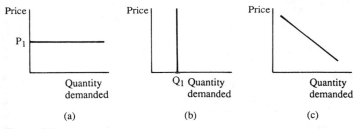

Figure 9.2

ucts lie. At one extreme we have a demand curve which is the result of perfect competition. This is illustrated in Figure 9.2 (a). From an individual firm's point of view, perfect competition implies that all that can be produced can be sold at the market price P_1, nothing would be sold if the price were above P_1, and there would be no point in selling at less than P_1. The other extreme is represented by Figure 9.2 (b). Here, a certain quantity, Q_1, is demanded no matter what the price. In this diagram demand is insensitive to price.

When there is imperfect competition, firms may sell products and services whose demand may temporarily resemble (b). However, relationship (c) will prevail after the market has had time to adjust. In this instance, which is by far the most common, an increase in price will result in a reduction in quantity demanded and *vice-versa*. It is this last case that we shall now examine more closely.

The most general statement that one can make concerning Figure 9.2 (c) is that there is a negative relationship (or correlation) between price and quantity – an increase in one implies a decrease in the other. At first sight it might also seem that the slope of the line would be important. The slope *is*

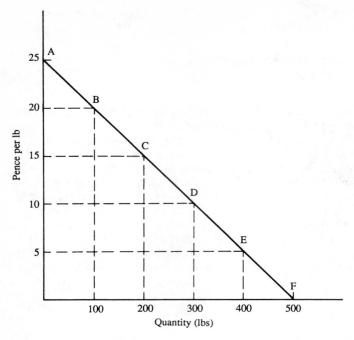

Figure 9.3   *Demand for potatoes*

important, but a direct measure is unfortunately affected by the units of measurement that we happen to choose. If Figure 9.3 represents the demand curve for a local shop selling potatoes, the slope may be described as −5p/100 lbs or −0.05, though if we chose kilos instead of lbs, the slope would be −5p/45.5 kilos = −0.11, and if we chose French francs instead of £ sterling, the slope would be −0.5F/100 lbs = −0.005. Clearly, the slope does not serve as a useful description of the price/quantity relationship, as it depends upon the scales used.

To avoid this problem, the numerator and denominator are expressed in terms of percentage change rather than the absolute amount. The measure is known as demand elasticity and is represented by the formula:

$$\text{Demand elasticity} = \frac{-\% \text{ change in quantity}}{\% \text{ change in price}}$$

(Note the reversal of quantity and price. Also, the negative sign makes our measure positive – a more convenient representation). Applying this formula to the movement from B to C in Figure 9.3, there is a 100 per cent increase in the demand for potatoes for a 25 per cent decrease in price. Therefore:

$$\text{Elasticity B} \rightarrow \text{C} = \frac{100\%}{25\%} = 4$$

If we choose the mid-point of the differences, then:

$$\text{Elasticity B} \rightarrow \text{C} = \frac{100/150}{5/17.5} \text{ or } \frac{66.6\%}{28.6\%} = 2.33$$

The first important observation to make is that elasticities differ at varying points on the demand curve, even though the slope is constant. Secondly, demand is termed elastic where the measure is greater than 1 and inelastic where it is less than 1. Thirdly, where demand is inelastic, an increase in price increases total revenue and a decrease in price decreases total revenue; where demand is elastic, an increase in price decreases total revenue and a price decrease increases total revenue. This is illustrated in Table 9.3.

Table 9.3   Elasticity

Point	Price	Quantity	Total Revenue (£)	Elasticity between points (using mid-point measure)	
A	25p	0	0		
				9.00	
B	20p	100	20		
				2.33	elastic
C	15p	200	30		
				1.00	
D	10p	300	30		
				0.43	
E	5p	400	20		inelastic
F	0	500	0	0.11	

Readers might like to confirm that elasticity would be the same if we were to measure the demand curve using francs and kilos or any other unit of measurement.

To understand the practical implications of this measure we must remind ourselves that firms normally have only a very vague idea as to the shape of their demand curve. The problem in practice is that they only have observations of price and quantity sold over a period of time. For these observations to be comparable, all other price and market characteristics should be unchanged. Of course, this is rarely the case. More typically, firms setting prices have to make more abstract judgements, such as: 'We believe we will sell X units if the price is £x and that we would sell Y units if we increased price to £y'. Observations of past prices and quantities are useful but are at best only an indication in what is, in essence, a subjective estimate.

Although useful for theoretical analysis, elasticity can also help managers in their more practical task as follows:

(a)   The optimum price will lie on the elastic part of the demand curve (assuming that costs are positively related to output). We have already demonstrated that where demand is inelastic total revenue can be raised by increasing price. Another direct consequence is that output is lowered and hence total costs will be less. Therefore, when demand is inelastic, prices should be increased, as increasing prices both increases total revenue and decreases total cost – hence profits increase. It is only where revenue decreases when a price is increased that we have to judge whether or not such a decrease is more than compensated for by a fall in cost. Or alternatively, whether the increase in revenue from a cut in price would outweigh the increase in costs. Such judgements only occur when demand is elastic.

(b)   Where demand is very elastic, customers may be described as being very price-sensitive. In such cases, it is essential that the error in pricing should be minimized, as overpricing can result in a dramatic decline in demand. Also, underpricing may result in damaging stock outs and loss of profits. As the optimum price will constantly be altering, owing to inflation and relative price changes in other goods, the price of such items should be subject to careful management control. The potentially drastic consequences of overpricing may also encourage firms to attempt to reduce the elasticity demand for their product. This may be achieved by advertising and promotional activities designed to create a preference for the product that is independent of the price.

(c)   Where demand is relatively inelastic, other elements in the marketing mix are likely to be important. By relatively inelastic we mean that elasticity is close to 1 but is still greater than 1. Here, customers are less price-sensitive than in case (b). This may be due to a number of factors, such as location, quality, service, image and flexibility, as well as advertising and promotional activities. In that prices are thought to be less important, one would expect these other factors to receive greater attention than in the previous case.

In conclusion, we can say that varying levels of elasticity have very different implications for pricing policy. Therefore, in an uncertain world where managers have to make difficult judgements as to pricing, the concept of elasticity can help to guide thinking towards crucial aspects of pricing policy.

9.3.2   The effect of changes in relative costs on decisions

We have established that a change in relative prices affects value. If values are significantly affected, then we may reasonably expect decisions to change as a result. We begin by looking at a very simple example of a relative cost change in example 2.

Example 2
Montonia Ltd has the capacity to produce one of the following products:

	Product A	Product B
Price	10	9
Direct Cost	8	8
Contribution per unit	2	1

The numbers of each item that Montonia could produce are about the same. All prices it is estimated will be subject to 10 per cent inflation, except for the cost of product B, which is constant.

Which product is at present preferable? Would the decision change in future years?

Since the volumes produced are similar, Product A yields the higher contribution per unit and is therefore preferable. After the first year, the contribution of Product A will have risen by 10 per cent to £2.2:

	After 1 year	After 2 years
	Product A	
Price	11.00	12.10
Direct cost	8.80	9.68
	2.20	2.42
	Product B	
Price	9.90	10.89
Direct cost	8.00	8.00
	1.90	2.89

After two years, Product B produces a relatively greater profit and would be preferable. This change in profitability is wholly accounted for by the relative reduction in the cost of Product B. If the cost had kept pace with inflation, it would have been $8 (1.1)^2 = 9.68$ at the end of year 2, and profits of B would have been 1.21 i.e. half of Product A's contribution – the same ratio as in the original figures. Relative price changes, therefore, affect profitability and decisions, unlike general increases.

In practice, it is unlikely that we would be able to predict future prices in the manner of example 2. Prices, as a rule, do not follow simple predictable trend lines over time, though we may yet be able to make useful statements about their future levels. In example 2, for instance, if the two products used identical resources, then an increase in the cost of Product A would always be accompanied by a similar increase in the cost of Product B. If this were the case, given the other details in the example, we would be able to say that Product A would always be preferable whatever the level of future prices.

In the following sections we examine how specific price movements affect two types of decisions: the make or buy decision and the competitive supply problem.

9.3.3 *Relative price changes: make or buy*

A common problem faced by firms is whether they should 'make' or 'buy in' the goods and services they use. A manufacturing firm building engines, for instance, may decide to make as opposed to buy the electrical components. Some firms have their own legal department, others buy in the service. An important element of all such decisions is the need to establish the cost of each option. There are two aspects to this problem: (1) the cost of current resources and (2) prospective price levels.

When making a component, or providing a service, a combination of internal and external resources will be used; some may be diverted from other activities, creating an opportunity cost, other resources may be 'free' in that they are surplus to current requirements. The concepts required to establish a relevant cost are discussed in section 4.5; in this section we examine the problem of incorporating future price-level changes in our decision. We cannot say that in future, other things being equal, we will choose the cheaper of the two options. The transaction costs of switching into and out of production and 'self-service' make such a policy impractical. Therefore, we have to take into account how the prices might vary in relation to each other as an integral part of the decision. This we can do by applying some of the techniques in chapter 3 – example 3 illustrates possible approaches.

Example 3
Pendlebury Ltd is considering adding Product A to its range. It will sell for £10 per unit and have an expected cost of £6 if made by Pendlebury. An alternative is to import the item at a cost of £5.80. The cost of the bought-in alternative is expected to vary considerably, as it is subject to exchange rates which are not fixed. The variation of the two costs can be described as follows:

Cost level	Subjective probability (%)	Costs per unit Made in (£)	Imported (£)
High	25	8	8.8
Medium	50	6	5.8
Low	25	4	2.8

The manager's reaction to risky choice may be described as decreasingly risk-averse (see section 3.4.3), and is modelled by the equation $U = 100 (\log_n x / 30,000)$, where x is the return and U is utility. It is expected that annual sales will be about 10,000 units. Will the manager prefer to make or buy Product A?

Using the expected value criterion, it would be preferable to import Product A. However, if this option is selected, profits will vary more widely than if Product A is made in. We therefore need to confirm our selection by using the expected utility criterion.

£000 Net cash flow or return	Made in	Imported
High cost	20	12
Medium cost	40	42
Low cost	60	72
Expected value	40	42
Standard deviation	14	21
Expected utility	22	16

In this case, the expected utility from making in is greater than the importing alternative, indicating that it would be preferable to make Product A. Clearly, the greater variance of importing has offset slightly higher expected value.

We should, however, be cautious in coming to this conclusion, as our calculations are only a partial view of the effect of price changes. The manager also has to take overall returns into consideration. For instance, when costs are high for making the product in example 3, what will be the level of other costs in Pendlebury Ltd? It is likely that they too will be high, assuming that there are common resources. Alternatively, when other costs are low, then Product A's costs should be low. In other words, we would expect there to be a positive covariance between the contribution from Product A and the contribution from other products. The effect of a positive covariance will be to increase the variance of the returns by more than the sum of the individual variances. Where X is the return on product A, and Y is the return on other products, as we have seen in chapter 2, $Var(X+Y) = Var(X) + Var(Y) + 2Cov(XY)$. By contrast, the imported substitute may well not have an especially strong covariance with other costs, as it is subject to the special influence of exchange rate fluctuations. In example 4 we continue with Pendlebury Ltd by looking at the general picture.

Example 4
In addition to the information in example 3, the returns of Pendlebury Ltd, apart from Product A, are expected to be as follows:

Costs	Probability	Return (£000)
High	0.25	2
Medium	0.50	30
Low	0.25	58

The manager estimates that the returns of the made-in option will be perfectly correlated with existing returns, as similar resources are used. Imports, by contrast, are expected to be independent of existing returns, as the exchange rate is the predominant cause of price changes. Which option is the more attractive?

The pattern of returns for the made in option are as follows:

Made-in costs	Other product costs	Probability	Return (£000)
High	High	0.25	22
Medium	Medium	0.5	70
Low	Low	0.25	118
	Expected return		70
	Standard deviation		34
	Expected utility		68.9

The imported option is independent of existing costs, so that the pattern of returns is:

Import costs	Other product costs	Probability	Return (£000)
High (0.25)	(0.25) High	0.0625	14
	(0.5) Medium	0.125	42
	(0.25) Low	0.0625	70
Medium (0.5)	(0.25) High	0.125	44
	(0.5) Medium	0.25	72
	(0.25) Low	0.125	100
Low (0.25)	(0.25) High	0.0625	74
	(0.5) Medium	0.125	102
	(0.25) Low	0.0625	130
	Expected return		72
	Standard deviation		29
	Expected utility		76.6

When considering the picture as a whole, the importing option has a higher expected utility (76.6 as opposed to 68.9), and is therefore preferable.

If the made-in option had returns that were independent of existing production, then the expected utility would have been 77.4; under such conditions Pendlebury Ltd would have marginally preferred the made-in option. Thus, the actual choice, that of importing, results solely from the statement that its costs are independent of other products.

Let us review the argument in Pendlebury Ltd, for ultimately it is a story of managerial estimates and judgement, rather than numbers and equations. Firstly, let us assume that the manager reviewed the position of the make or buy decision for Product A independently of other products. The expected returns and standard deviations are:

£	Expected return	Standard deviation
Made-in	40,000	14,000
Imported	42,000	21,000

The manager is risk-averse, so he would reason to himself along the following lines: 'Although I expect to earn £2,000 more by importing, this may not prove to be the case; the standard deviations, and what I have seen of the discrete estimates, suggest that there is a small but significant chance that the imported option will be less profitable. Although the accountant has pointed out to me that there is a better chance that importing will be more profitable, I feel that this possibility is not as important as the less profitable scenario. I think I will go for the made-in option in spite of the lower returns – it's safer'.

The accountant then, as in example 4, considered the picture:

	Expected return	*Standard deviation*
Returns including made-in option for product A	70	34
Returns including importing option for Product A	72	29

The manager's reasoning would be: 'Well, I'm glad we looked at the implications for the whole operation. I had rather assumed that variation of returns under the made-in option would also be less in the overall picture as well. I do agree with the accountant, we will not have high costs in A and low costs for the other products if we make A. They use the same resources. On the other hand, import prices will move on their own. There is now no contest; importing has the higher expected return and lower standard deviation; on financial grounds importing is the obvious choice.'

Readers may note the similarity between this argument and that in section 3.4.6 – in effect, importing benefits from diversification.

In this example, we have put aside the many other factors that need to be weighted along with the financial benefits. In practice, these might well outweigh the financial considerations: supply may be more reliable under the made-in option, quality may be superior, production may help retain valuable staff, the potential for new opportunities may be greater and so on. The accountant should not be surprised if the actual choice is to make, rather than import, product A. It might be argued that the financial effect of other considerations ought to be included in the original estimates of the expected return. In practice, as we have argued in chapter 1, putting a price on such intangible aspects is asking too much of our financial system. A more indirect method of scoring these attributes with respect to profits is preferable (see chapter 3).

9.3.4   Competitive supply

The make or buy decision is a part of the more general problem of competitive supply. Making the product, or indeed performing the service oneself (in-house lawyers, etc.), is simply a case of self-supply. When compared with making in, external supply has two special features:

(a)   costs are less likely to covary with internal costs, hence separate consideration is probably sufficient;

(b)   in a competitive supply position, switching between suppliers will incur fewer transaction costs than changing between self-supply and external supply.

The obvious implication of point (b) is that a firm should adopt a strategy of buying from the cheapest of a number of competitive suppliers, with the important proviso that the products or services are identical. We now examine this policy in example 5.

Example 5

Irlam Software retails packs of component X. It has identified two suppliers who have agreed to supply plain components to which Irlam adds its logo before selling. The price of component X varies between £3.5 and £5 in real terms for each supplier; there is an estimated 25 per cent chance that the price will be £3.5, £4.0, £4.5 and £5.0 at today's prices. The prices tend to vary according to each supplier's own production problems; they therefore move independently of each other. It is perfectly possible, for instance, that for a few months one firm may be selling at £5 and the other at £3.50; the prices will then change, there being no particular pattern.

Calculate the expected cost and standard deviation of Component X, assuming that Irlam always switches its supplier to the cheaper of two. Compare this with the costs of a single supplier.

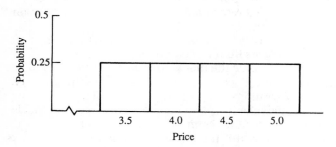

Figure 9.4

The distribution of costs is rectangular (see Figure 9.4). The average price of a single supplier is 4.25, with a standard deviation of 0.56. If Irlam could switch between suppliers, then, assuming price independence, the probabilities of each price would be as follows:

3.5: 7.0 $(0.25)^2 = .4375$
4.0: 5.0 $(0.25)^2 = .3125$
4.5: 3.0 $(0.25)^2 = .1875$
5.0: 1.0 $(0.25)^2 = .0625$

(Hint: draw up a matrix of all the possible combinations, and note the cheapest price in each combination – the probability of each combination is 0.25^2.)

The distribution is now skewed (see Figure 9.5). The new average is 3.94 and the standard deviation is 0.46.

As one might expect, the existence of competitive supply reduces the average cost and the spread of likely costs. Again we should stress that in practice the position is likely to be more complex. For instance, suppliers may

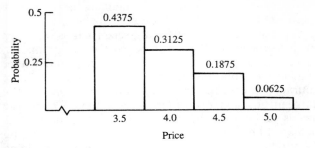

Figure 9.5

not always have the capacity to supply and there may be other hidden costs, such as delays when suppliers are switched or reduced flexibility in the product from having more than one supplier (joint development is more difficult).

9.4   Price-level changes and year-end accounts

Management accounting is principally concerned with the internal workings of the firm. In this light, the final accounts may seem beyond the immediate scope of the management accountant, as they are intended for investors and shareholders. In practice, firms very often are themselves the investors and shareholders. In fact, most large firms will have wholly owned subsidiaries reporting to head office. The management accounting activities of planning, decision making and control in such an environment necessarily entails the use of the year-end accounts. Inflation, and indeed any change in price levels, represent a major cause of distortion in such accounts.

The stated purpose of the published balance sheet and profit and loss account is to present a 'true and fair view' of the company. With this objective in mind, we shall now examine the effect of inflation on the principle aspects of the final accounts.

If there are no inflation adjustments, tangible assets such as land and machinery which may have been purchased over 50 years ago will be added together with assets purchased during the year. The resulting figure will be a meaningless mixture of prices at varying dates, providing little indication as to value.

Unlike tangible assets, the worth of monetary assets and liabilities will not be distorted by historic cost conventions. A debt of £100 whether incurred last month or 10 years ago is still a debt valued at £100. Similarly with creditors, if £100 is owed, then whatever the rate of inflation, the value of the liability remains £100. Although the monetary amount remains the same, there is nevertheless gain to the firm in holding such liabilities in times of inflation (the real value of what is owed decreases) and a loss in holding such assets (by the same measure, inflation reduces the value of all such debts). Most firms hold net monetary assets and hence experience net loss in real worth through the effects of inflation. To run a business at the same level in times of inflation requires ever-increasing investment in net monetary assets and a commensurate provision in the accounts.

Inflation also affects depreciation. Tangible fixed assets, such as buildings and machinery when depreciated on their historic cost value produce a depreciation charge that is woefully out of date. Such a charge would neither provide a reserve for replacement nor measure the value used. The effect of this practice is to encourage industry to keep out of date machinery, for the lower depreciation charge means higher short-term profits, though obviously long-term performance is endangered by not updating machinery. This author is no doubt not alone in having had the unenviable task of explaining to a director that his purchase, in this case, of a new rubber moulding machine meant a much higher depreciation charge!

Changes in the value of stock will also affect profit. An item purchased for £10 at the start of the year and resold for £15 at the end of the year, records a profit of £5. How much of this profit is simply due to the fact that prices have risen (a holding gain) and how much is due to reward for the service provided (an operating gain)? In other words, what cost should we record against this sale? Suppose that general inflation has been 10 per cent, and the current cost of the item is £11.50, we could then record three levels of profit thus:

	Historic profit	Profit adjusted for general inflation	Replacement cost basis
Revenue	15.00	15.00	15.00
Cost	10.00	11.00	11.50
Profit	5.00	4.00	3.50

There are justifications for employing each method. Historic cost, it is argued, records the actual events. The user of the accounts may then adjust for inflation as he or she sees fit. Something of this approach is current practice, for although firms only report historic cost profits, there is no doubt that investors and the stock market do make allowances for inflation.

Many investors will be principally concerned with the monetary value of their investment. As regards this transaction, they would wish to see the real value of the cost debited to revenue, i.e. £11. Their concern is not how managers spend the money but simply that they should endeavour to earn real profits, and that capital should not be repaid as dividends due to inflation. To explain this last point, suppose the £5 historic profit were returned to the investor and the manager retained the original investment of £10. As we have said, in end of year terms the £10 should be £11 to retain the real value. By distributing £5 instead of £4, the investor is effectively being given back £1 of his original investment in end of year terms. The element is wrongly termed profit under historic conventions.

The concern of replacement cost is, as the term implies, for a continuation of the activities of the business. In our example, £11.50 would have to be charged to enable the manager to purchase another item of stock. The argument for this practice is that such provision protects the operating activities of the company. In the example, if all profits are distributed, the activity can only be repeated if they are measured by this method. A counter argument is that adjustment for general inflation only is required to safeguard monetary rather than physical capital. Investors are concerned with their financial claim on the company, and not with the assets that represent that claim. The debate is an interesting one, and the different views were much discussed when the accounting profession and the government were considering how to adjust for inflation in the final accounts in the 1970s.

In the context of management accounting, the particular method chosen to adjust for inflation can vary according to the purposes of the user. In this sense, all methods are relevant. In practice, however, the replacement cost basis would appear to accord best with the usual requirements of management accounting in that it is the operations of the company which are normally the main concern of the management accounting report – the need to safeguard the assets is essential in this respect. For this reason we use the replacement cost basis, as suggested in SSAP 16, to illustrate the effect of changing price levels on the final accounts.

Example 6

Whitefield plc operates in the textile industry. In June 1981, it purchased land worth £1m, buildings for £0.5m and machinery for £0.1m. In 1983 a further £0.25m of machinery was acquired. The historic cost final accounts for the year 1989 are as follows:

Profit and loss account year ended June 1989 (£000)

Sales		5,000
less cost of sales		
opening stock	500	
purchases	4,500	
closing stock	1,000	4,000
gross profit		1,000
Expenses		
(including depreciation)		500
Net profit		500

Balance sheet as at June 1989 (£000)

Fixed assets: land			1,000
buildings	500		
less dep^n (4%)	160		340
machinery	350		
less dep^n (8%)	184		166
plus working capital			
Current assets	stock	1,000	
	debtors	400	
less current liabilities	Creditors	(200)	
	Overdraft	(100)	1,100
			2,606

Financed by

Shares	1,000
Reserves	1,006
Long-term loans	600
	2,606

opening balances included (£000s) Debtors £300 Creditors £150 and over-draft £80.

The relevant price indices are:

	1981	1983	1987	1988	1989
Land or buildings	100	150		180	200
Machinery	107	123		149	160
Stock	105	116	130	140	150
General Prices	295	335		426	447

Required:
Construct a profit and loss account and balance sheet which shows effect of inflation on the company.

We shall follow the methods of SSAP16.
Step 1
Restate the closing balance sheet at June 1989 prices (where a firm does not intend to replace the asset with one performing a similar function, the asset should be restated at the greater of its net realizable value or the amount recoverable for future use). Assets are revalued by the entry:

Dr: Asset to revalued amount Cr: Revaluation reserve

Asset/Reserve	Historic	Index* adjustment	Dr accounting	Cr entries	Replacement cost
Land	1,000	$\dfrac{200}{100}-1$	1,000		2,000
Buildings: cost	500	$\dfrac{200}{100}-1$	500		1,000
dep^n	(160)	$\dfrac{200}{100}-1$		160	(320)
Machinery 1981					
cost	100	$\dfrac{160}{107}-1$	50		150
dep^n	(64)	$\dfrac{160}{107}-1$		32	(96)

Asset/Reserve	Historic	Index* adjustment	Dr accounting	Cr entries	Replacement cost
Machinery 1983					
cost	250	$\dfrac{160}{123}-1$	75		325
dep^n	(120)	$\dfrac{160}{123}-1$		36	(156)
Stock	1,000	$\dfrac{150\dagger}{148}-1$	14		1,014
			1,639	228	
Revaluation reserve			228	1,639	
			1,867	1,867	

*Index adjustments are:

$$\frac{\text{Index when reported}}{\text{Index when purchased}}-1$$

† Closing stock was purchased before June 1989. Assuming a stock turnover of approximately 2.25 months (taken from the existing profit and loss account) the estimated index at purchase was:

$$150-(150-140)\,\frac{2.25}{12}=148.$$

Step 2
Calculate extra depreciation to be charged to the profit and loss account. This is the depreciation for the year only. The full adjustment, shown in step 1, includes increased depreciation for previous years (known as backlog depreciation) – this amount is debited directly to the reserve and does not go via the profit and loss account (see note in step 5). The depreciation attributable to the year ended 1989 is:

Depreciation account	Amount	Index adjustment	Amount charged to the year
Buildings	160	$\dfrac{200}{100}-\dfrac{180}{100}$	32
Machinery	64	$\dfrac{160}{107}-\dfrac{149}{107}$	7
	120	$\dfrac{160}{123}-\dfrac{149}{123}$	11
			50

The index adjustment is the value at end of the year less value at beginning of year.

Step 3

Calculate the cost of sale adjustment (COSA), that is the increase in stock value due to inflation:

	Historic cost	Index adjustment	Current cost
Opening stock	500	$\dfrac{145}{138}$	525
Purchases	4,500		4,500
Closing stock	1,000	$\dfrac{145}{148}$	980
Cost of sales	4,000		4,045

Debit profit and loss account with an extra $4,045 - 4,000 = 45$

We assume here that stock was sold evenly through the year and therefore the point of sale can be approximated to the half year. If sales are strongly seasonal, then the average month calculated as the month weighted by volume of stock sold, will serve as a better approximation. An exact calculation would be the accumulated difference between the values at the point of sale and the point of purchase, the point of sale being the assumed replacement time.

Step 4

Calculate the monetary working capital adjustment (MWCA). This is the loss of value through holding net monetary assets. To continue in business at the same level of activity, the business will incur higher debtors and creditors and also need higher cash levels – the adjustment makes an allowance for such an increase. Only the assets and liabilities that form the working capital should be included. The calculation is as follows:

MWCA = increase in debtors due to inflation less increase in creditors due to inflation

A stock index is preferred, though the retail prices index would be an adequate substitute.

Increase in debtors due to inflation = Closing debtors – opening debtors – (non inflationary element).

$$\begin{matrix} \text{Non-} \\ \text{inflationary} \\ \text{element} \end{matrix} = \begin{matrix} \text{Closing debtors} \\ \text{adjusted to the} \\ \text{mid-year value} \end{matrix} - \begin{matrix} \text{Opening debtors} \\ \text{adjusted to the} \\ \text{mid-year value} \end{matrix}$$

With both debtors and creditors we have assumed that the balances were acquired on average 1 month before the reporting date. Thus:

$$\text{MWCA debtors} = 400 - 300 - \left[\left(\frac{145}{149} \times 400 \right) - \left(\frac{145}{139} \times 300 \right) \right]$$
$$= 100 - 76$$
$$= 24$$

The same process applies to creditors and overdraft used for working capital. Therefore:

$$\text{MWCA creditors} = 300 - 230 - \left[\left(\frac{145}{149} \times 300 \right) - \left(\frac{145}{139} \times 230 \right) \right]$$
$$= 70 - 52$$
$$= 18$$

The monetary working capital adjustment is therefore

$$\text{MWCA} = 24 - 18 = 6$$

This is debited to the profit and loss account and credited to current cost reserves (note the similarity with the COSA adjustment).

Step 5   Put it all together!
First, the profit and loss account for the year ended June 1989

	£000
Historic cost profit	500
less:	
extra depreciation (step 2)*	50
cost of sales adjustment (step 3)	45
monetary working capital adjustment (step 4)	6
	399

Then: the balance sheet as at June 1989

		£000
Fixed assets: land		2,000
buildings	1,000	
less depreciation (4%)	320	680
machinery	475	
less depreciation (8%)	252	223
plus working capital		
Current assets: stock	1,014	
debtors	400	
Current liabilities: creditors	(200)	
overdraft	(100)	1,114
		4,017
Financed by:		
Shares	1,000	
Historic cost reserves (at start of year)	506	
Current cost operating profit	399	

Revaluation reserve†   1,512
Loans   600
                                                        _____
                                                         4,017

* The full treatment of the current year depreciation adjustment as follows:

	Part of step 1	Step 2
Depreciation account	cr 50	
Revaluation reserve	dr 50	cr 50
Profit and Loss account		dr 50

† Made up of: net credit to the balance sheet from step 1 $(1639-228)=1411$ plus the difference between the historic and inflation adjusted profits, which is the net effect of the depreciation, cost of sales and monetary working capital adjustments, i.e.

$$1411 + (500 - 399) = 1512$$

The current cost operating profit is a measure of the amount that can be distributed without affecting the operating ability of the company. SSAP 16 attempted to divide the reduction in profits between shareholders and long-term investors. We have omitted the adjustment, which was always controversial, on the grounds that the management accountants' interests, as discussed above, are company- rather than shareholder-orientated. In following SSAP 16 we do not infer that management accountants must follow its recommendations, but merely that it provides a useful starting point. We would particularly warn against the expense of such an exercise outweighing the benefits. In particular, accountants should use their experience in limiting the cost of step 1, which involves the ageing of assets.

Further adjustments may well be justified: for example, the sales figure may usefully be analysed to differentiate between revenue caused by volume changes as opposed revenue caused by price level changes. Similar adjustments may also be made to the various categories of cost.

The guiding principle in making adjustments for price-level changes in management accounting is, as ever, the needs of the user rather than any particular standard or practice.

References and further reading

CSO, *Annual Abstract of Statistics*, HMSO (annual).
Hinton, P. R., Westwick, C. A., *Current Cost Accounting*, Oyez, 1981.
Kaplan, R. S., Atkinson, A. A., *Advanced Management Accounting*, Prentice-Hall, 1989, pp. 412–30.
Koutsoyiannis, A., *Modern Macroeconomics*, 2nd edition, Macmillan, 1979.
Rowley, E. E., *The Financial System Today*, MUP, 1987.

10 Transfer pricing

10.1 Introduction

Most successful organizations become too large to be treated as a single entity and can only be managed efficiently by separating the operation into units, or divisions. This is the organizational counterpart of the division of labour. Managers are able to specialize in the problems of their own divisions, and the knowledge they develop will help them in decision making, planning and control. Performance evaluation can also be more easily gauged, as managers are responsible for the performance of their own division. These benefits must be weighed up against the danger of divisions pursuing their own goals to the detriment of the company as a whole, this is sometimes termed the problem of *goal congruence* (see section 1.5).

The benefits of divisionalization normally require that divisions are as separate in their operations as possible. It is rare, however, for the separation to be complete. In particular, there are likely to be transfers of goods and services between divisions. For example, in the car manufacturing industry, it is common for different parts to be made in different factories. These are then transferred, sometimes across international boundaries, to the assembly plant. Another example is where production and selling are treated separately. The production division will transfer its output to the selling division, which will then decide upon the pricing and marketing of the product. In each case a value has to be placed upon the transfer, and this is known as the transfer price. With each transfer, the company is in the unique position of being able to decide upon the selling price *and* the buying price. This forms, as it were, an internal market under the complete control of the company.

10.2   The transfer pricing problem

If a company is not divisionalized, goods and services that might otherwise have been transferred would be valued at cost. Is there any reason to change this practice merely because a company is organized into divisions? For a few firms the answer is no (see Table 10.1), but clearly the answer does not have to be no. A division can transfer or 'sell' an item at a price above cost and record a profit. The purchasing division can then treat the item like any other purchase.

A policy of transferring goods and services at cost would imply that the division is being controlled by a budget. In the traditional budgeting system there is no incentive to plan for a high or low budget, or indeed to co-ordinate with other divisions. Such budgets will therefore require central planning, decision making and control. The intended benefits of delegation and division of responsibilities would be largely lost in such a system.

By contrast, profit is the measure of worth that a division would earn if it were truly separate. A manager controlled by profits has the traditional incentive to maximize, which includes responding to the needs of other divisions. Whether or not this results in a benefit for the company as a whole is very much the problem of transfer pricing. It is not simply a technical measurement problem, as it may sometimes appear. For even where a profit measure has obvious drawbacks, it may yet serve as an incentive to achieve productivity levels, innovations and developments that may not have been achieved under a technically better system. Thus the choice of transfer price is guided by both technical and judgemental issues. Let us illustrate the problem with the following simple example.

Example 1

Selling division (S) transfers 25 per cent of its output, component X, to the buying division (B), which then uses it as input for component Y. Each Y requires one X. As yet, the company is undecided on the transfer price of component X and has assigned the letter A to the value of such transfers. The budget for the year (based upon the production of 100 units of X) is as follows:

Division	S		B	
	units of X	£ per unit	units of Y	£ per unit
Units sold externally	75		25	
Units transferred	25			
	£		£	
External sales	750	10	1500	60
Internal sales	25A	A		
Variable costs	500	5	750	30
Inter-divisional purchases			25A	A
Fixed costs	300	3	100	4
Profit	25A−50		650−25A	

In addition, the company is expecting an order from abroad for component Y (produced by B) of 10 units at £37 each – the order has not been included in the above figures. The managing director on viewing the budget comments: 'I want a transfer price that will motivate both S and B as well as benefiting the company as a whole.'

Discuss the possible solutions as well as their effect on the export order.

The first point to note is that any transfer price which will benefit S will be to the cost of B. The interests of the two managers are therefore diametrically opposed.

The choice of transfer price falls into two categories: cost-based and market-based. We will examine cost-based methods first, and make the assumption (to be relaxed later) that the 25 units transferred cannot be sold externally, nor can division B purchase X on the open market. In practical terms, we are saying that there is no effective intermediate market – the 75 units sold by S therefore form a special order in this context.

Marginal cost

If we make the approximation that the variable cost can be used as the marginal cost, then the transfers would be valued at £5 × 25 units = £125. The profit of S would be £75 and B £525.

But would S be motivated by such a price? If profit is our measure of motivation, the answer is no. If S did not produce 25 units for B, then it would save itself the variable cost of production, i.e. the £125. Profit would therefore be £75 for S with or without production and transfer to B. There would also be no incentive on the part of S to meet the export order, though B would correctly accept the order, as there would be a £2 positive contribution per unit (being the selling price less total variable cost $(37-(30+5)=2)$.

The marginal cost represents the lowest possible price from the transferor's point of view. Any less, and profits would decline on transfer of any units.

Thus the benefit of this method is that the decisions by B will not be distorted by the transfer price, as the marginal or variable cost will be the variable cost to the firm as a whole. The drawback is the lack of incentive given to S.

Full cost and cost plus

The manager of division S may argue that the 25 units transferred out should bear a portion of the fixed overhead burden. If fixed costs are allocated *pro rata*, then each unit would be charged with an extra £3. The transfer price would then be:

	£
Variable cost	5
Apportioned fixed cost	3
'Full cost'	8

Division S would gain by the fixed cost apportionment, the with-transfer total profit of S would be $(8 \times 25) - 50 = £150$ and the without-transfer (and production) profit would be £75. The gain of £75 is simply 25 units multiplied by the £3 fixed cost apportionment, which from S's point of view represents contribution.

At such a price there would be no incentive for B to meet the export order. If S can produce an extra 10 units and they are transferred at the 'full' cost of £8, then from B's point of view, the total variable or direct cost would be £38 per unit, a negative contribution of $-£1$ per unit. The order would be incorrectly rejected, for the costs and revenues *to the firm* have not changed from the marginal cost case.

In general, any price above the marginal cost of the transfer will potentially lead to the rejection of opportunities that increase the profitability of the company. In this sense, the transfer price is too high. In another sense it is too low, for the division S manager may claim, as with the marginal cost, that he or she is receiving little or no incentive to transfer component X. In addition, if divisional profitability is used to assess performance, the manager of division S might fairly claim that the decision to transfer at full cost (or indeed marginal cost) biases downwards the division's profitability, as resources are being used in S for little or no contribution. In other words, the measured profits of division S are not a fair reflection of the the division's contribution to general profits.

So often in transfer pricing there is an intermingling of 'fairness' or equity and economic arguments. When applied to a cost-based approach, the desire for a fairer price suggests that the transfer price should be on a cost plus basis. A fair mark-up on absorption costs might be deemed to be a reasonable percentage, say, 10 per cent, or the mark-up on external sales may be applied, i.e. 25 per cent. But although this is a fairer measure, in that some reward for effort is credited to division S, the price may well lead to the rejection by the firm of profitable opportunities such as the export order.

In a case such as this, where there is *no external market* for the 25 units that are transferred, the manager of S might, with considerable justice, argue: 'All the profits of the company depend on my division, therefore my profits should be at least as great as those of division B'. Equally, the manager of division B might argue: 'Without my contribution the company would earn £525 less'. Both arguments are in a sense correct, though both would have to admit an element of truth in each other's point of view. If we cannot satisfactorily resolve this problem, then it would seem that one of the parties will feel unfairly treated and hence demotivated.

*A game theory approach**
One possible solution is to apply game theory (Shubik, 1962). This approach measures profits as an 'average incremental profit' of the possible scenarios faced by each division. The possible scenarios for each of the two divisions are to either exist on their own, or combine with the other division, i.e.:

* CIMA see Preface

From S's point of view
  (i) S could be on its own
  (ii) S could join B

From B's point of view
  (i) B could be on its own
  (ii) B could join S

The incremental profits to the company produced by each division separately are S = £75 (i.e. excluding transfers); and B = £525 (i.e. component X transferred at marginal cost). The incremental profits for the scenarios are from S's point of view:

(i) 75 – If S were on its own, no transfers would be produced.
(ii) 75 + 525 = 600 – As S has argued, the company profits depend on S producing product X; therefore the addition of S to B will enable the company to produce and earn a contribution from B as well. Without the addition of S, B would have to close and contribution would be £0; the incremental effect of adding S is therefore the whole £600.

From B's point of view, the profits are:

(i) 0 – Division B cannot survive on its own; we would assume closure, and there would therefore be no profits.
(ii) 525 – This is B's argument; adding B to S increases profits by £525.

From each point of view there are two scenarios which we shall weigh equally. Therefore the 'average incremental profit' is:

$$\frac{(i) + (ii)}{2} \text{ or } \frac{b}{2} = \frac{525}{2} = 272.5 \text{ for B}$$

$$\frac{(i) + (ii)}{2} \text{ or } \frac{2s + b}{2} = \frac{2(75) + 525}{2} = 337.5 \text{ for S}$$

where s and b are the individual contributions from divisions S and B respectively.

In what sense, we might ask, is this approach equitable? Let us start with a slightly different case. If S could not survive on its own, it would have an incremental profit of £0 when considered separately. Scenario (i) for S would therefore have an incremental profit of £0 and scenario (ii) for B would be £600; the formula for each division would then be (s + b)/2. In other words, where the two divisions are totally dependent on each other, the 'judgement of Solomon' is applied and the profits are shared equally.

In this case division S is able to survive on its own, and by this method is given a larger share of the profit. In fact its profits are 337.5 − 262.5 = £75 higher, which is precisely the profit it would earn if the division were on its own. The transfer price that would distribute profits in this manner is £15.50. Unfortunately, the export order would be rejected if this transfer price were used.

A practical interpretation that reflects the game theory solutions, and would not lead to the rejection of the export order, would be to use marginal costs for decisions during the period. Transfer prices could then be set at the end of the period such that each division would be credited separately for profits earned independently, whereas profits earned by transferring goods (or the remaining profits) would be divided equally between the respective divisions. Where a division would make a loss if it were independent (as in division B), shutdown is assumed and independant profits would be £0. Remember that we are assuming no external market for the transferred items; component X itself could not be purchased externally (see above).

Divisions would, in fact, use the marginal cost without being ordered to by head office, for it is the only cost that indicates whether or not a positive 'share' will be earned. Under this arrangement, the export order would not be rejected – the contribution per unit of £2 would be shared equally.

As a cautionary note, however subtle one attempts to make these techniques, the problems are never wholly solved. In this case, the solution is dependent upon the divisional structure chosen. Suppose that most managerial skill and effort in S was required for selling. If production were transferred to B, the distribution of profits would change dramatically, with there being no great change of effort and skill. Equally, B might regard the existing sharing of its profits as being unfair, as the transferred item, in value at least, is a minor part. To distribute profits fairly under this method, one must first agree upon a fair structure, or negotiate a sharing rule other than 50:50 that both sides feel to be fair.

Linear programming

Another approach is to base the transfer price on linear programming (Biggs and Benjamin, 1989). The linear programme assigns contribution as shadow or dual prices to scarce resources. The transfer price is then the variable cost of an item plus dual prices associated with the scarce resources it uses. As the dual price is calculated from the most profitable use of existing resources, any proposal that does not at least cover the dual price plus the direct costs is suboptimal; hence such a price should lead to the most profitable course of action being chosen. In this simple form there are obvious problems, for the price can only be calculated after the best course of action has been determined (ideally we would like our price to lead the divisions to the best course of action). The price may still be relevant for additional marginal projects, but any significant change will require a reformulation of the linear program.

Nevertheless, the method does provide useful insights into the problem. In this example, suppose the manufacture of component X was limited by a machine whose capacity was 100 hours, and that each component requires 1 hour. Also assume that demand for Y is limited to 25 units and that the special order could be increased to 110 units. The initial tableau would appear as follows:

Maximize $5X + 25Y$
  subject to: $X + Y \leqslant 100$ machine hour constraint
          $X \leqslant 110$ the special order
          $Y \leqslant 25$ demand constraint
          $X, Y > 0$

One can see by inspection that the optimal solution is 75X and 25Y, i.e. the budget. The dual price of a machine hour is £5, as one extra machine hour would enable one more unit of X to be sold, increasing contribution by £5. The transfer price of product X to B would be £10, which is the variable cost plus the dual price. Such a price would ensure that if B could sell an extra unit, the price of that unit would be at least £5 above the variable costs to the firm. In other words, it will have to earn at least the same contribution as product X.

By varying the problem, the linear programme will produce other equally sound results. It therefore seems a natural extension to suggest that the dual price should be added to variable costs in order to derive a transfer price. However, this solution is unattractive for two reasons. First, as we have said, the linear programme solves the very problem that we are attempting to delegate (though linear decomposition methods can help delegate the problem). Secondly, it can encourage managers to act against the interests of the firm.

As a variation, suppose that bad management by division S means that only 24 hours of machine time are available. The initial tableau would now read:

Maximize
$$5X + 25Y$$
$$X + Y \leqslant 24$$
$$X \leqslant 110$$
$$Y \leqslant 25$$
$$X, Y > 0$$

Again, by inspection the solution is to make and sell 24 units of Y (remember that B cannot buy X on the open market). The dual price of 1 machine hour would be £25 – the contribution from producing and selling an extra Y. The transfer price would therefore be $5 + 25 = £30$. The profit shown by division S would be $(30 - 5)24 - 300 = £300$. In the previous scenario the profit of S would be $(10 - 5)100 - 300 = £200$. In other words, manager S has managed to increase his or her profits by restricting the resources! However, the total profits of the company would have declined from £600 to £200.

More generally, we can say that linear programming as a basis for transfer pricing has very poor motivational consequences and is in no sense a fair measure of performance. Despite this, the model has been suggested as a tool for helping to determine optimum output levels (the simple model is extended to non-linear versions) and as a basis for an organizational procedure to determine the optimum solution (again, linear decomposition methods). The practicality of these developments is dubious, as they are both very data-greedy. Thus, although linear programming provides an interesting commentary on the transfer pricing problem, it is not a basis for practical policy.

In general, cost-orientated approaches have the advantage of being relatively easy to calculate. Their main disadvantage is that they provide no incentive where there is no profit element, and any transfer price above marginal cost may lead to dysfunctional decisions where there is no external market. How dysfunctional these consequences might be is a matter of judgement by the companies concerned. For instance, in this example a transfer price of full budgeted cost plus 20 per cent, or £9.60, might be judged sufficient to allow division S to make a profit and encourage it to increase its profit by reducing its operating costs below the budget. If the 'cost' of this transfer price is the loss of the occasional order, then the incentives from setting such a price may well be seen as more important.

Market-based methods

Where there is an external market for component X, the market price may usefully serve as a basis for computing the transfer price. In the simplest case, there is perfect competition in the intermediate market for component X. Division S could then sell component Xs for £10 each instead of transferring them to division B. If division B were then unable to make a profit on its own product with X costed at £10, then it would be to the benefit of the company as a whole to close division B and sell component Y externally. In effect, the price is being used as an opportunity cost of producing component Y.

The external price may also be viewed as a fair price, in that B should at least compensate S for the loss of revenue. The export order ought to be rejected in such circumstances, as it is clearly more profitable to produce for the existing market.

Where there is imperfect competition, the problem is more complex. Division S would be unable to sell more than 75 units without lowering the price, and a transfer price of £10 would therefore be unrealistic. As we have seen in section 8.3.1, the decision as to whether to sell more than 75 units depends upon the elasticity of demand. For the 25 units that are transferred, the percentage increase in cost is $125/375 = 33\frac{1}{3}$ per cent; as variable costs are deemed constant, this is also the increase in quantity. The percentage fall in price must at least result in a total revenue that compensates for the increase in costs as well as maintaining existing revenue. The total revenue must therefore be at least $750 + 125 = £875$, or a price of £8.75 – a decrease in price of 12.5 per cent. The elasticity must therefore be at least $33\frac{1}{3}$ per cent/12.5 per cent $= 2\frac{2}{3}$ over the 25 units, for the manager to prefer lowering his price and increasing output sufficient to meet the needs of division B.

If the manager judges that division S could sell 100 units for £9, what should be the transfer price? One solution would be to sell 100 units for £9 and use that as the transfer price. Division S would then be indifferent between selling to B or selling externally. But this is not necessarily the best solution. An alternative would be, for instance, for division S to sell 75 units at £10 on the open market and offer division B 25 units of X at £9. The position of division B would not have changed, though division S would have increased its revenue by £25.

In practice, the problem is more complex than basic micro-economic analysis would suggest, for usually there is uncertainty over the price/demand relationship. A practical response in such circumstances would be to leave both parties free to negotiate, allowing B to purchase on the external market if necessary. Both managers would then have to make subjective judgements concerning their demand and supply curve. The need to allow B to purchase externally ensures that the market price acts as a real alternative or opportunity cost. Negotiation without this option is likely to lead to a solution that measures the respective manager's bargaining power rather than respective economic advantage.

The export order would again not be worthwhile. As with the case of perfect competition, any spare capacity can be more profitably employed selling to the home market, unless the market for X is very inelastic.

Finally, in this example we have not yet commented on the effect of selling costs where there is an external market. We might, for instance, include this element by regarding £1 of the £5 variable cost of X as being related to selling. Whether the intermediate market is perfect or imperfect, division S would save £1 per unit on all internal transfers. Should division S charge B with the market price, or the market price net of selling costs? In this example, the difference has no practical consequences, as B would accept in both circumstances. However, where the difference is critical to the pricing and output decision of division B, it should be noted that the lower price encourages B to exploit the final market further, to the benefit of company profits. In addition, as a practical matter, the net price would help to maintain the market share in the further processed product, as B's marginal costs would be lower, allowing for greater profitable output.

To conclude the rather lengthy discussion of this example, it is clear that further information is required, particularly as regards the intermediate market. Where this is an actively traded market, a market-based transfer price is preferable. This price serves as an opportunity cost for transfer, and for unexpected events such as the export order. Where there is no actively traded market, then the economic solution would be to transfer at marginal cost. The export order would then be correctly accepted. However, such a solution does not in any way motivate division S, and may well demotivate if it is regarded as being unfair. In practice, the consequences of a lack of motivation may well prove more costly than an 'economically correct' transfer price.

It is to a more general consideration of the selection problem that we now turn.

10.3   The transfer pricing decision

Ideally, a transfer price should be:

(a) simple to calculate;
(b) robust (not requiring frequent adjustment);
(c) fair (hence motivating to both parties);
(d) profit maximizing (for the company as a whole).

As we have seen in the previous section, attributes (c) and (d) are in conflict where there is no intermediate market. Where there is such a market, the price may not be simple to calculate, or indeed, robust. In other words it may vary greatly and the elasticity of demand be subject to great uncertainty. Clearly, no method meets all our requirements in all circumstances. At best we can hope for a reasonable 'fit' between the circumstances faced by the firm and the method chosen. Figure 10.1 gives an approximate picture of the problem as determined by normative analysis.

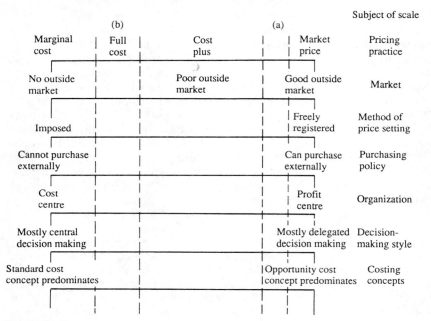

	(b)				(a)		Subject of scale
Marginal cost	Full cost		Cost plus			Market price	Pricing practice
No outside market			Poor outside market		Good outside market		Market
Imposed						Freely registered	Method of price setting
Cannot purchase externally						Can purchase externally	Purchasing policy
Cost centre						Profit centre	Organization
Mostly central decision making						Mostly delegated decision making	Decision-making style
Standard cost concept predominates						Opportunity cost concept predominates	Costing concepts

Figure 10.1

For any given situation, we imagine that the accountant is able to score the position as a point on the seven scales. We should stress that it is not a precise representation, as many of the attributes are in practice complex issues and difficult to measure. Nevertheless, if a reasonable 'fit' is to be achieved, the points on each of the scales should lie in a vertical band for each firm. For instance, where the points lie in band (a), there is a good outside market; the market price is used; as the parties can purchase externally, the rates can be freely negotiated; divisions can be profit centres; and decision making is largely left to the managers. In such circumstances, the opportunity cost concept predominates. However, there is a risk of inconsistency if one of the points should lie to the left of the band. For example, if there is a poor outside market, a realistic market price, as we have said, may be very difficult to determine. Similarly, if scores lie within band (b), it would be inconsistent to measure the divisions as profit centres (which is outside band (b)) unless the transfers were not significant in value. Thus using normative analysis, we can make general statements about appropriate transfer pricing policy in practice.

The choice of transfer price has also been extensively researched by means of questionnaires. Findings show that, apart from the linear programming and game theory approaches, all methods that we have discussed are actively used. In both the surveys of UK companies that we quote here, the most common practice is to use the market price.

Table 10.1

	Emmanuel (1976)	Whiting and Gee (1984)
No. of companies in survey	92	57
% where transfers between divisions were insignificant	0	34
No. of companies responding to detailed transfer pricing questions	92	38
	%	%
Market price	44	61
Negotiated	19	18
Cost related	37	16
Variety of methods	0	5
	100	100
The decision to trade externally		
has to be approved	69	44
never has to be approved	31	56
	100	100
autonomy in setting selling price		
Division alone	32	74
Reference to head office	39	17
Head office alone	29	9
	100	100

The least common is variable or marginal cost, 3 per cent in the Emmanuel survey and unreported per cent in the Whiting and Gee survey (but it will be less than the 16 per cent cost category and hence the smallest single category). Empirical attempts to discern clear reasons for the pricing policies adopted have, as Emmanuel and Otley (1985) reported, not been successful beyond rather obvious findings. We therefore have to rely on our normative interpretation to analyse the decision.

A final important practical element in the transfer pricing decision is the effect of taxation. Divisions situated in different countries, have to pay the corporation tax of the host, or foreign country. In that the transfer price, as we have seen in example 1, can critically affect the level of profits in divisions, so the liability for tax in the host country will be affected. In order to minimize tax liability, a multinational company will be tempted to set transfer prices such that little or no profit is reported in countries with relatively high rates, leaving higher profits to be reported in countries with similar or lower rates than the home country. There are double taxation agreements with most countries; in such cases, companies are given credit for taxation paid by its divisions in foreign countries up to the level of the home taxation rate. Therefore, where the foreign rate is below the home rate, the company will only be expected to pay the difference between the two rates, making the total tax similar to the home rate. Alternatively, where the foreign tax is above the home rate, the company will be fully exempt from the home rate, but no more. In practice the problem is rather more complex, for countries do not define income uniformly, nor do they have the same rules for deduction. We should also note that there are no such offsetting arrangements for other taxes, such as import duties and value added taxes.

These taxes, along with corporation tax, can play an important part in setting the transfer price. Taxation authorities are fully aware of these pressures, and taxation rules will specify acceptable bases for setting transfer prices. In general, the requirement is that transfers be treated as being 'at arm's length', i.e. as if the division were a third party. The favoured method is to use the market price, and the least favoured is cost plus.

It is difficult to determine in practice how important an influence taxes are on international transfer pricing. Certainly, companies list compliance with tax regulations very highly (Wu and Sharp, 1979), but the setting of the transfer price and disputes with foreign revenue authorities are not reported publicly for obvious reasons. However, there is limited evidence that transfer prices may be significantly affected by tax considerations (Rahman and Scapens (1986)). In this study of foreign multinationals in Bangladesh, it was clear that the profitability of multinational divisions was considerably below that of domestic equivalent companies. Obviously, such countries are in a weak position, for the benefits of employment and foreign earnings from exports outweigh the benefit of revenue from taxation.

10.4   Conclusion

Industrialization has seen a seemingly irreversible trend towards larger and larger companies. The exchange of goods and services between divisions within these companies has led to a corresponding increase in the importance of the transfer price. In this chapter we have outlined the fundamental aspects of the problem. The actual decision, as we have indicated throughout the chapter, will depend upon a number of detailed judgements concerning the state of the market, the motivational consequencies, international tax and trading regulations, as well as the company's style of management.

References and further reading

Biggs, C., Benjamin, D., *Management Accounting Techniques*, Heinemann, 1989.
Emmanuel, C., Otley, D., *Accounting for Management Control*, VNR, 1985.
Rahman, M. Z., Scapens, R. W., 'Transfer Pricing by Multinationals – Some Evidence from Bangladesh', *Journal of Business Finance and Accounting*, 1986, pp. 383–92.
Shubik, M., 'Incentives, Decentralized Control, The Assignment of Joint Costs and Internal Pricing', *Management Science*, 1962.
Tomkins, C., *Financing Planning in Divisionalised Companies*, Haymarket, 1973.
Whiting, E. A., Gee, K. P., *Decentralisation, Divisional Interdependence and the*

Treatment of Central Costs as Charges or Allocation Financial Control Research Institute monograph, 1984.

Wu, F. H., Sharp, D., 'An empirical study of transfer pricing practice, *International Journal of Accounting,* Spring, 1979, pp. 71–85.

11 Pricing policy

11.1 Policy determinants

11.1.1 Introduction

We conclude this section by examining pricing in its broader business environment. More has been written about price than any other variable in the marketing mix. Although the emergence of marketing as a separate discipline is a twentieth-century development, pricing has been a prominent feature in the literature from the very beginning. Economists have taken a formal academic interest in the subject for around 200 years, and accountants have been concerned with the practical impact for more than ten times that period.

The overriding aim of *business* organizations is profitability, and more particularly profit maximization. This is not to say that other objectives might not also be actively pursued in support of this, as we saw in chapter 1, but profitability must be the principal focus.

Businesses make profits by selling goods and services at a price higher than their cost. In most markets, the amount that they are able to sell will be largely determined by the price charged for the goods and services. There is a direct and tangible link between prices and profits, and the importance of the pricing decision lies in its pivotal contribution to the fundamental policy of profit maximization.

11.1.2 Markets

Markets can be classified according to the number of suppliers present, and according to the homogeneous or differentiated nature of the product sold. The ability of any individual supplier to determine the selling price will be a function of the particular market. The main categories can be described as follows:

1   *Many suppliers*
    (a)   Homogeneous product   PERFECT COMPETITION
    (b)   Differentiated product   MONOPOLISTIC COMPETITION
2   *Few suppliers*
    (a)   Sole supplier   MONOPOLY
    (b)   Few suppliers   OLIGOPOLY

The different nature of these individual market categories, and the relative manoeuvrability of suppliers in respect of selling prices in each of them are set out below. In each case, it should be borne in mind that economic theory states that profits will be maximized at the point at which marginal cost = marginal revenue (see section 11.4.3). However, the *size* of the profit will depend on the relation of price and average cost at this particular point, and therein lies the significance of the different market categories. Note that average cost includes a return to the suppliers of capital.

Perfect competition. Where there are a large number of suppliers of a homogeneous product, no single supplier can influence the market price, and thus there is no pricing decision to be made. Since *all* the supplier's output could be sold at the ruling market price, the only effect of a decrease in price would be a reduced profit. Similarly, any increase in selling price by any one supplier would result in no sales at all accruing to that supplier, as buyers could purchase the same product at a lower market price from any number of other suppliers (remember that we are dealing with a purely homogeneous product and *not* one differentiated by marketing strategies). Suppliers *must* accept the market price, which by definition is their marginal revenue. Profits will be maximized by producing and selling up to the point where the marginal costs of production and sales equal the marginal revenue, i.e. the market price. 'Maximized' in the context of perfect competition in equilibrium, however, means that profit will merely be sufficient to provide an acceptable return to the suppliers of capital, as Figures 11.1 and 11.2 show. Conditions of perfect competition are rarely met with in practice.

Monopolistic competition. This, and the remaining two categories, could be described as markets in which the individual supplier *is* faced with a pricing decision. In monopolistic competition, there are a large number of suppliers producing similar but not identical goods and services. Although product differentiation by such means as brand imaging will give an individual supplier a measure of monopolistic power, the fact that the products are similar in nature – and thus close substitutes – implies that the demand for them will be elastic. Despite the 'monopoly' that each supplier enjoys over his product, he will be faced with a downward-sloping demand curve, where changing prices will have a significant effect on the quantity sold. In view of the number of suppliers, there is an underlying assumption of *free entry* into such markets, such that long-run super-profits are impossible, because of the ability of other suppliers to set up and produce a different brand of the same product under identical cost conditions. This assumption also has the corollary that market forces will limit the manoeuvrability of any individual supplier to set prices which differ markedly from those ruling in the market. In the case of monopolistic competition, as with perfect competition, the application of the marginal cost = marginal revenue rule will lead to a price

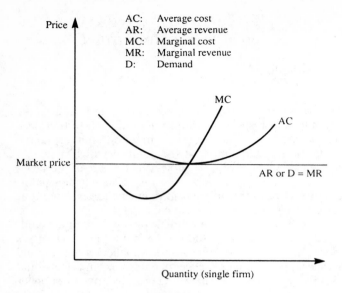

Figure 11.1 *Perfect Competition*

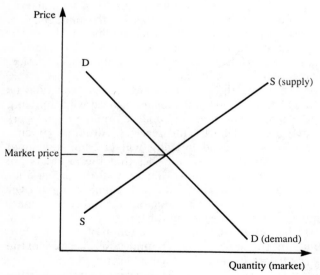

Figure 11.2 *Perfect Competition*

which corresponds to long-run average cost, and hence the absence of monopoly profits, as Figure 11.3 demonstrates.

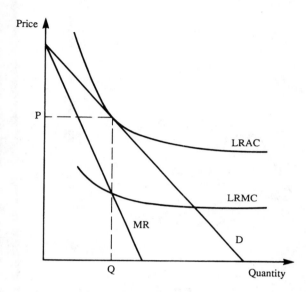

LRAC: Long-run average cost (which includes 'normal' profit)
LRMC: Long-run marginal cost

Figure 11.3 *Monopolistic competition*

Monopoly. If a product has no substitute, and there is only one supplier of it in the market, then a monopoly exists in that product, and super-profits can be earned. For the monopoly to be sustained, however, there must obviously be barriers to the entry of any new suppliers into the market. Such a barrier would occur where the original supplier corners or controls the available market in some essential input to the product; or it could take the form of a patent, which would give prolonged legal protection against potential competition, or some technical superiority that ensures a consistently and significantly lower production cost throughout the volume range, such that other interested suppliers are effectively precluded from entering the market. In a monopoly the demand curve for the supplier's output will be the market demand curve for the product. Faced with a relatively stable and predictable downward-sloping demand curve, the monopolist is in a perfect position to determine and set a price for his product that will maximize his profits. However, public opinion and the existence of bodies such as the Monopolies Commission will usually conspire to prevent the monopolist from actually being a profit maximizer in practice, and invariably he will be forced to settle for the more modest objective of achieving a 'satisfactory' return on his investment. This return should, nevertheless, be higher than the rate of return which a supplier in perfect competition or monopolistic competition is capable of earning, because of the potential for super-profits which is inherent in the marginal cost = marginal revenue equilibrium of monopoly, i.e. in a monopoly in equilibrium, marginal cost is *less* than average cost, as Figure 11.4 shows.

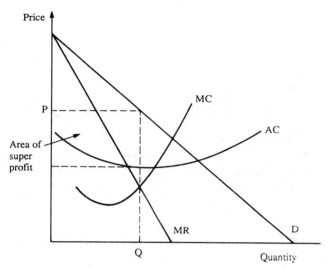

Figure 11.4   *Monopoly*

As with perfect competition, a true monopoly will rarely occur in the real world, and actual market structures vary in practice between these two extremes of perfect competition and monopoly.

Oligopoly. In an oligopoly, the market is dominated by a few major suppliers. Regardless of whether the product is homogeneous or differentiated, each individual supplier knows that an attempt by him to manipulate any market variable under his control will probably result in retaliation by his competitors, with potentially damaging consequences for all who operate in the market. A good example of this category of market would be fuel retailing: the UK has seen more than one instance of a price cut by one oil major being followed by a debilitating price war in which all the major suppliers have suffered considerable losses. Awareness of the mutual interdependence of variables, combined with enlightened self-interest and the relative ease of communication between a small number of major suppliers, will often lead to the establishment of a price cartel – in the presence of legal constraints, *de facto* rather than *de jure*. The oligopoly thus takes on the characteristics of a monopoly by virtue of the fact that the price can be kept artificially high by agreement among the dominant members, who will then effectively share out the resulting super-profits in proportion to their individual slices of the market.

11.1.3 *Profit maximization*

In each of the above market categories, there is an underlying assumption that suppliers are aware of their cost and revenue functions. Profit maximization occurs at the point at which marginal cost = marginal revenue, and the selling price which will optimize sales volume and thus maximize profits can be calculated by finding the value of the demand or total revenue curve at this optimal level. This is illustrated graphically in Figure 11.5.

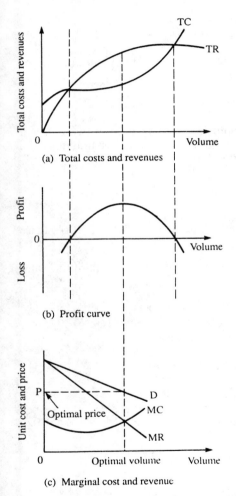

(a) Total costs and revenues

(b) Profit curve

(c) Marginal cost and revenue

Figure 11.5 *Profit maximization*

If, for the purpose of analysis, we accept the assumption of known cost and demand functions inherent in the microeconomic model, the optimal selling price can be determined mathematically with relative ease, as in Example 1.

Example 1

A supplier has calculated his demand and total cost functions as follows:

$$\text{Demand function } x = 50,000 - 20p$$
$$\text{Total cost function TC} = £100,000 + 40x$$

By solving the demand function in respect of p, we can find the price function p:

$$\text{Price function } 20p = 50,000 - x$$
$$p = 2,500 - 0.05x$$

We can now determine the total revenue function simply by multiplying the price function, p, by the sales volume, x.

$$\text{Total revenue function TR} = 2500x - 0.05x^2$$

From this stage, we can calculate the optimal sales volume in two different ways. We can either proceed via the derivation of marginal cost and marginal revenue (a), or develop and solve an equation for total profits (b):

(a)   Derive marginal cost from total costs $\left(\dfrac{\text{dTC}}{\text{dx}}\right)$ MC $= 40$

Derive marginal revenue from total revenue $\left(\dfrac{\text{dTR}}{\text{dx}}\right)$ MR $= 2,500 - 0.1x$

Setting marginal cost = marginal revenue, to determine optimum sales volume, we have:

$$40 = 2,500 - 0.1x$$
$$0.1x = 2,460$$
$$\text{optimal sales volume } x = 24,600$$

(b)   Total profits = total revenues − total costs:

$$\text{TP} = 2,500x - 0.05x^2 - £100,000 - 40x$$

Taking the first derivative of this equation, we have:

$$\frac{\text{dTP}}{\text{dx}} = 2,500 - 0.1x - 40$$

and setting this derivative to equal zero, we have:

$$0 = 2,500 - 0.1x - 40$$
$$\text{as above, } x = 24,600$$

We now substitute this optimal sales volume figure (however calculated) in the price function derived earlier, in order to calculate the selling price at this volume:

$$p = 2,500 - 0.05 \ (24,600)$$
optimum selling price $p = 1,270$

Note that when alternative (b) is employed, it will be necessary to go to the second derivation of the profit function in order to confirm that the slope is negative:

$$\frac{d^2 TP}{dx^2} = -0.1$$

If this second derivative had been *positive* rather than *negative*, we would have calculated the sales volume that maximized the *loss* for the supplier rather than the *profit*.

However theoretically attractive such a strict micro-economic approach to the pricing decision might be, the reader would doubtless wish to argue that the assumptions are so restrictive as to make it of very limited practical value as a prescriptive model (see Dorward [1987] for a full critique). As Nagle (1984) put it, '(Marketeers) are soon disillusioned if they look to economics for practical solutions to pricing problems' (p. S4).

In the real world, the variables which can influence both cost and demand are of such magnitude and quantity that the information required by the analysis is unlikely to be forthcoming at a reasonable price, if at all. Furthermore, as we saw in the section on monopoly, profit *maximization* will often not be achievable in practice even by those suppliers in the best position to realize it, and indeed it might not be the *only* objective pursued by the firm in any event, although as stated earlier, *profitability* – whether maximising or satisficing – must invariably remain the *principal* focus if other aims are to be met. In practice, in the absence of perfect information, the vast majority of suppliers, in any market category, will have no option but to set out to achieve a *target* profit rather than a *maximum* profit, and most pricing decisions will use formulae based on cost and desired profitability levels rather than the direct application of an economic model. However, familiarity with the academic theory behind the pricing decision, and the significance of the different types of market on the flexibility inherent in that choice, will enable the manager to gain a better appreciation of the forces at work, and thus improve the quality of the decision itself.

11.1.4 *Product life cycles*

Like human beings, products (and to a lesser extent services) have a recognizable life cycle, depicted in Figure 11.6. This biological analogy has considerable significance for the pricing decision, because different pricing strategies will be appropriate for different stages in the cycle, depending on levels of demand and market structures. It is worth examining each of the classic stages in some detail.

Introduction. When a product is first launched on the market, demand is likely

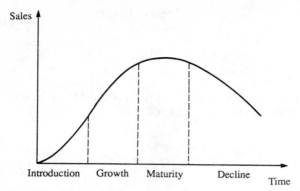

Figure 11.6   *Product life cycle*

to be small. Lack of familiarity with the new product and its sources of availability will militate against large initial sales, and it will usually be necessary to spend heavily on advertising to bring the product to the attention of potential customers. A combination of relatively high unit costs, relatively low sales volume, and the potential problem of rejection by the market conspire to make this the riskiest stage in the life cycle.

Growth. Assuming the product successfully negotiates the perils of the introduction stage it will enter the growth phase, where demand for the product increases steadily and average costs fall with the economies of scale that accompany the greater production volume. This stage should offer the greatest potential for profit to the producer, despite the fact that competitors will be prompted to enter the growing market (with or without slight product variants).

Maturity. By this stage the product has reached the mass market, and the increase in demand will begin to slow down. The sales curve will flatten out, and eventually start to decline. Profitability will generally be at a lower level than in the growth phase.

Decline. The fall in sales accelerates when the market reaches saturation point. Although it is still possible to make profits for a short period during this stage, it is only a matter of time before the rapidly dwindling sales volumes herald the onset of losses for *all* producers who remain in the market. The product has effectively reached the end of its life cycle, and more profitable investment opportunities must be sought elsewhere.

However, it must be pointed out that this is a very general model of sales behaviour over time. It is not possible to specify the length of any particular timespan within the cycle, or even the total length of the cycle itself, as these will obviously be a function of an individual product's characteristics. For example, at one extreme could be the market for souvenirs of a specific event, lasting a few months; at the other extreme, certain basic types of machinery could have a market lasting decades. The presumption is that the life cycle will follow the pattern of a bell-shaped curve, but as long as it begins with a sustained rise, levels out and then falls away, it can assume any shape. This last point is of considerable strategic significance, as the shape of the cycle will determine the requirement for new products and their development time. It is also important to distinguish between different *brands* of the same product type, different *types* of a particular product, and different *products*, as research has found evidence of life cycles at each of these disaggregated levels, with the possibility of different shaped curves and even diametrically opposed trends. Care must be taken with such definitions to ensure that like is compared with like, so that important, expensive, and often irreversible decisions are not taken on the basis of spurious and non-homogeneous data.

Oliver (1986) reproduces a table which summarizes the main characteristics associated with each phase of the cycle, and an adapted version is set out as Table 11.1.

In order to illustrate the strategic implications (other than for price, which will emerge *passim*) we may profitably expand this summary by adapting a second table from the same author. The statistics are based on an empirical research study of the emphasis of advertising at different stages in the life cycle on seven groups of objectives (Table 11.2).

It can be seen that the relative weighting of the objectives is consistent with the traditional theory of the product's life cycle. The provision of factual information on the product, the building of public awareness of it, and the use of trials were important during the first stage, when the product was introduced on the market. In the growth phase, when rival suppliers entered the market, the resulting increased competition created a need to differentiate the product in a qualitative sense and maintain a favourable public attitude towards it. This need is continued throughout the stage of maturity, when it was joined by a vigorous attempt to establish brand loyalty. The final phase of decline showed the different responses adopted by those suppliers still in the market – some left quickly, to look for alternative investment opportunities; others remained to take whatever profits were left in the face of rapidly dwindling demand. As might have been expected, branding and image was important throughout the cycle, but the statistics clearly show a differential emphasis consistent with the requirements of the different individual stages of the cycle. For a recent detailed review of this topic, the reader is referred to Kotler (1988).

Our own brief examination of the product life cycle has provided a further necessary economic and marketing basis to a consideration of pricing, but before we can finally turn specifically to this, we must draw attention to the significance of one additional related background factor: the choice of growth path adopted by the firm. This choice will determine the stage at which any individual product actually enters the life cycle. A completely innovative product will obviously appear at the lowest point on the curve; a competing product – a variation on an existing proven theme – will enter at a higher point on the curve. To a large extent, the choice will be determined for the firm by external factors: access to or lack of developmental expertise and technical know-how; the availability or shortage of skilled labour; the ability or inability to raise funds for equipment and working capital, and so on – these will alternatively facilitate or militate against the introduction of entirely new products. On the other hand, the attitudes of individual firms towards risk

Table 11.1   Implications and characteristics of product life cycles.

	Introduction	Growth	Maturity	Decline
General characteristics				
Sales volume	Low	Steady growth	Slow growth	Declining
Customers	Innovative	Mass market	Mass market	Laggards
Cash flows	Negative	Moderate	High	Low
Profitability	Negligible	Highest	High/ declining	declining
Strategic responses				
Focus	Market expansion	Market penetration	Defence of market share	Productivity
Marketing emphasis	Product awareness	Brand preference	Brand loyalty	Selective markets
Product development	Basic	Improved	Differentiated	Rationalized/ standardized
Price	High	Lower	Lowest	Rising

Original source: Doyle, P., 'The Realities of the Product Life Cycle', *Quarterly Review of Marketing*, Summer 1976.

Table 11.2   Advertising objectives through the life cycle.

Objectives	Introduction	Growth	Maturity	Decline
Brand and image building	1.0	0.54	0.77	0.5
Factual information	0.71	0.36	0.44	0.5
Public awareness	0.57	0.27	0.0	0.33
Trials	0.28	0.09	0.0	0.33
Differentiating/qualities info.	0.42	0.73	0.66	0.66
Maintaining favourable attitude	0.28	0.36	0.66	0.33
Brand loyalty	0.0	0.09	0.44	0.16

1 = high 0 = low
Original source: Corkindale, D. R., Kennedy, S. H., *Measuring the Effect of Advertising*, 1975.

will exercise an internal or philosophical influence: as mentioned earlier, the initial phase of the life cycle is the one which carries the greatest degree of risk, and many firms would positively prefer to forego the potentially higher returns offered by an innovative product with the whole cycle in front of it, in favour of the lower but more secure profits associated with entering an established market in the growth (or possibly, maturity) phase.

11.1.5   Summary

We are now in a position to summarize in general terms the policy determinants of the pricing decision:

(a) The demand for the product (also see section 10.3).
(b) The number of suppliers in the market.
(c) The nature of the product sold.
(d) The life expectancy of the product.
(e) The stage in the life cycle at which it enters the market.

It is evident from these five points that the pricing decision can only be taken against the much broader background of detailed marketing information and strategy, and the accountant can do no more than assist management in setting a price which reflects the company's objectives.

Earlier in the chapter, it was stated that most firms set out to achieve a *target* return, and their pricing decisions use formulae based on cost and desired profitability levels. We shall begin our review of the practical aspects of pricing with a consideration of those methods.

11.2   Cost-plus pricing

Simply put, this means adding a predetermined mark-up to the full cost of a product in order to arrive at a selling price. However, the full cost of a product will depend on the volume produced, and the volume produced will reflect the quantity that can be sold – and we know that this quantity is largely a function of the price charged for the product. It would thus appear that pricing on a cost-plus basis is an example of circular reasoning. This apparent illogicality is frequently pointed out in the academic literature, which emphasizes the importance of management judgement and market conditions in the selection of the mark-up to be added to cost, in order to give this approach the flexibility to respond to different demand circumstances.

Empirical evidence suggests that most cost-based pricing formulae use normal absorption costing principles, and thus 'cost' will be a full production cost containing fixed manufacturing overheads. It may also contain selling, distribution and administrative expenses, variable and fixed, in which case the mark-up required to give an acceptable income need not be as high as would otherwise be the case if these costs had to be recovered through the profit margin. Obviously, the long-term prosperity of any firm will depend upon its ability to generate sufficient revenue from sales to cover not only the cost of the products sold, however calculated, but also the total of all other costs, including an adequate return on the capital employed, however defined. These additional costs form the basis for the calculation of the mark-up on cost.

Although some businesses operate a standard mark-up – this is particularly true of contractors and companies in classic job-costing environments – most firms must vary the percentage to reflect different market conditions. In a multi-product firm, for example, it is highly unlikely that the mark-up will be the same for every type of product. Different products are faced with different markets and thus competitive circumstances; and individual products will require the measure of flexibility mentioned above if they are to respond effectively to the changing demand patterns of the various stages of their life cycles. Furthermore, it has also been pointed out that the adoption of 'normal' or 'customary' mark-ups within one industry or for particular product types is no guarantee of successful pricing in the long term, as local grocers found with the arrival of supermarkets, and retailers of electrical goods and furniture found with the advent of discount warehousing – classic examples of the triumph of simple volume over margins. Example 2 below shows the calculation of the base cost to be used in the formula, under different cost assumptions.

Example 2   Cost-plus pricing

Pricer Ltd is to begin the manufacture of a new product, X, and must calculate a base cost, to which will be added a mark-up in order to arrive at a selling price. The following direct costs have been established, although they will probably be subject to an error margin of ± 10 per cent under full production conditions:

	£
Direct material	4
Direct labour ($\frac{1}{4}$ hr @ £8/hr)	2
Variable manufacturing overheads	
($\frac{1}{4}$ hr of machine time @ £4/hr)	1
	7

It is estimated that 10,000 units of X could be produced within the existing manufacturing capacity, but the spare 2,500 machine hours currently available (of a total of 25,000 available hours) could alternatively be used to increase the production of Y, which shows a contribution of £30 per machine hour. However, additional advertising expenditure of £11,000 would be required to stimulate the additional demand for Y. Current fixed costs are £120,000 for the production facilities, £80,000 for selling and distribution and £60,000 for administration. These are likely to increase to £100,000 for selling and distribution, and £70,000 for administration, again with an error margin of ± 10 per cent for any increase. Pricer has spent £150,000 on developing X, and working capital of £70,000 will be required to support its successful manufacture. The company's cost of capital is 10 per cent.

Variation 1, using conventional absorption costing principles, building in the conservative error margin but ignoring opportunity considerations

	£
Direct costs (as above)	7.0
add allowance for underestimate 10%	0.7
	7.7
add Fixed manufacturing cost	
($\frac{1}{4}$ hr of machine time @ £4.8/hr £120,000/25,000 hrs)	1.2
Base cost	£8.9

Variation 2, as 1 but including selling, distribution and administrative costs

		£
	Base cost as under 1 above	8.9
add	Fixed selling and distribution costs (based on increase in costs– £20,000/10,000 units)	2.0
add	allowance for underestimate 10%	0.2
add	Fixed administration costs (based on increase in costs– £10,000/10,000 units)	1.0
add	allowance for underestimate 10%	0.1
	Base cost	12.2

Variation 3, as 1 but including opportunity considerations

	Base cost as under 1 above	8.9
add	Opportunity cost of machine time ($\frac{1}{4}$ hr @ £25.6/hr*)	6.4
add	Opportunity cost of working capital (£70,000 @ 10% = £7,000/10,000 units)	0.7
	Base cost	16.0

*Contribution from Y for 2,500 hours less additional advertising costs – 2,500 × £30 = £75,000 − £11,000 = £64,000/2,500 hrs = £25.6/hr.

Variation 4, as 2 but including opportunity considerations

		£
	Base cost as under 2	12.2
add	Opportunity costs as above	7.1
	Base cost	19.3

In our example, absorption of overheads was based on machine hours, which happened to be the same as labour hours. If these two were not the same, and absorption was based on *labour* hours rather than *machine* hours, different base costs would obviously have resulted. Depending on our analysis and costing assumptions, we can see a base cost varying from £8.9 to £19.3 (this range reflects a conservative view of the margin of error – a more liberal view would show a range of £7.5 to £17.3). As the base cost increases from variant 1 to 4, it covers an increasing proportion of the total costs. The percentage mark-up on base cost built in to the selling price formula by producers is likely to be decreased between 1 and 4 to reflect this.

The formula can easily be adapted to reflect a target rate of return, but, again, different assumptions will give rise to different mark-ups. For example, in calculating the return to be spread over the marginal units of production, the amount of the existing capital employed (a figure we do not have in our example) could be included, or we could merely use the increase in working capital due to the production of X – £70,000 – as our base; similarly, we might choose to ignore the £150,000 development costs of X, on the grounds that it is a sunk cost, or include it as an investment that must earn a return. The effect on selling price of these different interpretations will be readily appreciated by the reader, without recourse to further examples.

Several advantages have been claimed for the cost-plus/target return approach to pricing:

1   If cost structures are known, cost-plus is a simple exercise, which is quick to apply, and therefore cheap. It is an exercise which, by virtue of its routine nature, can easily be delegated, thereby saving management time: it thus has administrative benefits. Furthermore, where it is necessary to set a large number of prices for different products quickly, cost-plus is often the only practical solution to the pricing problem.

2   Any selling price in excess of full cost (if it includes selling, distribution, administration and capital costs) will ensure that a profit is made when budgeted volumes are achieved.

3   Where there is no foreknowledge of demand patterns for a range of products in a multi-product environment, the use of a standard mark-up on full cost can increase the probability of a profit being earned in the initial stages.

4   The use of cost-plus will avoid the danger of low short-run prices becoming the norm. The marginalist approach, while sensibly recognizing the opportunity cost of rejecting any order at a price in excess of marginal cost when there is no alternative use of spare resources, nevertheless can give rise to an expectation on the part of new customers that the same low price might continue in the future, when capacity could be more constrained. It can also cause dissatisfaction among existing high-price customers, and create an unwelcome pressure for a reduction in mainstream selling prices.

5   Cost-plus pricing is particularly useful in contracting industries, where large individual contracts can consume the bulk of the annual fixed costs.

6   It can be used to justify selling prices to potential customers and, indeed, increases in selling prices to existing customers, if costs are seen to increase.

7   If similar technologies and techniques are employed within an industry, such that there is likely to be broad comparability of cost structures between different firms operating in the industry, then widespread use of cost-plus methods can lead to a high degree of price stability.

The following problems are associated with the cost-plus/target return approach to pricing:

1   Insufficient consideration is given to the phenomenon of the life cycle. There is a danger that prices will be set too rigidly, effectively placing marketing managers in a commercial straitjacket that renders them impotent to respond to competition, and to adjust prices adequately to difficult and changing market and demand conditions. Customers may be lost and opportunities for increasing profits forgone. A very simple example, using the contribution (or marginalist) approach, will illustrate this point.

Example 3
The variable cost of a product, X, is £6. Fixed manufacturing costs of £400,000 are spread over an estimated production and sales volume of 100,000 units, to give a 'full' absorption cost of £10 per unit. The cost-plus approach used by the manufacturer of X, based on a standard mark-up of 60 per cent on the products 'full' cost, dictates a selling price of £16. Assuming all costs were as anticipated, and the company managed to sell 100,000 units at the fixed price of £16, a gross profit of £600,000 would be earned. Suppose, however, that a market survey had indicated the following price elasticity of demand for the product:

Price (£)	Demand
14	130,000
15	125,000
16	100,000
17	95,000
18	80,000

A more correct analysis of the pricing problem, *ceteris paribus*, would have been to concentrate on maximizing total contribution, and therefore total profitability, thus:

Selling price £	Variable cost £	Contribution £	Demand	Total contribution £	Fixed mfg. costs £	Total net contribution £
14	6	8	130,000	1,040,000	400,000	640,000
15	6	9	125,000	1,125,000	400,000	725,000
16	6	10	100,000	1,000,000	400,000	600,000
17	6	11	95,000	1,045,000	400,000	645,000
18	6	12	80,000	960,000	400,000	560,000

Clearly, the figures indicate that there is an opportunity cost associated with the decision to use a cost-plus price of £16; failure to take full account of market conditions when setting the selling price has cost the company at least £45,000 in additional profits (the difference between total contribution at £17 and that at £16), and possibly as much as £125,000 (the difference between total net contribution at £15 and that at £16), depending on the levels of fixed costs as production varies between 95,000 and 125,000 units.

2   Cost-plus fails to distinguish between those costs which are affected by a particular pricing/output decision, and thus are *relevant* to it, and those which are unaffected by the decision and therefore *irrelevant*. The classic example of this particular criticism was mentioned in the diametrically opposed context in 4 (p. 292). It occurs when a company with spare production capacity, and no other obvious competing uses for it, suddenly finds itself faced with an opportunity to fill some or all of the available production volume at a selling price which would, under normal operating circumstances, be considered unacceptably low. Strict adherence to any full absorption cost-based pricing model in these short-run situations, whatever flexibility is exercised in the amount of the mark-up on this cost, could lead to the outright rejection of orders which would in fact

have shown a profit. Full cost, under any definition, includes in its cost base a figure for *fixed* costs that are irrelevant in such situations which preclude their increase. Critics would quickly point out that *any* price which shows a positive contribution, i.e. any selling price higher than marginal cost, would increase profitability, assuming any *genuine* increases in fixed manufacturing costs or overheads are covered by the total contribution from the marginal business.

Example 4

A company with a production capacity of 60,000 units of X currently produces and sells 45,000. The unit variable cost is £8, and total fixed manufacturing costs are £180,000. The company sets its selling price by adding a standard mark-up of 25 per cent to the full unit cost, although this mark-up can be flexible in cases of marginal business.

The normal selling price can be calculated as follows:

	£		
Variable cost	8		
Fixed cost	4	£180,000	
	12	45,000	units of normal volume
Mark-up 25%	3		
	15		

The company receives an order for an additional 15,000 units, which could be produced within the existing capacity and without increasing existing fixed manufacturing costs. However, in view of the huge size of the order, the customer is unwilling to pay more than £11 a unit. The company rejects the order, arguing that it would be making no mark-up at all on the deal, and indeed only just covering its own costs if they are reanalysed to reflect the spreading of fixed manufacturing overhead over the increased volume, viz:

	£		
Variable cost	8		
Fixed cost	3	£180,000	
	11	60,000	revised volume
Selling price	11		
Gross profit	–		

Needless to say, this is a false analysis of the situation. The only relevant costs to be considered by management should be those that will be increased or decreased by the order, that is the *variable* costs:

	£
Variable cost	8
Selling price	11
Contribution	3

We can see that a contribution of £3 per unit would be made by accepting the order; more pertinently, there is an opportunity cost of £45,000 associated with its rejection.

3 The comparative disregard for life-cycle considerations noted under 1 above can give rise to a further problem. During the growth phase of the product's cycle, demand is relatively inelastic and most companies enjoy increasingly healthy margins as prices remain high and average costs fall with the economies of scale related to the greater production volume. However, under such buoyant and profitable trading conditions, there is always a danger with cost-plus pricing that insufficient attention will be paid to controlling the levels of costs, and the resulting complacency can lead to an uncompetitive manufacturing position when the product enters the maturity phase and prices eventually begin to fall.

4 Cost-plus pricing must ultimately be designed to produce a target return on capital employed. Critics often point out that a major element in capital employed is trade debtors, which cannot be known until selling prices are known; this brings us back to the circular reasoning mentioned at the beginning of this section.

5 Whenever a full absorption costing system is used, there are problems associated with the selection of a suitable 'absorption basis' on which to charge fixed manufacturing costs to products. Notwithstanding the academic argument that absorption can never be anything other than the arbitrary division of indivisible fixed costs, this point has particular relevance for a multi-product company that uses a cost-plus pricing system. As the reader will readily appreciate, selling prices under such a system could show tremendous variation, depending on the particular apportionment basis chosen to determine full cost price. This could easily lead to the overpricing of some products and underpricing of others, unless considerable flexibility is exercised in the amount of the mark-up on each, to properly reflect the different market conditions faced by each.

6 The choice of the *volume* or *capacity* base is critical in full costing. Wide fluctuations in product cost, and therefore selling price, can be seen to result from different concepts of volume as the definition moves from maximum capacity at one end of the range of acceptable interpretations to normal (or, if lower, to expected) capacity at the other.

7 A false sense of security can be engendered by cost-plus pricing, when prices are set on the basis of estimated full cost at normal volume and actual volume turns out to be considerably lower than this. Profits can unknowingly be more than offset by underabsorbed overheads. Figure 11.7 shows this situation, in which actual average cost is greater than selling price, and a loss results.

Ironically, unless the demand for the product is highly inelastic, any attempt to rectify matters by pricing products on the basis of estimated actual average costs at estimated actual volume is likely to be self-defeating, as the resulting higher price might affect demand adversely and reduce volume still further, simply exacerbating the existing problem.

8 When the costs of new products are being estimated, the use of cost-plus will worsen any errors in the estimating process, possibly to the detriment of the company's profitability and competitiveness.

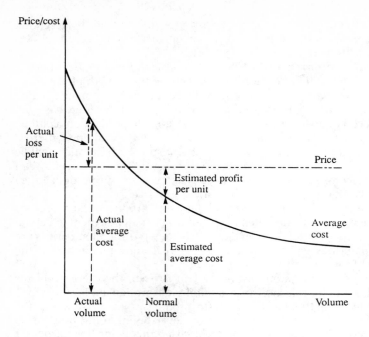

Figure 11.7   *Volume and cost-based policy*

A discrete delineation of the merits and demerits of a particular system, such as we have set out above for cost-plus pricing, should not lead the reader to the erroneous conclusion that those who operate the system live in a world of absolutes. Commercial reality will almost always exercise a beneficial effect on the cost-plus price setter (although in some cases it might impinge at too late a stage in the process), so that he is unlikely to lose sight of the fact that selling prices derived from cost-plus are *target* prices. Depending on the category of market in which the company operates, and the particular stage in the life cycle of an individual product, actual prices achieved for goods and services could be either higher or lower than those dictated by a simple formula. It has often been pointed out that managers are paid to *manage*, i.e. exercise their management judgement and discretion, and not simply to follow pre-set equations slavishly. If the target looks too low in comparison to what the market or individual will bear, then it can be increased, thereby increasing profitability. Similarly, these 'abnormal' gains will be more or less offset by the reduced margins which must be accepted on those lines which come up against competing and substitute products that are selling at lower prices than the company's pre-set 'target' price. In other words, in the real world, it would be naive to assume that the target prices set by a predetermined mark-up on full product cost would remain inviolate. They may reasonably be expected to fluctuate around the 'target', some higher and some lower, averaging out in such a way, it is to be hoped, that the *overall* target return required by the company is ultimately achieved.

11.3   Marginal cost-plus pricing

An obvious alternative to full cost-plus pricing and one that featured in the discussion of the pros and cons of the latter, is marginal cost-plus. A number of its virtues (and one of its vices) have already been mentioned in that discussion and thus require no further amplification. However, in view of the apparent superiority of the marginalist approach in the literature, and the (often uncritical) support it commands, it behoves us to preface our own positive remarks about its usefulness in certain aspects of the pricing decision with a healthily cynical *caveat*:

> Direct costing (marginal costing) emerged during the 1930s. It is ironic that it is more popular now, in a period of prosperity, capacity utilization, and expansion even outwardly ill-suited to many of its underlying assumptions. Depression period ad hoc business thinking logically was influenced by the existence of idle capacity of plant, equipment and labor. At least 15 per cent of the work force was usually unemployed: furthermore, labor unions had not yet reached their present strength, and employers had greater flexibility in hiring, lay offs, setting standards, cost control, etc. Fewer capital assets were committed to each worker and, from the point of view of the individual enterprise, insolvencies and quick changes in ownership of capital assets at distress prices had decreased dollar costs of investment per worker below the years immediately preceding. Brand identifications, markets and selling prices were less differentiated, on the whole and in many more markets than today intense price competition prevailed. Compare our current economic situation: little idle capacity in manpower or machines, a high and increasing ratio of machinery to labor cost, powerful trade unions, more restrictive labor laws and relatively inflexible labor costs, and rising costs of fixed asset replacement and management and administrative personnel.
>
> The special characteristics of the depression economy made it possible for management to emphasize variable costs and frequently neglect fixed cost in pricing decisions without apparent adverse consequences. In an economy of idle capacity, incremental costs tend to be small, and certain costs may not increase at all until capacity is absorbed. Graphically, the fixed cost plateaus were much longer relative to the existing operating levels of many businesses. However, as plant and equipment were replaced and as capacity was fully utilized on regular product lines, costs that appeared to be constant eventually became variable. Continuing an ostensibly 'logical' short-run policy into the long run would have been highly destructive.
>
> The peculiar problems of the depression gave direct costing a pragmatic justification that obscured its theoretical fallacies. The continuation – and even expansion – of the concept to a changed economic and technical

environment is an excellent example of a cultural lag (Herson and Hertz (1981), p. 231).

On the plus side, in addition to the situations mentioned earlier, the marginalist's emphasis on contribution and relevant costs can prove particularly useful in constructing *ab initio* a *demand*-based approach to pricing, and in recognizing the existence and importance to profits (and hence pricing structure) of scarce or limiting resources. An excellent illustration of the first of these is set out by Sizer (1980). He puts forward a method which combines CVP analysis and demand estimates to arrive at an approximate selling price. In the absence of precise data, best estimates of market demand at various prices in excess of variable cost are used to construct a series of profit lines on a PV chart. These lines are then joined to give a 'contribution curve', the highest point of which will indicate the selling price that makes the largest contribution to profits.

Example 5
The variable cost of product X is £10 per unit, and the manufacturer estimates demand for X as follows:

Selling price (£)	Demand (units)
15	12,000
16	11,000
17	10,000
18	8,500
19	7,000

Within the volume range of 7,000 to 12,000 units, fixed costs are expected to remain unchanged at £40,000.

From these data, a table can be prepared to enable the relevant points on the PV chart to be plotted and the contribution curve to be drawn:

	Selling price £	Variable cost £	Contribution £	Demand	Total contribution £	Fixed costs £	Net profit £
A	15	10	5	12,000	60,000	40,000	20,000
B	16	10	6	11,000	66,000	40,000	26,000
C	17	10	7	10,000	70,000	40,000	30,000
D	18	10	8	8,500	68,000	40,000	28,000
E	19	10	9	7,000	63,000	40,000	23,000

The contribution curve (Figure 11.8) would appear to confirm the figures in the table; a price of £17 maximizes profit. It would be better to extend the table and chart with some basic sensitivity analysis: by expanding the data to include estimated demand at intermediate points between £16 and £17 and £18, we can determine whether point C really *is* optimal, or whether this point lies some slight distance – and selling price – to the right or left.

Sizer acknowledges the problems associated with single-figure estimates,

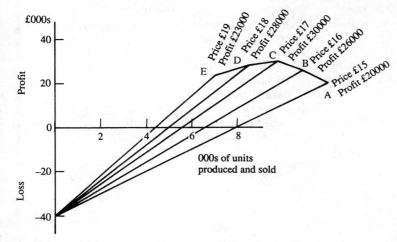

Figure 11.8   *PV Chart for X in the price range £15–£19*

and suggests the inclusion in the model, where possible, of the likely *range* of demand at each selling price. A similar chart can be constructed, joining all the lower and upper range points across the various profit lines; a visual inspection of the different contribution curves indicated by these limits should refine the analysis. A further refinement can be introduced by providing a probability distribution of sales demand for the various price levels, and calculating an expected value for profit at each of these to support the earlier contribution curve approach.

Obviously, it is axiomatic in all quantitative disciplines that the quality of the output from a process can be no better than that of the input, and in view of the approximate nature of demand estimates, however statistically refined, the selling prices indicated by such analyses can themselves only be regarded as approximations. However, notwithstanding the overriding importance of market circumstances, which will subordinate all other considerations, Sizer's model provides a useful starting point in the search for profit maximization.

The second situation in which the marginal costing approach to pricing can be particularly appropriate is where alternative products are competing for a scarce or limited resource. Here, profits will only be maximized where the total contribution from the limiting factor is maximized. The calculation follows easily from a computation of the contribution that each alternative product makes from each unit of the scarce resource. Where there is more than one limiting factor, the calculation is more complicated and calls for the use of linear programming or graphical analysis, but the principle remains simple – to maximize the contribution from the scarce resources. Obviously, contribution is a function of selling price and variable cost, and it is the former that we are interested in determining, in such a way that it satisfies the principle outlined above. Example 6 will illustrate how marginal costing can help in this situation.

Example 6

A company has been producing X successfully for a number of years, and demand appears to be relatively inelastic into the foreseeable future at a market price of £12 per unit. A market has just developed in product Y, which the company could produce without additional investment in plant, and without increasing or retraining the existing labour force. Unfortunately, however, Y uses the same basic direct material as product X – that is, units of Z – which is in short supply because of its particular nature. The company must determine a minimum selling price for product Y, below which it would not be worthwhile to divert resources from product X. Relevant data follow:

	X £		Y £
Direct material:			
4 units of Z @ £0.50	2.00	3 units of Z @ £0.50	1.50
Direct labour:			
1 hour @ £4.00	4.00	1 hour @ £4.00	4.00
Variable overhead	1.00		1.00
	7.00		6.50
Selling price	12.00		
Contribution	5.00		

X produces a contribution of £5 using 4 units of Z, i.e. a contribution per unit of Z – the limiting factor – of £1.25. Y uses 3 units of Z, so must therefore seek a minimum price of £6.50 + £3.75 (3 units of Z × contribution per unit of £1.25) = £10.25 if it is not to incur the opportunity cost of a net reduction in total contribution.

Obviously, if the company can obtain a selling price in excess of £10.25, profitability will be increased, but if the market will not even bear the 'minimum' price of £10.25, then the company is better off concentrating its resources in the production of X.

It might reasonably be argued that a single factor approach is simplistic, and overlooks the capacity constraints that could easily occur in other variable cost components if the production plan indicated by the model is implemented. For example, let us assume that only 30,000 units of raw material Z are available. Either 7,500 X could be produced and sold, which at a contribution of £5 per unit of X would generate a total contribution of £37,500; or 10,000 Y could be produced, which if sold at the minimum acceptable price of £10.25 would give a unit contribution of £37,500 – as we would have expected from our earlier computation.

Let us ignore any consideration of market saturation in the case of Y (i.e. would the market absorb the whole of our 10,000 units at a minimum price of £10.25?), which in the real world of course we could *not* afford to do, and concentrate simply on the fact that the production of 10,000 units of Y will require a labour input *one third* higher than that required to produce 7,500 X. Where are these extra hours to come from? Would they need overtime working, in which case should the variable cost of labour in our calculation not be higher than £4 per hour for Y? If the additional units can be manufactured without an increase in the total cost of labour – through gains in productivity, for example, or simply by the labour force working unpaid overtime – should our figure not be lower than £4 per hour? In such a situation, could we not legitimately regard labour as a fixed cost, and therefore exclude it from the calculation altogether? Is it not likely that any unrewarded productivity gains or unpaid overtime would give rise to problems in our labour relations? How can we quantify the effect of this in our calculation? From a strategic point of view, would we actually wish to withdraw completely from the production of the well-established X in order to manufacture a new – and therefore perhaps riskier – product Y? Would it not be more sensible to produce a mixture of X and Y, so that we retain a strong presence in our traditional, tried-and-tested market, while at the same time gaining a foothold in, and valuable experience of, the market in a new product that perhaps has considerable lucrative growth potential? If we were able to get more than £10.25 for Y, how would that affect our decision?

These are not perverse questions, raised in order to discredit the approach illustrated in example 6 – that approach is, and will remain, particularly appropriate where alternative products are competing for scarce or limited resources. Their purpose is rather to reinforce the remarks made at several points in this chapter, namely that no one technique presents a panacea to management in its search for the profit maximizing or satisficing selling price. By itself, each method can only represent a *starting* point, and certain methods will be more appropriate than others in particular sets of circumstances – like marginal costing in the last example, when it was important to emphasize the opportunity costs associated with the alternative use of scarce input factors. But they cannot be seen as providing simple black and white solutions; often they will raise as many questions as they answer.

Market considerations will override *all* others in the pricing of individual products, and the firm that believes otherwise is pursuing a chimaera that will ultimately lead to self-destruction. The sensible manager will assimilate and benefit from the insights provided by different costing techniques, but will not be a slave to any one of them; they will help him better to understand the circumstances surrounding a decision, and the consequences that can and may flow from it. They should therefore improve the quality of that decision – but the ultimate touchstone must always be the market itself.

11.4 Pricing and markets

11.4.1 Introduction

So far in this chapter, we have examined the background against which the pricing decision will be taken: the effect of price on consumer demand; the degrees of flexibility available in the different categories of market in which firms operate; and the attitudes of customers and competitors at the various stages in a product's life cycle. We have looked at the concept of profit maximization and the market reality of target return, illustrating and discussing the two basic accounting techniques that are used as starting points in management's search for the profit objective, and underpin any modification thereof. We are now in a position to consider specific pricing situations and issues, and shall begin with the launch of a new line on the market.

Although each product will have a full and unique individual life cycle, it is necessary to draw the distinction once more between different *brands* of the same product type, different *types* of a particular product, and different *products* themselves. In the first (and probably the second) of these, the new launch will be entering an *existing* market in the growth or maturity stage of that market, where competing brands are already established; the third (and only possibly the second) will represent an innovative product, which will form the basis of a completely *new* market at the introductory phase of that market. Obviously, in the case of an existing market, the presence of competitors with close substitutes that are already familiar and acceptable to the potential customer is likely to give a highly elastic demand curve for any undifferentiated new product; small price premiums or discounts will normally lead to large swings in the volume sold (assuming a successful initial launch). Three different approaches to pricing could be adopted in this situation: an average or going-rate price could be charged; a small discount or premium to the going-rate might consciously be selected; or a penetration price could be chosen. Let us examine each of these in turn.

11.4.1   Average or going-rate pricing

In a perfectly competitive market, where there are many suppliers of homogeneous products, and the new product does not differ (and cannot be differentiated sufficiently by marketing means) in terms of quality or design from existing products, then the firm has little choice but to charge the 'going-rate'. Departures from this price will lead to losses. There are also cogent reasons for accepting the 'going-rate' price in an oligopoly, inasmuch as any attempt to influence demand will be met by retaliation by competitors, with potentially damaging consequences for all. There is an implicit assumption that an acceptable return will be earned under conditions of average efficiency when a company enters either a perfectly competitive or an oligopolistic market, and the emphasis consequently will be on cost control and 'making to a price'. However, as mentioned previously, perfect competition is rarely met with in practice, and true oligopoly by definition does not easily lend itself to fresh competition on a large scale.

Although relying on a different category of market, we should not overlook here the case of the firm that attempts to capture a small share of the existing market by differentiating its product sufficiently to generate additional demand at the normal market price, the higher marketing costs being offset by the benefits of greater volume.

11.4.3   Premium pricing and discount pricing

In most situations, the new product will either differ, or be made to appear different, in a way which will justify a premium over competing products, thereby covering the additional production or marketing costs; or it will be put forward as being of comparable quality, so that at a discount price to the market norm it will procure a larger share of the market than it might otherwise do, thereby counteracting the reduction in selling price. However, in this latter case, care must be taken to ensure that potential customers' perceptions of the product are not prejudiced by the lower price – as the marketing literature frequently points out, the consumer will often view with suspicion a branded product that is priced at even a small discount to the prevailing market rate. Note, however, that with an obviously homogeneous class of products such as petrol or heating oil, despite the presence of a textbook oligopolistic market, it will often be possible for a relatively small firm to capture a tiny but sufficiently profitable slice of the market by discount pricing. As long as it never grows beyond the stage of being a very minor irritant to the majors operating in the market, and poses no real threat to their monopoly profits, there is every chance that the new entrant will prosper.

A number of factors can contribute towards successful *premium* pricing:

1 *High price prestige.* Market research constantly confirms the existence of a section of the buying public that blindly equates higher prices with better quality goods. These customers will happily pay a premium over competing goods, regardless of their relative intrinsic merits. Although acting from rather different motives, there is another type of customer for whom the payment of a premium becomes a *de rigueur* response to increased affluence and what is perceived as the concomitant rise in social status, again regardless of relative quality considerations. The manufacturers of luxury cars, and owners of private schools have benefited from this psychological phenomenon of 'conspicuous consumption'.

2 *Brand loyalty.* An extensive advertising campaign could seek to establish the brand on the market, and build up a loyal consumer following. Well-known branded goods will generally be capable of sustaining a premium over non-branded goods, thus justifying the heavy initial promotional expenditure.

3 *Quality.* If a supplier can convince the consumer that his product or service is of better quality than those of his rivals, then a higher price can be justified. This is perhaps the most obvious case of premium pricing. Needless to say, this 'better quality' can be either real or perceived, with the help of appropriate advertising in the latter instance. A successful extension of this is demonstrated by the 'produced in limited quantity only' market: advertising can exploit the production of goods in limited quantities, by implying that the small numbers are the result of a conscious policy to maintain the highest of standards in manufacture – and incidentally supporting the price premium with the added attraction of scarcity value.

4 *Reliability.* Most customers are willing to pay more for goods which are seen or perceived to be more reliable than the general run. This particular characteristic will often be subsumed under the more general 'quality' category in the company's marketing strategy.

5 *Durability.* If a particular good is likely to have a longer physical life than similar items on the market, then it can justify a premium price. This characteristic, too, is often seen as part of the 'quality' picture.

6 *After-sales service.* This is really the converse of the previous two points,

with the same premium outcome for the supplier: in the absence of general reliability or durability, or a reluctance to pay a very high premium for those goods with that reputation, the ready availability of spare parts or servicing facilities can be translated into a higher sales price than would otherwise be the case.

7   *Extended warranties.* If a supplier is prepared to offer a longer warranty period for his particular product than that offered by rival suppliers with comparable products, he can usually rely on the innate conservatism and risk-aversion of the public to justify a price premium.

8   *Geographical location.* As many consumers know to their cost, and many suppliers to their benefit, geographical location will affect prices. For example, retailers will often charge premium rates for goods and services sold in rural and outlying areas. The difference is due not only to higher transportation costs, but reflects the lack of competition in such areas, and thus the customer's inability to 'shop around'. Effectively, it is a form of price differentiation or discrimination, which we shall look at separately under section 11.4.11.

11.4.4   Penetration pricing

As mentioned earlier, a highly elastic demand curve is likely to greet any undifferentiated new brand launched on to an existing product market. If substantial offsetting economies of scale can be expected at higher levels of production volume, a firm may deliberately set a particularly low price in order to 'penetrate' the market and quickly secure a large enough share of it to guarantee the necessary reductions in unit cost. Obviously, for penetration prices to be effective, the total market in which the firm is operating must be substantial, and the anticipated market share significant. However, the company must not lose sight of the role of product quality in this equation – success will be a function of the ability to produce sufficient units of the desired quality standard. This is particularly relevant in high technology industries, where difficulties in the supply of raw materials may be experienced.

The search for market dominance, as opposed to the desire for a substantial market share, might lead a large firm with very considerable excess productive capacity to take penetration pricing one stage further. Instead of merely settling for the satisficing benefits of lower unit costs, as spare production capacity is taken up through the stimulus of the penetration price, the company reduces the initial price still further as its costs fall. The aim would be to dominate the market at the stage at which the whole of the firm's productive capacity is being utilized. Effectively, the strategy is to trade-off high early losses against what ultimately should be the lowest production costs in the market and the dominant share of it – with all that is implied by that in terms of future price manoeuvrability.

11.4.5 *Buy-response curves*

In an established market, a modest investment in consumer research should yield valuable information concerning the elasticity of demand for existing brands. The construction of a buy-response curve, to be used in conjunction with the strategic considerations outlined in the preceding paragraphs, can help a newcomer to select an appropriate price with which to enter the market. Buy-response curves are based on the work of Stoetzel (1954), who suggested that consumers associate with any given article a certain price *range*, rather than a *single* price. The data for the curve are obtained by establishing the top and bottom prices that individuals would be willing to pay for a particular product. For each price within this range, a cumulative distribution of the numbers giving it as their upper or lower limit is calculated. By subtracting from the *lower* limit cumulative distribution at a particular price the *upper* limit cumulative distribution of the price immediately *below* it, one can determine a buy-response percentage for the former price, which can be plotted on a graph.

As an illustration, let us take the response to a product price of 30p. If 90 per cent of the total sample of respondents considered that this price was their *lower* limit, and 5 per cent considered that 29p was their *upper* limit, the buy-response rate is 90–5 = 85, i.e. 85 per cent of the sample would be prepared to pay 30p for the product. By obtaining details of the last prices actually paid for the product by the sample members, and plotting this against the buy-response curve, it is possible to see whether the existing brands on the market are under- or over-priced. In Figure 11.9, it can be seen that the distribution of actual prices is well to the left of the buy-response curve, indicating that the public would be willing to pay considerably more than the prices being charged currently for existing brands; a distribution to the right would have signified that existing brands were overpriced. The strategic value to management of such analyses of consumer response is obvious.

A useful recent discussion of the buy-response technique can be found in Foxall (1981).

11.4.6 *Market skimming*

As noted earlier, an innovative product will form the basis of a completely *new* market, and the producer has all the advantages, and potential disadvantages, of participating in the introductory phase of the life cycle. Although sales at this stage are likely to be low, and will need to be bolstered by advertising, the demand curve will often be relatively inelastic, giving the producer the opportunity to adopt a 'skimming price' strategy. 'Market skimming' exploits the novelty appeal of a new product by charging a high initial price, in the knowledge that a lower price in the introductory phase would not lead to significantly greater sales. Recent examples of a successful 'skimming' policy would include pocket calculators, digital watches and video recorders. Obviously, one objective of 'market skimming' would be to maximize profitability when a product is first launched. However, it can also act as a form of insurance policy against unexpected increases in manufacturing or distribution costs, particularly where, in the absence of a product

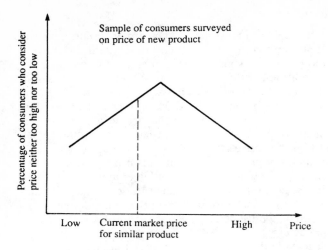

Figure 11.9   *Buy-response curve*
Adapted from Gabor, A., Granger, C. 'The Pricing of New Products', in Taylor B. and Wills G. (1969)

history, these costs are of necessity only estimates. It will also help to minimize losses in the unhappy event of a rejection of the product by the market.

It has often been pointed out that it is much easier to lower prices than to raise them, particularly if the demand schedule is uncertain; from a psychological point of view it is far better to begin with a high price, which can then be lowered if demand for the product appears to be more sensitive to price than had at first seemed the case. There are two particular circumstances that would dictate the *necessary* adoption of a 'skimming price':

(a)   when it is anticipated that the product's life cycle will be relatively short, making it desirable to recover development costs as quickly as possible;
(b)   when the firm has poor liquidity, and high cash flows must be generated as early as possible as a matter of necessity.

However, as we saw in the previous section, when alternative pricing strategies for new brands in an existing product market were discussed, high prices will inevitably tempt potential competitors to come into the market, possibly with a lower price that will give them a competitive advantage. Obviously, as in the case of monopoly, for profitable 'skimming' to be *sustained*, one or more significant barriers to entry must be present to deter these potential competitors. As we saw earlier, examples of such barriers might be patent protection, prohibitively high capital investment, or unusually strong brand loyalty. Nevertheless, where the profit motive is strong enough, even the most significant barriers will be breached eventually, and the innovative producer will inevitably be faced with a critical decision regarding future pricing policy. It can often be more difficult to determine when the time has come to *reduce* the 'skimming price' than take the initial decision to adopt 'market skimming' when the product is first launched. Strategy and timing will be a function of the strength or weakness of the barriers to entry. As seen in Figure 11.10, when entry barriers are high, prices can be maintained at the 'skimming' level for a considerable time, until the innovative upper share of the market becomes saturated. The price should then be reduced in order to appeal to a more sensitive part of the market, but by dropping the price gradually, as the benefits of the learning curve and increased manufacturing volumes are felt in product costs, margins can be maintained at a high level with relative impunity for some time – until the inevitable partial substitutions appear on the market.

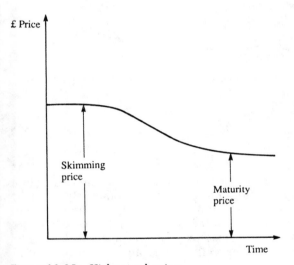

Figure 11.10   *High entry barriers*

In contrast, Figure 11.11 shows the situation when entry barriers are weak. The initial 'skimming' advantage of being first on the scene is only enjoyed for a short period, before the profit potential of the expanding market is recognized by competitors. The innovator must anticipate their actions by making a pre-emptive move from a 'skimming' to a 'penetration' price. A sharp reduction in price should lead to greatly increased demand, higher productive levels and lower unit costs. Obviously, any competitors entering the market could benefit from mass production and low costs, so the innovator must continue to make anticipatory price reductions until the stage is reached at which no further economies of scale or learning benefits can be achieved. The life cycle has effectively been accelerated, and the product has now reached maturity; further falls in price will be relatively modest.

In both situations, the timing is crucial – profits will be reduced unnecessarily if the price is reduced too quickly; reacting too slowly to market conditions, on the other hand, will lead to a loss of market share, and the concomitant loss of profits.

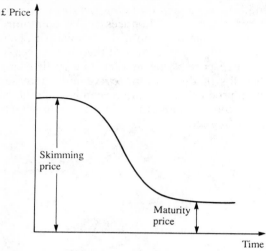

Figure 11.11   *Low entry barriers*

11.4.7   *Limit pricing*

Where a firm has certain advantages that provide barriers to entry, but those barriers are not high enough to block out competition completely, it might be able to sustain a market skimming situation by adopting a 'limit pricing' policy. In order to deter entry on the part of rivals, the limit price will be set at a level which reflects the firm's competitive cost advantage but falls short of that which would ensure short-run profit maximization. Dorward (1987) has pointed out that successful limit pricing requires a homogeneous product market, price leadership or collusion on the part of a few dominant firms, and a policy of long-run profit maximization on the part of both established firms and potential entrants. The models developed to determine the limit price are based on the so-called 'Sylos postulate', which assumes that potential entrants will expect established firms to maintain their existing output levels when new entry occurs, and that this is known to be the case by those firms. The effect of this is to restrict new entrants to operating on that section of the demand curve below and to the right of the existing limit-price output; and it is assumed that the new entrant will merely be able to serve the residual demand created by lowering price below the limit price, which it could only do at a loss. Interested readers are referred to Dorward (1987) for a graphical illustration of a limit price in the case of an absolute cost advantage, and one with the benefit of economies of scale, together with a critical discussion of the models and assumptions.

11.4.8 *Product line pricing*

A 'product line' can be defined as 'a range of related products', and the supplier of such a range is faced with a number of pricing problems. While the theoretical approach to be adopted by the firm in such circumstances is easily stated, namely, that profitability can only be viewed in relation to the range as a whole, and therefore the price for each individual product within the range should be fixed at the level which maximizes the profitability of the range as a whole, there is no practical way to translate this into the reality of the market place. In the absence of prescriptive solutions, we can only point to two additional factors which need to be taken into consideration by the decision maker:

1 *Joint products.* If two or more of the products in the range are *joint* products, i.e. they necessarily result from a common production process, their prices cannot be considered in isolation. In essence, this situation represents a microcosm of product line pricing – the price set for each individual product from the process should ideally result in a demand which will absorb *all* the available units, and leave none unsold. For example, if the production of X cannot take place without a given quantity of Y also being produced, profits would be suboptimized if the firm manufactures in order to satisfy the demand for X at a particular price, and the concomitant production of Y is *not* fully absorbed by the market because the price set for Y fails to generate sufficient demand.
2 *Interdependent demand.* If two or more products in the range are substitutes, or complement each other in any way, then a relation might exist between the demand for the different products. The effect of a price change on one product could be felt in the demand for another. Again, this situation emphasizes the basic point of product line pricing, namely, that profitability is inextricably linked with the line *as a whole*, and individual products cannot be looked at in isolation.

11.4.9 *Optional extras and loss leaders*

These represent a particular variety of product line pricing, in which the range consists of one or more main products, and a series of related optional products, or optional extras, and buyers are free to choose whether or not they wish to add on to the main product one or more of the ancillaries. There are two approaches to pricing in this context. The supplier could set a relatively low price for the main product and a relatively high one for the optional extras, hoping that sufficient numbers of the main product will be sold to guarantee a satisfactory return from the highly priced extras. This approach will be particularly successful in the case of 'captive' or 'after-market' products, when the manufacturer or supplier obtains a sale on the basis of a low price for the main product, and his profitability stems from the sale of the 'tied' extras; aircraft engines and their spares are a good example, where a highly competitively priced main product wins the order, and it can only be serviced by means of dedicated (and very profitable) spares. Restaurant chains frequently employ a variant of this approach: vouchers offering discounts against meals are issued in the expectation that the reduced contribution will be more than offset by the increased volume and the profit that will accrue from the highly priced drinks that are likely to be consumed during the visit; alternatively, a free bottle of wine might be offered as an inducement to purchase a relatively expensive meal. In the case of 'optional extras', some might be rather less 'optional' than others, despite the publicity material. One need only think of certain prestige cars, where the basic model without the (extremely expensive) optional extras is such a spartan vehicle that no potential owner would dream of acquiring it in that state: through skilful marketing, the manufacturer would seem to have his cake and eat it in this rare and extreme example.

Obviously, with a low margin/high margin approach to pricing, the supplier must be careful to ensure that he does not find his sales limited to the low margin products; there is an inherent risk that customers will 'play the market' and only buy the 'loss leaders', purchasing the highly profitable complementary products more cheaply elsewhere. The creation of a captive or tied market for the complementary products is one obvious way of avoiding this.

The alternative approach to pricing in this situation is to regard both main and subsidiary products as profit earners in their own right.

11.4.10   *Competitive price plans and decision trees*

Oliver (1986) mentions the use of decision trees in assessing brands in an established market, particularly an oligopolistic one in which competitors' responses can be anticipated with a reasonable degree of probability. He prefaces his example with some useful remarks on competitive price plans, distinguishing between *initiatory* and *response* strategies. The former includes precedence (being the first to take a particular action) and pre-emption (making a 'shut-out' move to exclude the competition). Precedence is used to catch rivals off guard, and make additional profits before retaliatory action by competitors; pre-emption is intended to make it difficult for rivals to follow a move, usually by cutting a price so savagely that competitors feel unable to match it. Response strategies comprise *imitation* and *exploitation*. An imitative response would be to match the first move, or 'better' it in kind – meeting a competitor's price cut with an even larger reduction, for example. An exploitive response would be one that contrasts with the original strategy, typically *cutting* prices in response to an *increase* by competitors. Obviously, the number of variables inherent in these different competitive stances lends itself to their examination in the form of a decision tree, in which the payoff can be expressed in terms of profits from expected sales under each alternative. Figure 11.12 is an adapted and expanded version of the example reproduced by Oliver.

For the sake of simplicity, only one competitor is assumed to exist (or all competitors act as one) and only two alternative prices are considered: 50p and 40p. If we choose an initial price of 50p, our competitor can respond with either 50p or 40p. The probability estimates that we assign to each response show that there is a 75 per cent chance that he will choose 50p, in which case we can meet his response by keeping to our original price of 50p or going down to 40p. Lowering the price to 40p gives us a 75 per cent

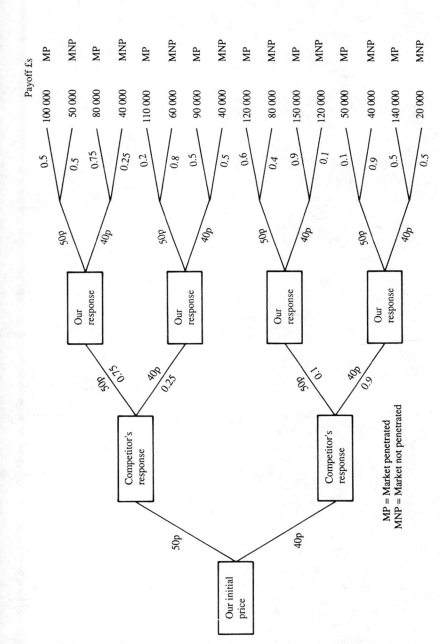

Payoff £s

100 000	MP
50 000	MNP
80 000	MP
40 000	MNP
110 000	MP
60 000	MNP
90 000	MP
40 000	MNP
120 000	MP
80 000	MNP
150 000	MP
120 000	MNP
50 000	MP
40 000	MNP
140 000	MP
20 000	MNP

MP = Market penetrated
MNP = Market not penetrated

Figure 11.12 *Pricing decision tree*

Expected strategy	Our initial price	Our response to competitor's response of 50p	Our response to competitor's response of 40p	Payoff*
1	50p	50p	50p	73,750
2	50	50	40	72,500
3	50	40	50	70,000
4	50	40	40	68,750
5	40	50	50	47,300
6	40	50	40	82,400
7	40	40	50	51,600
8	40	40	40	86,700

*Calculations of expected payoffs:

Strategy 1 $(0.75 \times 0.5 \times 100,000) + (0.75 \times 0.5 \times 50,000) + (0.25 \times 0.2 \times 110,000) + (0.25 \times 0.8 \times 60,000) = 73,750$

2 $(0.75 \times 0.5 \times 100,000) + (0.75 \times 0.5 \times 50,000) + (0.25 \times 0.5 \times 90,000) + (0.25 \times 0.5 \times 40,000) = 72,500$

3 $(0.75 \times 0.75 \times 80,000) + (0.75 \times 0.25 \times 40,000) + (0.25 \times 0.2 \times 110,000) + (0.25 \times 0.8 \times 60,000) = 70,000$

4 $(0.75 \times 0.75 \times 80,000) + (0.75 \times 0.25 \times 40,000) + (0.25 \times 0.5 \times 90,000) + (0.25 \times 0.5 \times 40,000) = 68,750$

5 $(0.1 \times 0.6 \times 120,000) + (0.1 \times 0.4 \times 80,000) + (0.9 \times 0.1 \times 50,000) + (0.9 \times 0.9 \times 40,000) = 47,300$

6 $(0.1 \times 0.6 \times 120,000) + (0.1 \times 0.4 \times 80,000) + (0.9 \times 0.5 \times 140,000) + (0.9 \times 0.5 \times 20,000) = 82,400$

7 $(0.1 \times 0.9 \times 150,000) + (0.1 \times 0.1 \times 120,000) + (0.9 \times 0.1 \times 50,000) + (0.9 \times 0.9 \times 40,000) = 51,600$

8 $(0.1 \times 0.9 \times 150,000) + (0.1 \times 0.1 \times 120,000) + (0.9 \times 0.5 \times 140,000) + (0.9 \times 0.5 \times 20,000) = 86,700$

Figure 11.12   *Pricing decision tree (cont.)*

probability of penetrating the market, in which case we shall make a profit of £80,000. We assign a 25 per cent probability to the alternative scenario that we will *not* penetrate the market at this price, in which case we would expect a much reduced profit of £40,000. From the table in Figure 11.12 it can be seen that eight alternative strategies are possible, and an expected value of the payoff associated with each strategy can be calculated from the decision tree. The expected payoff of strategy 8 – setting an initial price of 40p and sticking to that price regardless of our competitor's response – is highest. Needless to say, the usual *caveats* regarding expected values should be considered before a statistical technique such as this is employed in decision making. A more complex example, together with a discussion of the Bayesian theory underlying the model, can be found in Green (1967).

11.4.11   *Price discrimination (or differentiation)*

It is often possible to sell the same product to different customers at different prices. In order to do this, the market must be divisible into segments, each quite separate from the others, and each with its own degree of price sensitivity. The principle of market segmentation is not new – variations of standard product types have been designed for particular social classes or regional markets for several thousand years. Although mass production techniques lead naturally to homogeneity of products (the Henry Ford maxim), the trend in the last 40 years has been to recognize the profit potential of discrete market segments, with their different demand functions.

If natural demarcation lines already exist, so much the better; if not, they can be created by marketing techniques. There are five possible bases for segmentation.

1   *Time.* One example of differentiation by time has already been mentioned: market skimming. The customers who buy a product relatively early in its life cycle will pay more than those who buy later. More obvious (and personal) everyday examples include rail travel and telecommunications. A huge inelastic demand curve is presented to the suppliers of these services in the form of customers having little or no control over the time of day they use them. Other examples, exploiting a different section of the market, are seen in the reverse of the above situation. The concept of off-peak or low-tariff services is an attempt to maximize profits by attracting marginal income which will make an additional contribution to fixed costs. Hotel groups were one of the first successfully to discriminate in this particular way – low weekend tariffs for accommodation and food reflect the fact that any income in excess of the marginal cost of supply goes to reduce overheads that are incurred regardless of volume. Moreover, the weekend leisure customer represents a totally different market segment that poses no threat to the highly profitable weekday business trade.

2   *Quantity.* Discounts for bulk purchases are a long-established and well-known form of price discrimination, which reflect cost savings for the supplier in terms of lower handling and distribution costs. Customers can also be persuaded that the principle should be applied in reverse, namely, that small orders should carry a price *premium* (not always represented by concomitant additional supply or distribution costs).

3   *Function.* A common form of segmentation is based on differences in the *functions* performed by various groups of customers within the market. Different prices will usually be paid by wholesaler, retailer and the ultimate consumer. Like bulk discounts, functional discounts reflect the degree of cost savings to each supplier along the chain. However, if the difference in price departs significantly from the costs of performing the marginal functional service, the chain is likely to break, and prices obtainable from the ultimate consumer will be eroded. For example, too wide a band between wholesaler and retailer may prompt the wholesaler to sell directly to the consumer at a lower price than the retailer is able to quote.

4   *Location.* Products which are subject to high transportation costs may be successfully differentiated in price in different geographical locations. As long as the differential is less than the cost of moving individual cheaper priced goods to the more expensive market, there should be no risk of their filtering across boundaries and diluting margins. Retail price differentiation is also possible between urban and rural locations, and between wealthy and poor districts within cities: the support for higher prices in these situations is not so much the prohibitive transportation costs from one location to another, but the unlikelihood (for reasons of convenience or snobbery) of higher priced customers seeking out the lower priced outlets.

5   *Product content and presentation.* Relatively minor (in cost terms) physical

variations can be made of the same basic product, which is then sold to different market segments at significantly different prices. Cars are an obvious example: a more sporty look to a small saloon, a different finish to its paintwork and facia, or a more comfortable fabric for the seats. On the other hand, the difference may simply be in the presentation of the goods for sale to the consumer – the same basic products can be set out in more attractive showrooms, with more attentive and knowledgeable sales assistants, and no-quibble exchanges. The only requirement for successful segmentation in these cases is a sufficiently large number of customers who will value the differences highly enough to pay a premium price for them.

It is frequently pointed out that price differentiation has both private and public benefits. The *private* benefits to both supplier and low price consumer are obvious, but the *public* benefit is less so. It is seen when a 'single-price' policy fails to cover total costs, and would result in the supplier withdrawing the product from the market. Let us take a simple illustration of a retailer who buys a particular product for £125, and has shop overheads of £180 in total. Let us asume that there are only two customers in the market, one willing to pay up to £250 for the product, the other no more than £200. If the retailer is able to differentiate the price between the two customers, he will sell two units and make a profit on the deals:

$$\text{Revenues:} \qquad \text{£250} + \text{£200} = \text{£450}$$
$$\text{Costs:} \qquad (2 \times \text{£125}) + \text{£180} = \text{£430}$$
$$\text{Profit} \quad \underline{\text{£ 20}}$$

However, if the retailer can only set a single price for the product, he will lose money, no matter what price is quoted. If he says £200, he can sell two units, but will fail to cover his total costs:

$$\text{Revenues:} \qquad (2 \times \text{£200}) = \text{£400}$$
$$\text{Costs:} \qquad \text{as before} \quad \text{£430}$$
$$\text{Loss} \quad \underline{\text{£ (30)}}$$

If he quotes £250, he will only sell one unit, the second customer being unwilling to pay more than £200. A bigger loss ensues:

$$\text{Revenues:} \qquad (1 \times \text{£250}) = \text{£ 250}$$
$$\text{Costs:} \qquad (1 \times \text{£125}) + \text{£180} = \text{£(305)}$$
$$\text{Loss} \quad \underline{\text{£ (55)}}$$

The net result of his inability to exercise price discrimination would be his withdrawal from the market, so that *neither* customer has the opportunity to buy the product. Figure 11.13 is a graphical representation of this type of

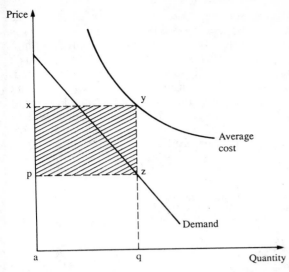

Figure 11.13   *Price differentiation: a single price model*

situation. It shows a conventional downward-sloping demand curve, and a downward-sloping average cost curve. At every feasible volume, average cost > price. If the price is set at p, the quantity sold will be q, and the loss is represented by the shaded rectangle xyzp, the area between average cost and price. Without price discrimination, the supplier will not offer the product to the market.

Now consider Figure 11.14, in which the market is divided into two segments, with a separate price – the maximum the customer is willing to pay (in our illustration £250 and £200 respectively) – being set for each. The price in the first market segment is p_1, and the quantity sold q_1. The total revenue from this segment is p_1q_1. The price in the second market segment is p_2, and the quantity sold is q_2-q_1. The total revenue from this second segment is $p_2(q_2-q_1)$. If the total area of the two revenue blocks (p_1acdq_2o) is greater than the total cost (xyq_2o) [or $p_1abx > bydc$, the rest of the area being common to both], the supplier will make a profit, and will thus be willing to continue to offer the product for sale; and the consumers of the product will be able to satisfy their requirements. Readers will recognize in this the theoretical justification for the 'off-peak' policy outlined above.

There are several prerequisites for the successful implementation of a policy of price discrimination:

(a)   The different market segments should be logical and easily measurable. Unusual bases for segmentation can lead to difficulties in data collection for both planning and control.

(b)   Where advertising plays a major role in the market, there must be a cost-effective match between the segment population and the audience for the advertising medium selected. For example, the whole of the audience for one particular television programme or daily newspaper is unlikely to have the same attitude towards an individual product; and mass advertising can be prohibitively expensive. Each segment should be of sufficient size to justify the specifically targeted advertising campaign.

(c)   There must be an adequate flow of accounting data for both planning and control purposes. Accounting information must be capable of being disaggregated, and costs and revenues assigned to segments with a reasonable degree of accuracy. Aggregate company accounting information is at best useless; at worst dangerous.

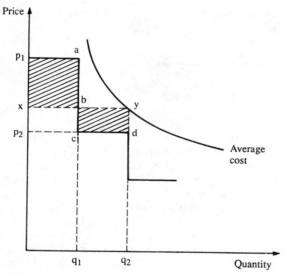

Figure 11.14   *Price differentiation: multiple price model*

For a recent theoretical discussion of price discrimination, the interested reader is referred to Dorwood (1987); Kotler (1980) contains an excellent overview of market segmentation.

11.4.12   *Product bundling*

This is a form of price discrimination which comprises 'bundling together' several goods or services at a lower aggregate price than the total of the separate parts. Obvious illustrations are the 'luxury packs' of optional extras sold with certain new cars, and an 'all-in' price for the different facilities offered by clubs or hotels. Dorwood (1987) gives good examples of the profitable use of both 'pure bundling' and 'mixed bundling', which we have modified slightly in the discussion below.

1   *Pure bundling.* Film X is more valuable to exhibitor A than exhibitor B, and film Y is more valuable to exhibitor B than exhibitor A, thus:

A would pay £8,000 for film X and £2,500 for film Y
B would pay £7,000 for film X and £3,000 for film Y

Obviously, if the two films were booked separately, X would be rented out at £7,000, so as not to exclude B, and Y at £2,500, so as not to exclude A. The distributor's revenue would be £19,000 in total. However, bundling the two films together for £10,000 (the lower of A and B's valuations for X and Y together) will increase the revenues to £20,000. The revenue gain comes from the inverse relation in the valuation of the two films by A and B, and the fact that their separate valuations are not too far apart – only £500 in our example.

2   *Mixed bundling.* This is more profitable than pure bundling whenever some buyers value one of the items in a bundle relatively highly, but the other(s) slightly above or below cost price, and there are further buyers who place a relatively high valuation on both or all the items in the bundle. Let us extend the number of film exhibitors to four:

A values X at £8,000 and Y at £2,500 (as before)
B values X at £7,000 and Y at £3,000 (as before)
C values X at £5,500 and Y at £5,000
D values X at £5,000 and Y at £5,500

Under a pure bundling strategy, the same £10,000 bundle would be offered to all four. If the distributor's marginal cost of supplying each film is £4,000, then he will make a profit of £40,000 − £32,000 = £8,000. Note that, under pure bundling, A and B hire film Y, despite its marginal cost exceeding their valuations. With *mixed* bundling, the profit would be higher. The distributor could offer X and Y separately at £7,000 and £4,000 respectively, or the pair as a package for £10,500. The result would be A, C and D hiring the package, and B hiring film X only, as the cost of both the bundle and film Y exceed his particular valuations. The profit would now be (£10,500 × 3) + £7,000 − (£4,000 × 7) = £10,500.

However, A might also prefer to hire film X for £7,000, instead of taking the package, as the extra cost of the bundle exceeds his valuation of Y by £1,000. If A did choose this option, the distributor's profit would rise to £11,000, as he does not have to supply either A or B with film Y, which has a supply cost in excess of their valuations: (£10,500 × 2) + (£7,000 × 2) − (£4,000 × 6) = £11,000.

Mixed bundling is a particularly efficient means of exploiting price discrimination. Buyers are offered a pricing structure in which they are charged higher prices for buying the items separately (X + Y = £11,000) than in a package (X + Y = £10,500). Mixed bundling works as a discriminatory device by (a) using the package to extract the most from those customers who value it most (in our example C and D, who placed relatively high valuations on both films), and (b) charging a relatively high separate price for that item in the package that is valued very highly by some particular buyers (in our example film X, which was valued very highly by both A and B).

It should be noted that a *non-bundling* policy would have resulted in a profit of only £6,500 – A, B and C would have been charged £5,500 for X with a marginal cost of £4,000 (the contribution from three sales at £5,500 is higher than four sales at £5,000, the lowest valuation placed on X by exhibitor D), and C and D £5,000 for Y (A and B having a valuation for Y below its marginal cost).

The assumption underlying the economic analysis of product bundling is that customers will evaluate the package by adding together their valuations of the individual components. Whenever the supplier's price for the bundle exceeds the buyer's valuation, it will be rejected in favour of the separate purchase of those individual items within it that are valued more highly than their separate selling price.

11.4.13   *Competitive bidding*

This occurs when competing firms are asked to submit their individual bids for a particular contract. Obviously, the problem facing a firm in this situation is the uncertainty regarding the prices at which the competition will tender, because a supplier will wish to pitch his own quote at a figure which is sufficiently attractive to secure acceptance, but at the same time not so low that a loss might ensue (unless the contract is regarded as a loss leader). In other words, the bidder will wish to increase his probability of winning the job, without sacrificing more profit than is absolutely necessary. Models employed in this situation will take explicit note of the possible positions adopted by competitors, and use simple probability theory to determine the most profitable course of action to adopt. Table 11.3 is an example of such a model. The firm's own marginal costs must be calculated, together with the probability of a bid being successful within a particular price range – this latter will be the major variable, and could be estimated from past bidding behaviour by competitors and a knowledge of previously successful bid prices for similar contracts. Note that costs should include opportunity costs, if a successful tender would prevent other, profitable, work from being under-taken during the life of the contract.

As can be seen, a quote of £860,000 gives the highest expected profit, and provides the most satisfactory trade-off between probabilities and profit.

Whenever a quantitative model of this type is employed, it is worth empha-sizing that the future will always be uncertain; probabilities are often only *estimates*; and the 'expected profit' will almost never be a feasible outcome (the *actual* profit on a bid of £860,000, according to the table, could *only* be £80,000, *ceteris paribus*). Finally, it is worth noting that there are very few business problems that can be reduced to a simple quantitative analysis – qualitative factors must *always* be taken into account. In this situation, for example, the contract might not necessarily be awarded on the basis of the lowest bid; reliability and a reputation for good quality work might also be considered by the firm awarding the contract.

For a detailed discussion of this topic and its theoretical underpinnings, the reader is referred to Oxenfeldt *et al.* (1961) and Edelman (1967).

Table 11.3   Competitive bidding (all in £000s)

Price range	Probability of lowest bid being in this price range	(a) Cumulative probability of bid in this price range being successful	Our bid	Our MC	(b) Profit	(a) × (b) Expected profit
over 1000	0.10	<0.10	1010	780	230	<23
950–1000	0.20	0.10	960	780	180	18
900–950	0.25	0.30	910	780	130	39
850–900	0.30	0.55	860	780	80	44
800–850	0.10	0.85	810	780	30	25.5
Below 800	0.05	>0.95	790	780	10	>9.5
	1.00					

11.4.14   Inflation

If increases in costs cannot be offset by greater productivity (which they rarely can), increased prices will be the only way to maintain existing profit margins. In the case of long-term contracts, if cost inflation is anticipated, the tendering company will be torn between:

(a)   a natural desire to win the contract;
(b)   an equally natural reluctance to enter into any fixed price contract which might lead at best to reduced margins, at worst to a loss;
(c)   the knowledge that building anticipatory increases into the quoted price could lead to the loss of the contract to a more modestly priced competitor who might face a different cost profile.

The two usual approaches to this problem are:

1   To write an 'escalation clause' into the contract, pointing out that competitors who do not do likewise will either cut corners (which could have quality and perhaps safety connotations), or will seek to recover their losses through overpricing of any subsequent modifications or additions to the original contract specification.
2   To adopt one of the two policies criticized under 1 above, viz. to quote a non-inflationary tender price in the expectation of obtaining compensatory increases in revenues by means of highly priced amendments.

In more normal trading situations (i.e. those not involving fixed-priced contracts), our earlier discussions of markets and demand curves would indicate the difficulties faced by many firms in obtaining a suitable price increase, and therefore alternatives must be sought when inflation is experienced or expected. These might include the following strategies:

(a) *Marketing.* Producing a 'new' or differentiated product, with a price structure that is designed to cover both the inflationary costs and the marginal costs of differentiation. Alternatively, or additionally, those products which show the highest contributions under the revised cost structures could be consciously promoted in an attempt to shift the sales mix in a favourable and compensatory manner.

(b) *Distribution.* Restructuring the system of quantity discounts and minimum order quantities so that the 'break point' occurs at a much lower level.

(c) *Physical adjustment.* Reducing the quantity of the product in an imperceptible and cost-effective way. Well-known examples include putting fewer peas in a tin, and less chocolate in a bar.

Of course, if a price increase is acceptable to the market, then it might be possible to build into it a certain 'cushion' against future cost increases. This also has the merit of avoiding loss of customer goodwill (and business) by having more frequent price revisions.

11.5   General policy issues

11.5.1   The promotion mix

In modern, highly industrialized societies, where oligopoly or near oligopolistic markets are common, non-price competition is of great importance to the supplier. It can assume four separate forms:

1 *Personal selling.* This is the classic salesman–customer relationship, where personal communication is used to sell the product, usually on a face-to-face basis but sometimes by telephone.

2 *Publicity.* This is non-personal communication in the mass media, not paid for by the supplier (although perhaps subtly influenced by him). Examples would be news stories or programmes including the company's products (either in a central or peripheral role), or favourable editorial comment in the specialist press.

3 *Advertising.* This is paid non-personal communication in the mass media, and will often be the largest single item in selling costs.

4 *Sales promotion.* This could be defined as any persuasive activity not included in the first three categories, such as exhibitions, demonstrations, money-off coupons, samples, or sponsorship.

The effectiveness of each of the four promotional means in the sales process can be seen in Figure 11.15.

Personal selling is a powerful tool, and its potential for actually creating sales is considerable, but it is time-consuming and limited by the size of the sales force. Publicity has the benefit of greater credibility than any house campaign or comments, but its use lies largely out of the firm's control. Advertising provides the mass exposure that personal selling lacks, and its strength lies in heightening consumer awareness and understanding. However, its potential for converting this into a sale is less than the direct

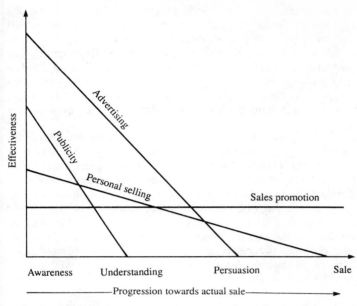

Figure 11.15 *Promotional effectiveness*

personal approach. Sales promotion can be very variable in its effects: sponsorship can stimulate awareness of a product, exhibitions and demonstrations can increase the public's understanding, and money-off coupons and samples can encourage the all-important first trial that can lead on to further full-priced sales. Reliance on any one of these four methods would obviously be exceptional; more usually, the firm will combine them, and the so-called promotion mix will be the specific combination selected by the firm for its own particular circumstances.

Factors which will affect the individual mix would be as follows:

1   *Product life cycle.* The characteristics of the different stages in the life cycle will demand changes in the promotional mix, as Table 11.4 demonstrates.

Table 11.4   The promotion mix and the life cycle

Ranking	Introduction	Growth	Maturity	Decline
1	Publicity	Advertising	Advertising	
2	Personal selling	Personal selling	Sales promotion	Gradual
3	Advertising	Sales promotion	Publicity	Phase out
4		Publicity		

Adapted from Wasson, C.R., *Dynamic Competitive Strategy and Product Life Cycles*, 1974, Challenge Books, p. 248.

2   *Market size and geographical location.* Large, geographically diverse markets will obviously have different promotional requirements to those which are smaller or more geographically concentrated. As an example of the former, a branded confectionery or grocery product would normally use mass media advertising and sales promotion as the prime elements in the mix; in the latter category, a local bakery or dairy would rely largely on personal selling. In a similar way, the relatively small market for an industrial machine will lend itself to a mix in which personal selling predominates.

3   *Product type.* Where a product is homogeneous, sales are largely a function of the service offered by distributors, and personal selling is likely to be a major feature of the mix, although promotional material such as diaries and calendars can play a useful part. For non-homogeneous products, the mix will reflect the technical complexity of the individual item in the hands of the consumer: at one end of the spectrum will be the highly complex and specialized industrial product that requires the detailed technical communication that only personal contact will provide; at the other end, the promotional needs of a product which is either readily understandable or, if complex in design, is not so in use, can be met largely by advertising.

All forms of non-price competition aim to shift the firm's demand curve to the right (note that a change in price influences the amount sold *within* a given demand curve; it represents a movement *along* a demand curve, but not a *shift* in that curve). Obviously, the choice of promotional mix will reflect not only the factors outlined above, but also the firm's assessment of the relative cost-effectiveness of the various elements within it. Unfortunately, although most promotional costs can be estimated with a considerable degree of accuracy, formidable measurement problems face any attempt to determine the real *effectiveness* of the promotional expenditure. In theory, if the sales response to each promotional element were known with certainty, an optimal mix could be derived by plotting cost and revenue curves and flexing the variables within cost in turn until we reach the classic stage of $MC = MR$. However, as Dean (1951) pointed out many years ago: 'The economist's assumption that the entrepreneur knows the least-cost combination of production factors is rarely correct for marketing activities' (p. 134). Despite the existence of several mathematical models, the level of uncertainty surrounding the input variables to them is such that they are largely eschewed in favour of rule-of-thumb alternatives. In sales promotion, perhaps more than any other area of management decision making, the extent of the interdependencies between the demand determinants, exacerbated by the time-lag element inherent in most forms of advertising, precludes a simple mathematical solution to the calculation of an optimal mix.

Interested readers are referred to Dorward (1987) for a recent critical discussion of the various advertising models that have been put forward.

11.5.2 *Psychological pricing*

This is designed to encourage purchases based on emotional reactions rather than rational responses, and is seen most frequently at the retail level. One type of example would be the prices £6.49, £9.99 and £249.99: the theory is that the customer would *perceive* a considerable difference between these prices and £6.50, £10.00 and £250.00, with the former representing a desirable buying opportunity. Similarly, there are a number of well-documented examples of an unsuccessful product being withdrawn and successfully relaunched at a *higher* price, merely because consumers' perceptions had erroneously equated the earlier lower price with an unacceptably low quality.

A different approach is based on the 'attractiveness' of the numbers themselves. Psychologists believe that certain numbers are physically more attractive to people – the symmetrical figure 8, for example, is seen as more appealing than the numbers 7 and 4, with their harsh edges and points. An extension of this theory has its roots in the work of Morris (1967), who suggests that human beings are attracted to round letters and figures, such as O, because the primal self is always alert for eyes that might belong to a predator. Thus, an advertising sign reading GOOD FOOD outside a snack bar is more likely to catch the attention of passers-by than one which reads EAT WELL HERE. Interestingly, an implication of this approach to is that a price of £100 is more eyecatching that one of £99.99, and the marketeer must therefore determine the appropriate mix between the visibility of a price and its psychological buying impact mentioned above.

11.5.3 *Multi-stage pricing*

Some 30 years ago, Oxenfeldt (1960) developed his now famous six-part pricing method. The first stage calls for the selection of the target consumer group, and research into its price awareness and sensitivity. Next comes the choice of a brand image, designed to appeal to the class of customer previously identified. The third stage is the composition of the appropriate marketing mix for that image and market. The determination of a broad pricing policy is the fourth step, followed by the choice of a particular pricing strategy; Oxenfeldt distinguishes these two stages by regarding the former as being concerned with the 'normal' situation, and the latter with specific (and by definition) short-lived variants thereon. A certain price bracket should have emerged as a result of steps 1–5, and the final stage is the selection of an actual price or prices within that range. The multi-stage approach does not necessarily lead to a single price: '... one must beware of any pricing method that does ... for such a method could not possibly take into account all the special circumstances which are relevant to a price decision and which vary so greatly from market to market and from time to time' (p. 133). Its aim is simply to narrow down the number of possible prices, by adopting a logical and sequential progression of decisions that will exclude more and more of the variables and options.

11.5.4   *Information for the pricing decision*

Obviously, different information will be required for new products than for an existing product range. In the latter case, the firm can extrapolate from an historical analysis of costs, prices and demand, taking into account the likely changes in cost structures over the coming period, and any other relevant factors, such as competitors' marketing strategies, and the product's position within the life cycle. However, no historical data are available for new products, and forecasting errors can be high if the firm relies solely on management judgement.

The determination of costs will usually be much less of a problem than estimates of demand, and for this reason, whenever possible, consumer research should be carried out in order to provide reliable data on the effect of different prices on sales. However, market research, in the form of test marketing of a product, is not always feasible, and does not necessarily give completely reliable data when it is carried out. For example, pricing experiments with complex, high value industrial products can be impractical simply because it is impossible to separate test markets adequately – the buyers in the high-priced test area invariably hear of the low-priced experiments and demand price parity. For some products it can be difficult to identify wholly comparable test markets, and even wholly comparable ones are susceptible to data corruption through extraneous actions and events. Finally, price-sensitive customers take longer to reach, and important test marketing information will be missing if management is unwilling to delay the launch of a new product until all the results are available for analysis. For these reasons, test marketing is often limited to low-priced consumer products of little technical complexity, but management should not forget that other forms of market research can and must be carried out quite independently of these field tests.

11.5.5   *Price and demand: future perspectives*

In a classic article, Kjaer-Hansen (1981) suggested that traditional demand curve theory would need to be revised:

> The heavy increase, absolute as well as relative, in the real income of the man in the street, and the influx of women into the labour market, have enabled consumers to satisfy new desires while at the same time intensifying the old. One effect of this has been that the demand has shifted from an increase in quantity to an improvement in quality. This development has resulted in a corresponding shift in the importance of the two primary parameters of marketing action, price and quality.
>
> If the present development continues, I think the young generation may live to see the classical price demand curve undergo a radical change. It will flatten out, or may perhaps be reversed, so that a rise in price results in an increase in demand. This latter extreme situation may arise if price, in increasingly affluent societies, comes to serve merely as an indicator of quality.
>
> Competitive conditions today make it more important for a firm to offer the product which best satisfies the wants and desires of the consumers

than the one which sells at the lowest possible price and, consequently, present and future pricing policy must necessarily be governed more by the relative than by the absolute height of prices.

It is no longer a question of determining what is the lowest possible price at which a product can be offered, but what price will give the best possible balance between the performance which consumers desire and the costs incurred by the business firms in supplying such a performance. Therefore, the result must be that price determination will come to be based on factors relating to demand rather than on factors relating to supply (p. 216).

He goes on to suggest that traditional pricing systems, based on product costs, will not be capable of satisfying these changed demand conditions, and notes that there is already a trend in the field of personal consumer goods towards 'retrograde costing'. This is simply a system in which a product's price is based entirely on estimates of what consumers are able and willing to pay for it. Costing is then made retrogressively – the firm makes an assessment of whether this is high enough to cover costs of purchasing, production, marketing and administration. These calculations of cost are thus not used directly for the purpose of setting selling prices, as in the traditional model, but for determining whether a particular product whose price was set solely by demand should be included in the product line or not. Kjaer-Hansen argues that this form of pricing is perfectly consistent with the changed conditions of demand in affluent First World countries, but calls for more facts and estimates regarding the individual categories and variations of costs than normal accounting systems provide, and in particular for the recognition and control of marketing costs, which his own researches have shown to represent an increasingly large percentage of total turnover.

11.5.6 The empirical evidence

A number of studies have been carried out to determine pricing objectives and pricing methods employed in practice, and a most useful recent review of their findings is presented in Dorward (1987).

In a major study of the pricing objectives of 728 British manufacturing firms, carried out in 1979, Shipley (1981) found that while most firms had more than one pricing goal, two-thirds specified a target profit or return on capital as their principal objective. The next most popular goals were 'prices fair to the firm and customers', 'price similarity with competitors', and 'target sales revenue'. Almost 50 per cent of the firms surveyed included one of these three non-profit-based goals in their set of pricing objectives, although only some 10 per cent specified any of them as a principal objective. These findings are consistent with those of Lanzillotti (1958), who published the results of a Brookings Institution study of twenty large US corporations and also found that profit, in the form of a target return on capital, was the most popular objective. Other frequently cited pricing objectives in the Brookings study were 'stable price and margin', 'target market share', and 'matching the competition'. Although target market share fared badly in Shipley's survey, it was one of the most popular objectives, along with profit, in Hague's (1971) comprehensive study of thirteen UK manufacturing firms.

The importance of profit as a pricing objective is not really surprising, given its prominence as an objective or constraint in most theories of the firm. However, as Dorward points out, this is *not* the same as profit *maximization*. Although nearly 50 per cent of Shipley's sample claimed to be motivated by profit maximization, only a third of that number were classified as 'true maximum profit motivated firms' in the sense of the profit objective being of overriding importance. Moreover, some 60 per cent of Shipley's sample had a long-term profit preference as compared with only a third of that percentage preferring short-term profits.

Dorward summarizes the results of one pre- and six post-war investigative studies of pricing *methods* employed in practice. The weight of evidence does not support an *explicitly* marginalist approach to costing and pricing, but an overwhelming majority of firms demonstrated an important demand orientation, best described as *modified full cost pricing*. Starting with a full cost price, their allocation of overheads and the size of the profit margin were ultimately demand-determined. The response to bad trading conditions was to write off part of the allocated overheads as losses, and in buoyant trading conditions they either reduced their discounts or increased the proportion of product variants carrying higher margins. Only 11 per cent of the firms surveyed had pure cost-based pricing policies (and, perhaps significantly, the bulk of this 11 per cent is contributed by the pre-war survey), leaving 89 per cent with demand-adjusted or demand-determined policies, weighted very heavily towards modified full cost as compared with a contribution margin type of pricing policy.

The two major British questionnaire surveys in recent years have been those of Skinner (1970) and Atkin and Skinner (1975), the latter being unusual in that the questionnaire was addressed to the marketing director rather than the managing director or chief accountant. They both support the findings of the interview studies, that full costing is predominant in the initial stage of the pricing process, and is then adjusted for market demand and competition to give the actual selling price. The former showed 70 per cent of firms using cost-plus pricing, with almost 70 per cent of that figure applying different percentage mark-ups between products, based predominantly on strength of competition and demand. In the latter survey, of those firms which determined price by cost-related methods, only 14 per cent appeared to stick rigidly to the cost-based price; 63 per cent used full cost pricing and 35 per cent direct or marginal costing, and in approximately 40 per cent of all cases, firms 'usually' or 'frequently' adjusted the cost-based price to accommodate non-cost factors. Furthermore, this pattern was said to be broadly consistent regardless of product type.

Interestingly, 70 per cent of Atkin and Skinner's respondents offered discounts on normal trade prices, with the proportion rising to 85 per cent for those firms publishing price lists. This led them to conclude that 'There is, therefore, some reason for believing that, in industrial selling (the basis of the survey), list prices often exist as a basis for discounting rather than as prices that customers in general are expected to pay' (p. 24). With such large proportions of firms using marginal costs for pricing, amending the cost-based price to take account of non-cost considerations, applying widely different margins between products, and engaging in regular discounting, this latter study provides strong evidence against the conventional full-cost theory of pricing. In general, respondents were heavily orientated towards demand factors, even when employing full-cost practices.

These two UK questionnaires support the hypothesis that implicit marginalism is the predominant business pricing behaviour. Further support is obtained from published research into pricing practices in the rest of Europe, the USA and Australia, which largely replicates the UK findings that the general pricing behaviour is implicitly marginalist, with rigid full-cost pricing being a minority practice. As managers do not, in general, have suitable information to make *explicit* marginalist pricing decisions, they practice an *implicit* form of marginalism, using direct standard costs as a low information cost surrogate for constant average variable cost, and allocating overheads and profit according to demand. Although such an approach is obviously far from ideal, it is difficult to offer management a practical alternative when faced with imperfect cost and demand information.

Let us conclude by quoting Tucker (1966):

> Pricing is at once an art as well as a science, combining internal cost and capital data, external market information, and the judgement of management regarding effects, both economic and strategic. Pricing is influenced by a host of factors, some objective as relating to internal information, the uncertain externals regarding market factors, and behaviour and types of competition. It is not difficult to understand, therefore, why management people are unable to describe their pricing policy in definite terms. Not that a rigid pricing formula is desirable; quite the reverse. Instead, pricing should be a continuous process of scrutiny, test of alternatives, and balanced decisions that mesh the variables of internal and external factors (p. 61).

References and further reading

Atkin, B., Skinner, R. C., *How British Industry Prices*, Industrial Marketing Research, 1975.

Cannon, T., *Basic Marketing: Principles and Practice*, Holt, Rinehart & Winston, 1986.

Chisnall, P. M., *Marketing Research: Analysis and Measurement*, McGraw-Hill, 1981.

Dean, J., *Managerial Economics*, Prentice-Hall, 1951.

Dorward, N., *The Pricing Decision: Economic Theory and Business Practice*, Harper & Row, 1987.

Edelman, F., 'Art and Science in Competitive Bidding', in Mulvihill, D. F., and Paranka, S. (eds), *Price Policies and Practices: a Source Book in Readings*, Wiley, 1967, pp. 261–85.

Enis, B. M., Cox, K. K., *Marketing Classics: a selection of influential articles*, Alyn & Bacon, 1988.

Foxall, G. R., *Strategic Marketing Management*, Croom Helm, 1981.

Green, P. E. 'Bayesian Decision Theory in pricing Strategy', in Mulvihill and Paranka *op cit*, pp. 213–30.

Hague, D. C., *Pricing in Business*, Allen & Unwin, 1971.

Herson, R. J. L., Hertz, R. S., 'Direct Costing in Pricing: A Critical Reappraisal', in Wilson, R. M. S. (ed), *Financial Dimensions of Marketing*, Macmillan, 1981, pp. 223–34.

Kjaer-Hansen, M., 'Marketing Costs and their Importance in Pricing', in Wilson, *op. cit.*, pp. 214–23.

Kotler, P., *Principles of Marketing*, Prentice-Hall, 1980.

Kotler, P., *Marketing Management: Analysis, Planning, Implementation and Control*, Prentice-Hall 1988.

Lanzillotti, R. F. (1958), 'Pricing objectives in large companies', *American Economic Review*, 1980, pp. 921–40.

Morris, D., *The Naked Ape: a Zoologist's Study of the Human Animal*, Jonathan Cape, 1967.

Nagle, T., 'Economic foundations for pricing', *Journal of Business*, 1984, 23–26.

Oliver, G., *Marketing Today*, Prentice-Hall, 1986.

Oxenfeldt, A. R., 'Multi-stage Approach to Pricing', *Harvard Business Review*, 1960, pp. 125–33.

Oxenfeldt, A. R., 'A Decision-Making Structure for Price Decisions', *Journal of Marketing*, 1973, pp. 48–53.

Oxenfeldt, A. R., *Pricing Strategies*, American Management Association, 1975.

Oxenfeldt, A. R., Miller, D., Schuchman, A., Winick, C., *Insights into Pricing from Operations Research and Behavioural Science*, Wadsworth, 1961.

Pride, W. M., Ferrell, O. C., *Marketing: Basic Concepts and Decisions*, Houghton Mifflin, 1985.

Shipley, D. D., 'Pricing objectives in British manufacturing industry', *Journal of Industrial Economics*, 1981, pp. 429–43.

Sizer, J., 'The accountant's contribution to selling price decisions', in Arnold, J., Carsberg, B., Scapens, R. (eds), *Topics in Management Accounting*, Philip Allan, 1980, pp. 148–77.

Skinner, R. C., 'The determination of selling prices', *Journal of Industrial Economics*, 1970, pp. 201–17.

Sonkodi, L., *Business and Prices*, Routledge, 1969.

Stanton, W. J., Futrell, C., *Fundamentals of Marketing*, McGraw-Hill, 1987.

Stoetzel, J., 'Le prix comme limite', in Reynaud, P. R. (ed), *La Psychologie Economique*, Bilans de la connaissance économique 4, Paris, 1954, pp. 184–8.

Taylor, B., Wills, G., *Pricing Strategy*, Staples, 1969.

Tucker, S. A., *Pricing for Higher Profit: Criteria, Methods, Applications*, McGraw-Hill, 1966.

Tull, D. S., Hawkins, D. I., *Marketing Research: Measurement and Method*, Collier-Macmillan, 1987.

Winkler, J., *Pricing for Results: How to wage and win the price war*, Pan, 1984.

Questions for Part Three

1   A group includes two divisions that trade with each other and with companies outside the group. Division 1 sells three products X, Y and Z. Its major customer for all products is division 2, but up to 20,000 kgs of product X can also be sold outside the group at a price of £32 per kg, though special packaging costs of £1 per kg are incurred in supplying such orders.

The capacity of division 1 is 150,000 hours per annum. All products are made on the same equipment. The processing times and variable costs for each product are:

Product	Processing time (hours per kg)	Variable cost* (£ per kg)
X	2.5	12
Y	3.0	25
Z	2.0	34.5

*Includes the cost of processing time.

The marketing policy of the division is to sell a minimum of 12,000 kgs per annum of each product. Its fixed overhead is £300,000 per annum.

Division 2 sells four products, L, M, N and P, to customers outside the group. Their selling prices, the usage of X, Y, Z in their production, and the other variable costs incurred in Division 2 are:

	Products (per tonne)*			
	L	M	N	P
Selling price	£31,000	£37,000	£24,000	£35,000
Usage of product:				
X (kgs)	220	400	—	—
Y (kgs)	400	—	250	150
Z (kgs)	—	300	200	450
Other variable cost	£4,680	£5,570	£3,305	£5,635

*1 tonne = 1,000 kgs

Division 2 can buy product X from outside the group at £26 per kg but it is of inferior quality and the division has to reduce its selling price by 5 per cent if it uses the outside material.

It can also buy up to 10 tonnes per annum of product Z at a cost of £38 per kg delivered.

Division 2's capacity is 100 tonnes of output. Its policy is to sell a minimum of 15 tonnes per annum per product. Its fixed overhead is £600,000 per annum.

The group's rules for fixing transfer prices between divisions are:

1   Where a product is sold outside the group, the average external price (less any special packaging costs) is to be used.
2   If the product is not sold outside the group, the transfer price per kg comprises the sum of

– the variable costs,
– the fixed cost that would apply if equal quantities (in kgs) of each product were sold,
– 5 per cent margin on the total of variable cost plus fixed cost.

You are required to state, with supporting evidence,

(a)   whether the transfer pricing rules make for goal congruence between the Divisions;
(b)   what arrangement of production, purchasing and selling of products achieves the most profitable outcome for

  (i)   the group as a whole,
  (ii)   Division 2.

(CIMA, May 1987)

2   Current cost accounting seeks to make adjustments to the profit and loss account as drafted for publication to shareholders.
   You are required to discuss the situations in which each of these adjustments might be applied to the purposes of management accounting.

(CIMA, May 1987, adjusted)

3   A group of companies has hitherto used historical costing in the performance evaluation of its investment centres.
   Whilst a few of those investment centres (class A) have replaced their fixed assets fairly regularly, the majority (class B) have, among their fixed assets, plant and equipment bought at a fairly even rate over the past 25 years. During that time their manufacturing technologies have changed very little, but these technologies are expected to change much more rapidly in the near future.
   The group now wishes to evaluate its investment centres on a current cost basis.
   You are required to prepare notes for a paper for the executive management committee to show

(a) the impact for performance evaluation of the differences between class A and class B investment centres that are likely to result from the change to a current cost basis in respect of
   (i) their depreciation charges,
   (ii) their relative standing as measured by their return on capital employed.
(b) what steps would be needed to revalue the plant and equipment.

(CIMA, May 1987)

4 A company has two divisions. The output of division X is product Xen. There is a market outside the company for product Xen, but this product is mainly used by division Y, which has first call on division X's output.

Division Y's output is product Yang, all of which is sold outside the company. For each unit of Yang, two units of Xen are used.

The maximum capacity per annum of the divisions is

X	130,000 units of Xen
Y	50,000 units of Yang

Each division maintains a stable level of stocks throughout the year.

The company has examined the results of four different scenarios shown below using for each the following bases of transfer pricing for product Xen:

Market price (M),
Absorbed standard cost (A),
Variable cost plus a lump sum of 80 per cent of division X's fixed cost (V).

The senarios are:

	Product Xen		Product Yang	
Scenario number	Market price (£ per unit)	Total demand (000 units)	Market price (£ per unit)	(Total demand (000 units)
1	60	100	200	40
2	50	70	180	30
3	70	130	180	30
4	70	130	230	30

Standard costs per unit:

Variable cost	£40	£24 (excluding 2 units of Xen)
Direct materials cost included above	£12	£8
Fixed cost	£10	£36
based on budgeted volume (units per annum)	100,000	40,000

The resulting profits are shown in the following table:

Transfer price		Scenario	Division X (000)	Division Y (£000)
(M)	Market price	1	1,000	800
		2	(300)	240
		3	2,900	1,860
		4	2,900	(960)
(A)	Absorbed	1	200	1,600
	standard cost	2	(300)	240
		3	900	3,860
		4	1,700	240
(V)	Variable cost	1	200	1,600
	+ 80% fixed cost	2	(100)	40
		3	700	4,060
		4	1,900	40

You are required

(a)   assuming that a major objective of setting a transfer price is to achieve goal congruence, to recommend which basis of transfer price should be used for product Xen, and justify your recommendation using the data in the profits table;

(b)   assuming that Division Y receives an overseas order for 20,000 units of Yang that will in no way influence its other clientele, to recommend, with supporting calculations, acceptance or refusal of the order under each of the following two scenarios:

Scenario 2   Price per unit (ex factory) £110 Transfer price basis (A)
Scenario 3   Price per unit (ex factory) £130 Transfer price basis (M)

   (i)   as manager of division Y,
   (ii)   as managing director of the company;

(c)   assuming that no market price for product Xen existed, to

   (i)   calculate a transfer price for product Xen, explaining the reasoning behind the calculation,
   (ii)   calculate what profits would result from using that transfer price under scenario 1 (using the figures in respect of product Yang only).

(CIMA, May 1987)

5   A company has developed a new product which it is about to launch on its local market.

   The new product will be in competition with a large number of products from some 25 to 30 companies and particularly from one product selling at £65 per unit in quantities of 6,000 per month which represents some

30 per cent of the potential market for this new product. The company manufactures and sells other products, none of whose local market share is less than 5 per cent or more than 35 per cent. Prices in this local market have been fairly steady for some years.

The new product involves an advanced technology and is demonstrably better in performance and quality than its major competitor. The company believes that it has at least 12 to 18 months before competitors could achieve a comparable quality of product

The company estimates that its production costs for the new product will be:

Direct materials	£12 per unit*
Direct labour	£28 per unit*

For each of its three production departments, the following data apply:

(1)	(2)	(3)	(4)	(5)	(6)
				Fixed and/or allocated	*Department time on*
		Full cost overhead	*Normal monthly volume on which*	*overhead*	*new*
Production department	*Unit of m'ment*	*rate*	*(3) is based*	*in (3)*	*product**
X	Machine hours	£2.40	12,500	£5,000	2
Y	Direct labour hours	£1.80	15,000	£6,000	1.5
Z	Direct labour hours	£0.80	25,000	£7,500	3

* All these estimates are subject to an error of ± 10%

Selling and administration expenses for the new product are expected to be £20,000 per month and will be virtually unaffected by the price or sales level achieved by this new product.

The company generally sets its selling prices by adding a mark-up on factory cost of between 30 per cent and 45 per cent, mostly towards the upper end.

You are required to

(a) advise, with brief explanations, what type of pricing strategy the company should adopt for its new product;
(b) recommend a selling price for the new product, with supporting figures, explaining briefly the reasons for your recommendation.

(CIMA specimen questions)

6   As management accountant to a group of companies manufacturing footwear, you have been asked to consider the following two subjects that are to be discussed at the next group pricing committee meeting.

(a)   the possibility of differential pricing for different sizes of shoes;

(b)   the levels of prices at which contracts with a large multiple retailer for 'own label' shoes might be negotiated.

You are required to describe *briefly* the major topics under each of the above headings that you would include in the agenda for discussion.

(CIMA, November 1987)

7   Fred Roda commenced business on January 1985 selling a limited range of home computers with £40,000 from his own resources plus a loan of £20,000, both of which were paid into a current account at the bank. On that day he purchased a 10-year lease of shop premises for £30,000 and 200 computers for £20,000. A further 100 computers were purchased on 1 July 1985 for £90,000. All were paid on the day.

250 of the machines were sold on a FIFO basis for £75,000, expenses of £2,000 were paid and drawings of £8,000 were made all at an even rate throughout the year. 10 per cent interest on the loan is due but not paid at 31 December 1985. 10 per cent on the loan is due but not paid at 31 December 1985. The replacement prices of the computers at 31 December 1985 are quoted at £80 per machine and that of the shop is estimated at £35,000.

Retail price index numbers are:

1 January 1985   100
1 July 1985   103
31 December 1985 105

Required

(a)   Prepare Trading and Profit and Loss Accounts for the year to 31 December 1985 together with a Balance Sheet at that date using:
(i)   conventional historic cost accounting,
(ii)   current purchasing power (price level) accounting.

(b)   Discuss the relative usefulness and limitations of the results shown by the financial statements in (a).

(c)   Briefly explain how it is possible for a company to gain or lose on monetary items and loans during periods of inflation.

8   A group has two companies:

K Ltd, which is operating at just above 50 per cent capacity,
L Ltd, which is operating at full capacity (7,000 production hours).

L Ltd produces two products, X and Y using the same labour force for each product. For the next year its budgeted capacity involves a commitment to the sale of 3,000 kgs of Y, the remainder of its capacity being used on X.

Direct costs of these two products are:

		X		Y
		(£ per kg)		(£ per kg)
Direct materials		18		14
Direct wages		15 (1 production hour)		10 ($\frac{2}{3}$ production hour)

The company's overhead is £126,000 per annum relating to X and Y in proportion to their direct wages. At full capacity, £70,000 of this overhead is variable. L Ltd prices its products with a 60 per cent mark-up on its total costs.

For the coming year, K Ltd wishes to buy from L Ltd 2,000 kgs of product X, which it proposes to adapt and sell, as product Z, for £100 per kg. The direct costs of adaptation are £15 per kg. K Ltd's total fixed costs will not change, but variable overhead of £2 per kg will be incurred.

You are required to recommend, as group management accountant,

(a)   at what range of transfer prices, if at all, 2,000 kgs of product X should be sold to K Ltd;
(b)   what other points should be borne in mind when making any recommendations about transfer prices in the above circumstances.

(CIMA, May 1989)

9   PT Ltd supplies an imported consumable component to distributors who, in turn, sell it to industrial users.

PT Ltd's selling prices range from £0.40 to around £5.00 per 100, according to size. There is a range of about 600 items, available in two materials. The cost of the component from PT Ltd.'s suppliers, and similarly the selling price to its customers, is lower as the quantity bought increases.

Market research has shown that an important factor in the ability to sell this component is its availability for quick delivery (especially ex stock). This is particularly so for small orders (say, under 500) but much less so for large quantities, where prices are keen and crucial to the purchase from any supplier.

PT Ltd has made a speciality of holding very large stocks and has always been in a strong position to give quick delivery. However, it charges about one and a half times the prices of its competitors on the grounds that customers for small quantities (average price £0.60 per 100) will be prepared to pay for quick delivery. In consequence, PT Ltd is a peripheral supplier, used mainly for small quantities when quick delivery is crucial. It currently holds about 3 per cent to 5 per cent of the market.

PT Ltd buys from two major sources overseas. Supplier A is extremely cheap, and is PT Ltd's major supplier. However, A will sell to almost any customer, including PT Ltd's competitors, though such customers will need to place a large enough order to justify importing.

Supplier B, though more expensive than A, holds very large stocks and can generally offer quicker delivery. Until two years ago it was PT Ltd's main supplier, but it has recently established a UK company, B(UK) Ltd, through which all sales to the UK will be placed.

PT Ltd is about to review its selling prices. It is concerned that B(UK) Ltd will, by holding large stocks in the UK, be able to offer distributors quick delivery at selling prices below those of PT Ltd, yet still make a good margin. There is still some doubt as to how much B(UK) Ltd will wish to invest in stock.

At present PT Ltd sets its selling prices at a mark-up of 150 per cent to 220 per cent on its costs from A. This mark-up yields a contribution roughly equal to PT Ltd's total overheads, while other products not connected with the component provide a further contribution that makes PT Ltd a profitable company.

You are required to

(a) List *three* major options available to PT Ltd regarding its selling prices if it is to increase its profit from the sales of the component. In respect of *each* option, explain what you consider would be its major effects on PT Ltd's sales, costs and profit.

(b) Recommend the pricing option that you consider should be adopted, giving briefly the main reasons for your choice.

(CIMA, November 1989)

10   AB Ltd produces a special chemical whose quality is regarded in the market as superior to that of the competition. It has two smaller, but important competitors, CD and EF, who are roughly equal in size to each other. These three companies account for 85 per cent to 90 per cent of the market, with the remainder being supplied by five smaller companies.

For each year, AB Ltd is usually the first to announce its selling price, on which contracts with customers for the year are signed. CD, EF and the other competitors then announce their prices.

The recent history of prices (after adjusting for inflation) and sales volume for this market, and the projections for 1989 based on four possible price scenarios, are as follows:

	Price				Sales volume		
	AB Ltd	CD	EF	Total market	AB Ltd	CD	EF
Year to	(£)	(£)	(£)	(000)	(000)	(000)	(000)
30 September,	per kg	per kg	per kg	tonnes	tonnes	tonnes	tonnes
1985	0.75	0.75	0.75	2.9	1.1	0.8	0.8
1986	0.75	0.75	0.75	3.2	1.1	0.75	0.7
1987	0.75	0.75	0.75	3.7	1.8	0.75	0.8
1988	0.90	0.75	0.75	3.9	1.5	1.0	1.0
Projections for 1989							
Price scenario							
1	0.90	0.90	0.90	3.7	1.8	0.75	0.75
2	0.90	0.90	0.75	3.9	1.5	0.6	1.4
3	0.90	0.75	0.75	4.0	1.3	1.2	1.1
4	0.75	0.75	0.75	4.1	1.8	1.0	0.9

AB Ltd estimates that its costs per kg for this chemical are:

Volume (000 tonnes)	1.3	1.5	1.8
	(£ per kg)	(£ per kg)	(£ per kg)
Direct materials cost and wages	0.273	0.273	0.273
Departmental costs:			
Directly variable with output	0.027	0.027	0.027
Depreciation	0.245	0.212	0.177
General works overhead			
(apportioned at $\frac{1}{3}$ direct costs)	0.091	0.091	0.091
Manufacturing cost	0.636	0.603	0.568
Other costs (apportioned at			
20 per cent of manufacturing cost)	0.127	0.121	0.114
Total cost	0.763	0.724	0.682

AB Ltd maintains its stocks at the same level from year to year.

For planning purposes, AB Ltd assumes CD's and EF's costs per kg to be equal to its own, though in practice it believes them to be somewhat higher.

AB Ltd also believes that there is a 0.8 probability that CD and EF will adopt a pricing policy that yields the largest profit to those companies.

You are required, in respect of 1989 to

(a) Calculate which of the four scenarios will yield the highest profit possible for

    (i)   CD
    (ii)   EF

(b) recommend, with supporting calculations, whether AB Ltd should charge £0.75 or £0.90 per kg if its objectives are to maximize its profit;

(c) comment on the other considerations that AB Ltd will need to take into account when making its eventual decision as to the price that it should charge.

(CIMA, May 1989)

Part Four   Performance Feedback

Successful decisions should lead to successful performance. Monitoring performance is therefore important to the decision-making process. It can also, as we shall see, affect the process it is measuring. We begin by considering performance measurement within the organization, and then go on to consider external performance measures.

12 Internal performance measurement

12.1 Decentralization

In any organizational structure, some authority will be delegated to lower-level management. In this sense therefore almost every firm could be described as 'decentralized'. However, the term is usually reserved for those firms which give individual managers responsibility for *profit*, and not just costs or revenues. Decentralization will normally be based on geographical location, or a specific business activity, such as the production and sale of a particular product or group of related products. A number of advantages are claimed for this approach:

1 *More informed decision making*. The manager who is directly involved in the day-to-day running of the business is able to apply his first-hand knowledge to the decision (which also has behaviourial implications). Furthermore, experience of decision making at a decentralized level gives good career training to management.
2 *Speed of decision making*. Decisions can be made more rapidly when delegated to the local level. In the modern business environment, this can give a competitive edge to the firm.
3 *Specialization*. If a decentralized management is left to concentrate on the operating decisions, top management has more time to devote to the broader policy and strategic issues facing the organization as a whole.

In highly decentralized organizations, the operating units (often called divisions) are more or less autonomous, and it is the degree of autonomy enjoyed by divisional managers that creates the four basic problems associated with this form of structure:

(a) Obtaining a sufficient number of competent divisional managers to operate the system successfully.
(b) Selecting an appropriate system of performance measurement.

(c) Ensuring that divisional management will operate in a way which is consistent with the goals of the organization as a whole.

(d) Transfer pricing (see chapter 10).

A discussion of the first of these lies beyond the scope of this book, and we shall direct our attention to the second and third of the problems, which are clearly interrelated: an inappropriate performance measure can motivate managers to act in a dysfunctional and suboptimal manner, and *vice versa*. The reader should be aware that evaluating the performance of a division is *not* the same thing as evaluating the performance of its manager. For example, a highly efficient and effective manager could be put into an ailing division to improve its performance, and might succeed in increasing its profitability by, say, 200 per cent; this may well reflect a brilliant effort on the part of the *manager*, but if the improved profitability still falls below a given standard level, the performance of the *division* could still be unacceptable.

There are two commonly used measures of divisional performance: return on investment (ROI) and residual income (RI), with the former enjoying much greater currency. We shall consider each in turn.

12.2   Return on investment

This measure expresses divisional profit as a percentage of the firm's investment in the division, and is the equivalent at local level of the global 'return on capital employed' measure used in the external interpretation of accounts (see chapter 13):

$$\text{ROI} = \frac{\text{Divisional profit}}{\text{Divisional investment}}$$

It recognizes that a critical test of efficiency is not the absolute size of a division's net income, but rather the relation between that income and the assets employed in its generation – for example, a profit of £100,000 on an investment of £500,000 represents a more efficient use of capital than a profit of £200,000 on a £5m investment, *ceteris paribus*. Capital always has alternative uses, and the firm must determine whether the returns being earned on the capital invested in a particular division exceed its opportunity cost (i.e. the returns which could be obtained from an alternative use of the capital). ROI represents a logical corollary to investment appraisal: as Kaplan and Atkinson (1989) have pointed out, most companies have elaborate systems for authorizing capital expenditures, and without some form of measurement of the *ex post* returns on the capital, there is little incentive for accurate estimation of the further cash flows during the capital budgeting process. Furthermore, it is argued that use of the ROI measure focuses management's attention on the control of costly items of working capital in the decentralized unit, such as stocks and debtors, whose financial impact is usually felt at central, rather than divisional, level.

12.2.1 Breakdown of ROI

For analysis purposes, as with return on capital employed, the basic formula is often broken down into the product of return on sales and investment turnover:

$$\text{ROI} = \frac{\text{Divisional profit}}{\text{Divisional investment}} = \frac{\text{Divisional profit}}{\text{Divisional sales}} \times \frac{\text{Divisional sales}}{\text{Divisional investment}}$$

It can clearly be seen that this 'expanded' version will produce the same ROI, because 'divisional sales' cancels out as both the denominator in the first factor and the numerator in the second, but the two following numerical examples will illustrate the significance of the breakdown for analysis and decision purposes.

Example 1

A retailer of electrical and electronic equipment has franchises in several high-street department stores, as well as operating its own out-of-town discount warehouses. The same ROI of 20 per cent is earned on both businesses, but in quite different ways:

	Department stores	*Discount warehouses*
Divisional profit	£200k	£320k
Divisional investment	£1m	£1.6m
Divisional sales	£2m	£4.8m

Department stores

$$\text{Overall ROI} = \frac{\text{Divisional profit}}{\text{Divisional investment}} = \frac{£200k}{£1m} = 20\%$$

$$\text{Expanded ROI} = \frac{\text{Divisional profit}}{\text{Divisional sales}} \times \frac{\text{Divisional sales}}{\text{Divisional investment}}$$

$$= \frac{£200k}{£2m} \times \frac{£2m}{£1m} = 10\% \times 2 = 20\%$$

Discount warehouses

$$\text{Overall ROI} = \frac{\text{Divisional profit}}{\text{Divisional investment}} = \frac{£320k}{£1.6m} = 20\%$$

$$\text{Expanded ROI} = \frac{\text{Divisional profit}}{\text{Divisional sales}} \times \frac{\text{Divisional sales}}{\text{Divisional investment}}$$

$$= \frac{£320k}{£4.8m} \times \frac{£4.8m}{£1.6m} = 6.67\% \times 3 = 20\%$$

The store franchises earn a higher profit per £ of sales, but only turn over capital twice, whereas the lower prices charged by the discount warehouses lead to a higher sales volume for every £ invested, boosting the capital turnover to 3.

Example 2

In the current period, the investment in a particular division of CIMA Ltd is £1m, and it generates net income of £100,000 on sales of £500,000.

$$\text{Current ROI} = \frac{\text{Divisional profit}}{\text{Divisional investment}} = \frac{£100k}{£1m} = 10\%$$

$$\text{Current expanded ROI} = \frac{\text{Divisional profit}}{\text{Divisional sales}} \times \frac{\text{Divisional sales}}{\text{Divisional investment}}$$

$$= \frac{£100k}{£500k} \times \frac{£500k}{£1m} = 20\% \times 0.5 = 10\%$$

Let us say that divisional management reports an increase in ROI in the following period to 12.5 per cent. How are we to interpret this? Would we assume that any increase in ROI is a cause for unqualified congratulation? Further analysis reveals that the 12.5 per cent is derived from a turnover of £575,000, which generated profits of £150,000 on an investment of £1.2m:

$$\text{Basic ROI} = \frac{£150k}{£1.2m} = 12.5\%$$

$$\text{Expanded ROI} = \frac{£150k}{£575k} \times \frac{£575k}{£1.2m} = 26.1\% \times 0.479 = 12.5\%$$

The breakdown reveals a *deterioration* in investment turnover (from 0.5 to 0.479) which happened to be more than offset by a dramatic increase in profitability (from 20 per cent to 26.1 per cent), thus producing an increased ROI. Further investigation reveals that there is no cause for either congratulation or complacency: the decrease in investment turnover is due to an unwelcome and expensive build-up of finished goods stocks, caused by excessive production levels in the period; and the steep rise in profitability was merely the result of using an absorption costing system which had conspired to defer much of the period's fixed manufacturing costs in the vastly increased closing stocks, thus improving the level of profitability on those goods actually sold in the period.

The vagaries of alternative accounting systems notwithstanding, the breakdown of ROI provides top management with two additional measurement criteria by which the performance of a division can be evaluated. Further, at the operational level, by showing the different factors which influence ROI, it can give clues to the kind of strategies that may be adopted by divisional management to improve performance. Let us expand this last point by making several generalizations. ROI will be increased by any of the following actions taken individually, all other factors held constant:

(a) *An increase in sales price (for a given volume) or volume (at a given price)*
(b) *A reduction in operating costs (fixed or variable).*
(c) *A reduction in divisional investment.*

(a) and (b) will increase the level of profitability per £ invested; and (c) will increase the investment turnover. Obviously, any combination of these would also give an increased ROI, as would a combination which involved opposite movements but contained sufficient compensatory factors to more than offset the adverse trend, as we saw in the second example.

These two examples also serve to emphasize an extremely important general principle, which we shall return to in the next chapter: ratios, such as ROI and its constituent parts mean nothing *by themselves* when simply viewed in isolation; they only take on signficance when used for *comparative* purposes – when compared to a company standard, a trend, an industrial average or a competitor. When used comparatively, the reasons for any change in ratios need to be investigated thoroughly before any sensible management conclusions regarding performance can be drawn from them, and, even then, both ROI and RI are best used in conjunction with other evaluation techniques, as will emerge *passim*.

12.2.2   *ROI and dysfunctional behaviour*

We noted at the beginning of this chapter that selection of an inappropriate performance measure can lead managers to act in a manner that is inconsistent with the goals of the organization as a whole. In chapter 5, we saw that, *ceteris paribus*, the firm should accept *all* proposed investments which show an expected return in excess of the cost of capital (i.e. which would give rise to a positive NPV at this rate of return), and that the use of a *ratio* (in the case of capital budgeting, IRR) is unreliable for ranking alternative investments. It follows therefore that appraisal of divisional performance on the basis of ROI alone could give rise to decisions which are dysfunctional. This point is easily demonstrated when one considers that ROI represents an *average* return on divisional investment. An average will be *reduced* by adding individual investments that offer a return *lower* than the existing average, and *increased* by the divestment of similar *existing* individual investments. Obviously, divisional management would be motivated to reject (or never bring forward for consideration) investments of the former type, despite the fact that their acceptance might actually *increase* the firm's economic wealth; and it would tend to adopt the latter policy of divestment, despite its potential for making the firm worse off as a result. The problem centres on the firm's cost of capital, as the following simple examples illustrate:

Example 3
A division currently earns a profit of £20,000 on an investment of £100,000, giving an ROI of 20 per cent (£20k/£100k). The firm's cost of capital for investments of this type is 10 per cent. An investment opportunity appears that offers a profit of £3,000 on an outlay of £20,000, a return of 15 per cent. The return is clearly well in excess of the cost of capital, but its acceptance will reduce the division's ROI:

$$\text{ROI} = \frac{£20k + £3k}{£100k + £20k} = \frac{£23k}{£120k} = 19.1\%$$

If divisional management is judged solely on the basis of ROI, it would be inclined to reject this proposed investment, not wishing to see a decline in its performance measure, notwithstanding the fact that the firm's economic wealth would actually increase by £1000 (£3k − [10% × £20k]) as a result of its acceptance (and, indeed, we could say that there is an opportunity cost to this firm of £1,000 in rejecting it).

Example 4

Let us assume that, among the investments of the same division, there is an asset which earns £4,200 on its carrying cost of £30,000. Even though this represents a return of 14 per cent, which again is well in excess of the relevant cost of capital of 10 per cent, divisional management would be motivated to divest itself of the asset, because it is able to significantly increase its ROI by so doing:

$$\text{ROI} = \frac{£20k - £4.2k}{£100k - £30k} = \frac{£15.8k}{£70k} = 22.5\% \text{ (as compared with the earlier 20\%)}$$

Again, we can see that the firm would be £1,200 worse off (£4.2k − [10% × £30k]) by disposing of this asset, despite the increase in divisional ROI that would result from the move. Indeed, the *reductio ad absurdum* of this divestment policy is that the divisional investment base is ultimately reduced to the one asset that generates the highest individual ROI.

A similar problem is seen when the performance of two divisions is compared by means of ROI, as example 5 demonstrates.

Example 5

A company with 2 divisions, A and B, has a cost of capital of 10 per cent:

	Division A	*Division B*
Profit	£21k	£40k
Investment	£70k	£200k
ROI	30%	20%

Division A appears to be more profitable, with a 30 per cent ROI as compared with the 20 per cent of B. However, the incremental investment of £130,000 in B (£200k − A's £70k) generates incremental profits of £19,000 (B's £40k − A's £21k). The incremental ROI is therefore £19k/£130k = 14.6 per cent, well above the 10 per cent cost of capital of the firm. Thus division B is actually more profitable, after deducting capital costs, than division A, and contributes more to the firm's economic wealth:

	Division A	*Division B*	*Difference*
Profit	£ 21k	£ 40k	£ 19k
Capital cost	(7k) [10% × £70k]	(20k) [10% × £200k]	(13k)
Net increase	£14k	£20k	£6k

As the last three examples illustrated, concentrating on maximizing a ratio can distract attention from the importance of increasing the firm's wealth in *absolute* terms. In fact, the objective of maximizing ROI will be consistent with profit maximization only when investment in the division is a fixed constraint; obviously, in that case, for any given denominator in the ROI calculation, the maximization of the ratio will involve maximizing the profit numerator. If investment were centrally determined and controlled, and fixed over the short term, ROI maximization must by definition coincide with profit max-imization – but the ROI becomes redundant. In the real world, the working capital element in divisional investment makes it highly unlikely that such investment could be fixed even over a short control period.

The more perceptive reader will not have failed to recognize that the use of a cost of capital in the secondary calculations performed in examples 3–5 effectively turned ROI into RI, the alternative performance measure to which we now turn.

12.3   Residual income

We can define residual income as the net income produced by a division in excess of an imputed 'capital charge' made for the use of the assets invested in it. The 'capital charge' is calculated by applying a required (or target) rate of return to the division's investment base. Theoretically, rate of return should be the division's cost of capital; in most cases, however, it is a cut-off rate based on the firm's objectives and strategies, and will be somewhat higher than the divisional cost of capital, for reasons which will later become apparent. However, there are two important points to note here: it must be *at least* equal to the true cost of capital, or the real earnings of the firm could decline and investors would move their capital elsewhere; and any target rate in excess of the true cost of capital runs a risk (however small) of dysfunctional decision making, in that potentially profitable projects – whose return is actually in excess of the cost of capital and thus their acceptance would increase the economic wealth of the firm – could be rejected if the cut-off rate is set *above* this rate.

Nevertheless, the RI approach eliminates the very considerable potential for dysfunctional actions asssociated with the use of a ratio in ROI, as we saw in examples 3–5. By focusing attention on the absolute contribution made by a division to the financial well-being of the firm it produces goal congruence between divisional objectives and evaluation, and actions that would max-imize the economic wealth of the firm. Obviously, a higher residual value would always be preferred to a lower one, and the anomalous behaviour exhibited by ROI – where an increase in ROI can actually make the firm worse off – disappears.

Referring back once more to chapter 5, RI can be viewed as analogous to

NPV, whereas ROI is similar to IRR: the terms analogous and similar as used as the book values on which RI and ROI are usually based are incompatible with the DCF measures used in NPV and IRR. However, in the same way that maximizing IRR is considered to be inferior to maximizing NPV, divisional performance evaluation based on ROI is generally inferior to that using RI. Furthermore, as we saw in chapter 7 to be the case with NPV, the RI measure gives greater flexibility to management than its alternative, as different rates of return can be applied to investments which exhibit different levels of risk. Obviously, not only may the cost of capital for divisions in different areas of activity differ, but assets within the same division may also be in different risk classes – to use Kaplan and Atkinson's (1989) example, contrast the risk of cash or debtors with that of long-lived, highly specialized fixed assets. Evaluation by means of RI allows management to accommodate difficult risk-adjusted capital costs in the model in a way that ROI cannot do.

However, precisely because it does measure the absolute increase in a firm's economic wealth, which is unaffected by the actual size of the particular division under consideration, there is an element in which RI can be a less convenient performance yardstick for management than ROI. After all, a large division will probably find it easier to earn a given level of residual income than a small division, *ceteris paribus*. Example 6 illustrates this point.

Example 6
A company has two divisions, A and B, with investments of £500,000 and £2.5m respectively. Division A is highly profitable, generating net income of £200,000 – representing an ROI of 40 per cent – and RI, after the firm's specific capital charge of 10 per cent, of £150,000 (£200k − [10% × £500k]). In order to provide the *same* RI, division B needs merely to produce £400,000 of net income (£150k RI + [10% × £2.5m]), which represents an ROI of only 16 per cent as compared with the 40 per cent of division A.

In order to make valid comparisons between divisions of different sizes, but wishing to eschew the type of problems associated with ratios that we have pointed out above, firms using RI would tend to set *target* levels of residual income for divisional management. The targets will reflect the different investment structure of each division, and performance will be judged on the extent to which the division exceeds or falls short of these budgeted levels.

Interestingly, as Kaplan and Atkinson (1989) have pointed out, despite the fact that senior executives' bonus plans are frequently based on an ROI-type measure (the bonus 'pool' is defined as a percentage of net income in excess of a prespecified rate of return on invested capital), RI seems to be much less popular than ROI, despite its obvious attractions. Although a number of firms supplement their ROI measure with RI, very few appear to rely on it entirely to evaluate their divisional performance. Several reasons have been suggested for its relative lack of popularity:

1 The potential for dysfunctional behaviour associated with ROI does not pose a real problem in practice.
2 Most companies wish to see consistency between internal and external accounting numbers, and this is impossible with RI: the aggregate of the

divisions' residual incomes will always be considerably lower than the profit reported in the published financial statements.

3   ROI is extensively used as a performance yardstick by external analysts; this prompts top management to motivate divisional managers to maximize that particular ratio.

4   A percentage measure of profit such as ROI is found by management to be more compatible and comparable with other financial measures, such as external/internal rates and the rate of inflation.

5   Top management is unwilling or unable to supply an (accurate) cost of capital, especially in circumstances in which explicit calculations regarding risk adjustments for different divisions or classes of assets must be made.

Having discussed the distinguishing features of ROI and RI, together with their relative merits and weaknesses, we must now turn to a consideration of the problems associated with *both* measures of performance: what items should be included (and which excluded) in the calculation of divisional profit and the divisional investment base; and how the latter should be measured.

12.4   Divisional profit

At the beginning of this chapter, we referred to the dichotomy between the evaluation of divisional performance and that of the manager in charge of the division. We return to that dichotomy when we seek a satisfactory definition of divisional income. Although there would be general agreement on what should be *excluded* from it under all circumstances – corporation tax, for example, which not only reflects regulations outside the control of the firm as a whole, but will also be a function of the performance of *all* operating divisions within the firm; and interest on long-term corporate debt – there is disagreement as to what should be *included*.

If the performance of the *manager* is being assessed, then it would seem reasonable to base that assessment only on costs and revenues that are controllable by him. Thus, apart from those service costs that are clearly identifiable with the activities of an individual division, the expenses of the central head office should *not* be included, even if the absence of an administrative centre would cause additional expenses in the division. The vast majority of central expenses are uncontrollable by divisional management, and their joint nature makes any allocation arbitrary and unfair. However, if the performance of the *division* is being evaluated, then it is perfectly reasonable to allocate all the operating expenses of the head office, together with the cost of say short-term financing undertaken by it, although the usual *caveats* regarding the decision value of such indirect costs should be observed by top management. The measurement of depreciation in both cases calls for a consideration of asset values, which is treated in the next section.

12.5   Divisional investment

12.5.1   *The contribution of the investment base*

We must consider the different elements which go to make up a division's investment separately from the alternative bases on which they may be measured. In considering the former, however, we must once again draw the distinction between measuring the performance of a division and that of its manager. If the purpose is to evaluate the *manager's* performance, then we should include in the investment base only those assets which are directly traceable to the division and controllable by the manager. Assets which represent the investment in corporate headquarters, as well as any divisional assets which are controlled centrally by head office, should be excluded from this calculation.

The fixed assets and stocks of a division are obvious candidates for inclusion, although there could be some dispute over non-productive assets such as vacant land or construction in progress. Similarly, when central management directives force the local management to carry extra stocks or production capacity, there is an argument for excluding the excess amounts.

The other elements of working capital – debtors, cash and creditors – can present problems. Although head office might control the day-to-day maintenance of division's sales ledgers, to allow a greater level of efficiency in invoicing and cash collection, if the individual manager sets the sales terms and credit policy for his division, then debtors should be included in the investment base. Invariably, the total cash requirements of all divisions acting as independent units will exceed those of the organization taken as a single entity. In view of the considerable operating economies that can be achieved thereby, many decentralized organizations choose to control their cash centrally. While the theoretical approach to allocating cash under such circumstances is simply to determine the incremental amount needed to support each individual division as part of the firm as a whole, it is far from clear how this calculation could be performed satisfactorily in practice, and any alternative basis of allocation – such as relative levels of sales – would be open to objection on the part of divisional management. The simplest solution is to disregard all but those cash balances actually held and managed within the division itself. If the divisional manager controls the payments for stock purchases and supplies (including services), he should be encouraged to maximize the use of short-term credit by being allowed to deduct such creditors from his asset base. The treatment will have the effect of increasing both ROI and RI for the division, as example 7 illustrates.

Example 7
Division A has the following financial data:

	Assets employed in division	£15m
	Current liabilities of division	£5m
	Divisional profit	£2.5m
	Capital charge	12%

	Performance measures excluding CLs	*Performance measures including CLs*	*% change*
Investment in division	£15m	£15m	
Current liabilities	–	(5m)	
Net investment in division (1)	£15m	£10m	
Divisional profit (2)	£2.5m	£2.5m	
Capital charge @ 12%	(1.8m)	(1.2m)	
RI	£0.7m	£1.3m	+86
ROI (2 ÷ 1)	16.7%	25%	+50

Obviously, certain constraints must be placed upon the manager to ensure that he concentrates on seeking out the most favourable credit terms from suppliers rather than jeopardizing the organization's credit rating by simply withholding payments due under the normal terms of trade. This could be achieved by restricting the deductibility of trade creditors to the number of days' purchases represented by the supplier's credit terms, which would not only remove any incentive to unilaterally extend them, but would also (from the individual manager's viewpoint) draw the unwelcome attention of top management to undesirable local activities.

The alternative to an asset-based definition of divisional investment would be the 'equity basis', which attempts to measure the shareholders 'equity' in the division (total assets less specific liabilities). Although this might be an appropriate definition for evaluating the operating and financial management of an *independent* firm, it has little to commend itself in the case of divisionalized activities. In a decentralized firm, the divisional manager is concerned with the management of *assets*, and not with the long-term sources of finance for those assets, which will normally result from a head office policy decision. Horngren and Foster (1987) demonstrate how the use of an equity basis can distort a comparative performance assessment of two otherwise comparable divisions, and we have adapted this illustration in example 8.

Example 8
A company has two operating divisions: X, which was set up on a 50:50 debt:equity basis; and Y, which was financed entirely by equity.

	1	2	3	4	5	6	7
	Total assets less current liabilities (£)	Longer-term debt (£)	Shareholders' equity (1–2) (£)	Divisional profit before interest (£)	10% debtinterest (£)	Divisional profit after interest (4–5) (£)	ROI(6 ÷ 3) (%)
Div X	1m	500k	500k	200k	50k	150k	30
Div Y	1m	–	1m	200k	–	200k	20

* Debt/tax shield has been excluded for the sake of simplicity.

We see in these figures the effects of financial leverage, or 'trading on the equity' in a result not dissimilar to that obtained in example 7. The 30 per cent ROI fails to distinguish between the operating and financing functions of management. Division X has benefited from a head office decision to trade-off a fixed 10 per cent cost to use £500,000 worth of assets with a (current) return on those assets of 20 per cent (£200k total return before interest ÷ £1m total assets less current liabilities). This decision was quite independent of the operating performance of the divisional manager, which should be judged for comparative purposes on the profit *before* financing costs, and on assets which do *not* include the effect of different form of finance.

It will readily be appreciated that an evaluation based exclusively on assets controllable by the divisional manager will overstate the actual profitability of the division itself. A division could not operate without the services represented by the investment in head office assets. A comparable *independent* firm would incur considerable additional running expenses and capital outlay in order to provide the same level of operational capability and administrative back-up enjoyed by the division. For this reason, top management would expand the definition of 'investment base' where the division rather than the manager was being assessed, and an attempt would be made to allocate to individual divisions the perceived value of their investment in head office assets. Obviously, such allocations must by their nature be arbitrary, and we would reiterate our earlier remarks concerning their decision value for top management.

Nevertheless, that inclusion in the division's investment base in some suitable form within the performance report, can serve as a useful reminder to local management that the aggregaqte return from individual divisions must cover the cost of the investment in head office assets. However, this must not lead to the arbitrary raising of the so-called 'hurdle rate' for divisions, which could result in an undesirable opportunity cost through the rejection of profitable assets that offer only a marginal return over the true cost of capital. If a sufficient number of divisions are able to offer a positive return at the true cost of capital, the cost of this investment in head office or centrally administered assets should be adequately covered.

Exhibit 12.1 shows an evaluation report which reflects, however imperfectly, the differences that we have referred to in this chapter between the performance of the division and that of its manager, by highlighting those costs and assets which are controllable at divisional level and those that must be covered at overall group level.

Exhibit 12.1: Performance report for managerial and divisional calculation

	(£000s)
Divisional sales	800
Variable costs	(300)
Contribution margin	500
Controllable fixed costs	(100)
Controllable profit	400
Non-controllable costs	(150)
Divisional profit	250
Current assets less current liabilities	380
Controllable fixed assets	470
Controllable investment base	850
Non-controllable net assets	130
Total divisional investment	980
ROI on controllable investment base (400 ÷ 850)	47.1%
RI on controllable investment base @ 10% capital charge (400 − [10% × 850])	315
ROI on total divisional investment (250 ÷ 980)	25.5%
RI on total divisional investment @ 10% capital charge (250 − [10% × 980])	152

12.5.2 The problem of intangibles

Before we turn to the measurement of assets, we must address the problems
raised by the alternative treatments of intangibles in accounts. It is still
possible to choose between capitalizing and expending certain intangibles,
and even when SSAPs and SORPs lay down a definitive treatment for *external*
reporting purposes, the decision maker is perfectly entitled to adopt whatever
policy suits *his* purposes when it comes to the preparation of *internal* statements. However, writing off to his income statement expenditure which is
expected to provide future benefits to the division will deflate profits and
understate ROI and RI in the early years, and overstate ROI and RI once the
steady state is reached (if a roughly equal outlay is made each year, the
steady state will be reached when the sum of the amortization of previous and

current expenditure approximates to the annual outlay). We can illustrate this situation with the help of the following example.

Example 9
A division currently has profits of £25,000 on an investment base of £100,000; its cost of capital is 10 per cent. It begins to incur expenditure on intangibles of £5,000 per annum, and each outlay of £5,000 brings in a profit of £2,000 per annum for 4 years from the year following the expenditure. For convenience, the ROI calculation is based on the investment base at the end of the year under consideration:

$$\text{Current ROI} = \frac{£25k}{£100k} = 25\%$$

Current RI = £25k − (10% × £100k) = £15k

Variant (1) – Expensing the intangibles (write off to P & L)
£000s

Year	1	2	3	4	5 (steady state)
Divisional profit	25	27	29	31	33
Intangibles	(5)	(5)	(5)	(5)	(5)
Net profit for ROI	20	22	24	26	28
Capital charge @ 10%	(10)	(10)	(10)	(10)	(10)
Residual income	10	12	14	16	18
ROI	$\frac{20}{100}=20\%$	$\frac{22}{100}=22\%$	$\frac{24}{100}=24\%$	$\frac{26}{100}=26\%$	$\frac{£28k}{£100k}=2$

Variant (2) – Capitalizing the intangibles and amortizing the expenditure in equal instalments over 5 years

Year	1	2	3	4	5 (steady state)
Divisional profit	25	27	29	31	33
Amortization	(1)	(2)	(3)	(4)	(5)
Net profit for ROI	24	25	26	27	28
Capital charge @ 10%	(10.4)	(10.7)	(10.9)	(11)	(11)
Residual income	13.6	14.3	15.1	16	17
ROI	$\frac{24}{104}=23.1\%$	$\frac{25}{107}=23.4\%$	$\frac{26}{109}=23.9\%$	$\frac{27}{110}=24.5\%$	$\frac{28}{110}=25.5$

If the annual outlay is *expensed*, (variant (1)), divisional profit, ROI and RI are artificially reduced in years 1–3, because of the absence or low level of associated inflows. By year 5, the full benefits of the inflows are felt, but because the associated expenditure has been excluded from the investment base, ROI and RI are unrealistically high. If the annual outlay is *capitalized*, and amortised over 5 years (variant (2)), a much more gradual transition to the steady state is observed, with the ROI and RI more accurately reflected within a much narrower range.

This example has important implications for the comparative evaluation of divisions engaged in different activities. Manufacturing divisions, whose income-yielding expenditure is largely in the form of *tangible* assets, will tend to show lower ROIs and RIs, *ceteris paribus*, than those divisions with a high proportion of their expenditure on *intangibles*, such as marketing, with heavy promotional outlays, or management services, with a large number of professional employees whose human capital is excluded from the balance sheet. As Kaplan and Atkinson (1989) note, these later divisions are not as profitable as they appear (assuming the steady state), as the current benefits they enjoy from the previous investments in intangibles are not being related to the intangible investment base developed over the years. Divisional ROI and RI are higher merely because they have assets that do not form part of their investment base.

12.5.3   The measurement of assets

The surveys of Mauriel and Anthony (1966), Reece and Cool (1978) and Vancil (1979) found only a small minority of organizations using any basis other than net book value derived from historical cost to measure their assets in ROI and RI calculations. This might appear surprising in view of the well-publicized distortions in the comparative values of ROI and RI that result from the conventional application of this basis. Example 10 illustrates the problem.

Example 10
A division buys a machine for £1m, which will yield a constant £300,000 per annum over its 5-year life and have no residual value. The division uses straight-line depreciation, and a cost of capital of 10 per cent. All figures are in £000s. Tax ignored.

Year	NBV @ beg. of year	Average NBV during year	Increase in income	Depreciation	Increase in net income	Beginning ROI	RI	Average ROI	RI
1	1,000	900	300	(200)	100	10%	0	11.1%	10
2	800	700	300	(200)	100	12.5%	20	14.3%	30
3	600	500	300	(200)	100	16.7%	40	20%	50
4	400	300	300	(200)	100	25%	60	33.3%	70
5	200	100	300	(200)	100	50%	80	100%	90

Despite the fact that the Net Cash Inflows (NCIs) remain unchanged each year, ROI and RI (using either version of historic NBV) rise dramatically, simply because of the shrinking investment base.

Our example used uniform NCIs, but obviously if the cash flows follow a more normal pattern – with lower initial inflows followed by increasing flows, which gradually reduce towards the end of the investment's useful life – then the rise in ROI and RI will be even more spectacular (and, depending on whether the NBV of the investment declines more rapidly than that of the NCIs, the ROI and RI could continue to increase, though at a slower rate, until the asset is scrapped).

We saw in chapter 5 that the correct decision rule for new investments was to accept those that offer a positive NPV at the appropriate cost of capital; any other decision would be dysfunctional, *ceteris paribus*. If we modify the data in example 10 very slightly, and say that the appropriate divisional cost of capital is 14 per cent rather than 10 per cent, and assume that the NCIs occur at the end of each year (for simplicity), we can demonstrate an important behavioural corollary to the use in managerial ROI and RI calculations of divisional income and investment based on normal financial accounting depreciation methods and NBVs derived from historic costs, which could lead to just such a dysfunctional decision.

Example 11
The same data as example 10 apply, except that the cost of capital is now 14 per cent.

PV of £300k p.a. for 5 years @ 14% = £300k × 3.433 = £1,029.9k

Cost of investment	(1,000 k)
NPV = £	29.9k

IIR = £1,000k/£300k = 3.33 = IRR of just over 15% (from annuity tables)

The investment is worthwhile and should be accepted.
However, ROI and RI for years 1–3 show the following pattern:

	Case 1 ROI using opening NBV (as before)	Case 2 ROI using average NBV (as before)	Case 1 RI using opening NBV	Case 2 RI using average NBV
(£000s)				
Year 1	10%	11.1%	(40)[a]	(26)[b]
Year 2	12.5%	14.3%	(12)	2
Year 3	16.7%	20%	16	30

[a] (100 − [1,000 × 14%]) etc.
[b] (100 − [900 × 14%]) etc.

Book ROI is below the minimum required in years 1 and 2 in case (1), and in year 1 of case (1), with year 2 showing only a very marginal positive return. The RI is strongly negative in years 1 and 2 in case (1), and in year 1 of case (2), and is barely positive in year 2 of the latter.

The divisional manager, seeing that the acceptance of the project in example 11 would penalize his performance in the first 2 years under (1), and in the first year of (2), with little compensation in year 2 of the latter, might be tempted to ignore the returns after this period and reject the investment, particularly if he is hoping for a promotion or transfer before year 3 is through. Obviously, the performance indicators would be worse, and the motivation to reject even stronger, in the more normal situation, where some considerable 'lead time' is required by a new investment – to launch a new product, build a plant, install machinery, test a new operation adequately and remove any 'bugs', and generally reach peak profitability.

There are actually two factors militating against his acceptance of certain worthwhile projects under such circumstances: the lower income and returns in the early years, which we have just discussed; and the natural tendency (seen earlier in example 10) for ROI and RI to rise as depreciation causes the book value of the investment to decline. This second factor will give a false impression of increasing profitability on the existing investment that new investment could jeopardize. In other words, there is a dangerous incentive to keep investment on new assets to a minimum. In defiance of logic, a lack of new investment will not cause a deterioration in the division's performance over the years – quite the reverse!

The result that can be said in favour of using NBV based on historic cost in ROI and RI calculations is that it conforms to financial accounting practice – if that is sufficient recommendation in management accounts – and that it recognizes (however imperfectly) the deterioriation in asset values and productivity that often accompany increasing age. Furthermore, given that the net income figure used in the calculation includes a charge for depreciation, it would be inconsistent not to also deduct depreciation from the asset base. The unfortunate result of this 'consistency' was seen in the inexorable and meaningless rise in ROI and RI.

The continued use of *original* cost (i.e. *gross* book value) has been suggested as a way to eliminate this last problem. However, as noted above, virtually all assets lose productivity as they age, leading to a drop in cash inflows; gross book value does not consider this decline, and in fact penalizes divisions with older assets. Nevertheless, original cost will remove any incentive to avoid investment in new assets; indeed, it creates a new incentive to replace existing assets, because the increase in the investment base will be limited to the difference between the historic cost of the old asset and that of its replacement – a figure which is likely to be considerably less than the actual net outlay for the replacement.

The correct theoretical solution to the problem of increasing ROI and RI is compound interest depreciation. The IRR of a new asset is calculated, and this rate applied to the written-down value of the investment to determine the 'income' for a particular period. The difference between this 'income' figure and the actual net cash inflow is the depreciation in the value of the asset. Example 12 illustrates the process, and the ROI and RI that result.

Example 12
A division purchases an asset for £317,000. The investment is expected to yield net cash inflows of £100,000 per annum for each of the 4 years of its useful life. At the end of the 4 years, the asset will be scrapped, with no expected salvage proceeds. For the sake of simplicity, we shall assume that the inflows occur at the end of each year, and ignore taxation.

The investment/inflow ratio is $\dfrac{£317k}{£100k} = 3.17 =$ IRR 10%

(from annuity tables)

(£000s)

Year	WDV at beginning of year (a)	NCI	Inputed income @ 10% of WDV (b)	Depreciation	ROI on WDV ([b] ÷ [a])	RI ([b] − [10% × [a]])
1	317	100	31.7	68.3	10%	0
2	248.7	100	24.87	75.13	10%	0
3	173.57	100	17.357	82.643	10%	0
4	90.927	100	9.0927	90.907 (difference rounding)	10%	0

The compound interest method must (by definition) provide a constant ROI and RI (assuming actual net inflows correspond to the expected pattern in the IRR model). It thus avoids the misleadingly low ROI and RI in the initial years of a new project as well as the rising figures later, and thereby removes that particular disincentive to new investment. If the cash flows turned out to be lower than expected, ROI would fall below the original IRR, and RI would be negative. Obviously, with higher inflows, the reverse would be the case. Either way, a useful signal is given to management that operations are not proceeding as planned.

An alternative way to calculate compound interest depreciation is to determine the present value of the future net cash inflows at the beginning and end of each year. The difference between the two PVs will be the depreciation for the year in question. The reader will appreciate that the WDVs in column (a) of example 12 represent the PVs of the investment at the beginning of each year, so that the two approaches give the same outcome. Thus the use of compound interest depreciation results in investments being shown at their present value in divisional 'balance sheets'.

Despite the undoubted ability of most organizations to calculate it (the principle is the same as a loan repayment schedule, for example), compound interest depreciation is rarely met with in practice. We cannot speculate as to why this should be the case.

The reference to present values in the preceding discussion reminds us that historical cost (whether gross or net) suffers from a very familiar defect – the failure to reflect changes in price levels. Our examples so far have assumed stable price levels, but inflation will obviously give another element of distortion to the figures of ROI and RI. Net cash inflows will be measured in current year values, whereas the investment base and depreciation charges under conventional historic cost accounting are measured in terms of monetary values at the time of the asset's acquisition. Depreciation based on historical costs will be considerably lower than a charge based on current values, and will then cause current income to be overstated. Concomitantly, the investment base will be understated because of the acquisition of assets at price levels lower than those currently prevailing.

Although it is dangerous to generalize, this understatement of the investment base will usually be much more significant than the increased maintenance costs and lower productivity that often accompany older plant. Thus the combination of overstated income and understated assets will conspire to inflate ROI and RI, and it would be wrong to evaluate a divisional manager on the basis of such spurious increases in profitability. Furthermore, comparative evaluations between divisions will be rendered meaningless by the failure to compensate for the impact on ROI and RI of assets acquired by divisions at different dates – obviously, divisions with recently acquired assets will show a lower ROI and RI *ceteris paribus*, than equally (or even less) profitable divisions which happened to have obtained their assets at much lower price levels. Finally, the dysfunctional motivational tendencies we saw earlier will also accompany a failure to neutralize influencing biases in a division's investment base: there will be a tendency to delay the replacement of existing assets, because of the misleadingly high ROI and RI produced by them; and a reluctance to acquire new investments, because of the adverse effect on ROI and RI of investments at current values.

Several alternatives to historical cost have been suggested: present value, which we mentioned briefly earlier; replacement cost, which reflects the specific nature of the individual asset; and price-level adjusted value, which emphasizes the change in the general purchasing power of the funds invested in the individual asset. These different bases were discussed in chapter 9, and do not need further elaboration here. However, where price-level adjustments provide a reasonable surrogate for replacement costs, all three will lead to more sensible and economically significant ROI and RI measures for individual performance evaluation purposes, and to greater comparability between different divisions (after taking into account the different types of activity and risk). They will also remove the potential for dysfunctional behaviour associated with historical costs. That they are not more widely observed in practice is surprising and regrettable.

12.6 Alternatives to ROI and RI

So far, this chapter has been a catalogue of *caveats* regarding the use of ROI and RI. Even when historic cost is abandoned, it is not unreasonable to suggest that any attempt to measure a division's performance by means of a single all-encompassing, summary figure is a chimaera. We have discussed this point in relation to decision making; we now consider the issues in relation to performance measurement.

12.6.1 Non-financial measures of performance

In Part One we demonstrated that decisions in both the commercial and non-commercial sectors can include financial and non-financial objectives. Consistency demands that the criteria by which decisions are taken are also the criteria by which performance is measured. If, for instance, a football club buys a player for his ability to tackle, then his performance should be measured by the same criterion. Of course, circumstances may change and other attributes *may* become important. The player's ability to pass may subsequently be deemed more important. But good management should be able to anticipate such uncertainties by using multi-attributable measures in decisions.

It is true to say that until recently little attention was given to non-financial performance measurement. The example of Japanese industry, combined with a change of heart by leading academics, has subsequently radically altered opinions. The new approach is summed up by Johnson and Kaplan (1987):

> More important than attempting to measure monthly or quarterly profits is measuring and reporting a variety of non-financial indicators. The indicators should be based on the company's strategy and include key measures of manufacturing marketing and R & D systems. For example, a company emphasizing quality could measure internal failure indicators – scrap, rework, part-per-million defect rates, unscheduled machine downtime – and external failure indicators – customer complaints, warranty expenses, and service calls. Rather than attempt to extract such information from a system designed primarily to satisfy external reporting and auditing requirements, we should design systems consistent with the technology of the organization, its product strategy, and its organizational structure.

The problems of non financial performance measurement are, not surprisingly, similar to those of using non-financial measures in decisions. For example, the measures that Kaplan cites represent the attributes of quality. To build a measure of quality, there will be the same problems of measurement and association as discussed in chapters 1 and 3. Some measures will be cardinal – the differences will be meaningful. Other measures may be more ordinal in nature – the differences may not be especially meaningful other than their sign (an increase or decrease). An organization's attitude to movements and levels of the various measures may vary considerably over the range of any one measure. A movement from 0 to 1,000 defects parts per million may be viewed as less serious than movement from 10,000 to 11,000 defect parts per million. How should these attitudes be measured?

One method would be to develop target levels or constraints. If, in our example of defect parts per million, a target level of 9,000 parts is set, then the latter movement will be regarded as more serious than the former (in practice zero defects is the target for many firms). Another method would be to map the measure on to a scale of utility which weights movements in defects at the upper end more heavily than at the lower end of the scale – again we refer the reader to chapter 3.

Performance measurement inevitably calls for comparison. Where non-financial measures are being used, management seeking to evaluate, say, quality is faced with difficult questions such as: 'Has quality improved if customer complaints are up by 10 per cent, warranty expenses down by 30 per cent, defects up by 5 per cent and service calls are unchanged?' One approach would be to refuse to recognize improvements in quality until all the indicators of quality had improved. In effect, this would be applying the concept of dominance in measurement (see section 3.3.2). Although the problem of trade-offs between the measures is avoided, the cost will be the many situations where management is unable to say whether there has been an improvement or deterioration in quality.

An alternative approach would be to weight the various attributes. Thus, in our example, changes in customer complaints may be seen as twice as important as changes in defects and so on. To some managers such weights are a welcome chance to give priority to certain aspects; to others it may be unwelcome, in that they may not wish to give the impression that some measures are less important than others. The choice of measurement is itself a management decision. For a fuller analysis of the issues, the reader is once again referred to chapter 3.

In practice, the renewed emphasis on quality, just-in-time production, marketing, innovation, service and flexibility all argue for the development of non-financial as well as financial measures to gauge performance. More recent texts and research are now giving a renewed emphasis to this aspect. For instance, Kaplan and Atkinson (1989) quote McDonalds as evaluating performance on the basis of:

> Product quality
> Service
> Cleanliness
> Sales volume
> Personnel training
> Cost control

Horngren and Foster (1987) quote a semiconductor firm as including the following measures:

Yield: Ratio of wafer chips in to wafer chips out
Production: Percentage of delivery commitments met
Productivity: Wafer chips produced/payroll dollars
Equipment: Percentage of hours with no unscheduled downtime
Financial: Cost per chip: revenue per chip

It is a moot point whether or not the finance and accounting function has rediscovered those aspects of measurement which were always present, or whether recent developments have promoted these measures. In any event, it is now recognized that non-financial measures have an important role to play in measuring performance. In the future, the accounting and finance function will, no doubt, regularly report both financial and non-financial data.

References and further reading

Dearden, J., 'The case against ROI Control', *Harvard Business Review*, May–June 1969, pp. 124–35.

Dearden, J., 'Measuring Profit Center Managers', *Harvard Business Review*, Sep–Oct 1987, pp. 84–8.

Fitzgerald, L. 'Management Performance in Service Industries', *International Journal of Operations and Production*, 1988.

Horngren, C. T., Foster, G., *Cost Accounting: A Managerial Emphasis*, Prentice-Hall, 1987.

Johnson, H. T., Kaplan, R. S., *Relevance Lost: The Rise and Fall of Management Accounting*, Harvard Business School Press, 1987.

Kaplan, R. S., Atkinson, A. A., *Advanced Management Accounting*, Prentice-Hall, 1989.

Mauriel, J. S., Anthony, R. N., 'Misvaluation of Investment Center Performances', *Harvard Business Review*, March–April 1966, pp. 98–104.

Reeece, J. J. and Cool, W. R., 'Measuring Investment Center Performance', *Harvard Business Review*, May–June 1978, pp. 28–46.

Scapens, R. W., Sale, T., Tikkas, P., *Financial Control of Divisional Capital Investment*, CIMA, 1982.

Solomons, D., *Divisional Performance: Measurement and Control*, Irwin, 1968.

Vancil, R., *Decentralisation: Managerial Ambiguity by Design*, Irwin, 1979.

13 Ratio analysis

13.1 Introduction

Published accounts are the only regular source of detailed financial information on a company to the vast majority of people interested in its affairs. It is possible to supplement this information from a number of external sources (see Holmes and Sugden (1986) and Collier *et al.* (1988)), but as the data tend to be drawn from the same published statements, the value of the additional information lies more in the convenience of its presentation. The data are often summarized in the form of a time series analysis (data relating to the same company over a period of years) or a cross-sectional analysis (data relating to other firms in the same sector as the target company). In many of these summaries, the information is set out in the form of ratios, which not only remove any potential problems of scale between companies of different sizes, but also highlight important relations between different accounting numbers and indicate the direction in which further analysis might profitably be aimed.

This chapter will briefly examine the use (and limitations) of such ratios in the interpretation of a company's accounts. Our examples will be based on the following published statements of CIMA plc, a small quoted company whose shares stand at a mid-market price of 310p:

£000s	Balance sheet as at 31 December			
	Year 2		Year 1	
Fixed assets				
Factory fixtures and fittings at cost	500		400	
Accumulated depreciation	(200)	300	(150)	250
Office fixtures and fittings at cost	200		180	
Accumulated depreciation	(100)	100	(80)	100
		400		350

£000s		Year 2		Year 1
Fixed assets brought forward		400		350
Current assets				
Stock	250		230	
Debtors	200		180	
Cash	50		20	
	500		430	
Less creditors due within one year	(200)	300	(180)	250
Net assets		700		600
Capital and reserves				
Called-up share capital (£1 shares)	250		250	
Profit and loss account	250	500	150	400
Creditors due after more than one year				
10% loan		200		200
Capital employed		700		600

Profit and loss accounts for the years ended 31 December

£000s	Year 2	Year 1
Turnover	2,000	1,600
Cost of sales	(1,200)	(1,000)
Gross profit	800	600
Distribution and admin. expenses	(590)	(460)
Trading profit	210	140
Loan interest	(20)	(20)
Pre-tax profit	190	120
Taxation	(65)	(40)
Profit after tax	125	80
Dividends	(25)	(20)
Retained profit	100	60

13.2   Liquidity ratios

The two ratios most commonly used to assess a company's liquidity position are the current ratio and the quick ratio (otherwise known as the acid test). They are both concerned with the ability of a firm to cover its short-term liabilities from those assets which the working capital cycle will turn into liquid form in the short term.

13.2.1   *Current ratio*

This is $\dfrac{\text{current assets}}{\text{current liabilities}}$: Year 1 $\dfrac{430}{180} = 2.39$

Year 2 $\dfrac{500}{200} = 2.5$

Unfortunately, the current ratio can never give more than a very broad indication of a company's short-term financial position. There cannot be a 'norm' for the ratio below which a danger signal is sounded. Manufacturers could be expected to have higher ratios than high-street retailers, simply because of the sheer length of the working capital cycle in the case of the former, and the financing of stocks through creditors, coupled with the relative absence of debtors, in that of the latter. Rather than indicating increasing financial strength or liquidity, a high or increasing current ratio may indicate poor or deteriorating credit control, or an unwelcome build-up of stocks that will prove expensive to finance and difficult to sell. Again, because companies may prefer to have their year end at a time which is most convenient to them in terms of low activity and stock levels, balance sheet ratios will not reflect the typical situation, and a completely different picture might be observed if the following month's management accounts were used for the calculation of the current ratio.

We must also recognize that the composition of 'creditors falling due within one year' could range from 100 per cent items that are due on the first day of the following financial year, to 100 per cent items that are due exactly 12 months less a day from the present balance sheet date: both extremes would present current liabilities for the purposes of the current ratio calculation, but there is obviously a vast difference in their *real* impact on a company's short-term financial position. Finally, an extreme example will illustrate the susceptibility of the current ratio (and the quick ratio, seen in 13.2.2), to 'window dressing':

Example 1
Extract from balance sheet

	£		£
Other current assets	12,000		
Cash	10,000	Current liabilities	11,000
	22,000		11,000

The current ratio is $22,000/11,000 = 2$. Suppose the company uses the cash to pay off £10,000 of the current liabilities. This would have the dramatic effect of increasing the current ratio from 2 to 12:

Other current assets $\dfrac{12000}{12000}$ Current liabilities $\dfrac{1000}{1000}$ Current ratio $\dfrac{12000}{1000} = 12$

No accountant would argue that this increase represents an *improvement* in the company's financial position, despite the inferences which might be drawn from a superficial analysis.

Lewis *et al.* (1981) have pointed out the simple mathematical basis for this form of 'window dressing' – if a ratio is greater than 1, the subtraction of the same amount from both numerator and denominator will make the ratio larger: if $A/B > 1$, then $(A-x)/(B-x) > A/B$. Conversely, if the initial ratio is less than 1, it would become smaller as a result of this action: if $A/B < 1$, then $(A-x)/(B-x) < A/B$. $[B \geqslant x > 0]$.

13.2.2   Quick ratio

This is simply a modification of the current ratio. In order to show the ability of a company to meet its more immediate financial obligations from those current assets already in cash or near cash form, stocks are removed from the numerator, thus:

$$\frac{\text{Current assets} - \text{stocks}}{\text{Current liabilities}} \quad : \quad \text{Year 1} \; \frac{200}{180} = 1.11$$

$$\text{Year 2} \; \frac{250}{200} = 1.25$$

Although a ratio of less than 1 might be considered a sign of imminent problems, it should be borne in mind that many companies with rapid turnovers, such as supermarkets, are in a position to convert purchases into cash sales before the normal terms of trade with their suppliers require them to pay for the goods: a ratio of considerably under 1 would be perfectly acceptable in such circumstances. Care must be taken with the classification of bank overdrafts – although they will appear in current liabilities, a number of companies effectively use them as long-term sources of finance, relying on the bank to regularly renew the facility. If this situation is discernible, overdrafts should be excluded from the denominator in the calculation. Attention should also be directed to the notes to the accounts, for additional short-term demands on liquidity can often be identified in notes on items such as contingent liabilities, capital expenditure already contracted, and other capital expenditure planned for the coming year. Obviously, there can be no substitute for an outline cash budget for the year ahead; unfortunately for external users of accounts, this will always remain an internal document.

13.3 Operating ratios

It is axiomatic that a ratio taken in isolation means nothing; only *changes* in a ratio (in a time series analysis) or differences *between* ratios (in a cross-sectional analysis) have informational value. However, strictly speaking, these changes and differences can do no more than point towards areas that require detailed investigation; they cannot in themselves provide a basis for internal management action, although, of necessity, they must form the basis for external users' decisions.

It is usual to seek explanations for comparative movements in ratios at one level by reference to the ratios at the level immediately below it, which break down the numerator or denominator of the higher level ratio into its constituent parts: this demonstrates the so-called 'pyramid approach' to ratio analysis. We set out in Figure 13.1 the 'pyramid' of operating ratios, and discuss several of them in sections 13.3.1 to 13.3.3.

13.3.1 Return on capital employed (ROCE)

As we saw in some detail in chapter 12, profit must be related to the size of the assets used in its generation before we can determine whether it represents a satisfactory figure. ROCE, expressed as profit over assets, brings together the two elements of profit and underlying resources, and is the measure of profitability most frequently encountered.

The pyramid of ratios shows us how we can analyse this primary ratio further, in order to explain relative differences in the ROCE. The problem we are faced with, however, is one of definition: for example, we could use profit before interest and tax, profit after interest but before tax, or profit available for ordinary shareholders; we could take gross assets or net assets, total capital employed or long-term capital employed (if there is a difference), or simply shareholder's equity. Obviously, the choice of any particular asset base will dictate the choice of profit numerator in the calculation, as it would be inappropriate to compare a profit figure which excludes the financing effect of a particular form of funding with an asset base of which that funding forms a part. A decision must also be made as to whether opening or closing balance sheet figures are to be used, or some average (weighted or otherwise) of these two.

For our present purposes, let us include in capital employed the effect of any long-term debt, and therefore take as our definition of profit the figure before deduction of loan interest. We would have the following ROCE for CIMA:

Year 1
$$\frac{140}{600} = 23.3\%$$

Year 2
$$\frac{210}{700} = 30.0\%$$

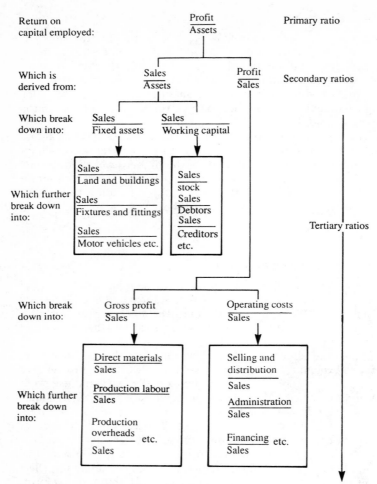

Figure 13.1   *Pyramid of operating ratios*

13.3.2   *Profit margin and asset turnover*

A company's ROCE can be larger or smaller than that of another firm, or have increased or decreased from the ratio for the previous year, for one of two reasons: the profitability per £ of sales has been higher or lower; or the productive capacity (assets) has been used to greater or lesser effect. Obviously, corporate life is rarely simple, and it will usually be a combination of these two reasons.

The profit margin on sales will be profit/sales, where the numerator is the same as that used in the ROCE computation:

Year 1 $$\frac{140}{1,600} = 8.75$$

Year 2 $$\frac{210}{2,000} = 10.5$$

Thus, the increase in CIMA's ROCE from 23.3 per cent to 30 per cent is partly explained by the increased profitability of sales, i.e. a greater profit per £ of sales has been generated in year 2.

The effectiveness of the utilization of productive capacity is seen in the asset turnover, expressed as sales/assets, where the denominator is the one used to calculate ROCE:

Year 1 $$\frac{1,600}{600} = 2.67$$

Year 2 $$\frac{2,000}{700} = 2.86$$

We can see from this that a further contributory factor to the increased ROCE in year 2 has been an improved asset turnover: CIMA has generated more sales per £ of capital employed, as well as raising the margin of profitability on each £ of sales.

13.3.3   *Asset ratios and expenditure ratios*

The analyst would now examine, by reference to the tertiary level of ratios in the pyramid, which constituent elements within the two secondary ratios have contributed to their increase in year 2. We shall direct our attention to just four of these.

Management should attempt to maintain a proper balance for a given sales between the amount of funds invested in fixed assets and the amount tied up in working capital. The fixed asset:turnover ratio measures the number of £ of sales generated by each £ invested in fixed assets, and is calculated by sales/fixed assets:

CIMA Year 1 $$\frac{1,600}{350} = 4.57$$

Year 2 $$\frac{2,000}{400} = 5$$

Unless there is a good match between the activities of two different companies, cross-sectional analysis can give rise to misleading comparisons with this ratio: in any given industry, a vertically integrated company will have a much greater investment in fixed assets than one which simply buys in from outside. Furthermore, as we saw in chapter 12, there is an unfortunate tendency in historical cost accounts for this ratio (and therefore ultimately ROCE) to increase by default, merely because of the shrinkage in the investment base due to the effects of depreciation. Other problems of comparability notwithstanding, cross-sectional analysis will also be complicated by the fact that different companies have fixed assets of different ages, and therefore net book values (although productivity might provide a counterbalance of sorts).

Let us now turn to measures of working capital utilization. The stock: turnover ratio indicates how quickly products are being converted into sales. Except when stocks are built up to avoid sharp price rises on the part of suppliers, companies would prefer to carry stocks at a level which will minimize financing, handling and storage costs, and the risk of deterioration and obsolence. Although the ratio has hitherto been calculated as sales/ stocks, as set out in the pyramid, this is not as satisfactory a measure as cost of sales/stocks; after all, stocks are valued at cost in the balance sheet, and not selling price. This alternative calculation has been facilitated by recent Companies Act requirements for listed and large companies to disclose cost of sales figures, and we are able to do this for CIMA:

Year 1 $$\frac{1,000}{230} = 4.35$$

Year 2 $$\frac{1,200}{250} = 4.8$$

The denominator in our example has been taken to be closing stock. A more accurate measure might be average stock, but this can smooth out the effect of any dramatic change in year-end stock levels.

A useful indicator of the effectiveness of a company's credit control procedures, and therefore their contribution to the general level of asset utilization, is the debtors:turnover ratio, which can be calculated in two ways, Sales/Debtors or Sales/Debtors × 365 – the latter expressing closing debtors in terms of the number of days sales they represent:

Year 1 $$\frac{1,600}{180} = 8.89 \qquad \frac{365}{8.89} = 41.1 \text{ days}$$

or

Year 2 $$\frac{2,000}{200} = 10.0 \qquad \frac{365}{10.0} = 36.5 \text{ days}$$

In general terms, unless the company has recently adopted a more generous credit policy, to tempt customers away from more stringent competitors, there is no reason to expect an increase in sales to be accompanied by a reduction in the ratio (or an increase in the number of days' sales in debtors). Alternatively, an increase in the ratio would not necessarily be cause for congratulation if it resulted from a desperate need for cash, which had led the company either to offer huge discounts for quicker payment, or to put undue pressure on customers to the potential detriment of future business. Obviously, the term 'debtors' refers to credit sales; the numerator should therefore be limited to credit sales. If a company has cash as well as credit sales, their relative proportions are unlikely to be revealed by the accounts, and the higher the proportion of cash sales, the less useful the ratio becomes to an outsider.

The recent statutory provision of cost of sales figures, referred to above, has also enabled a more sensible creditors turnover than that shown in the pyramid to be calculated, namely cost of sales/creditors. This can also be expressed in the alternative form of number of days' sales, as we saw with debtors. The figures for CIMA are

Year 1 $\quad \dfrac{1,000}{180} = 5.56 \quad$ or $\quad \dfrac{365}{5.56} = 65.6$ days

Year 2 $\quad \dfrac{1,200}{200} = 6 \quad$ or $\quad \dfrac{365}{6} = 60.8$ days

This is not entirely satisfactory, however, as creditors refer to *purchases* rather than to the cost of goods actually *sold*, but the problem can be easily overcome by adjusting the cost of sales numerator to take account of the movement in stocks over the year. Such a refinement might be considered unnecessary if the user is seeking merely to identify trends that will help to predict potential liquidity problems as well as explain part of the change in the secondary asset turnover ratio.

13.4 Gearing ratios

These ratios relate to the basic financial structure of the organization, and concern themselves with the relative proportions of capital provided by equity shareholders and outside lenders, and the effect on earnings on this capital 'mix'. A 'low-geared' company is one that is financed predominantly by equity, whereas a 'high-geared' company relies on outside suppliers for a large part of its capital employed.

Gearing produces a risk/reward trade-off, because of the disproportionate effect that it creates in shareholders' earnings when profits fluctuate. When profits increase, the fixed interest charges of loan capital will represent a smaller proportion of a bigger cake, leaving a disproportionately large slice of the available cake for the ordinary shareholder; when profits decline, the same fixed interest charges will obviously represent a larger proportion of a reduced cake, leaving a disproportionately smaller slice of the available cake for the equity shareholder. Obviously, the higher the gearing, the greater the potential rewards to the equity holders when profits are rising – and the greater the downside if profits should fall. However, as gearing increases, the security offered by owners' equity contracts, and the risk to the lender increases. Thus the company is likely to find that opportunities to make further borrowings will diminish.

There are two types of gearing ratios: income-based and capital-based. The first is most commonly expressed in the form of interest cover, and measures the number of times the fixed interest charge is covered by available profits; The calculation is profit before interest and tax/interest:

Year 1 $\qquad \dfrac{140}{20} = 7$

Year 2 $\qquad \dfrac{210}{20} = 10.5$

The standard capital-based gearing ratio is the debt:equity ratio, which can be calculated in two ways – borrowings/owners' equity:

Year 1
$$\frac{200}{400} = 50\%$$

Year 2
$$\frac{200}{500} = 40\%$$

or $\dfrac{\text{Borrowings}}{\text{Borrowings} + \text{owners' equity}}$ Year 1 $\dfrac{200}{600} = 33.3\%$

Year 2 $\dfrac{200}{700} = 28.6\%$

The effect of a particular company's gearing level on the profit attributable to its ordinary shareholders can be demonstrated by means of the ratio known variously as the degree of capital gearing or degree of financial leverage – profit before interest and tax (PBIT)/pre-tax profit (PTP):

Year 1
$$\frac{140}{120} = 1.167$$

Year 2
$$\frac{210}{190} = 1.105$$

With this ratio, we can predict the increase in PTP that would be achieved for any given percentage increase in PBIT (and *vice versa*). For example, a 10 per cent increase in PBIT would lead to an 11.67 per cent increase in PTP in year 1 (10 per cent × 1.167) and 11.05 per cent in year 2 (10 per cent × 1.105). The reader might care to prove these figures for himself, although the mathematics are intuitive.

Similarly, if it is possible to break down the operating expenditure into fixed and variable elements, so that a contribution figure can be obtained, a further useful predictive ratio can be derived, called variously the degree of operational gearing or the degree of operating leverage: contribution/PBIT. If we assume, for the purposes of illustration, that CIMA's total operating expenditure in year 2 of £1·79m (i.e. cost of sales £1·2m + distribution and administration expenses £590K) was made up of £1·4m variable and £390,000 fixed costs, then the contribution would have been £2m turnover – £1·4m variable costs = £600,000. The ratio for year 2 becomes 600/210 = 2.857, and we can use this figure to predict the increase in PBIT that would be expected from any given percentage increase in turnover (and *vice versa*). For example, a 10 per cent increase in turnover would translate into a 28.57 per cent increase in PBIT (10 per cent × 2.857). Once the reader recognizes that contribution is a surrogate for turnover, the mathematics again become intuitive.

These last two ratios can be combined to produce a figure which can predict the increase in PTP which would follow from any given percentage increase in turnover (and *vice versa*), thus: degree of capital gearing × degree of operational gearing. For CIMA year 2, the calculation is 1.105 × 2.857 = 3.157.

A 10 per cent increase in turnover would give rise to a 31.57 per cent increase in PTP (10 per cent × 3.157). At this remove, the mathematics are perhaps not intuitive, so we shall briefly prove the figure: a 10 per cent increase in turnover = £60,000 additional contribution = £60,000 additional pre-tax profit (the fixed operating costs and interest charges remaining static). £60,000 additional profit on the original £190,000 = 31.57 per cent.

13.5 Stock market ratios

We shall look briefly at the four ratios most commonly encountered in connection with quoted companies: earnings per share, price:earnings ratio, dividend yield, and dividend cover. Two of these – price:earnings ratio and dividend yield – are a function of a factor external to the accounts: the market price of the shares. For the purposes of this section, we shall look only at CIMA's year 2 figures, using the current mid-market price of 310p mentioned in section 13.1

13.5.1 *Earnings per share (EPS)*

The calculation is as follows: earnings attributable to ordinary shareholders over total number of ordinary shares in issue:

$$\frac{£125K}{250K} = £0.50$$

The numerator will be the earnings after tax, minority interest and preference dividends, but before extraordinary items – the 'net' basis of EPS required by SSAP3. Adjustments must be made to the denominator for any changes in share capital during the period to which the earnings relate, and a figure for diluted EPS must be disclosed where the possible dilution exceeds 5 per cent of the basic EPS. Blake (1989) and Collier *et al.* (1988) provide excellent summaries of the alternatives.

13.5.2 *Price:earnings (PE) ratio*

The main use of EPS figures for quoted companies is as the denominator in the calculation of the PE ratio:

$$\frac{\text{Market price}}{\text{EPS}} : \frac{310}{50} = 6.2$$

This figure of 6.2 is the 'historic' PE ratio, i.e. based on the previous year's EPS. It is the so-called 'exit multiple' referred to in takeovers. A 'prospective' PE ratio can be calculated, using the analyst's own estimate of EPS for the current year. Obviously, any change in the share's market price will bring about a change in the multiple, historic or prospective.

On the face of it, the PE ratio simply represents the number of years' historic earnings reflected in the current market price, or the capitalization of the EPS. However, this is to understate the influences which underlie the market's view of individual share prices, a topic which lies outside the scope of this book. Generally speaking, however, a high historic PE ratio compared to the section average (as set out in the FT Actuaries Indices) suggests either that the share has above-average prospects (including dividend prospects) for the current year (if the market has judged it correctly), or that it is overvalued (if the judgement is flawed), or that the company is a sector leader. A PE ratio lower than the sector average suggests either that poor results are expected (if the market is right), or that it is an undervalued share (if the market is wrong).

13.5.3   Dividend yield

This is *dividend per share over market price*. The dividend should be based on the *gross* distribution, i.e. including the associated tax credit. This latter will be a function of the basic personal tax rate in force at the time of the actual payment. CIMA's net dividend is 10p (£25K dividend/250K shares in issue), which translates into a gross equivalent of 13.33p at a 25 per cent basic rate of tax. At the market price of 310p, therefore, the yield is

$$\frac{13.33}{310} = 4.3\%$$

Again, any change in the market price will give a revised yield.

13.5.4   Dividend cover

This ratio measures the number of times that the most recent dividend could have been paid out of the available profits; it is a 'safety measure', i.e. the higher the cover, the safer the dividend for future years (or the potential for an increase in its size). Assuming that the company is in a normal tax position, the calculation uses the *net* dividend per share, thus:

$$\frac{EPS}{\text{Net dividend per share}} : \frac{50}{10} = 5$$

Complications can arise, however, when foreign tax on overseas earnings becomes significant, and the reader is referred to Holmes and Sugden (1986) for a full worked example of this situation.

13.6   Univariate and multivariate analysis

Financial accounting texts (including the present one) have tended to adopt a univariate approach to ratio analysis, i.e. only one ratio at a time is examined, and after a sufficient number of individual ratios have been calculated and analysed, a picture of the operating performance and financial position of the company is formed. This is the predominant approach in practice. However, the last 20 years have seen the development of a multivariate approach, in which statistical techniques such as multiple regression analysis and discriminant analysis are used on several ratios simultaneously. As Blake (1989) has pointed out, most research in this field has concentrated on the prediction of liquidity problems. By weighting a number of ratios, a so-called 'Z' score is produced, and from an analysis of firms in the particular industry under consideration which have become bankrupt, a score is set below which bankruptcy is predicted.

13.7 Users of accounts

The various users of published financial statements have different information needs, and will therefore direct their attention to different aspects of the profit and loss account and balance sheet. An obvious example is that of short-term creditors, who will be concerned with a company's liquidity, and will concentrate on the quick and current ratios. A comprehensive recent discussion of users and the ratios that correspond to their areas of interest is contained in Farmer (1986).

Because the law required a company to file its accounts annually with the Registrar of Companies, all users have access to them – with a greater or lesser degree of inconvenience – and are thus in a position to calculate most of the ratios contained in this chapter. However, some users will have access to considerably more information than is contained in the financial statements – for example, the management of a company can draw on the resources of the total information system; the company's bankers may see the monthly management accounts (indeed, may even insist on the disclosure of more internal data before granting a loan or a facility); and existing suppliers have first-hand trading experience, which enables them to form certain judgements as to the financial strength or otherwise of the company. These users are fortunate in not having to rely on published information, and the necessarily imperfect and inadequate ratios based on them. It is to this last point that we devote the next section of this chapter.

13.8 Some general problems of ratio analysis

At various points in this chapter, we have indicated the need for caution in the use of ratios. This need is most acute when a cross-sectional analysis is employed, but considerable problems can be encountered in the external examination of the accounts of an individual entity, either for a single period or over time. The latest balance sheet available for analysis could be up to 22 months old, and even this legal limit can be extended with relative impunity: the information on which ratios are based may thus be significantly out of date. Moreover, the amount of information available will be limited by the size of the company and the reporting format it happens to adopt, thus limiting the actual number of ratios than can be calculated in some cases, and the usefulness of certain ratios in others. Finally, inflation has an insidiously distorting effect in both the profit and loss account and the balance sheet, and attempts to counter this effect in published accounts have been unsuccessful; the informational value of ratios must suffer as a result of this failure.

When a second company is added to the analysis, the problems are compounded by the critical issue of comparability. Although the implementation of SSAPs has done much to reduce the variability in accounting treatment of a number of contentious items, it should be borne in mind that they are not uniquely or wholly prescriptive: alternative treatments are suggested in some cases, and legitimate departures are not ruled out in any technical case, if the implementation would jeopardize the 'true and fair view'.

We have already referred to the problems of finding perfect 'matches' between companies in section 13.3.3. The point must be reiterated here that without a *perfect* match – in terms of both size and activity – invalid conclusions might be drawn from a comparison of ratios. There are a number of obstacles in the way of such comparability, not least of which is the fundamental problem of definition of industry type, which is not just a question of initial identification (Blake, 1989) gives the example of a shipping company running passenger services – is the correct classification 'shipping', 'travel' or 'holiday'?), but also involves the likely absence of relevant disaggregated data in the case of large companies operating in a number of different industries.

There is no doubt that using ratios under the benevolent aegis of an organization such as the Centre for Interfirm Comparisons will remove much of the uncertainty, but sufficient scope for ambiguity is likely to remain, and a healthy cynicism is called for by all who use accounting ratios – with the probable (but by no means guaranteed) exception of management conducting a purely internal time series analysis.

References and further reading

Blake, J. D., *The Concise Guide to Interpreting Accounts*, van Nostrand Reinhold, 1989.

Collier, P. A., Cooke, T. E., Glynn, J. J., *Financial and Treasury Management*, Heinemann, 1988.

Farmer, E. R., *Making Sense of Company Reports*, Gee, 1986.

Foster, G., *Financial Statement Analysis*, Prentice-Hall, 1986.

Holmes, G., Sugden, A., *Interpreting Company Reports and Accounts*, Woodhead-Faulkner, 1986.

Lee, T. A., *Company Financial Reporting: Issues and Analysis*, Nelson, 1976.

Lewis, R., Pendrill, D., Simon, D. S., *Advanced Financial Accounting*, Pitman, 1981.

Morley, M. F., *Ratio Analysis*, Gee, 1984.

Reid, W., Myddleton, D. R., *The Meaning of Company Accounts*, Gower, 1988.

Westwick, C. A., *How to Use Management Ratios*, Gower, 1987.

14 Value-added statements

14.1 Introduction

Most organizations would like to describe themselves as adding value to society, in other words, using the resources of labour, materials and services in such a way as to produce a product or service that is more valuable than the total value of the inputs. The CIMA Terminology defines it thus: 'Value added: the increase in market value resulting from an alteration in the form, location or availability of a product or service, excluding the cost of bought out materials or services'. The similarity with the profit and loss account is apparent. Indeed, the difference between the two is, in essence, one of emphasis. Profit in the profit and loss account is exclusively the return to the shareholders; 'value added' is the return to all interested parties, namely, the shareholders, employees and government.

To many, this less partial representation of the effect of an organization's activities is both a truer and fairer view. Others would argue that the information market is efficient: as long as the information is published, whether in the form of a value-added statement, profit and loss account, or some other form, the interested parties will be able to interpret the information in their own way. In particular, they will not be affected by whether information is from a value-added statement, or profit and loss account. Such an argument implies that unless new information is contained in the value-added statement, the difference between a profit and loss account and a value-added statement is trivial. As the following pages reveal, the contribution of the value-added statement is a matter of controversy.

Organizations are not required to report value-added statements as a part of the year-end reports. Such statements are therefore rarely included in the final accounts, though they are often the basis for a separate, less formal presentation – especially to non-skilled users. Such reports may take many forms, the common element being an emphasis on the broader distributional aspects. For instance, reports in employee journals explaining 'how we spent our money', or 'who gets what' are very much in the spirit of the value-added statement.

As a historical note, it is worth recalling that in the late 1970s up to one-fifth of leading firms reported value-added statements in their year end accounts (Gray and Maunders, 1980). This high point was largely due, one suspects, to the Corporate Report – a discussion document published by the Accounting Standards Steering Committee – which advocated such statements. In addition, the climate of opinion at that time was rather more questioning of the capitalist ethic than to-day.

No doubt the future will hold further changes. The increasing use of computer graphics as well as the emergence of the concept of a 'corporate image' will ensure that statements based upon the concept of value added will remain popular.

14.2   Method

The main purpose of the value-added statement is to show the difference between revenue and bought-in goods and services. Despite the apparent clarity of this goal, it is nevertheless possible to justify several different value-added statements from the same set of figures. In this section we will use examples from Cox (1979) to illustrate the difference found in practice.

14.2.1   The Corporate Report method

We begin with the manufacturing and trading account for Example Ltd in Table 14.1 (Cox, 1979, p. 32).

The first column may be used to formulate a value-added statement as recommended in the Corporate Report (Table 14.2). We shall assume that 45 per cent of the profits are distributed as dividends and that tax is £25,000.

The materials figure in this statement represents the amount spent in the period, (£250) adjusted for the change in stocks (£100). This is something of an approximation, for the value of stocks is a mixture of bought in materials (or non-value-added items) and labour costs (or 'value added by the firm' items). By effectively increasing the total value added by the value added put into stock, the resulting measure includes productive effort during the period which has not resulted in sales – a violation of the matching principle.

14.2.2   The cost of sales method

This method attempts to correct for the approximation of the previous technique by separating stock costs into materials and value aded items. The materials figure is now:

	£000
Direct materials	200
Materials in overheads	50
Less material costs put into stock	45
Materials used in period	205

Table 14.1   Example Ltd, manufacturing and trading account.

	Total (£000)	Materials (£000)	Value-added (£000)
WIP at start	110	50	60
at end	−150	−65	−85
Finished stock			
at start	300	100	200
at end	−360	−130	−230
Increase in stocks	−100	−45	−55
Input this period			
Direct materials	200	200	
Direct labour	200		200
Overheads:			
labour	150		150
materials	50	50	
depreciation	100		100
Cost of sales	600	205	395
Profit	100		
Sales	700		

Table 14.2   Value-added statement as in the Corporate Report.

	£000
Turnover	700
Materials	150
Value added	550
Applied the following way:	
To pay employees	350
To pay providers of capital	45
To pay government	25
To provide for maintenance and expansion of assets:	
Depreciation	100
Retained profits	30
	550

The value-added figure is accordingly revised to:

$$700 - 205 = £495$$

The decrease of £55 is represented by value-added costs (in this case labour) that have been put into stock. The statement would now read:

Table 14.3   Value added – the cost of sales method.

	£000
Sales	700
Materials	205
Value added	495
Applied in the following way:	
To pay employees	295
To pay providers of capital	45
To pay government	25
To provide for maintenance and expansion of assets:	
Depreciation	100
Retained profits	30
	495

14.2.3   The national accounts method

A problem with the previous two methods is that productive effort is being unequally measured. If production results in a sale for the retail value, then the full value added is recorded. Alternatively, production may be for capital goods for the firm's own use, or the goods may be put into stock (recording a lower total value added than if the items were sold), or they may be sold on hire purchase with, again, a delayed effect on sales. The national accounts method adjusts for these differences by treating these alternative transactions as though they were sales. In this example only items that have been put into stock have been treated differently; finished stock and work-in-progress items have increased by £100, and if the profitability remains the same, then the value added will be about £17. Hence, the total value added will be as in Table 14.4.

14.3   Applications

The most suitable method of measuring value added (section 14.2) depends upon the circumstances that the statement is attempting to represent. For measuring value added by a productive unit, the national accounts method would seem to represent more fairly the effort involved. Alternatively, if the intention is to show how wealth is distributed, then either the Corporate Report method or the cost of sales method is a better approach, in that they are related to the value added realized in the period.

Further innovations may be made to suit the particular purpose of the statement. For example, in a market where sales prices fluctuate, the use of value added to measure productivity by means of value added per £1 of assets, or per 1 hour of labour, may be distorted. An apparent increase in value added due to greater productivity may, in fact, be due solely to a favourable price increase which is unrelated to productive effort. In such a scenario, standard selling price, or even standard value added, may be regarded as a fairer measure. Clearly, we need to consider carefully the purpose of the

Table 14.4 Value added – the national accounts method.

	£000
Sales	700
Increase in stocks	117
Gross output	817
Less materials	250
Value added	567
Applied in the following way:	
To pay employees	350
To pay providers of capital	45
To pay government	25
To provide maintenance and expansion of assets:	
Depreciation	100
Retained profits	47
	567

value-added statement before deciding on its form. We offer the following broad purposes as candidates for value added statements:

(a) *Value added as measure of social contribution.* Corporations may wish, for varying reasons, to remind society of the contribution that they make. In this respect the value-added statement is better than the profit and loss statement, as it shows that employees and government benefit as well as shareholders. If anything, the statement underestimates the contribution, for the wages and salaries will be spent largely within the community, thereby creating further wealth (known in economics as the multiplier effect). In addition, the materials purchased provide further employment and business and also represent value added to the community. Nevertheless, the format of the statement, de-emphasizing profit and highlighting the wider distribution of wealth, does much to remedy the rather limited view of a firm as given by the profit and loss statement.

(b) *Value added as a measure of effort.* Value added is a readily understood concept and therefore provides an attractive base for bonus schemes. Schemes may gauge effort, using a productivity ratio such as value added per £1 payroll cost, or value added per employee. Alternatively, they may deem the difference between actual value added and value added from standard cost data to be an increase in productivity which may then be used as a pool for bonuses (for a detailed explanation, see Cox (1979)). More efficient use of materials and capital goods as well as greater effort may well result in increased value added for the firm. However, as we have noted, value added may be affected by non-productivity-related factors. Changes in the price of input materials and of goods and services sold are not related to production effort but will nevertheless affect value added. In general, where these other factors are likely to be significant, a value-added basis may well be inappropriate.

(c) *Value added as a return on capital employed.* A company generates a return for the owners or shareholders through a combination of resources, including materials, wages, bought-in services and even the infrastructure provided by government, as represented by taxes. Value-added statements deduct only one of these resources – bought-in materials. This partial approach can create distortions when using the ratio for investment decisions or for inter-temporal comparisons. For instance, suppose that instead of making a product in the factory, a firm decides to buy in the finished product. The value added will be reduced by virtue of the increase in material costs. Other factors being equal, there will be a reduction in the workforce, as some of their effort is now being bought in. If this action results in a greater profit, with no significant increase in capital, then *reducing* value added as a return on capital may *increase* the return to the shareholders (or the 'providers of capital').

(d) *Value added as a corporate objective.* Shareholders, employees and government would all benefit from an increase in value added due to an increase in selling price, greater productivity, lower material costs and greater efficiency. To this extent, it may seem that value added is a preferable goal to the more narrowly defined profit and loss account, as it would appear to unite the differing interests of the parties concerned. Unfortunately, this 'unifying effect' is limited. As we have seen above, shareholders may increase their returns by reducing the share of labour in the value added by the firm. Similarly, labour interests may be furthered by favouring products with high labour content irrespective of their profitability. Value added fails to measure goals at a sufficiently detailed level to reveal such conflicts of interest.

14.4   Conclusions

The main advantage of the value-added statement is that it is a simple, easily understood measure. When applied to business, it has a particular appeal as a means of demonstrating contribution to society, as a basis for incentive schemes and as a measure of return. In each instance, though, value added can communicate a misleading signal. The contribution to society is a rather broader concept than value added, even when our consideration is limited to the financial effects. As a measure of effort, value added has been shown to be not wholly isolated from non-effort-related events. Finally, profit or cash flows are superior as measures of return on capital, for these measures correctly treat labour as a cost for such purposes. Its less controversial role is perhaps as a post-decision measure, reporting in an attractive manner the effect of combining resources to pursue an acceptable objective.

References and further reading

ASSC, The Corporate Report, 1975.
CIMA, Terminology, 1988.
Cox, B., *Value Added: An appreciation for the accountant concerned with industry,* CIMA/Heinemann, 1979.
Gray, S. I., Maunders, K. T., *Value Added Reporting: Uses and Measurement,* Association of Certified Accountants, 1980.

Questions for Part Four

1   You have been asked to evaluate the performance of a department store in a retail group. The quality of the store's merchandise is fairly high and its image with its clientele is largely based on the interdependence of the merchandise in its different departments.

The four departments are Garden Equipment (GE); Dining Furniture (DF); DIY Decorating Products (DIY); Crockery and Glassware (CG).

The following data have been prepared by the store accountant for the year ended 31 October 1987.

	Basis of apportionment	GE (£000)	DF (£000)	DIY (£000)	CG (£000)	Total (£000)
Sales actual		1,240	900	600	560	3,300
Gross margin actual		440	450	200	280	1,370
Direct costs:						
Supervision		15	20	20	25	80
Sales staff actual		135	216	81	108	540
Advertising actual		12	6	8	14	40
		162	242	109	147	660
Gross contribution		278	208	91	133	710
Costs apportioned:						
Rents and rates floor space at £4 per sq ft.		30	48	18	24	120
Heat and Light weighted floor space		10	12	3	10	35
		40	60	21	34	155
Net contribution		238	148	70	99	555
Other overhead sales		83	60	40	37	220
Net profit before tax		155	88	30	62	335

A new managing director with retailing experience has been appointed from outside the group. He has said that he considers that a department should achieve a net profit before tax of at least 7.5 per cent on sales and that he is prepared to close any department not meeting that criterion.

You are required to

(a) (i) identify which departments, if any, qualify for closure under this criterion,

(ii) state whether or not you would recommend their closure, explaining the reasons for your recommendations;

(b) recommend briefly what changes management might consider to improve the store's total profitability;

(c) advise what other departmental data might be fairly easily provided that would enable more comprehensive recommendations to be made.

(CIMA, November 1987)

2 A group consists of three separately located operating companies:

Company A, the oldest, manufacturers and markets fast-moving consumer goods;

Company B, manufactures and sells heavy machinery made to customers' specifications;

Company C, the youngest, provides technical advice and service to industrial and commercial customers.

The group headquarters treats the operating companies as investment centres and evaluates their performance by means of return on capital employed (ROCE). This is calculated before interest and tax, as follows:

(a) The ROCE numerator consists of the operating company's net income less a share of group HQ expenses;

(b) the ROCE denominator consists of its fixed assets at cost less cumulative straight-line depreciation plus its net current assets plus a share of group HQ net assets;

(c) each operating company's share of group expenses and assets is based on that company's sales as a proportion of total sales by all three operating companies.

For the year ended 31st December the ROCE for each operating company was:

A 8.0%
B 5.5%
C 15.0%

Group HQ is rather dissatisfied with the results and, in the hope of improving them, sets a target of 14 per cent ROCE on all new investment proposals and requires operating companies to obtain group HQ approval for any proposals for new investment above £60,000.

Company A submits to group HQ the following proposal for a new investment:

Investment: fixed assets £37,500 (with a capacity of 13,000 units p.a.)

Net current assets £37,500 (incremental)

Income: this is dependent on the price obtainable, as follows:

Price per unit	Expected annual sales
£3.00	11,500 units
£3.50	9,000 units
£4.00	6,500 units

Costs: Variable costs per unit £1.50

Incremental fixed cost p.a. £8,500 (including depreciation on new fixed assets)

You are required, using relevant data from the question to support your answer, to:

(a) state whether Company A's investment proposal would pass group HQ's qualifying test;

(b) explain what you consider to the *three* major deficiencies of group HQ's ROCE evaluation system;

(c) recommend any *two* important changes you would propose to group HQ's ROCE evaluation system;

(d) state whether you would pass Company A's investment proposal under the changed system recommended at (C) above.

(CIMA, specimen questions)

3   A boatyard is divided into three profit centres whose managers are rewarded according to results. Transactions between these profit centres are frequent.

Sales centre (S) buys and sells new boats. If it needs to take part-exchange from a customer in order to sell a new boat, it transfers the part-exchanged boat to B at an agreed price.

Brokerage (B) buys and sells second-hand boats (i) in part-exchange from S (B names the price at which it can buy a comparable boat that is in a suitable condition for resale to an end-user customer, but deducts the likely cost of repairs) and (ii) from other sources, on a normal trading basis.

Repairs (R) does repairs for (i) B (to put boats into a saleable condition) and (ii) other customers.

The following situation arises:

S can sell to a customer for £35,000 a new boat which would cost £29,000. To do so, it needs to offer £16,000 in part-exchange for the customer's old boat. However, the customer's boat is estimated by R to need repairs that will cost:

Materials   £300
Labour   60 hours at £15 per hour

B can buy for £15,000 a boat comparable to the one being offered by the customer in part-exchange but which needs no repair. B could then sell that boat for £19,000.

Other data:

R's labour rate per hour is made up as follows:

	£	
Variable cost	6.00	
Fixed cost	4.50	(based on 20.000 budgeted hours p.a.)
Profit	4.50	
	£15.00	

45 per cent of R's time is reserved for work from B.
Annual fixed cost is budgeted at:

S,   £70,000
B,   £80,000

You are required
(a) in relation to the above situation, to set out the contribution to profit for each profit centre that would result,
  (i)   assuming that all estimates and budgets materialized as expected,
  (ii) assuming that all estimates and budgets materialized as in (i), except that the repairs undertaken by R took an extra 10 hours and £100 of materials due to a problem not noticed by B or R;
(b) to identify *two* situations where the profit centre arrangement, insofar as it has been outlined, might cause problems between any two of the three managers and indicate what you recommend should be done in *each* case;
(c) to discuss briefly what major merits and what management accounting problems there might be in establishing investment centres in place of the existing profit centres, and recommend what the boatyard should do.

(CIMA, November 1989)

4   Ramanujan Ltd's profit and loss account appears as follows:

Sales	£8,500,000
Opening stock	400,000
Production	6,000,000
Closing stock	2,000,000
Gross profit	4,100,000
Expenses	2,500,000
Net profit	1,600,000
Taxation	400,000
Dividends	500,000
Reserves	700,000

Sales represent a range of products with differing stock levels. As a rough approximation, the management accountant estimates that the mix of costs is as follows:

	Labour (%)	Material (%)	Depreciation (%)
Opening Stock	30	50	20
Production	20	70	10
Closing Stock	40	40	20

Required:

(a)   Calculate three different forms of value-added statement explaining the rationale for each statement.

(b)   'The four principal uses of value added in a company are:

(i)   informing shareholders,
(ii)   improving public relations,
(iii)   informing management and shopfloor,
(iv)   as a basis for employee incentives.

(Cox (1979))

Evaluate the statements you have prepared in relation to these uses.

Index

Accounting rate of return, 137
Agency, 21
Aircraft noise, 102
Analytical ability, 34
Arrow's Impossibility Theorem, 12, 27
Attributes, 4
Availability effect, 35
Average pricing, 302

Backlog depreciation, 261
Bayes Theorem, 30
'Beta', 176
   calculation, 180
   project, 189
   use of proxy company data, 192
Borda count, 43
Bottom up modelling, 94
Buy-response curves, 305

Capital asset pricing model (CAPM), 171
   CAPM discount rate and cost of capital, 203
   multi-period, 186
   real asset investment, 184
Capital market line, 172
Capital rationing, 150
   linear programming, 152
Cardinal measures, 41
Cash flows in capital budgeting, 153
Certainty equivalent, 58, 62
Common cost, 115
Competitive bidding, 318
Competitive supply, 255
Compound interest depreciation, 357
Condorcet's Paradox, 12
Contribution curve, 298
Cost apportionments, 113
Cost benefit analysis, 101

Cost of capital, 190
   CAPM discount rate, 203
   debt, 190
   equity, 190
Cost effectiveness, 3, 104
Cost-plus pricing, 289
Cost of sales adjustment, 262

Decentralization, 341
Decision conferencing, 98
Decision trees in pricing, 310
Decisions, 15
   accounting information, 108
   constraints model, 19
   information for decisions, 27
   levels, 24
   models, 93
   muddling through, 20
   multiple goals, 44
   political model, 20
   process, 15
   qualities, 25
   rational model, 16
   risk, 53
   single goal, 44
   uncertainty, 53
   under certainty, 43
Default free manufacturing, 106
Demand analysis, 247
   elasticity, 248
Dillon and Nash effect, 114
Discount pricing, 302
Divisional investment, 350
   asset measurement, 355
   compound interest depreciation, 357
   intangibles, 353
Divisional profit, 349
Double taxation, 275

Efficiency, 104
Elasticity of demand, 248
Estimating techniques, 97
Expected value, 58
Extended Pearson Tukey, 97

Goals, 3
  congruence, 11, 265
  formal, 7
  group, 11
  individual, 9
  informal, 7
  managerial, 6
  non-operational, 6
  operational, 6
  organizational, 6
  proxy, 7
Going-rate pricing, 302

Hawthorne effect, 37
Heuristics, 96
Human judgement, 33
  analytical ability, 34
  anchoring and adjustment, 35
  compounding estimates, 35
  concreteness, 35
  imaginability, 36
  insensitivity to prior probabilities, 34
  insensitivity to sample size, 34
  over confidence, 34
  regression to mean, 34
  retrievability, 35

Incremental cost, 114
Indices, 243
Indifference curves, 47
Inflation, 240
Inflation and pricing, 319
Information, 27
  gathering, 32
  value, 27
Internal rate of return, 141
  interest rate changes, 149
  multiple IRRs, 148

Just in time, 106

Lease evaluation, 212
  equivalent loan method, 214
  IRR method, 215
  PV comparison with borrowing/buying,
    212
Leasing, 208
  capital budgeting and leasing, 212
  discount rates, 212
  financial, 209
  operating, 209
  separation theorem and leasing, 209
Lexicographic ordering, 46
Limit pricing, 308

Limiting factor analysis, 299
Loss leaders, 309

M form hypothesis, 21
Make or buy, 252
Marginal cost-plus pricing, 297
Market categories, 278
Market skimming, 305
Marketing mix, 25
Maximax, 54
Maximin, 54
Mean variance rule, 77
Measurement, 40
Modelling, 93
  game theoretic, 96
  normative, 94
  numerate/non-numerate, 94
  static/dynamic, 95
  stochastic/deterministic, 95
Monetary values, 240
Monetary working capital adjustment, 262
Monopolistic competition, 279
Monopoly, 281
Monte Carlo simulation, 95
Moral hazard, 10
Multi-objective decisions, 44, 85
Multi-stage pricing, 323
Mutually exclusive projects, 144
  unequal lives, 146

Nemewashi, 11
Net present value, 41, 130

Objectives, 4
Oligopoly, 282
Opportunity costs, 108
  in capital budgeting, 157
Optional extras, 309
Ordinal measures, 41
Outranking, 51

Pareto optimal set, 45
Payback, 41, 135
Pearson Tukey estimate, 97
Penetration pricing, 304
Perfect competition, 279
Portfolio theory, 161
  correlation coefficient, 165
  covariance, 164
  expected return, 163
  expected value, 163
  standard deviation, 162
Post audit, 223
Preference independence, 48
Premium pricing, 302
Price differentiation, 312
Price discrimination, 312
Price level changes, 239
  general, 240
  specific, 247
  timing of changes, 245

Pricing out, 53
Probability, 56
Product bundling, 316
Product life cycle, 285
Product line pricing, 309
Profit, 3
Profit maximization, 283
Profitability index, 152
Projects:
  abandonment, 224
  definition, 218
  implementation, 220
  internal audit, 222
  manager's rôle, 220
Promotion mix, 320
Psychological pricing, 323

Qualitative factors, 42
Quality, 106

Ratios:
  asset turnover, 368
  capital gearing, 372
  cost of sales turnover, 370
  creditors turnover, 371
  current, 365
  debt/equity, 372
  debtors turnover, 370
  dividend cover, 374
  dividend yield, 374
  earnings per share, 373
  financial leverage, 372
  fixed asset turnover, 369
  interest cover, 371
  operating, 367
  operational gearing (leverage), 372
  price/earnings (PE), 373
  profit margin, 368
  quick, 366
  return on capital employed (ROCE), 367
  stock market, 373
  stock turnover, 370
  univariate and multivariate, 374
Real assets, 129
Real values, 240
Regret, 54
Relative risk aversion, 71
Relevant cost, 112
Replacement cost, 258
Residual income (RI), 347
Retail Prices Index, 244
Return on investment (ROI), 342
  dysfunctional behaviour, 345
Ringi, 11
Risk, 53
Risk attitudes, 60, 68
  averseness, 63

measurement, 67
neutral, 65
prone, 66
relative, 71
Risk premium, 66, 177
Roskill Commission, 102

SSAP 16, 259
Scenario analysis, 54
Security characteristic lines, 180
  alpha value, 181
Security market line, 178
Semi-variance, 77, 83
Separation theorem, 132, 175
  and leasing, 209
Social influences, 36
Social Judgement Theory, 51
Stochastic dominance, 72
  first order, 72
  second order, 72
  third order, 74
Surclassement, 51
Systematic (diversifiable) risk, 176

Target pricing, 291, 296
Tax and Price Index (TPI), 245
Tax shield, 196
Top down modelling, 94
Transfer pricing, 266
  cost plus, 267
  full cost, 267
  game theory, 268
  linear programming, 270
  marginal cost basis, 267
  market based methods, 272

Uncertainty, 53
Unsystematic (unique or non-diversifiable)
  risk, 175
Utility:
  marginal, 70
  measurement, 60
  Neumann–Morgenstern, 61
  traditional or classical, 70

Valuation of components rule, 202
Value added statements, 377
  corporate report method, 378
  cost of sales method, 378
  national accounts method, 380
Value analysis, 104
Value function, 48

Willingness to pay, 101, 111

Yield, 141

Zero based budgeting, 23